FRONTIERS IN LIBRARIANSHIP:
PROCEEDINGS OF THE
CHANGE INSTITUTE, 1969

*Contributions in Librarianship and
Information Science*
SERIES EDITOR: PAUL WASSERMAN

CONTRIBUTIONS IN LIBRARIANSHIP
AND INFORMATION SCIENCE, NUMBER 2

FRONTIERS IN LIBRARIANSHIP: PROCEEDINGS OF THE CHANGE INSTITUTE 1969

SCHOOL OF LIBRARY AND INFORMATION SERVICES
University of Maryland

GREENWOOD PUBLISHING COMPANY
WESTPORT, CONNECTICUT

Library of Congress Cataloging in Publication Data

Change Institute, University of Maryland, 1969.
    Frontiers in Librarianship.

    (Contributions in librarianship and information
science, no. 2)
    1. Library conferences. I. Maryland. University.
School of Library and Information Services.
II. Title. III. Series.
Z672.5.C5   1969   021   78-149958
    ISBN 0-8371-5823-0

Library of Congress Catalog Card Number: 78-149958

ISBN: 0-8371-5823-0

First published in 1972

Greenwood Publishing Company
A Division of Greenwood Press, Inc.
51 Riverside Avenue, Westport, Connecticut 06880

Printed in the United States of America

Designed by Peter Landa

CONTENTS

SERIES PREFACE NOTE

The essential purpose and anticipated contribution of this series is to influence for the better the intellectual currents of the field. On the assumption that the level of substantive contribution available to thoughtful practitioners and to students of the field stands in need of improvement, the mission of these publications will be to elevate this standard. The expectation is that the present publication program may achieve these ends under the aegis of an energetic and ambitious publishing organization firmly committed to libraries and to the intellectual concerns of their supportive professional discipline. Every effort will be made to influence those who, individually or in combination, have the capacity to add to the ideological, theoretical, pragmatic, and problem-solving perspectives of the field, to share their insights through this open-ended series, "Contributions in Librarianship and Information Science."

The range of material covered will vary widely. Its limits are set only by the capacity of the series editor to identify and to attract those of sufficiently broad and imaginative cast of mind who will treat the many areas and issues which stand in need of thoughtful discussion, analysis and elaboration. The nature of the work published in the series will span a wide continuum. There will be monographs and advanced or upper-division texts treating subjects of significance. Collections of essays and papers upon topics that transcend the capacity of single authors will be included. Proceedings of institutes, conferences, and symposia on significant issues of dynamic or topical concern will also receive hospitality in the series. Monographic reports of research, based upon individual or group efforts, on subjects in librarianship and information science will also be encouraged. The precise form and specific framework of the published titles may be expected to vary from work to work. But the primary criterion for accepting a prospective volume for inclusion shall remain focused upon whether the manuscript or the material makes a genuine contribution to the knowledge base of the field. In bringing "Contributions in Librarianship and Information Science" into being, we have attempted to inspire the very best efforts from the most thoughtful in librarianship and information science.

College Park, Maryland   *Paul Wasserman*
                                                      March 25, 1970

PREFACE

This conference was inspired by Mary Lee Bundy. Prompted by a sense of inadequacy in relating the dramatically shifting societal scene to the educational preparation of librarians, she prodded and then catalyzed her colleagues to convene a group of intellectuals from disparate disciplines to ponder this problem.

The concept of the institute became a reality only after Gilda Nimer, then a research assistant on the University of Maryland Manpower Research Project, agreed to accept responsibility for planning and arranging the program. She conceptualized the general lines of the program and assumed managerial responsibility for preparing the proposal for the Office of Education, which sponsored the week-long institute. Mrs. Nimer worked continuously from the earliest planning stages in the winter of 1969, to identification and invitation of the speakers, and then through the laborious processes of contract negotiation, screening and choice of applicants, and finally the arduous day-to-day management of the institute while it was convened. The preparation of the biographical sketches of the speakers in the program was another of the many contributions that Mrs. Nimer made to the institute and to these proceedings.

As part of the original design, Mary Lee Bundy and Paul Wasserman assumed responsibility for advising the conference director during the planning stages and then for conducting the program during the institute. Ruth Ann Edwards contributed to the success of the institute by assisting in numerous ways with program planning and arrangements before and during the conference.

The difficult, enervating, and time-consuming task of translating the tape recordings of the sessions to legible prose typescript was performed by Evelyn Daniel. She was aided in this effort by Mrs. Virginia A. Irby, who listened and typed.

Ultimately, the record of the institute is a result of the overall contribution of the speakers and panelists and of the participants drawn from librarianship who came to join the program personnel during the week-long seminar. These proceedings are thus testimony to the spirit and the effort of all those who came and bared their minds and their passions for the enterprise.

PART ONE
THE PROGRAM

INTRODUCTION

The essential purpose of this institute was to bring together librarians drawn from a wide range of backgrounds, types of library situations, geographic regions of the country, and ages, to join with lecturers and discussants in examining some of the fundamental issues in society and the effects of such issues on the practice and philosophy of library service. The institute was designed as a learning experience for librarians, so that the ideas and issues brought into focus might be cast in a context germane to their fundamental concerns as individual practitioners and as responsible agents for change in their libraries.

Speakers from a wide range of backgrounds and orientations were chosen on the basis of their potential for formulating a picture of some of the more important currents of political, social, and intellectual currents in the society that bear upon library practice. The speakers selected were those perceived as being on the cutting edge of social and political change, as informed representatives of movements and activities that are or might be significant for thoughtful librarians. Intrinsically, the plan of the program was to encourage each speaker and each panelist to help identify the specific issues with which he was most comfortable, and then to discuss with the participants the relevance, significance, and practical implications of such phenomena for library practice.

The conference followed the academic format. Typically, there was a guest lecturer who spoke formally or informally, according to his own proclivity, followed by panel discussants who responded to and analyzed the introductory lecture or the general topical theme for the session, and then general discussion. A consequence of this design was that the speakers and panelists came to control and influence the discussion far more than did the librarian participants.

Not all of the conference proceedings were captured on tape. Because of equipment failure, the welcoming address and a portion of the first session were not picked up; but the substance of the first session was reconstructed from notes. In some cases during the program, the recorder did not pick up exchanges.

It must be acknowledged that the typescript version of the proceedings can only partially capture the dynamics and the fidelity of a conference, which, despite its traditional format and arrangement, underwent a very great variety of diversions, forceful encounters, and other unanticipated consequences in the heat and the passion of the participants and of the lecturers and panel discussants.

In editing the typescript for publication, the number of changes made was minimal. In every instance, there was a conscious attempt to retain as much of the fidelity of the proceedings as possible; portions were adapted or reduced only when necessary. There has been no attempt to censor any portion of the content.

Because there was no record kept of the names of individuals who spoke at particular times, it has not been possible to identify the participants with their remarks. It is for this reason that the word "participant" is used to identify all of the nonprogram speakers during the proceedings. Only the lecturers and panel discussants are specified by name. Unfortunately, therefore, elements of the exchanges and interesting dialogues that took place during the course of the institute have been lost.

The prime purpose in publishing the proceedings of this institute is to illuminate issues only seldom treated in the annals of librarianship. It seems to those who convened and participated in this week-long seminar that the essential issues before librarianship are less those matters of technological import and more those issues that relate to choices and alternatives. The organizers believe that in selecting the political, economic, and sociological stance for library service, students and practitioners of librarianship will profit from the insights reflected in the comments and perceptions of the discussants in this institute.

AGENDA

SCHOOL OF LIBRARIANSHIP AND INFORMATION SERVICES,
UNIVERSITY OF MARYLAND

SUNDAY, AUGUST 10

WELCOME BY PAUL WASSERMAN: Purpose, Rationale, and
Procedures of the Institute*

RECEPTION

MONDAY, AUGUST 11

MORNING: The City as Change Milieu: Social, Economic, and
Political Factors
LECTURER: Horace Busby
PANELISTS: Isaiah T. Creswell, Jr.
Mary Lee Bundy
Paul Wasserman
John Forsman

EVENING.   The Disadvantaged: Reorienting the Urban Setting to
New Goals and New Commitments
LECTURER: Preston R. Wilcox
PANELISTS: Annie Reid
Mary Lee Bundy
Ernest M. Kahn
Joseph C. Donohue

* Not included in the transcript of the proceedings.

TUESDAY, AUGUST 12

MORNING: Dissident Elements in the Culture
CHAIRMAN: John Berry
PANELISTS: James Welbourne
                Stanley Segal
                Edward Taylor

AFTERNOON: Shifting Philosophical Perspectives in Public Education
LECTURER: William M. Birenbaum
PANELISTS: Paul Wasserman
                Annie Reid
                Mary Lee Bundy

WEDNESDAY, AUGUST 13

FREE MORNING

AFTERNOON: Responses from the Establishment: Models and Cues from Other Fields (Part One)
CHAIRMAN: Mary Lee Bundy
PANELISTS: Sidney Galler
                Jonathan Freedman

EVENING: Responses from the Establishment: Models and Cues from Other Fields (Part Two)
LECTURER: Rev. Geno Baroni

THURSDAY, AUGUST 14

MORNING: The Publishing Industry in Transition
LECTURER: Dan Lacy
PANELISTS: Paul Wasserman
                Mary Lee Bundy

                The Rise of the Information Utility
LECTURER: David Goldberg
PANELIST: Jordan Baruch

AFTERNOON: Information Transfer, Dissemination, and the Evolving Structure
LECTURER: Jordan Baruch

PANELISTS: Mary Lee Bundy
Joseph C. Donohue
Paul Wasserman

FRIDAY, AUGUST 15

MORNING: The Library Profession: Politics, Power, and Collective Bargaining

CHAIRMAN: Mary Lee Bundy

PANELISTS: Eldred Smith
Ralph Blasingame, Jr.

AFTERNOON: Change Responses from Librarianship: Education, Research, and Practice

PANELISTS: Mary Lee Bundy
Paul Wasserman
Brooke Sheldon

GUEST LECTURERS, PANELISTS, AND INSTITUTE PERSONNEL: DESCRIPTIVE NOTES*

REVEREND GENO C. BARONI

Reverend Baroni was born in western Pennsylvania, where his father worked in the coal mines. He worked in a plywood factory before entering Mount Saint Mary's College in Emmitsburg, Maryland, where he earned his degree. He continued his studies at Notre Dame University and Catholic University and was ordained to the priesthood in 1956. He then became an assistant pastor and taught in Altoona and Johnstown, Pennsylvania.

Father Baroni came to Washington in 1960 as assistant pastor of SS. Paul and Augustine Church. He was instrumental in establishing a parish center, a day camp, a tutorial program, and family counseling services for the community, and he formed a community organization in cooperation with Howard University and the late Rev. James Reeb. He founded several parish credit unions, and prepared a national low-income credit union program for use by the poverty program and the Credit Unions National Association.

In 1965, Father Baroni was appointed executive secretary of the newly established Archbishop's Committee for Community Relations. In 1967 this became the Office of Urban Affairs, Archdiocese of Washington, with Father Baroni as its executive director.

* Prepared by Gilda Nimer.

Father Baroni resigned as executive director of the Archdiocesan Office of Urban Affairs in December 1969. On January 1, 1970, he joined the staff of the United States Catholic Conference as program director for the National Task Force on Urban Problems.

Father Baroni serves on the boards of both national and local civic and religious groups concerned with jobs and training, race relations, education, welfare, housing, and related urban problems. He is a member of the D.C. Commissioners' Council on Human Relations and the Mayor's Committee for Economic Development; he is founder and president of the Urban Rehabilitation Corporation, a nonprofit corporation sponsored by the archdiocese to rehabilitate inner city houses for home ownership; he has strongly urged and is a major supporter of the formation of an Urban Coalition in Washington; and he is among those national religious leaders who have formed the Interreligious Foundation for Community Organization, a group seeking funds to support community organizations to become spokesmen for the poor.

JORDAN BARUCH

Dr. Baruch is currently a consultant to industry and government in the effective use of information systems. He was, at the time of the conference, president of EDUCOM, the Interuniversity Communications Council, which functions to facilitate the extra-organizational communication of the universities.

He received his B.S. and M.S. in electrical engineering, and then his D.Sc. in instrumentation, from Massachusetts Institute of Technology. Since then he has been on the faculty of MIT, as assistant professor of electrical engineering until 1955 and afterwards as lecturer. In 1949, he helped form Bolt, Beranek and Newman, a consulting, research, and development firm. He became the firm's vice president for research, and is now on leave of absence. Having initially worked in the field of acoustics, he holds several patents and is the author of numerous papers on methods and systems.

His wide range of activity brought him into the computer sciences, and he has directed projects in biomedical engineering, development of a cardiac surgery console, and automation of a clinical pathology laboratory. More recently, Dr. Baruch has been involved with direction of work on a time-shared system to provide for storage, retrieval, processing, and communication of information, with particular emphasis on its application to the needs of hospitals. In 1966, he was instrumental in establishing MEDINET, a program for a computer-based hospital network in New England.

Jordan Baruch has been the recipient of fellowships in acoustics and was given the Eta Kappa Nu Recognition Award in 1956. He is a Fellow of the Institute of Electrical and Electronics Engineers, the Acoustical Society of America, The New York Academy of Science, the American Academy of Arts and Sciences, and Sigma Xi.

JOHN N. BERRY III

John Berry, editor of *Library Journal,* is alert to sensing and articulating the currents of change, both as they evolve within and as they impinge upon librarianship. He joined the Bowker Company in 1964, and was assistant editor of *Library Journal* and managing editor of Bowker New Book Projects before assuming the post of editor-in-chief.

Mr. Berry's entry into the publishing end of librarianship was preceded by posts in both academic and public libraries. He was a youth-reference librarian at the Reading, Massachusetts, Public Library, and then became reference librarian and assistant director of the Simmons College library and a lecturer in the Simmons School of Library Science. During this period he was editor of *Bay State Librarian,* official journal of the Massachusetts Library Association.

Mr. Berry has been active in many associations, both within and on the periphery of librarianship, and is chairman-elect of the Special Libraries Association Publishing Division. He is the compiler of the *Directory of Library Consultants* (1969).

Mr. Berry was born in New Jersey, majored in history at Boston University, and received an M.S. in library science from Simmons College.

WILLIAM M. BIRENBAUM

Discarding the conventional wisdom frequently voiced by college presidents, William Birenbaum is a critical participant-observer of the college administrative scene. President of Staten Island Community College, Dr. Birenbaum has recently published *Overlive: Power, Poverty, and the University,* which states his views on the urgent need for the reform of urban higher education in the United States.

Born in Macomb, Illinois, Dr. Birenbaum earned his Ph.D. at the University of Chicago's humanities division and law school. In addition to serving as director of student affairs and dean of students in the University College at Chicago, he taught in the fields of political philosophy and American history. While assistant to the president of Wayne State University, he created Detroit Adventure, an association of thirty major cultural and educational institutions in the city. In 1960, Governor G. Mennen Williams appointed him as the first chairman of the Cultural Commission of the State of Michigan.

Dr. Birenbaum moved to New York to become dean of the New School for Social Research, a position he held until he became vice president and provost of Long Island University's Brooklyn Center. In 1967, he was president of the Bedford-Stuyvesant Development and Services Corporation.

Dr. Birenbaum currently is a member of the board of many organizations, among them the American Civil Liberties Union, Brooklyn chapter, where he is also chairman of the academic freedom committee; the national governing committee of the American Jewish Congress, metropolitan council; and the Brooklyn Academy of Music. He was elected in 1970 to the Board of Trustees of Friends World College, based in Westbury, Long Island, the Quaker-founded four-year liberal arts institution that stresses learning through direct involvement.

In 1965, Dr. Birenbaum was a member of the Salzburg Seminar faculty in Austria, where he lectured on problems of urbanism in the United States. He is the author of "Cities and Universities: Collision of Crises," in *Campus 1980: The Shape of the Future in American Higher Education.*

RALPH BLASINGAME
As a member of the executive hierarchy of the American Library Association, Ralph Blasingame has been a perceptive critic of the association's policies and practices. His service has extended over a period of about fifteen years. He was the organization's treasurer for four years, after a year as president of the Library Administration Division and a term on the Council.

After a number of years in state library administration, Dr. Blasingame joined the faculty of Rutgers University's Graduate School of Library Service in 1964. As a consultant, he has continued to utilize his expertise in library systems. His research has resulted in published surveys of the public libraries of West Virginia, of public and state library services in the state of Ohio, and *Feasibility of Cooperation for Exchange of Resources Among Academic and Special Libraries in Pennsylvania.* Since coming to Rutgers, he has directed several study and research projects. One resulted in the monograph, *Research on Library Services in Metropolitan Areas: Report of a Rutgers Seminar, 1964–65.* He also participated in the preparation of New Bases for Library and Information Services.

Dr. Blasingame, who has been awarded an honorary Doctor of Letters at St. Francis College, received his undergraduate degree in English literature from Pennsylvania State, and two library degrees from the Columbia University School of Library Service. After working in the City College library, he returned to the Columbia library school, first as a research assistant, then as assistant dean. He left Columbia to become the assistant state librarian for California, and after five years became the state librarian for Pennsylvania, a post which he held for seven years. During this time, the Library Code was formulated and enacted. In addition to his affiliation with ALA, Dr. Blasingame has been an officer in other library associations, both national and local, and has been a special editor for the Crowell-Collier Corporation.

MARY LEE BUNDY

Since receiving her doctorate in library science from the University of Illinois in 1960, Mary Lee Bundy has devoted a major portion of her time to research. She has studied a number of new developments in the public library field for the Illinois State Library, the Missouri State Library, the Massachusetts Division of Library Extension, and the Maryland Division of Library Extension. She was co-director of the first phase of Maryland's High John project (see p. 96) and is associate director of a national study of manpower in the library and information professions.

At present she is on the faculty at Maryland's School of Library and Information Services, and prior to that she was a professor at the Library School of the State University of New York at Albany. Her earlier professional experience included work in reference and administration at Rensselaer Polytechnic Institute.

HORACE BUSBY

Horace Busby of Washington, D.C., is a consultant, writer, and lecturer working with both the public and the private sectors on the long-range implications of urban and technological change to our society. In 1964 and 1965, during the first two years of the Johnson administration, he served at the White House as a special assistant to the President, secretary of the Cabinet, and deputy special assistant for national security. Currently, he is a member of the National Advisory Council on Economic Opportunity, which has the supervisory role in relation to the war on poverty; the President's Committee on Mental Retardation; and the Panel of Conciliators of the International Centre for Settlement of Investment Disputes. In private life, Mr. Busby has served as a consultant to the National League of Cities and the International City Managers' Association as well as to corporations, universities, and other organizations. A native of Fort Worth, Texas, he attended the University of Texas and Texas Christian University. He is author of *The Thirty-first of March,* to be published by Harper & Row.

ISAIAH T. CRESWELL, JR.

Isaiah Creswell not only has consistently utilized his legal training and skills in the promotion of civil rights, but can speak with the sophisticated knowledge of a government insider. He currently serves as the assistant staff director for community programming in the United States Commission on Civil Rights. There he directs the field activities and community relations functions of the Commission, and directs and coordinates the activities of its six regional offices and fifty-one State Advisory Committees. Prior to this appointment, he was executive assistant to the chairman of the District of Columbia City Council, and its legislative counsel. As first and ranking staff member, he assisted in the formation of substantive and procedural policy of the Council in meeting such complex urban problems as housing, police-community relations, taxation, and consumer affairs. Mr. Creswell has also been a partner in the first racially integrated law firm in Tennessee, where the primary focus was on civil rights; director of a community action agency in Tennessee; and an attorney for a federal committee on education and labor.

Though the settings have varied, the pattern of purposeful legal activism has been maintained. Mr. Creswell's activities include service as a consultant for the Office of Economic Opportunity, and on the boards of the Law Center for Constitutional Rights (a private civil liberties advocacy group) and the Tennessee Voters Council (a coalition of local and predominantly black political action organizations).

Mr. Creswell, a graduate of Amherst College, was born in Nashville, Tennessee. He received his law degree from Vanderbilt University, and also attended the University of Oslo.

JOSEPH C. DONOHUE

Joseph Donohue is an assistant professor at the University of Maryland's School of Library and Information Services and director of the Public Information Center Project, a cooperative effort of the school and the Enoch Pratt Free Library of Baltimore. The purpose of the project is to provide within the public library special information on subjects pertinent to the needs of the urban community.

Mr. Donohue is an information systems specialist with experience in a wide range of specialized libraries and information services. As a member of the Technical Staff of Informatics, Inc., he worked on analysis of information systems for effective communication of research results. He was previously assistant librarian of the RAND Corporation and reference librarian at General Electric-TEMPO.

Mr. Donohue received his B.A. from the University of California and an M.S. in library science from Simmons College, and is currently completing his dissertation for a Ph.D. in library and information science at Case Western Reserve University. His research concerns the development of a formal method for the analysis of subject literatures for application to library management. His publications include guides to information sources in a number of subjects, and articles on the development of information science as a discipline.

RUTH ANN EDWARDS

Ruth Ann Edwards is presently director of continuing education at the School of Library and Information Services at Maryland, where she completed her M.L.S. in January 1970. Mrs. Edwards has been heavily engaged, even while still a student, in a number of School activities, notably the Colloquium Lecture Series and the Committee on Recruitment of Black Students. Mrs. Edwards returned to the academic world after rearing two children. Between times, she has held a number of temporary and part-time positions in education and librarianship. Originally from West Virginia, she has made her home for a number of years in Chambersburg, Pennsylvania. Her prior academic work was done at Fairmont State College, where she received a B.A. and did graduate work in history.

JOHN FORSMAN
John Forsman is now assistant director of media services at Federal
City College. It was in an academic library, at the University of Southern California, that he began his professional career, but the intervening
years have been spent primarily in a municipal setting.

As city librarian of Richmond, California for three years, John Forsman handled his office with commitment and imagination. The March
1969 issue of *Library Journal* carried news of his resignation. Under
rightist attack because of his selection policies, Mr. Forsman resigned
because "he was anxious that the intellectual freedom controversy not
'be used as a weapon to deprive the black community of needed library
services.' "

Mr. Forsman has also held various positions in the Los Angeles
Public Library, and spent some years in the field of data processing,
experience which he was able to apply as a member of the Bay Area
Library Working Committee on Computerized Procedures. He partici-
pated actively in the organization of the East Bay Cooperative Library
System.

A native of Minnesota, Mr. Forsman received his B.A. degree in
philosophy from the University of Minnesota and his professional
degree from that university's Department of Library Science.

JONATHAN A. FREEDMAN
Innovative approaches to the solution of social problems are characteris-
tic of the projects with which Mr. Freedman has been associated.
Mr. Freedman, who has been a lecturer in the School of Social Work,
Syracuse University since 1965, is currently serving as adviser to Black
Youth United, a youth group establishing an Afro-American cultural
center (which includes a library).

Mr. Freedman's earlier professional activities included the creation
and direction at Brandeis University of a Crisis Research Team to
observe fast-breaking events, and serving as senior research analyst
and research coordinator of a Community Action Training Center.
He has acted in a consultant capacity for a community foundation
of neighborhood residents in Ohio to provide services that the residents
control, and for the Syracuse Psychiatric Hospital Storefront Mental
Health Center, and has served as a member of a social environment task force which is designing a central city for 259,000 in
Minnesota.

Mr. Freedman is a graduate of Wesleyan University and received his M.A. in sociology from Brandeis University, where he expects to receive his Ph.D. shortly. He was also a student at the Committee on Communication, University of Chicago, and held a traineeship at the National Institute of Mental Health.

SIDNEY R. GALLER

As assistant secretary for science of the Smithsonian Institution, Dr. Sidney Galler represents one facet of an institution which is changing and expanding its functions to meet new communication and information needs.

Dr. Galler was formerly head of the Biology Branch of the Office of Naval Research. Among his many awards, he holds the Navy Distinguished Civilian Service Award, the highest conferred by the Department of the Navy on civilian employees. It was presented to Dr. Galler for his outstanding contributions in the fields of hydrobiology and biological orientation and for the establishment of highly effective communication between the United States Navy and the community of biological scientists in Europe and Latin America as well as in this country.

He has carried over his interest in marine biology from the navy to the Smithsonian, and his idea for the increased use of commercial ships as "research ships of opportunity" has been as effective for Smithsonian oceanographers in need of ocean-going research platforms as it was for navy biologists.

While it is his interest in scientific communication that is most germane to this institute, Dr. Galler has been a creative and prolific pioneer in bio-instrumentation and has many designs to his credit that serve to improve biological research field instrumentation. He has been a member of many governmental, national, and international committees and panels. For his role in advancing international scientific collaboration, he has received letters of commendation from the secretaries of the Navy of Mexico, Argentina, Chile, Peru, and Brazil.

At the Smithsonian, Dr. Galler has expanded his interests in communications beyond the strictly biological. He established the well-known Center for Short-Lived Phenomena, a network for the rapid dissemination of information about natural events of scientific interest. The Center has been remarkably successful internationally for alerting the scientific community to important occurrences which might have been missed entirely or not discovered until too late for effective on-site study.

Dr. Galler is a graduate of the Baltimore City College, and received his Ph.D. in hydrobiology from the University of Maryland. He is the author of numerous technical publications and a member of many scientific organizations.

DAVID H. GOLDBERG

Dr. David H. Goldberg, a private educational consultant and encounter group leader, has a multidisciplinary background which enables him to work in areas that defy categorization.

He received his Ph.D. in experimental and physiological psychology from the University of California at Los Angeles in 1964 and later taught at Yale University, San Francisco State College, and Goddard College. For several years he was the "futurist-in-residence" at the U.S. Office of Education. More recently, he has lectured òr led seminars on radical educational reform, psychedelics, black rights and white racism, futuristics and alternative educational futures, affective education, mysticism and Eastern philosophy, environments for expanding human potential, and social change, as well as conducted encounter groups at colleges, universities, and "growth centers" throughout the country. He is a member of the American Association for Humanistic Psychology and a founding member of the World Future Society.

He resides with his wife and two children in Plainfield, Vermont, where he is attempting to live his life organically.

ERNEST M. KAHN

Mr. Kahn is particularly concerned with directing social work expertise to ameliorate problems of the disadvantaged in the inner city. From June 1965 until August 1967, Mr. Kahn served as director of the VISTA Training Center conducted by the University of Maryland, the first in the country set up for the training of VISTA volunteers in urban areas.

Since June 1968, Mr. Kahn has served as director of admissions for the School of Social Work of the University of Maryland, where he is an assistant professor. He teaches courses in social strategy and works with groups.

Mr. Kahn is a graduate of the City College of New York and holds an M.A. from the School of Social Service Administration of the University of Chicago. In addition to other responsibilities, he is preparing for his doctorate, and he recently received a grant for a study of the involvement of urban universities in the urban crisis.

Mr. Kahn has had professional experience as a social worker and branch director with the Jewish Community Centers of Chicago. While on leave from this agency, he served on the staff of the Hyde Park Youth Project in Chicago, one of the first antidelinquency projects in the nation. Before coming to Baltimore, Mr. Kahn was director of a community center in Stamford, Connecticut. He has also directed a number of projects developing group services for mentally ill, retarded, and delinquent young people.

Mr. Kahn has served as a consultant and has designed and conducted a large number of in-service training programs for various public and private agencies. Among these were six institutes on problems of the inner city for the senior policy-making staff of the Department of Health, Education, and Welfare. He recently completed a manual on the supervision of staff in antipoverty programs.

He is vice president for social policy and social action of the Maryland chapter, National Association of Social Workers.

DAN LACY

Dr. Dan Lacy, senior vice president of the McGraw-Hill Book Company, has also been a member of the President's National Advisory Commission on Libraries. From 1953 until he assumed his present position, Dr. Lacy was managing director for the American Book Publishers' Council. After beginning his professional career as an instructor in history at the University of North Carolina, he held various posts in the Works Projects Administration, eventually becoming assistant national director of its Historical Records Survey. He has been associated with the National Archives, was deputy chief assistant librarian of the Library of Congress, executive secretary of the Committee on Conservation of Cultural Resources of the National Resources Planning Board, and received the Superior Service Medal from the Department of State during his tenure there with the International Information Administration.

Dr. Lacy received both A.B. and A.M. degrees in the field of United States history from the University of North Carolina, where he was awarded an honorary doctorate in 1968.

Dr. Lacy was born in Newport News, Virginia. He has written and lectured extensively. His publications include *The Library of Con-*

gress, a Sesquicentenary Review (1950); *Books and the Future—a Speculation* (1956); *Freedom and Communications* (1961); and *The Meaning of the American Revolution* (1964).

GILDA V. NIMER

Gilda Nimer received academic degrees from three institutions—her B.A. in sociology at the University of Chicago, her M.S. in child development at the University of Rhode Island, and her M.L.S. at Maryland in 1968. Prior to her work as director of the Change Institute, she had served as research associate in the School of Library and Information Services following the completion of her library degree. During earlier periods, in addition to her family responsibilities as wife and mother, Mrs. Nimer gained experience as nursery school teacher in Rhode Island and New York, served as research assistant at Columbia University's Bureau of Applied Social Research, and was interviewer in the University of Illinois project on families of retarded children. Mrs. Nimer is author of "The Suburban Reality and Its Implications," in *The Library's Public Revisited,* and compiler of *Professions and Professionalism: A Bibliographic Overview,* both issued by the School of Library and Information Services at Maryland.

ANNIE T. REID

Mrs. Reid is an associate professor in the Department of Education at Bowie State College, Maryland. She has been on leave to the School of Library and Information Services at the University of Maryland, to direct the educational program for the High John Project. She has also been deeply involved in the school's black recruitment program.

Throughout her professional career, Mrs. Reid's primary focus has been the underprivileged. Initially a classroom teacher in the high-deprivation areas of Washington, Mrs. Reid both taught and developed special programs, and then served as a counselor. After service as the director of manpower programs of the United Poverty Organizations for the Washington area, Mrs. Reid joined the U.S. Commission on Civil Rights. She was assistant director of a study which resulted in a two-volume report, *Racial Isolation in the Public Schools.* From 1966 to 1968, Mrs. Reid was deputy director, Research Division, for the Commission, and she has continued with the Commission in a consultant capacity.

Mrs. Reid received her undergraduate degree from Simmons College and an M.A. in sociology from Boston University. She completed three years of graduate study in Harvard University's Department of Social Relations, was a National Science Foundation Fellow at Howard University, and also studied at George Washington University.

STANLEY J. SEGAL

Dr. Stanley J. Segal can comment on the phenomenon of dissidence, not only as a psychologist, but as one who has recently probed the psyche of librarians. He is currently associate dean of students and professor of college counseling and college student development at Hunter College in New York City and is a senior investigator in the Library Manpower Study under the overall direction of Dr. Bundy and Dr. Wasserman. Dr. Segal's study investigates personality and ability patterns related to work specialties in the information professions.

Dr. Segal previously held positions at the University of Michigan, where he was an assistant professor of psychology and assistant chief of the Counseling Center; the State University of New York at Buffalo, where he was associate professor and director of the Student Counseling Center; and at Columbia University, where he was senior research associate with the Conservation of Human Resources Project. He has also been a research associate at the Center for Research in Careers, Harvard University, and his professional publications have been in the areas of vocational choice, psychological measurement, and counseling.

A graduate of City College, New York, Dr. Segal holds M.A. and Ph.D. degrees in psychology from the University of Michigan.

BROOKE SHELDON

Brooke Sheldon is currently head of public library development for the New Mexico State Library in Santa Fe. In that capacity she works with public libraries all over the state. Previously she served with the Los Griegos Branch Library in Albuquerque.

Mrs. Sheldon attended Acadia University in Nova Scotia for her undergraduate work and completed graduate studies at Simmons College in Boston. After graduation she held a variety of posts including special services work with the U.S. Army in Stuttgart, Germany. She also served with the Detroit Public Library and as base librarian at ENT Air Force Base in Colorado Springs.

A deep concern with social problems and the need to extend library services to ever-widening circles of clientele is evident in many of Mrs. Sheldon's activities. She was chairman of the Library Service to Disadvantaged Children's Committee and recently participated in an institute in Pullman, Washington, on school and public library cooperation in providing library service to minority groups. Her article, "The Time of the Gringo," appeared in *American Libraries* for February 1970.

ELDRED SMITH

Eldred Smith is currently head of the loan department of the library of the University of California at Berkeley. He has been an active participant in a variety of librarians' organizations. He served as president of the University Federation of Librarians (AFT) on the Berkeley campus during 1967. In 1968, he was president of the statewide Librarians' Association at the University of California. He has also been active in the American Library Association (currently a member of the Academic Status Committee of the Association of College and Research Libraries) and the California Library Association (current president-elect of its College, University, and Research Libraries Division). During 1968–69, he was chairman of a UCB Library Task Force on Academic Library Personnel.

Mr. Smith received A.B. and M.A. degrees from the University of California at Berkeley and an M.S.L.S. from the University of Southern California. He worked in the California State College libraries before joining the UCB library staff. He has published articles on library operations, librarians' organizations, library management, and the role of the academic librarian.

EDWARD K. TAYLOR

Edward Taylor, executive director of the Harlem Cultural Council, was born in Sylvania, Georgia, and has lived most of his life in Harlem, New York, receiving his education in New York City institutions. While attending Frederick Douglass Junior High School, Mr. Taylor helped to plan and raise money for a student lounge at the Countée Cullen Branch Library. This involvement with libraries enabled him to pass the entrance examination for Stuyvesant High School, the New York City honor school; he went on to become president of its student body.

After graduating from the Mannes College of Music and having studied with John Browlee and Martial Singher, Metropolitan Opera stars, Mr. Taylor went on to perform with the New York City Opera, the music theater of Lincoln Center, and the Harlem Opera Society, of which he eventually became executive producer. While in the army he was stationed at Fort Carson, Colorado, was the director of entertainment for the United States garrison there, and was the director of the U.S.A.G. "Singing Soldiers" as well as founder and singer with the "Garrisonaires," a prize-winning barbershop quartet.

After returning to Harlem, he became vice president of Jazzmobile and executive director of the Harlem Cultural Council. When informed of the intended removal and mistreatment of rare documents in the Schonburg Collection of the New York Public Library, Mr. Taylor mobilized the community to help prevent any wrongdoing and became chairman of the Citizen's Committee for the Schonburg Collection. As chairman, he spent months negotiating with the Public Library and analyzing the problems of the Schonburg Collection.

In addition to his involvement in stage direction, Mr. Taylor is giving a lecture series on "Black Art: The New Experience" at New York University. He is also a voice teacher, stage director, actor-singer, and member of the following organizations: Screen Actors' Guild, American Guild of Musical Artists, Actors' Equity Association, American Federation of Television and Radio Artists.

PAUL WASSERMAN

Paul Wasserman served as dean at the Maryland School of Library and Information Services until recently, when he resumed a teaching role in the faculty as professor. He had served as professor and librarian in the Graduate School of Business and Public Administration at Cornell University until coming to Maryland in 1965. Still earlier, he was assistant to the business librarian and then chief of the Science and Industry Division of the Brooklyn Public Library. He holds degrees from the City College of New York, Columbia University, and the University of Michigan. During 1963/64, he was a postdoctoral student at Western Reserve University in data processing and information retrieval. His publications have concentrated in the fields of management and bibliography. Professor Wasserman is series editor for Greenwood Publishing Company's "Contributions in Librarianship and Information Science" series.

JAMES WELBOURNE

In a single individual, James Welbourne can represent the perspective of a student, a black, and a librarian. Working for change within the bureaucracy, he is prepared to work outside it if necessary.

Mr. Welbourne's activist bent is amply illustrated by the activities in which he has participated since he came, as a graduate fellow, to the Maryland School of Library and Information Services. As president of the Library School Student Association, he initiated planning for a national association of library school students. A planning council held in March was followed in June by a national convention entitled "Congress for Change," held in Washington. Mr. Welbourne was one of the students who addressed the national American Library Association as representatives of the "Congress." As an articulate spokesman for the current generation of professional library students, Mr. Welbourne has addressed and participated in meetings of several additional library associations.

A native of Baltimore, Mr. Welbourne received his undergraduate degree from the University of Maryland and spent four years with the Enoch Pratt Free Library.

PRESTON WILCOX

Having taught social work at the Columbia University School of Social Work, directed the Maria Lawton Center for Older People, the P.S. 68 Evening Community Center, and the East Harlem Project, Mr. Wilcox turned to full-time consultation in the fields of public and higher education, community development, and societal humanization. His prime intellectual interest is helping those he encounters either to develop an alternative to standing on the backs of others and/or to develop the ability to get others off their backs.

His volunteer activities currently include the following. chairman, Board of Directors, Talents Corps; co-chairman, Michael Schwerner Memorial Fund, Inc.; chairman, National Association for African American Education; and founding board member, Manhattan Country School.

Born in Youngstown, Ohio, he attended Youngstown College; Morehouse College; City College, New York; New York University; Columbia University School of Social Work; and Columbia Teacher's College.

PARTICIPANTS*

ALFORD, THOMAS E.—Mideastern Michigan Library Cooperative, Flint, Michigan

ARONSON, RUTH M.—School of Library Science, State University of New York at Albany, New York

BERGEN, DANIEL P.—Department of Library Science, University of Mississippi, University, Mississippi

BONN, THOMAS L.—State University of New York at Cortland, New York

BOSE, ANINDYA—Knowledge Availability Center, University of Pittsburgh, Pittsburgh, Pennsylvania

BRENTLINGER, HOWARD R.—Tompkins County Public Library, Ithaca, New York

BURNS, JOHN A.—Anne Arundel County Public Library, Annapolis, Maryland

CARROLL, EDWARD C.—Witchita State University Library, Witchita, Kansas

DAVIS, LEILA S.—Graduate School of Library Science, Syracuse University, Syracuse, New York

DOHERTY, AMY S.—School of Nursing, Syracuse University, Syracuse, New York

GREEN, JOSEPH H.—Fiske Free Library, Claremont, New Hampshire

HAMILTON, JAMES H.—Prince George's County Memorial Library, Hyattsville, Maryland

* Individuals' affiliations are given as of the time of the institute, except where a new location is known.

HUGHES, MARY M.—California State Law Library, Sacramento, California

HUNTER, JULIE V.—School of Library Service, Atlanta University, Atlanta, Georgia

JACKSON, MARGARET J.—Technical Library, System Development Corporation, Falls Church, Virginia

KASH, DIANA S.—Montgomery County Board of Education, Rockville, Maryland

KERR, VIRGINIA P.—Public Library of Cincinnati, Cincinnati, Ohio

NITECKI, JOSEPH Z.—University of Wisconsin at Milwaukee Library, Milwaukee, Wisconsin

PARKER, EVELYN—High John Library, Prince George's County, Fairmount Heights, Maryland

ROWLAND, CLARISSA M.—Mary Helen Cochran Library, Sweet Briar College, Virginia

SAGER, DONALD J.—Elyria Public Library, Elyria, Ohio

STREAMER, WILLIAM A.—Enoch Pratt Free Library, Baltimore, Maryland

TABORSKY, THERESA—University of Utah Libraries, Salt Lake City, Utah

WILSON, LOUIS C.—Maryland Division of Library Services, State Department of Education, Baltimore, Maryland

PART TWO
THE PROCEEDINGS

1

THE CITY AS CHANGE MILIEU: SOCIAL, ECONOMIC, AND POLITICAL FACTORS

MONDAY MORNING, AUGUST 11

LECTURER: HORACE BUSBY

PANELISTS: ISAIAH T. CRESWELL, JR.
             MARY LEE BUNDY
             PAUL WASSERMAN
             JOHN FORSMAN

BUSBY: I am grateful for your invitation and welcome the opportunity to consider with you the subject assigned: "The City as Change Milieu: Social, Economic, and Political Factors."

If, at the moment, the issues of our electorate are part war, part peace, part spending, part race, these together are not the sum. The larger and more pervasive part of the issue is a matter of perception, for it is increasingly evident, at every level, that between the people and the public sector there are tensions—tensions over the perception of these times. The times are times of change—but the nature and meaning of the change lie in the eye of the beholder. If I may, I would like to offer my own personal perception of the change coming in America.

As I see it, change is coming at us in America wearing a false face. We are quaking before the hippies and the yippies, the garish and bizarre. We are quailing before the hairlines and the hemlines—and groveling before the absurd and the extreme.

I respectfully suggest that we are putting ourselves on.

While we go tracking through the backwaters and swamps of this society seeking the meaning of our times, I contend that it is out in the mainstream of American life that we are beginning to run the wild water. It is my thesis that our future is being shaped not by this society's violence, but by its velocity—not by the disorder in our streets, but by the disarray spreading throughout our system.

Let me explain this view.

Over the years since World War II, we have brought into being a high-velocity, high-intensity, turned-on society, hurtling along with a momentum all its own, working more change in half a decade than some other societies on this earth will experience in half a century, or even half a millennium.

Much of what this society has wrought has been good—so good, so beneficent, so awesome, so much the fulfillment of our aspirations from the past that we have been slow to recognize the society for what it is: an anarchist in our midst.

All the forces and characteristics of this postwar American society are anarchical in their influence and effect—from knowledge to nomadism. Year by year, the past has been coming down. If there have been revolutions in morality and manners, revolutions in manufacturing, manpower, and the media—to name only a very few—have had far more telling effect upon our organization and functioning. Whatever the change in outward appearances of our life, changes in the inner realities of this complex America have been the greater by far, and many are passing unidentified.

The city is the crucible where these forces have done their work. For the last ten years, we have been observing the changes wrought among us—not merely growth and sprawl and congestion, but far more subtle and more significant changes. We are living a new life—a life man has never lived before, forming ourselves into a new society, beginning a new history, becoming a new people. It has been our special opportunity in growth cities to watch the power structure of Main Street, U.S.A., come down, the old power brokers go bankrupt, the establishment drift away. We have seen the old banks, the old department stores, the old dealerships sell out, lose out, or give up. We have watched the old families and the old neighborhoods, the old churches, old schools, and old ties slowly die. We know that when the demonstrators and the protesters shake their fists at the power structure or the establishment, they are confronting an empty shell.

The reality of our nation may be less what we see than what is no longer here to be seen.

Not merely the America of the 1930s is gone; even the America of the 1950s has been swept away. In a literal sense, this is a new America. Since the decade of the 1960s began, we have grown by more than all the Irish and Israelis, Belgians and Bolivians—plus all the Swiss. Sometime soon, before the decade ends, half of all the Americans who have ever lived will be alive; all that has been done before will need—already needs—doing again. By a 51 percent majority, Americans living next year will hold the casting vote on what America is to be.

But as our velocity has wrought such newness, it has also wrought a growing disarray.

In the America of today, our institutions are new. Our roles, relationships, and experiences are new—new, tentative, and insecure. If there is to be a purposeful, governable society, we need to come together. Yet we have all but lost communications among ourselves. The icons and images of a coherent and cohesive society are missing. Even the language is disintegrating: it has different meanings, city to city, neighborhood to neighborhood. The same is true for our values, and for authority. Not only government, but churches, universities, employers, labor leaders, commentators, certainly parents, are suffering credibility gaps—not because the character of the people has declined, but more because their knowledge has so increased.

Changes such as these, disarray such as this, reach very deeply into our capability to function as a social organization, whatever our purposes may be. These are changes for which we too little allow.

But there is more.

Despite America's pace, despite its growth, despite the seemingly infinite capacity, the truth is that, as now organized, our society is stretched taut. The tolerances are drawn fine. The elasticity is gone. The margins have disappeared. We are short of talent, short of people, thin on experience, thinner on patience. This new American life is strangely hard. Affluence is a vast irrelevancy; as a people, we are overworked, overburdened, overwrought, and, on many things, overanxious. Yet the American pace is unrelenting. Knowledge is our great industry, but the knowledge we are capable of utilizing is falling farther and farther behind the sum of knowledge we possess. Increasingly, ours is a society slipping out of phase. In sector after sector, from the delivery of medical services to the delivery of the daily mail, we are barely able to do what we are doing, with no assurance of how long we can continue.

What I am describing, our statistics don't—and can't—describe.

The point is simply this: in the United States, we are beyond the familiar times when the state of our nation could be measured by the annual increase in the GNP, the monthly levels of the Consumers' Price Index, or the daily reports of the Dow-Jones averages.

In politics and government, and throughout all aspects of our private sector and private lives, these times are, as Jefferson said of our earliest years, "like new times." It is not the garish and bizarre that should be occupying us. The fundamentals and the imperatives of organizing and governing a new society should be our concerns. As a nation, as a people, we are at a time of beginning again.

In the earliest days of the Republic, Alexander Hamilton warned of a time when, as he put it, "every vital question of state will be merged in the single question, who will be the next President of the United States?" Last year, in the national campaigns for that office, "every vital question of state"—domestically, at least—was merged into a single concern for "law and order."

I mean nothing I say to disparage that issue. The need for order in the streets and in the courts—and in the lives of all the people—is simply an indispensable requisite for any organized society. We have been late in our national life coming to grips with the realities of this responsibility. But my point is larger.

In our obsession with the false faces of change—not always the bizarre faces but sometimes the orthodox and conventional faces which have come to be so familiar—I believe we are neglecting a far greater issue: a classical issue of this society's order as a functioning organism. Our political focus is elsewhere. We are simply not allowing for the prospect that while we leave the fundamentals unattended, while we run on the momentum of other decades and other generations, our system, in its totality, may be almost daily becoming less and less able to survive the velocity which has been generated. Certainly, we are not, as I see it, allowing for the increasing possibility that as the balances become more delicate, the institutions and arrangements of the society more fragile, abrupt changes in our politics could have serious consequences to the orderliness of our society's performance.

Let me illustrate and underscore what I am suggesting.

Out of the traumatic experiences of the past two years, it has become the fixation of the public dialogue that the danger to America domestically is division. The imagery and the dialogue of two Americas is pervasive: two Americas—one black, one white; one poor, one rich; one peaceful, one militaristic; one illiterate, one learned; one ill, one robust; one alienated, one involved—and on and on. To every domestic question, this is the formulation which may immediately apply.

Certainly, the formulation is correct in identifying the disorder on one side of each division. But is it correct in inferring that order is the condition on the other side? Can two Americas—one orderly, one out of order—exist side by side? For myself, I believe not, and that is why I would pose the question:

Is our greater American danger division, or is it disruption?

In the context of these remarks (and, on this, there is a far larger context in which the question should be considered) I would like to read several passages from Roy Franklin Nichols' neglected study of another period in our history, the decade of the 1850s, a period which ended in the disruption of our society.

In those years, Nichols writes, the United States became "super-charged" and "hyperemotional." He explains:

The basic reasons for this hyperemotionalism cannot be neatly formulated and weighted. Fundamentally the process was an illustration of what Machiavelli describes as the "confusion of a growing state." The popula-tion of the United States was rapidly multiplying . . . . Many Americans were creating new communities, others were crowding together in older urban centers. In old and new, change was continual . . . .
Characteristic [of the social growth] and dominant in it were pervasive, divisive and cohesive attitudes which Whitman described as a grand upheaval of ideas and reconstruction of many things on new bases. The social confusion in itself was the great problem confronting statesmen and politicians. Turn where they would, they could not escape it . . . .
A great disruptive fact was the baneful influence of elections almost continuously in progress, of campaigns never over, and of political uproar endlessly arousing emotions. The system of the fathers might possibly bear within itself the seeds of its own destruction. This constant agita-tion . . . raised to ever higher pitch the passion-rousing oratory of rivals. They egged one another on to make more and more exaggerated state-ments to people pervasively romantic and protestant, isolated and con-fused. The men and women exhibiting these different attitudes were not isolated and separated by boundaries—they dwelt side by side, and the same person might be moved by more than one attitude at a time, or by different attitudes at different times . . . . The baffling problem

was not how to maintain a balance among the states but how to preserve a balance among a number of emotional units or attitudes. It was this that proved beyond the political capacity of the time.

The parallels hardly need to be drawn. We are "supercharged." "Hyperemotionalism" is rising. We are experiencing "a grand upheaval of ideas and reconstruction of many things on new bases." Certainly we are under "the baneful influence of elections almost continuously in progress, of campaigns never over . . . ." In this tense, taut, high-velocity society, none who work closely with it need have the point belabored: disruption is an ever-present worry throughout this complexity we call America—not merely social disruption, but disruption in the capacity of this organism to accomplish what we expect and the future demands of it.

In these times, our kinship is not so much with the year 2000 as with the year 1776. We are back to the basics of organizing a new society and providing for its governance. If what we have done in years past has succeeded—and much of it has succeeded beyond all expectations—that very success requires of us that we do anew much that we have done before and build larger on stronger foundations for new dimensions we have not yet faced.

We have created an economic republic. Now our challenge is to govern it.

A new people, of new experiences and new values, must decide anew what we mean by "order," by "freedom," by "justice."

We need new concepts of law and of politics.

We need, I believe, basic structural changes in our governmental system.

We need new thought, as a society, about science, agriculture, and energy supplies, about the roles and rewards of both labor and business, about the strength and competency of our professions, about the values and ends of education.

We are back to very basic questions about how our society and system are to function—and, indeed, whether either can continue to function as now organized. Many of the questions we have regarded as long closed—questions settled thirty or even sixty years ago—are coming open again, to be rethought, redecided in the bias of the present, not the past. Increasingly, it is apparent that the political decisions which helped bring order yesterday are enemies of order for tomorrow. Under the weight of political, administrative, and even judicial decisions long accumulated, under the burden of private choices which have become mere rote and ritual, our system may not even now be performing as we assume it to be.

The question, then, is this: Are the tasks the times require beyond the political capacity of a managed society?

I would like to offer some personal comments on several aspects of the political challenge.

It is true that we are gripped by a mythology of power in this country. A monarchical impulse runs among us. Much of what is asked and expected of the public sector is unreal, romantic, and ridiculous. But it is also true that too much of government is anonymous, insulated, and inaccessible. Its ears are stuffed with the cotton of its own concerns; more and more, its doors are closed. It is parochial. At the higher levels of most government, there is an air of meritocracy; at the lower reaches, an appearance of caste. Governments communicate best and correspond most with other governments; redundancy grows between the levels. An institutional rudeness is endemic throughout government, and it is not all confined to the lower echelons. There is a saying, "If a citizen wants to be insulted, ignored, or dealt with rudely, all he needs to do is to try to do business in person with any government office."

Winston Churchill once said that when one is close to the heart of great events, it is hard to realize "how damnable life is for the average citizen." While I know many of you realize it, I sincerely believe all of government suffers because so many, at some reaches of public management, fail to realize just "how damnable" many citizens feel the attitudes of their 80,000 governments have become.

Over recent years, our public dialogue in the United States has become increasingly "supercharged" and "hyperemotional." It is all too often borne along on wholly erroneous facts and irrelevant assumptions. It is a period of political vacuum, when old wisdom is falling aside and new wisdom is forming.

The popular perception is that the cities are failures, that their directions are precipitately downward. But is that perception correct? Only in the past thirty years have we actually begun to manage our cities. Only in the past forty years have the organized police forces actually come into control of most major cities. Only in the past fifteen years have we finally begun to design and build highways for modern automobile traffic, instead of for the horses and carriages of our grandfathers. Only in the past ten years has a glass of water begun to taste much the same in every city.

Socially, politically, and governmentally, cities are the most complex of governments. Other than at the Pentagon or the White House, Washington can quit at 5:00 P.M. A city's government can never rest. There are valves to turn, gauges to watch, infinite mechanical and social mechanisms to maintain. A city is never more than thirty minutes from riot. Fire, explosion, pestilence, contagion, and disaster are always near. Objectively, the simple fact that America's cities have been kept functioning through one of history's great migrations and growth must rate them as showpiece successes of the American system. But it is critically important that all the people, all the policy makers at every level, recognize that the complex city is always acutely vulnerable to disruption, in the sense I have been discussing. We must be far more sensitive, I believe, in our handling of policies toward America's cities.

In that regard, I would like to offer these specific comments.

• The founding fathers did not envision Washington as society's plumber nor city hall as the fountain of its philosophy. Too many national problems are called city problems today, and far too many local problems are described as national.

• It is very clear that the continuing success of our cities is imperiled by the imposition upon their resources—and their true priorities—by the burdens of the welfare sector. The problems of human welfare, as much as the problems of human rights, are problems of and for the whole society. The central government was established and constitutionally ordained to promote the "general welfare." The responsibility for public welfare must be vested at the national levels.

• If there has been too much nationalization of local government, there has been, I believe, too much localization of the national government. The highest responsibilities of the national government cannot be met if its chief executive is transformed into the nation's mayor-in-chief. The broad consensus required to support and sustain our foreign policies, and our ultimate national purposes, cannot be achieved by a central government "marking the sparrow's fall" in thousands of cities and neighborhoods. The national government must, in shaping its new urban role, avoid the morass of local entanglements from which cities themselves are trying to escape.

Further, I would like to suggest that in the eagerness to obtain national assistance for local needs, those in the urban field have a responsibility to guard against distortion of the federal role. It comes easily to the political tongue to berate the federal participation in space activities as proof of negligent and inhumane federal priorities. In reality, over the span of the age of space, which began ten years ago this month, federal spending has totaled $44 billion, and of that, $14.8 billion has gone to the Apollo program to put a man on the moon. In just this decade, since President Eisenhower's last fiscal year, federal outlays for urban aids have exceeded $60 billion.

In a broader view, let me make this observation. In its orientation of recent years, public management at every level has emphasized the priority of those "social programs" which most readily quantify. But the burden of what I have been saying today is that the challenges and the coming crises of this society are not all encompassed in such a line of vision. No single factor seems more alienating to public support than the people's perception that government is consumed with its own conception of social problems, to the neglect of society's other challenges. All programs which serve society's needs are social programs. A concerted effort must be made, I suggest, to enlarge the concept of "social action" and to direct our society's energies and capacity, as well as its resources, into many other areas now neglected.

In the private sector, there are systems analysis organizations which say, very bluntly, that their work consists of disinterring "dead executives" from the computers of corporations. Public management must develop the capacity—and the interest—to extricate dead visions, dead purposes, and dead politics from its technology and techniques.

The technology and techniques of public management are trouble areas. Technology is not the enemy of democratic values; it may be their salvation. But in these times, information is power. Public management's absolute control of information—by which policy is developed and by which policy might be evaluated—is absolute power, a power incompatible with democracy. It is the gathering storm that if the price of a managed society is such a delegation of power, many citizens are unprepared to pay it. Opening the policy processes to greater public participation is the urgent responsibility of your profession.

The library is a center of information, a source of information retrieval about the society. The library perhaps is the greatest underdeveloped potential among the many American public services. The two institutions which we want to send our young people to are the library and the jail. We should really know more about both.

My message, then, is this: In these times, we are experiencing what Whitman described in other times as "a grand upheaval of ideas and the reconstruction of many new things on new bases."

Whatever the appearances, there is much in America on which to build. I reject the vision that ours is a society coming apart; rather, I believe, it is a new society trying to come together. It is a new, forming society yearning for order, not rejecting it—yearning to create values, not destroy them. In our governance, there cannot be two Americas—one old, one new. "The earth belongs to the living," and government cannot belong to the dead past.

Americans living now are demanding the right to participate in their own governance. While it is spoken in many ways by many voices, what the people are saying, I believe, is what Emerson spoke for Americans of his time:

Our age is retrospective. It builds the sepulchres of the fathers. It writes biographies, histories and criticism. The foregoing generations beheld God and nature face to face; we, through their eyes. Why should not we also enjoy an original relation with the universe?

You cannot be partisan, but neither can you be neutral. You—and your role—are in the crucible.

There is a crisis, but it is my perception that it is not so much a crisis of our cities as it is a crisis of our society. In this period, we shall be walking the rim of the abyss, a "supercharged, hyperemotional" society, capable of creating the greatest good but capable also, by self-deception, of bringing chaos upon itself.

I would conclude by recalling the words John F. Kennedy spoke in his first State of the Union Address, as this decade began, when he said, "Before my term is ended, we shall have to test anew whether any nation organized and governed such as ours can endure." It is the organization and governance of this nation which are being tested in these years. And we can add now, as President Kennedy did then, "The outcome is by no means certain."

CRESWELL: Change does not affect many of the peoples in this country and the world. The society in which we live, known as America, really is a process and a structure. The government of this country does not so much set the pace as it does follow the support and the economy. Too often, change does not affect many lives. The library is somewhat of a system of information gathering. Libraries enjoy a great deal of status, yet they are selective. Libraries exclude many important facts.

BUNDY: Things don't work any more. Our sense of professional identity seems gone; rather, there is a new sense of professional identity criticizing the traditional methods and practices but without anything to replace the old ways.

WASSERMAN: I suppose this is one of the difficulties of living and trying to educate in times of change. Who sets the agenda? One of the fundamental frustrations of our time is that we all are questioning everything, but we don't have the sages of old to direct us to what is appropriate. Our responsibility is not only that of questioning but also that of assuming the responsibility of identifying alternatives. Mechanisms have not been utilized. We have not yet got consensus on the way to grapple with these problems.

BUSBY: I agree with Mr. Creswell about libraries' having status. Everywhere we have a library it has too much status. It is an awesome institution. I would like to see the libraries leading the public schools rather than the schools leading the libraries, which have been withdrawn institutions devoted to books. We are in an age in which the book is no longer the sole source of wisdom from the sages of the past. There are many other media. A neighborhood library should encourage the residents of the area to contribute a live vocal history of their community. Libraries should keep a record of the language as we use it today. There is so much we can do to bring people into the library for purposes other than reading. We can display such things as births and deaths. It can be a mirror in which people can see themselves.

FORSMAN: The vast majority of this nation doesn't know who it is. It is a large, money-making animal. The goal is personal gain— building a house, owning a swimming pool, buying gadgets of all kinds. The power structure of the city does not see the library as a source of important change. The library is a local institution. Until the library actually takes its role seriously of finding relevant information, directly related to war and race, it will remain a local institution. If it gets appropriate help, it may start helping the man in the city.

CRESWELL: It is my observation that in the supposedly nontroubled segment of our society we are beginning to discover that there is much that is not apparent and not current in our dialogue. One of the most important facts about the functioning of our society is the fact that it has never been and is not an integrated society. Congress has traditionally been a reservoir of continuity. Change has come to many of our structures. It has virtually obliterated our political parties. Change does not necessarily mean we are going ahead. We might be moving backward. The library itself, in order to be a related, committed, involved part of society, must change its own image of self. Therefore, those in the profession of library science must change. You don't get political power or backing before change.

PARTICIPANT: We are talking about the tremendous increase in change. We are still discussing change within a given society. Mr. Busby, you referred to Jefferson. Are we really in such bad shape that we must start completely anew?

CRESWELL: New institutions are beginning. The family is important, but we are approaching a great welfare state, a military ghetto. There is a conflict in the churches. We are bound to emerge with new and stronger religious institutions. The university will emerge anew.

PARTICIPANT: I have two questions. Mr. Busby, on the issue of centralization, and at the same time decentralization, the question, as far as the library is concerned, is which will be more relevant to us?

Second, on this matter of change, the urban area for a long time and the rural area more recently have one thing in common. Both are experiencing a loss of political power in relation to the suburb. In the Midwest the suburb is the area that is growing more rapidly. Cities are decreasing. How is the urban area affected by the change? A suburb is really an area that is supported by a city but not a part of it. Suburbs do not really feel tied to a particular city.

CRESWELL: No matter what you call the city, every city is probably composed of five, ten, or twenty metropolitan areas. Power in suburban areas is a reaction to centralization.

BUSBY: The word "city" is basically a code word. The suburb *is* the city.

PARTICIPANT: An extremely difficult question for any administrator or librarian today to face is how much centralization and decentralization can be achieved in his system. In one local library, there is less involved, but even there, centralization comes into the picture because of alliances with the state library association, or a telecom system, or whatever, wherein some centralization is necessary. It seems to me one of the most acute decisions an administrator needs to make is what operations will he agree to centralize and how much can he lessen that centralization so that there will be effective operational control at the local level.

That's a comment, but I do have a question. I keep wondering about one thing that Dean Wasserman has said. We raise questions today in the library school and elsewhere, but there aren't the sages of old to turn to for the answers. Why? Is it our educational system? Is it a comment on our life today? Why don't we have these sages?

WASSERMAN: That's a good philosophical question; perhaps it was rhetorical. Where are the wise men who can chart the path, direct us along the right lines?

PARTICIPANT: I assumed they were the library deans.

BUNDY: You assumed wrong.

WASSERMAN: If we look for authoritarian direction, this would be one potential source, but I don't think that's what the person who asked the question had in mind precisely.

CRESWELL: The comment, which may have been made facetiously, may be as close as you can come to a valid answer. The library dean certainly doesn't have all the wisdom of the world within his head, but as nearly as anyone he should be able to direct you towards an answer, or at least an area of inquiry.

WASSERMAN: I suppose this comes in conflict with the notion that direction comes from a community of scholars rather than the coercive effect of one among them. Although this is a school of thinking in which I classify myself, we have relatively few statesmen. The library field is bereft, more bereft than most, I would suggest, of such qualities of leadership and intelligence. It would be foolhardy in the extreme to look here for salvation.

BUNDY: Let's put it another way. Once we accept the fact that the great men are gone—or if they are still around, they're keeping a throttle on organizations, the very ones they may have founded—then we're ready to talk about democracy. Then we're ready to talk about group leadership. But as long as we cling to the notion that some people know better than other people just because we've given them some kind of status in administration, we can't grow.

PARTICIPANT: To me, the sages of the past are sages of the past because they are the past. What makes us think that they were sages when they were alive? I'm sure that they were granted as many problems as anybody now. I think we tend to look at them as sages of the past because they are removed in time. The basic problem today is that everybody is looking for *the* answer to the problem. Everyone looks for one person or one group to provide salvation. I think that's ridiculous.

PARTICIPANT: Hear, hear! That expression "old sages" reminds me of Mark Twain's definition of a classic: a book that everybody respects but nobody reads.

BUNDY: We do have our sacred cows in librarianship.

WASSERMAN: From old sages you get old answers.

BUSBY: I would offer this perspective. Take this "great men are sages" question and apply it somewhat more broadly than just to librarianship. In our society we show an instinct for almost a worship of royalty, a kind of monarchical impulse. We want to run out and create saviors and messiahs at every opportunity to deal with political questions of all sorts. One of Washington's leading correspondents, whom you would all know, told me very recently that he is going through a great personal trauma as a journalist. As a man occupying a responsible position, he feels that the press over the last eight years has been responsible for five misjudgments about the five most important Americans of that period. I won't get into names because we could get into an all-day discussion of that, perhaps.

But I think that there is an effort to create sages out of sow's ears, as it were. We're trying to find, as you said, *the* answer to *the* problem! If we can't find a person who qualifies, we want to find a foundation, or a university-affiliated study organization, or some such thing to give us *the* definitive word.

The whole truth of our times must be that we have had this great investment in education in this country. We have produced a society with the largest proportion of educated, supposedly enlightened people that any society has had. We are supposed to be the sages. We're not quite bringing ourselves to make the judgments that the sages made. We're not sitting down and saying, "This is the wisdom." We keep looking over our shoulders for somebody else to tell us. It takes a lot of responsibility to become a sage.

BUNDY: May I try it another way? Maybe in this profession right now we don't need sages, but people willing to go out on a limb, willing to stand up and be counted, willing to do something that seems daring to the profession. A good share of them will fail, but we need people to move us from this dead center position. I don't know if you would call these people leaders.

BUSBY: Back up their judgments with action.

PARTICIPANT: How did the sages of the past get to be the sages of the past if they weren't both willing and ready to go out on a limb?

PARTICIPANT: There are some sages today. The name of Paul Wasserman is just as well known on the East Coast as it is on the West Coast. There is more to it. These leaders are very important whether we recognize this or not. Changes are coming when exceptional men happen to be where they are.

BUNDY: That's a very nice accolade.

WASSERMAN: I wonder, Mr. Busby, if you would say something about your notion of a library's response to the local clientele, about the way in which it can be an information and a communication center in the culture, which it hasn't normally considered itself.

BUSBY: I do feel I'm way out on a limb in talking to you about libraries and library science, but it has seemed to me that the library is peculiarly suited for many functions that would serve beneficial purposes, which no other organization or institution within our urban culture either is performing or perhaps is able to perform, such as a place in which the young can express themselves.

A library in close proximity to the ghetto areas (I hate to use the word "ghetto" because it also is a very big and dangerous code word right now) could be a place in which the ghetto children could exhibit drawings, art work. We have seen the use of that, for example, in New York City for a time. Allow people to express themselves and then put up their work somewhere so that they can come and bring other people with them—their friends, adults, or children—to show them. Then they can say, in effect, "I'm part of something here."

That's one kind of participation. I also feel that libraries can be a logical place to sponsor the kind of competitions or organized activities in which people of all ages and all stations could write about their experiences, write about their history, pry into and develop the history of their block, or their neighborhood, or some institution.

I gather I'm seeing the librarian's role in a way in which librarians don't see it. The generation of information is a valuable exercise, along with that of cataloging it and disseminating it. You serve a community function by giving outlet to and encouraging constructive programs of this sort in many different directions, not just the kinds of things that come readily to mind, but in many different directions—churches, business institutions, high schools, all our modern schools, the public schools—where we must cope with this great growth.

In the early 1950s, they were busy building new elementary schools, and then new junior high schools, and then new high schools. And now, within a rather short time period, the problem of a lot of school districts is what to do with the elementary schools that have been built since World War II, the new schools which now must be phased out, closed within the next few years because the clientele is gone. We need to preserve our community in terms of information, but much more important than preserving the history, we also need to give the people in the community some place in which there is an opportunity to express themselves, and in the process to learn about where they live, and what they are, and how to interact. There is no racial line. There is no color line to this activity. It would be a benefit to society, I believe, for the library to be much more a community resource than the past conception of libraries leaves them to be. I'm speaking very amateurishly in saying that.

PARTICIPANT: I have a question. I'm interested in finding out where you would draw the line. Would you say a library can go this far and stop, or is it something invisible in your mind about how far you can go?

BUSBY: Go where on what?

PARTICIPANT: I mean getting involved in the community, which is going to happen. You can go so far and you run into a problem that probably will step on somebody else's toes in their field.

BUNDY: It isn't a problem we usually have because we don't usually try to do anything.

BUSBY: I've heard only a very little conversation like what I've heard this morning in relation to coming here. I don't know whether this is the proper thing to say or not, but, among librarians in this profession, there seems to me to be an inordinate concern over just this question: "How far can we go?" I won't say "fear" because that's an ugly word and probably an unfair word, but there seems to be some sense that there is a line circumscribing librarians. I believe the meaning of our times is that those lines are coming down.

PARTICIPANT: This is what I want to know. I have always been in arguments about the way I feel, but I don't think there should be a line. In education there should be no line, but really there is a line. I think we are in the middle trying to break down the line.

BUSBY: There is always going to be a line, yes. But the point is whether you're going to test the line and have a valid cause for expanding it, for pushing it out, or whether you're just going to say, "There's the line" and sit and look at it your whole career. It may not be there.

PARTICIPANT: I think the earlier question is very much to the point. It seems we're always talking about librarians' going out and doing something, but yet you really don't involve the institution, the library itself. How do we put those two factors together? Where is the line? Where is the line for librarians and where is the line for the libraries? It seems to me this is a rather neutral area. I'm interested in the panel's reaction to this particular point.

WASSERMAN: I would suppose that the library as institution is nothing more than the sum total of the perspectives, the commitment, the zeal, and the enthusiasm of the library people who make up its staff. We seem to harbor within us the limiting notion that there is a sort of monolithic body that keeps us from doing things.

In reflecting on my own experience and my own perceptions of librarianship, I see it as an open business in which almost everything and anything is possible if it is calculated within the framework of the individual psyche. A librarian has a great deal more freedom than he typically perceives of himself as having. The limits are limits of the imagination and limits of enthusiasm as much as they are limits of institutions, institutional history, and the culture of librarianship.

PARTICIPANT: I will argue that point with you because I've seen staff really get worked up about certain projects. I've seen things go into the mill, through the chain of command all the way up, and finally the director comes back and says, "The board will not go along with this." Somebody always does not go along with this.

BUNDY: We're getting a function of Paul's personality. Wherever he practices, he does what he thinks needs to be done. He doesn't ask the bureaucracy. Some of us who are better bureaucrats have asked and faced what you're saying. Ultimately, we are told no.

PARTICIPANT: Are you saying that this is a frontier, that we should be innovators rather than following the conservative chain of command?

BUNDY: The branches of public libraries have been doing it for a long time. They just don't ask permission to put up a different exhibit or do some things differently. The change is greater in libraries than it looks, if we study their policies and procedures at the headquarters.

PARTICIPANT: That's not really a change. So many exhibits in the library are not important.

WASSERMAN: Let's take some cases in point. Mr. Busby has identified a couple of things. As one looks at the public library and as one looks at the community library service, one tends to see a kind of book deposit center where people come and get things. One doesn't see a library conceived by librarians as a committed agency tied to the destiny, the needs, and the life styles of people around that library. There isn't that identification with it.

Now, in the folk mythology of librarianship, the branch library is attuned and acculturated to the requirements, the habits, and the needs of that culture within which it functions. In fact, we know that that is not the case. We know that librarians don't really get into that culture, don't interact with it. Mr. Busby used an interesting illustration when we talked during the coffee break: tell people what's going on in it, go out and get the information, and bring it into focus for that community. Play a communication or an informational role within that culture.

I'm suggesting that there are no constraints. There is no library administration that says no.

FORSMAN: I disagree with you completely, Paul. Practically everyone I have ever seen sets barriers. The bigger they are, the worse they are. You take any state that I've been in, and the administration will come down on a librarian who steps out and starts doing these things, because every one of them takes time, every one of them takes money. The administrator is put in the position of hanging on to time and money. He cannot keep people on the desk and have them going out and doing these jobs that you're talking about, that they should be doing, that you are training them to do. After a couple of years of it, with administration all the way from the top down coming down on them, they stop doing innovative things. That's what happens to the innovation. It goes away from librarians constantly throughout this country.

PARTICIPANT: Your point is very well taken here. I think Dr. Wasserman is saying, "Administration does not say no." John's point is apropos. Administrators say, "You know there is only so much money, and what you're talking about is a very expensive service."

WASSERMAN: If we follow this to its logical conclusion, we can never change anything. I'm suggesting that we come back to what comes first, the resource or the manifestation that there is an alternative. I'm saying you'll never get the resource until you do something otherwise and demonstrate that there is an alternative. If you wait for the resource, you'll never, never in a million years, do anything different.

FORSMAN: I want to be paid for what I'm doing. I'm getting tired of people telling me . . .

BUNDY: Yes. I'm working twelve hours a day. They look the other way when you're giving it all.

CRESWELL: But isn't that the question that faces almost any person who works within a structure that has some rules and regulations, *any* person who works within a bureaucracy that is dependent upon somebody else for funds? It's a question that you can look at practically and theoretically. Maybe theoretically there are no limitations and there are no guidelines. But practically, you know that there are. You know it because you have experienced it. If you don't think there are, try to move and you will find that you run into the wall.

If there is a solution, it's as Dr. Wasserman says. Maybe I'm trying to say it a little differently. Within that framework, you have to find out where the wall is, first of all, and then, within the structure of the institution, you begin to try to change it.

There are a couple of different ways to change it. The one that comes to my mind, and it's a simple kind of explanation, is that of a political process. You're talking about a state legislature that appropriates funds. You're talking about a community library that can build a constituency that will be its support. You're talking about a school library that has to play off students against the administration, but the students are gaining a lot more power now.

It's what the government worker faces. It's what a private practitioner of law faces with his bar association. Just because you know that sometime you're going to run across a wall shouldn't mean that you don't move. You move up to it. You push against it a little bit and try to find out what can give on the other side of it. Maybe you need to move somebody who is on your library board. Maybe you need to get on the board yourself, or maybe you need to go from the head of a branch library to the head of the city system.

BUSBY: Saul Alinsky said a few years ago something that I copied down. From my perspective, it's a real gem of wisdom. He said that so-called power institutions get away with a lot because they're not challenged. You see, power is not just what the status quo has, it is more what we may think it has. I want to speak from the perspective of having had the opportunity, the experience, and all that, to feel that I know what the power structure is. I don't think there is one, only what everybody thinks the power structure is. I've seen it. I know it is not this formidable thing that a lot of people build up in their minds that it is. If there is any concern about it, it is the very lack of strength there, more than its great powerful hold on things.

If you look back at the experiences of this decade, we have done an enormous number of things politically and socially and otherwise that, at the beginning of the decade, would have been thought impossible. It couldn't be conceived of being done in a lifetime. We have done it by lots of ways, not just by confrontation, not just by physical approach, but by simply saying, "This is what ought to be. This is the right thing. Let's go do it." All too often, you see experts in the departments and the agencies of the federal government coming up with a recommendation or a new program. By the time the program gets all the way up the channels to the point of ultimate sale, it's all confused, because the people who are experts on the subject have been making their own political judgments along the way—we can get this through or we can't get this through.

This is what was happening on foreign aid, for example. It became a joke that every foreign aid bill was double the amount actually wanted and expected because there was some little wisdom that you had to ask for twice as much in order to get half what you asked. As a result, you ended up getting about one-fourth because nobody believed the bureaucracy's statement on anything.

In this current discussion, you're talking about a political impasse, a political problem. The professional has a great obligation, not to make the political judgment, but to keep coming at the political barrier, which we're all too much inclined not to do. Either we tack our sails before hitting that barrier, or else we come up to it and just want to make a speech against it, knowing that it's there, and it's evil, it's wrong, and it's not going to give us what we want.

There is a great deal of power in the competent professional, the man or woman who proves and practices his competency and is uncompromising in that regard. He is indeed compromising at the final point, perhaps, in order to reach an agreement, but he says, "This is what this library ought to be doing and this is the support of it. It's not just my bias. It's not just my opinion. This is what we can do." You need to come on a little stronger.

BUNDY: Okay. I agree with you. You come on strong and the bureaucracy answers "No!" or gives you a very weak compromise. You can't afford to keep asking and keep getting no, so you must have alternatives. If not, then in the end, they know they can say no to you and you have weakened your position.

BUSBY: You always have alternatives.

BUNDY: You must have alternatives!

BUSBY: But you keep on with your ultimate goal.

BUNDY: Then you're nagging, unless you're prepared to find alternatives.

BUSBY: This gets back to my layman's impression of the profession as having some kind of built-in fear of the challenge of the confrontation. If you need it, well, don't ever say no.

BUNDY: One of the fears is that libraries don't want to accept the consequence for doing anything. If they're told no, they accept it.

BUSBY: You may have to accept the "no" on the budget this year, but that doesn't mean that you give up on next year.

BUNDY: No, but if you have a history of every year letting a university administration say no to more than a 10 percent budget increase, when it comes around to your budget and somebody has to give, well, they know the librarian will take the cut. I agree with everything you say, but it's more complex.

BUSBY: By continuing to push, I don't mean all you do is go ahead and redesign next year's budget asking for a 50 percent increase.

BUNDY: All right. That's what I want to get at.

BUSBY: There may be other things that don't lead to a compromise solution but which are the things that might lead to what I refer to as a political solution. In other words, you come up against the wall. You only get your 10 percent. To keep on pushing means that maybe next time you try to flank the wall. Not so much in terms of your demands, but you try to do something with what's behind the wall.

If you're a neighborhood library and you're not getting the budget increase that you need, maybe you need to violate whatever the local Hatch Act is, to let the people know that they should tell the city councilmen they want more money in the library. Going around the wall is a political process.

BUNDY: Traditionally, we have allowed our public library administrators to engage in this form of political activity. But for the reference librarians, for example, in a public library to band together and engage in this activity would be novel.

BUSBY: There are all kinds of ways to exercise political muscle. I don't know whether reference librarians have a union.

BUNDY: You're saying "Build a stronger professional group." I couldn't agree more, because many of our administrations are sitting in the libraries now and we're trying to find ways to go around them.

WASSERMAN: Let me comment on this in a somewhat different way. I think it's important to the discussion, and it relates to what John Forsman is saying about resources and the need for resources before you can do anything different. I want to make it clear that I don't concede this.

In librarianship, we are in a kind of peasant culture. That's one in which you live very frugally. All you have is bread, and you sort of hold it, and you nurture it, because it's so rare and scarce that you must make that resource go all the way. It may be that many libraries were once in this kind of culture where they had so very, very little that they were like the peasant culture. Every little bit they had had to be nurtured and put to work, used and reused and used again, like the kids used to use paper on both sides in school when I was a kid.

But I don't believe that large and complex libraries with large work forces have so little resource flexibility or leverage that they can't make some variations within the organization in the application and allocation of resources to problem solving and to doing their work. I just don't believe that we are so stringently controlled within libraries that our resources are so tightly drawn, that we are a peasant culture any longer. We use this argument as a rationalization for not doing otherwise. I just don't believe we are that thin. We're not stretched.

When I walk into a library and I see people reading magazines or doing all sorts of irrelevant things like filing cards, I know we're not using our resources well. Now, until we do that, nobody is going to give us more.

PARTICIPANT: This has to do with who's to decide on the budget, right? Why can't the people decide the budget? Can somebody answer that? These are the people being served; why can't they decide it?

CRESWELL: I can suggest an answer. It may be because democracy is probably working less and less than it has in the past. People don't decide an awful lot of things. Look at the people in the District of Columbia. They don't decide anything very much about what goes on around them. There are so many layers in government structure that between whatever may be the Jeffersonian theory of the right coming out of the mass and that point where the execution takes place, you've got all these experts like me who make the political judgments here and there about what's going to get through.

PARTICIPANT: I recall reading recently a book called *The Learning Society*. The author is extremely critical of our existing educational institutions. He says that this will not change, though, until the community makes a political decision that there should be some other kind of educational arrangement. Now, Mr. Creswell, you suggested in the beginning that perhaps political change is directed by the economic system. If that's the case, when you're talking about political change, maybe we're talking about secondary matters which are very, very circumscribed by something more basic. Would you care to say anything more about that?

CRESWELL: I'm not quite sure I follow you. What I hoped to say earlier is that the government that I see, particularly the federal government, is a reflection of an economic process that doesn't control it so much as it does react to it, and possibly even support it. I guess that the corollary to this is that many of the decisions that are made, are made for economic reasons, no matter what kind of tag or label we put onto them.

I see possibly three kinds of power that people exercise. One is an economic power; I think that's very clear. The other is political power, whether it's great or in a lesser degree. The third is a military power, the power of might and arms. I think the government is much more responsive to economic power than it is to political power.

PARTICIPANT: That is sort of what I had in mind. Mr. Busby this morning indicated that he doesn't see any force like perhaps John

Forsman saw, or Mr. Creswell has suggested, that sets certain circumscribed limits within which institutions have to operate.

BUSBY: Over the last forty years, basically in this country, we've been engaged in the creation of what Adolf Berle called the American economic republic. As a response to the collapse of the economy and the depression of 1929 and the 1930s, most of the thrust of the centralization of power, the whole development of the federal government as we know it today, has been oriented, as Mr. Creswell is saying, to things economic.

Our institutions have been geared that way. The government is responsive to this. In other words, this is not all bad. I don't think that you're saying that government is solely responsive to crass materialistic motives. In order to maintain the welfare programs of our society, or the educational programs, or any number of other worthy things, the government policy is oriented to maintaining the high level of employment and the high level of capital investment and all that sort of thing.

I think we are coming to a time now in which we have created a national economic republic, but man does not live by economics alone. In this decade, we are beginning to realize that there are a lot of other aspects to the spectrum of life that are not really part of a national republic. Everything, all economic power, for example, basically lies in Washington. When the cities seemed to be blowing up in 1967, it was very fashionable to say, "All the power is in Washington. Why don't we do something in Washington?" Well, actually the power wasn't there. The police power wasn't there. The power over firemen, the power over insurance, the power over all sorts of things has been retained at the state or at the local level. The educational power has been retained at the local level, at least until this decade.

We have created an economic republic. Now we must learn how to govern it, and we have a political upheaval, a revolution to go through. The institutions of this society have been occupied with that economic process through the 1930s, 1940s, 1950s, and 1960s. They have been oriented to it. I think that we are seeing in this decade, the last half of this decade, a great deal of challenge to those institutions saying, "This isn't adequate! This isn't enough!"

Young people come in and look at our society. They see it today and they don't appreciate the fact that a congested expressway out here is a vast improvement over what would have been there if we hadn't built it. They just see the congested expressway and say, "It's one heck of a big mess. Our society ought to be able to do better than that."

That's where the people in power in the society have had an awfully hard time understanding what all the commotion is about. They've been saying, "We have improved things so much." And they have. There's no falsity in that statement, but the point is the improvement has brought us to the point where we have a new base. We've got to start all over. It's no longer an improvement.

PARTICIPANT: People like Rap Brown, for instance, or some of the other more militant individuals, say they don't want any part of what affluent America is, because they don't like that life style for any-body—white or black.

PARTICIPANT: You don't have to go to black militants to find this. In fact, there are probably more white militants among the students who are willing to say, "I don't want any part of this system" than there are black folks right about now who will say that. Maybe I'm the wrong person to say this, but I wonder if behind all that there is somewhat more rhetoric than reality. All these students, and probably Rap Brown too, to an extent greater than they would admit, are living off the fat of this society. Yet they feel they have to change it.

If there's going to be any hope, it's going to come through some balance between these two different kinds of tension so that there can be a government that makes decisions recognizing economic realities but that does not disenfranchise people so terribly through a whole elaborate process. The democracy that we are all taught about in school is left in shambles. It is a sham. This revolution of the 1960s is composed of all kinds of people, not just students or black folks, but all kinds of people saying, "We don't need the ABM! Let's get out of Vietnam, because it's just an economic war!" Maybe this will cause the system to shift, not totally, but enough so that it becomes responsive to a plebiscite. I don't know that that kind of democracy is the best kind of system to have either.

BUSBY: I think we have had a great deal of repression of the demo-cratic impulse. We have invested the resources of this country heavily over many generations, trying to create better citizens for a democracy, better citizens better able to engage in self-government. Yet the drift of representative democracy has been more and more away from continuing democratic participation.

I'm not just talking about participating democracy, but in business, for example, the role of shareholders as influences over corporate policy is largely mythological. The concept of the faculty as the university has drifted away in this decade. All along the line, I'm often impressed by the fact that you can go across the country and sit at banquet tables and people on either side of you express opinions about problems all over the world, but they don't know how many governments they are governed by or what the power of confrontation is in the city.

I don't mean to leave you with the idea that I am saying things are fine as they are now. We had made vast improvements in the society by 1930, but now is the point to see that yesterday's advances are not today's answers. We are challenged to do more than we have done.

BUNDY: Are we not going to find unsolvable problems? Sometimes we seem to be demanding, "Do you see unsolvable problems ahead of us?"

FORSMAN: It is almost a mistake to believe we have done very much. The military-industrial complex is one place where democracy has not really done anything. The library has to change the basic economic structure.

CRESWELL: It seems to me to be somewhat irrelevant to be where we are. The relevances of the past are only in the eye of the beholder. If you agree that that needs change, or if you disagree that that needs change, no matter what you say, it doesn't make any difference whether I am better off today than I was ten years ago, or that I am not as well off today as I might have been ten years ago.

FORSMAN: That's true, but Mr. Busby said a few minutes ago that locally the power was in the local hands. He said when these cities were burning, the power wasn't in Washington. I would say the power was in Washington, and still is, because Washington is draining most of our natural resources. It has not left any to help solve the problems of these cities. Until it does, the cities can't solve their problems. Mr. Lindsay [mayor of New York City] has made this very clear, I believe.

BUSBY: In the 1930s, we felt much the way we are beginning to feel again now, about the military and munitions makers and that sort of thing. I personally feel that there is a great danger of self-

deception in attributing the problems of the cities and the social problems of our society solely to the root cause of the military-industrial
complex siphoning off the resources.

Our cities were in trouble before World War II. They weren't
going anywhere. They didn't go anywhere in the 1920s. They weren't
engaged in social activities. The things that we have seen fester for
thirty years are problems that originated way back. The group-against-
group type of situation that you run into in the management of a
city, such as Lindsay has run into, is a great hazard, a great hazard
to all social progress, a great hazard to the kind of library programs
that you might want to implement in your own community.

Take away the war economy, and I don't know if we have the
momentum socially to simply absorb that money and put it back into
social purposes. I wish that we did, but I am afraid that if you obliterated the war economy, it would not happen. Of course, I would like
to get rid of the war, but I am saying when that is done that does
not automatically insure this other. You still have to have administrators. You still have to have people in all fields who are able to go
across the line that we have drawn in order to lead the people across
to accomplish this social progress.

CRESWELL: I understand what you are saying, but I know many
library administrators who have had these programs on the drawing
boards for years. The reason they haven't been able to get them is
primarily because the funds are just awfully hard to come by, because
most of them are going in this other direction. So, I feel that we
do have the leadership available. It is around and ready to go. The
libraries' job, I think, is primarily to organize politically to make sure
that we change that economy and do redirect this money. That's where
our role locally is particularly important because the newspapers are
not doing this job, on the whole.

PARTICIPANT: It seems to me that I keep hearing David Riesman
speaking here and that we are speaking with a postindustrial mentality.
Neither the majority of the American people nor our economic interests
are set up in order to support the kinds of ideas that are coming
out. I think that is what you all are saying, like Mr. Forsman was
saying, about having to change the economic situation a great deal
in order to get the political power.

WASSERMAN: Can we separate out two things? Can we separate our
responsibilities, our commitments, and our consciences as citizens from

our functions, our commitments, and our responsibility vis-à-vis our professional roles? This is a hard thing to do. Can you differentiate your conscience from your professional role?

But there is a zone here where you can play a useful functional role in the culture which may sometimes be short of an advocacy role, yet still do a lot more than librarianship is now doing. Presently the library is a passive sort of repository function for the culture, where we get some things and we have them and people come and use them if they choose to. There is a wide range between the assumption of that commitment, that responsibility, and the whole range of opportunity that lies beyond it.

Some of these things that Mr. Busby has just identified very briefly form a zone between that and going to the point that John Forsman has suggested, which is a partisan, activist role, an advocacy role in the utilization of our knowledge base for change, and for making change come to pass. I suppose that I would be a little more sanguine about librarianship if I felt that we had begun even to shift beyond the passive, repository, sort of anal role, and move more toward a use-of-intelligence role, a furthering of it, enhancing the access to information, if not necessarily at this point for advocacy or partisan purposes, but simply to better inform our culture.

BUNDY: I must agree with John Forsman then. That's fine. Some of us think we might want to move, but then we ask the question, "What's the impact?" When you consider the amount of effort to get us to be a little better than we are in terms of the problems that we are facing, why move? It makes us better, but it isn't going to be good enough.

WASSERMAN: Because I am afraid that we can't get consensus on that kind of role in this profession or any other profession, but I hope we could get consensus on shifting the professional responsibility beyond the passive role. I think there we can hope to get consensus. That's an aspiration which we may share. We don't share it. Librarianship hasn't moved that far. I don't think there is consensus for doing anything more than just getting the books and saying, "What do you want from me?" or "Why don't you come and get it?"

We've got a long way to go even to shift the stance of librarianship that far. If we do that, I'll be satisfied with my life work. But I'm not even comfortable with that aspiration about its potential for being achieved in my lifetime. Now, maybe I am confused.

PARTICIPANT: I don't think you are. Here is something else. I am trying to digest several things you have said, but there are so many people who are trying to say something. One of my dreams is to be a legislative advocate for libraries, because I think a lot could be done, a lot could be said to the legislature. I think that if more people were interested there is a lot that could be done. Many people are afraid. They don't know how. They don't know the right people.

Here we are discussing issues, but nobody has said, "Where do we go?" There are all sorts of things to do if one has imagination. In my case, it is much easier because I am in a state library, and California is a smaller place than Washington. It has only eighty assemblymen and thirty-eight senators, so it is much easier to work with. Imagination tells you where to find change.

PARTICIPANT: Dean Wasserman, this is merely a personal observation, but I find it very difficult to find a middle ground between a passive stage and an active one. Once you become active you become an advoccate of something or other. I don't necessarily mean an advocate of one political party, or one economic system, or anything like that, but activism is advocacy of some form.

WASSERMAN: To that extent, yes.

FORSMAN: But to start thinking in terms of neutral activity, neutral activism, may be somewhat conflicting. If you begin to think about going only part of the way, that may cause you to fall back into a state of passive existence.

PARTICIPANT: I must protest that. I'd like librarianship to pass that proposition, and I don't think it will. It would take recruitment of an altogether different type of person into the profession than we now have. I don't think that librarianship, as it presently exists, appeals to the type of person that you are talking about, the kind that goes into the active realm.

Dr. Wasserman, you said you would be satisfied if you could just get the profession to move from this passive repository stance to an active stance.

WASSERMAN: Yes, but I'm suggesting something short of advocacy.

PARTICIPANT: I don't think this profession has sufficiently emerged for that, either salary-wise or personality-wise. You may be getting a few of that type, the Congress for Change type, at Maryland, but most library schools are going along pretty well as they were, appealing to the book lovers, the kind who more or less want to get out of the traffic of life rather than into it. If you can change the profession, more power to you, but you've got to change some other things first.

FORSMAN: We've got our share of Uncle Toms. But just like the black people, maybe once we start doing something, others will change their minds. After all, the knowledge that we are supposed to be conserving is humanitarian knowledge. By its very nature, it gives us some goals in life. The fact that we have organized ourselves in such a way that we can't do anything about it is our fault to a very large degree.

Regardless of how much I may protest against the economic structure of the present society, I do think it can be changed. I think it is our job. It is not only our job; it is our duty, as a result of the job we have chosen professionally, to see to it that it is changed and to organize ourselves so that we can do it. That involves taking political power to the point where we can get what we need to do the job that our profession demands of us.

BUNDY: Interestingly enough, I agree with you, John. I think social commitment is evolving out of public librarianship, but the mature information services are evolving out of a group of people who are putting it to work for government and industry, not for the city. I feel there must be a team-up of the two groups—the people who are exploring better ways to get people information when they need it and the people who have a social commitment to even up the information, to balance it.

CRESWELL: I keep visualizing the image of the kindly, well-respected, great college professor who doesn't deal neutrally with the knowledge that he has. He doesn't impart it with his eyes blind to his students. He tries to change their lives. He has to make some decisions about the way he presents it. He is not doing it just to store it, or make it easily available, or even to sell it. He is trying to do a little bit more with it. He is not just taking an active role in putting knowledge before his students. He is shaping minds.

WASSERMAN: One can have a sort of sub rosa agenda. To the extent that librarianship has this, to the extent that it has a social commitment, to the extent that it conceives of itself as having a social responsibility and a social opportunity, it then does certain things which it hasn't done yet. The point that Mary Lee Bundy makes is a very, very essential one. It's not enough to be committed. It's not enough to care. It takes something more than that. Otherwise, you are just a do-gooder who doesn't know anything more than the fact that you would like to do something, but you don't know precisely what. It takes the capacity to master the technology, to invent and devise the information systems that are viable now in a time when things are breaking down, when people need intelligence more than they ever needed it before.

This is really what we have to offer, if we have any professional contribution. It's that capacity to order, to organize, and to make intelligence available at the points where it is necessary. Our end may be social betterment, and I would hope this would be our end. All I am saying, in effect, is we can't announce *our* political purpose as *the* political purpose and then expect everybody to agree that that's what we are for.

BUNDY: Then don't claim to be a public institution.

CRESWELL: Maybe the profession that includes all librarians and all people connected with libraries is going to end up no better and no worse than the profession of lawyers, some of whom are very liberal, are changing the laws every day, others of whom with their social commitment are taking just the opposite direction. Maybe there is no one ground, or one tack, or one direction, except the direction towards activity. But within each individual, there is something beyond the activity. There is some advocacy.

BUNDY: If a professional group doesn't have social aspirations far beyond what they will ever achieve in their lifetime, then they won't achieve very much.

I recently visited a college that had just built a four-story library which no one was using. At the librarian's request, they called a meeting of some students and faculty to discuss how they could get the students to use the library. The students didn't talk for a while, but then they began to say things like "It's too quiet in here! Why can't we have music? We can't study when it's so quiet " "Well, yes, but it disturbs some of the students who want it quiet." And someone said, "Well, there's your front door. People have to come all the way around for a mile to get in your front door. Your back door is right across from the student union. Why don't you make your back door your front door?" "Oh, no. I want people when they come to a library to come for a serious purpose." Still the librarian kept saying, "Tell me what you want." Some students said, "Why don't you get some books on subjects we are interested in?" He said, "I've told you over and over again that I'll get books on subjects you are interested in. What are you interested in?" One student said, "Sex, drugs, and Vietnam!" "Oh," said the librarian. "Do you know what would happen to me if we put those books out?"

A librarian who couldn't take those steps isn't going to take the next step, but maybe another type of person could turn that library on. Why settle for a half measure in your lifetime?

PARTICIPANT: Perhaps librarians need to rid themselves of the circumference of the library building. Perhaps a librarian should become more like a social worker, or a psychologist, or a psychiatrist who is a member of a team in a multifaceted agency, where he contributes his own special kind of competence to a total effort, so he doesn't need to feel that in his own isolated library he needs to act as an art critic, as a museum curator, as a social worker, and as a group director.

PARTICIPANT: But if he wanted that, I don't think he would go into librarianship, this institution which we've suggested is rather confining to begin with. Why did this man become a college librarian? He felt secure. In this case, he said he wanted suggestions, but really, he didn't want them. If he had wanted to do what you're suggesting, that is, be a change agent, I don't think he would have become a librarian.

PARTICIPANT: Well, as some suggested, there is a possibility for librarians, like other professionals, to develop in different ways. There may be some librarians who will be purely surface librarians; there will be others who will be custodians of large buildings who guard collections.

WASSERMAN: There already are.

FORSMAN: What we heard this morning actually sets the framework within which a professional must operate. We are caught with anarchy, and we are caught with anarchy for quite a few reasons. Mr. Busby and I might disagree as to some of the reasons.

Our function is to provide information, relevant information. Your professional function is not to get a job where you are secure. If you are doing that, you are merely getting a job. You might just as well be selling shoes, because you are not professional. When we talk about our profession, we are talking about fulfilling this commitment, providing relevant information to the people of this society to solve their problems. Their number one problems are war, peace, poverty, and the ones that have come before it.

There are technical relationships, technical methods and means, which are handy and helpful in solving these problems, and it is up to us as librarians to know what they are and to be able to provide that information. There is room for all kinds of workers within our profession, but if we are not functioning in terms of providing the relevant information required in terms of the basic problems before us, then we are not professional and we are not doing our job.

BUNDY: We don't have the kinds of people who want to do this—or if we do, they get the hell out of the library and go where the people are. Then they come back and tell their library to change.

PARTICIPANT: I'd argue with that a little bit. I don't know how many of these people here were compelled to come. You didn't hold a whip over them.

BUNDY: Oh, but these are a select group here.

PARTICIPANT: Nobody's saying anything about the change starting in the educational part of it. I'm interested in seeing a change in the educational part because I can see where you could bring in all these different things we've talked about. Then once the student becomes a librarian, he'll know what direction to take.

WASSERMAN: It's easy to ascribe the role of change to the university, but I would say the problem is more complicated, as I am sure you are all aware. You can't draw people to be educated or acculturated to something they don't perceive as a fact of life. We can lie like everyone else who sells lies in the culture by saying, "Come here and do such and such" when everybody knows that this is not what they do there, because he sees every day of his life they are doing something different. That complicates our plight in education all the more. While we would like things to be otherwise and while we would like to attract people to join us in helping the cause, so that libraries would be otherwise, they are not drawn by sloganeering, but by . . .

BUNDY: We can stop giving in to them. We can stop having library school curricula that make them think that because they learn the names of some ready reference books they are going to give reference service. We can stop teaching that the book is the important thing and putting numbers on books is important. We don't have to play the game with them. Wouldn't you agree? We can't change the types of people, but we can refuse to play the game with them. Even if they wanted to play it, we would say, "No, we don't play that here any more, even though 90 percent of you would like that game."

SEGAL: You are saying it's got to come from both sides. The universities have to do something significant in terms of curriculum and recruitment, and at the same time, as professionals, they must agitate for actual change out in the field.

PARTICIPANT: There is another side, too, that I don't think you have considered. That is the professional organization that is supposedly behind us. That's the ALA. I don't think it is performing its function at all.

PARTICIPANT: There is another side, too. What about the library board or the librarian who really doesn't want an activist on his staff or doesn't want an activist as a librarian, period?

BUNDY: The only thing that gets protected is the head librarian, and even he doesn't get protected well. Would we get protected if we argued with our head librarian? Not by our professional association!

PARTICIPANT: If a person is an activist, there are a considerable number of hazards involved, because unfortunately, as has been said, one couldn't seek a secure position today in librarianship. How many times can we get fired and still get another job? Not very many, because you always have to go back to the places you worked before for a recommendation. Before too long, you would be dead.

BUNDY: That's one function the library schools can perform for their alumni. You can always come back and get another recommendation.

WASSERMAN: A more active placement service?

BUNDY: The schools could help put people in institutions where people want what they have to offer. Make a better match.

BUSBY: Without reopening the discussions we have had about whether we have had progress or advance in this society, I think it's a fair and an important perspective to keep in mind that the library, and thus librarians, has had an enormous impact upon this society over a long period of time. This is not as though this has been an American library experiment or example. It has not been a bunch of mush. It seems to me that, in your present context, as best I know it, or can see it, or feel that I know anything about it, there is a vital element of professional questioning, particularly at the university level, as to whether what you are doing is keeping the profession in the mainstream of what it is you are working with, or whether you may be engaged in habits or traditions, or any number of other words we might string together, that are actually taking the profession out, pulling it aside. In other words, this is a good point of self-examina-

tion. We are having this tremendous revolution in the whole information field and in the media of communication. There seems to be
a thrust in the library profession, in the library education programs,
reaching out to embrace the revolution. Or is it coming off to the
side and not embracing it?

WASSERMAN: These are very fundamental questions. They are part
of our rationale for having these discussions together. What is it that
libraries can do that no other agency can, or will, or should be doing?
What can libraries do by virtue of their experience, their history, their
professional expertise? What are the unique things? Maybe the unique
things are the things that the library has been doing, but maybe by
virtue of the changing technology, the changing culture, the changing
pressure points in the society, there are new opportunities open to
libraries and to librarianship which have not been realized, or if realized, have not been seized upon.

Many of us feel that this is the case. We tend to be reasonably
comfortable about the things we have always done, but as we look
at new, potential alternatives or additional opportunities, we are not
taking advantage of them actively enough to remain an important
force. You talk about our history and our contribution. Perhaps this
is valid. But perhaps to continue to make a contribution, and to be
important in the culture in these times, with the changes that have
been wrought, we need to identify and chart our responsibilities in
new zones of operation.

BUSBY: I did think at the beginning of the decade, at the beginning
of the electronic revolution in information, that the direction that it
would take would be a great enhancement to the library field, that
librarians would become the masters of the new information media.

FORSMAN: In the war department, yes, where they can get the funds
to get access to these new electronic devices.

BUSBY: I'm talking about the corporate world.

FORSMAN: And in the corporate world, where it is a matter of making
money for acquiring information for a chemical company. I can show
you advertisements in *The New York Times* every Sunday for librarians
who are acquainted with electronic devices. But, to find a public library
where they will be supported with public funds, to do this job for
the people, no. When it is tied directly to the economic structure
for a profit-making motive, yes. Then we can get our hands on this
equipment.

BUSBY: There is a similar motive in most cities. The city has great need for this electronic information.

BUNDY: According to the ex-president of the Special Libraries Association, you are giving librarians in these milieus too much credit. There is a real danger that in these settings there will be both a conventional library and a newer information service, so it is not true that automatically by virtue of being in any other setting the librarian performs differently.

FORSMAN: All right. Let's just look at any of these tools as merely tools for doing the information job. You use that tool only when it is applicable to the particular situation. I would never get far from the fact that the one thing the library has that nobody else has in education is the direct, one-to-one relationship with its clients. We are very much like lawyers in this respect. It gives us an opportunity to function very effectively, not only in schools, but in the total democracy that we are in. I certainly wouldn't want to do away with that. If we could have access to these tools as well, we could even do a better job of it.

BUNDY: On the other hand, in my years of practice, this access to our patron was a very fleeting one across the desk. I didn't even know the guy the next time he came in. We really haven't got a mature client relationship where we can spend a whole hour with a guy.

FORSMAN: You were restricted by rules and regulations as to how far into the information problem you could go.

BUNDY: Yes. "If we can't do it for all, we can't do it for some."

CRESWELL: In cities now, the mayor wants to know instantly x amount of demographical data on this ward or that ward, on this section or that section of town, on who moved in or who moved out. Both of you are suggesting that, at one point in history, the librarians were the people who gathered information and retrieved it and that instead of being aggressive and jumping on this new technology and using it for whatever ends it needed to be used for, the librarians have let a new set of professionals grow up outside your structure. The suggestion is that maybe those machines, the electronic devices which are now being used for profit making, could have been used for the other purpose also, had the librarians been the ones who said, "This is our baby."

BUNDY: Let me try this possibility on you. As this new profession has evolved, it is in the process of professionalization where it is looking for schools. Could the library school, by taking on the education for these new roles, become the merging force between traditional librarianship and the newer forces? Could this process then evolve information workers who would work in the public sector?

CRESWELL: I bet if a library school came up with a hell of a big package asking for an awful lot of money from foundations to do just this kind of thing, you would be surprised, because the doors would probably open a lot more easily and the money would be a lot more accessible.

BUNDY: You're so right. We always want just a little more to do what we have been doing, instead of saying, "We want $10 million more to do what we have never done."

CRESWELL: In this kind of problem, you have to be very careful that your own self-conception doesn't cause your profession to become a backwater to a bigger profession.

BUNDY: It could happen to the libraries, but the library schools might transform themselves and become schools for the information people.

CRESWELL: But what difference does that make? What I am saying is library schools are something separate and apart from all this other. Expand your concept of what a library school is! Expand your concept of what a librarian is! So that even if, instead of books, the main things that you deal with are television tapes, records, movie films, you are still librarians, but you have caught up to the twentieth century.

BUNDY: To some extent we are in it. The interesting thing is, of course, sitting on the side of Washington, we really see it. The money is over in the newer field. There is going to be a drain from the conventional library unless it can respond by wanting people enough to find the kind of person who can go this way. The best thing is to get a library to hire a computer person. They would have to pay $5,000 more than they pay the librarian. Then let the librarians agitate for more money.

WASSERMAN: On this aspirational note, perhaps we can conclude this first of our many sessions this week. Let me take this opportunity to thank our visiting panel members, Mr. Forsman, Mr. Creswell, and Mr. Busby, for stimulating and provoking us, and getting us off to a very interesting start.

2

THE DISADVANTAGED: REORIENTING THE URBAN SETTING TO NEW GOALS AND NEW COMMITMENTS

MONDAY EVENING, AUGUST 11
LECTURER: PRESTON R. WILCOX
PANELISTS: ANNIE REID
             MARY LEE BUNDY
             ERNEST M. KAHN
             JOSEPH C. DONOHUE

WILCOX: I have never been invited by a group of librarians to do anything before except return books. I have been thinking about my experiences with librarians. I thought about my role as a student and my role as a faculty member, and I felt that librarians were people who were very important to me. Number one, they saved me a lot of time by helping me to reach the kind of sources I wanted. Second, there were several librarians I can recall in my own experience who had actually read the books that were on the shelves. The other thought I had was that recently I found myself involved in trying to develop a bibliography on the issue of white institutional racism. What I was trying to do was to find books written by people who happen to be white who really believed that they were superior to black people, or books written by colonialists who really believed that they were superior to the natives. What I found was that there were very few library catalogs that listed the category "white institutional racism." People were sending me to things like "human relations," "Negro discrimination," "Negro intergroup relations," and what have you, all of which, by the way, have a different kind of slant. They suggest that if black people become like white people, the world will be O.K.; or if the lower class becomes middle class it will solve all of our problems; or if the stupid people start learning our schools will be O.K. I happen to think that it's just those kinds of definitions that are contributing to the kinds of problems we are having in the urban areas today.

People are clinging to old ways, to traditions that produce many of the kinds of problems that we have today. For instance, we might start out talking about the issue of the disadvantaged. There are many sociologists who have tried to throw that term out, but it keeps coming back. So I would like to start out by maybe defining what I think the word "disadvantaged" means. A disadvantaged person is one who is illegally deprived of opportunities to acquire the skills, resources, and insights to become the person he wants to become. I think the people who have a need to use a term like this in a sense also have a need to define people who are different from them as having a lesser quantity or lesser quality of humanity. It seems to me that what blacks are talking about is: How can we redefine the nature of the society so as to include black people as human beings? When I use the word "black" I mean human. I don't necessarily mean the replica of white. I hope I am not implying that all white people are inhuman, but our traditional definitions have defined white people as being human and black people as being inhuman.

That's the rhetoric of this country. And it has been done without any criterion other than the fact that people are white. What it really has done has been to make white people really insure that they never behave black. That is, white in America really means nonblack. If you go into white suburbia, the criterion for the high status in the white suburban areas is that there are no black people there. People make decisions on that basis. If there are fifty black people there they won't consider moving into it. If there are no black people they move into it automatically. The status of schools is largely based on how many black people are in the schools. Many of the opportunities that white people have received have been received largely because they were not black. On many levels they never really have had to compete with black people for any of the affluence of their society.

In fact, the problem now is that blacks are switching from a kind of subordinate relationship where whites patronized them to essentially a competitive relationship. Blacks are really concerned about the right to define themselves in the way in which they want to be defined rather than the way in which people who have control over their lives want to define them. The point that I am really trying to make is that in order to understand this issue that we are trying to talk about on a human level, one has to begin to redefine a large number of terms. Many of the words we have used, as far as I am concerned, have oppression built into them. We talk about brotherhood. Most black people know that when white people talk about brotherhood, they are either talking about once a year, or they are really talking about big brother and little brother. Or when you talk about the open society, most blacks know the real message is that there are a series of closed doors for black people, that much of the rhetoric does not really include black people. In fact, I will even go so far as to say that when sociologists talk about nonwhite, they are frequently talking about nonexistence.

There is powerful evidence of this kind of interpretation because, for instance, most of us who have been educated have not been educated to understand black people as people. Many of the white kids who call themselves educated are never educated to relate to blacks as people. Our integration programs have failed largely because there was no serious attempt in the classrooms to help black kids and white kids to develop and understand how to negotiate a coequal relationship. But there was no intent to really integrate the curriculum so that black kids could learn about themselves and white kids could learn to deal with the privilege of white skin, that is, to learn how to unlearn the racism which they learn in their daily lives. So integration in this country has largely been a substitute for white supremacy. It has not been a restructuring of a school organization to increase the possibility that as black and white kids learn cognitive material they also learn how to relate to each other as people, and they begin to take on some sort of joint responsibility for holding society accountable. So if you listen to the young white radical kids, it seems to me that they are saying they don't want to grow up to be white racists. They want to learn now how to turn themselves into human beings. They want to learn now how to get their pasts off their minds so they can get involved in planning for and shaping their own futures.

The best way I know of expressing this concept of humanity is a Dick Gregory statement that as a black man he doesn't want the kind of equality which will give him the same length of sentence for raping a white woman as a white man would get for raping a black woman. He would like to find a way to deal with the question of why people have to rape each other. In other words, he's talking about a new kind of humanity. Or, if you look at the push on the white college campuses for black studies programs, what black kids are really saying is they don't want to be integrated into racist institutions. Also, institutions that really want to be human have to look at themselves first and begin to humanize their own curricula. Not only are black kids rebelling; so are the sons and daughters of the faculty members. We are really talking about humanizing the system. If you look at a lot of the sociological writings, many of them are contaminated by what I would call racism interpretations. This is largely because I think that racism is much more than the encounter between black and white people.

Racism has affected everybody who lives in this society. It has affected how people feel about themselves, how they feel about their loved ones. It has affected their frames of reference. It is much more than the encounter between black and white people. William F. Whyte's *The Organization Man* describes the way in which young white executives are excessively loyal to their places of employment. I would say that had William F. Whyte understood my definition of humanity; had he also understood the model of the black Uncle Tom, the obsequious guy who survives by becoming excessively compliant to the rules and regulations of his oppressor, William F. Whyte might have named the Organization Man the white Uncle Tom, as this behavior really is no different. Or, if Moynihan had my interpretation when he made his study of the Negro family, in the first place it should have been called the victimization of black families rather than just the Negro family. What he was talking about was how they adjusted to oppression. More important, I think he was implying that since black families are matriarchal, ergo white families are patriarchal, and second, that patriarchal families should be valued more. He was talking about male superiority. If you go into any white suburban area, you won't find patriarchal families. You may find men in the home, but it's not patriarchal. I say to some of my friends in Scarsdale (who feel bad that I don't move to Scarsdale because I may face discrimination) that it is the content of the life in Scarsdale that I don't like. When

I stand on a platform in Scarsdale and see guys getting off a train, a station wagon driving up, the car door opening, and the guy getting into the car, dropping *The New York Times,* kissing his wife, picking up *The New York Times* again, I'm really not sure whether he's kissing the right wife and going to the right home.

The whole issue of male superiority is a very interesting kind of distortion when one considers that that person holding up the torch on Bedloe's Island is wearing a dress, or when one considers that if you review the Dun and Bradstreet records you would find the names of more women in it than men. One wonders whether male superiority isn't another kind of racism where people define themselves in positive ways by standing on the back of someone else.

By the way, this may be the reason for the movement of the women for liberation. I think these women have some hangups. It's almost like a civil rights movement as far as I am concerned, in that the women who are trying to become equal to men are like the blacks who really believe that all white people have a conscience and that they can be saved by the consciences of white people. One of them has written an article recently where she made an analogy between integration for blacks and marriage for women. She seemed to say it was like making peace with your master. It was not really developing a coequal relationship.

Much of the writing on racism, including the report of the National Commission on Civil Disorders, is very quiet on the issue of sex even though the studies on racial discrimination show that the sex issue ranks number one in the minds of whites at least, not in the minds of blacks. Myrdal's *American Dilemma* demonstrated this along with Bogardus' study earlier. Yet the National Commission report is silent on the issue of sex. My own feeling is that racial discrimination is really organized to protect the white vagina for white men. The ultimate policy decisions are made around this issue. I'm not so sure the urban crisis doesn't stem from the fact that for the first time in the history of black people the majority of them are concentrated in urban areas up North. Twenty or thirty years ago they were on the rural farms, in rural areas, and down South. When you consider that the large urban areas are the places where young white girls go to attempt to break an umbilical cord, there may be a connection which really has never been seriously investigated. I'm raising it as a possible question.

In trying to understand the nature of what goes on in black communities, which has been the subject of my intellectual interests now for about fifteen or twenty years, I think I have read practically everything that has ever been written about a poor community despite the ethnicity of the residents there. I have been largely concerned with how to change the relationship between such communities and the larger cities in which they are embedded. I have spent maybe fifteen years working in poor communities on some kind of continuous basis. I have worked in the South. I have worked largely in East Harlem and Harlem. I know of some activities in every large ghetto in the country. I am saying this because the more I spend time in them, the more I try to understand them intellectually, the more I understand how difficult they are to understand.

Just recently I happened to pick up a book on maximum security prison systems. So far I would say that's the closest sociological analogue I have been able to find in helping me to understand what goes on in black communities. That is, look at the kinds of homosexual behavior that goes on in prisons, largely because women are kept out, and the kinds of behavior people have to get involved in even though they don't have that problem as a personal problem. Or, look at the relationship between the inmates and guards. Look at the issue of power. The effective decisions are made outside the community. Decisions that sometimes are largely personal are made outside the community. It seems to me that this model may give a lead to understanding the nature of these communities. Most of the literature, by the way, talks about the communities in vacuo. They don't talk about the nature of the relationship between these communities and the communities that are surrounding them, that is, the exploitative relationship. Many of the people who live in better communities are able to do so because they are living off the backs of people in poor communities.

Look at the poverty program. The people who really have gotten help have not been the people who were really poor. It was the do-gooders. The do-gooders began to do well doing good. In a sense they needed poor people. They needed problems in order to get and keep their jobs. When I was a student in school, my wife was typing a paper for me one night. I had been asked to describe all the members of a group. Although I had been programmed to find problems in all of them, there was one kid who didn't have any problems. I had dozed off to sleep when my wife got to little Howard. Everything I said about him was fine. She woke me up to see if something was wrong. She was interested in my getting a good grade and she just couldn't figure out how I could describe any kid who didn't have problems. If you talk with many people who are in subordinate positions they tend to describe people who are lower than them in some negative way.

I think what I have said has a lot of implications for a whole network of social relations. For instance, I think I have used the word "programmed." I happen to think most of us are programmed. We were computerized the moment we were born to learn certain kinds of things. Education has to deal with this programming in some kind of way. We are programmed into not even wanting to think for ourselves. When you come into the library school at the University of Maryland there are signs that say "THINK." What they really mean is think the way the University of Maryland Library School wants you to think. Those people who really think for themselves find themselves on the outside.

I don't think that most of us know what it really means to be human. I know of no ongoing opportunities to learn how to be human. By being human I mean being able to engage in a mutual relationship with another human being without a need for power, without a need for brownie points, without a need to put the other person down and without a need to qualify, to ask yourself, "Is this person on welfare? Does he have a Ph.D.?" I mean to relate to another human being on an instinctive basis. I say that if you are human this can happen across sex lines, across age lines, across ethnic lines. In fact, part of you as humanity is embedded in another person. You really can't know that you are a human being unless someone else confirms it. If a man lived on an island all of his life by himself and you told me he was a human being, I would have to assume he was a CIA agent. You know what happens. You get three people together and one of them wants to be chairman. People don't really know how to have mutual relationships.

I am saying that we haven't really learned how to have mutual relationships. Now just on the individual level, it seems to me that the thing I am concerned about now is how people begin to get involved in liberating themselves. There is a whole network of relationships in which people are embedded and in which they are entrapped without even knowing it, because the same kind of effect that is used to help one enjoy it is also used to help control him and keep him in that relationship—the way maternal love is used to love and also to control.

I remember some of the kids I met down in Mississippi in 1964. I really felt that if many of them could go back home and resolve their problems with their parents, they would probably leave the movement. That's why many of them wouldn't want to go back home: because they didn't want to leave the movement. So when I meet with young people now, I suggest that they go home and take on their parents and still love them. I say that you are not liberated unless you can kiss your mother or your father in the same way you kiss your girlfriend or your boyfriend.

I think there is another network of relationships, the relationships between male and female. Do we really know how to have coequal relationships across sex lines? Some of us are now beginning to try to experiment in schools. This whole thing of separating boys and girls in schools, all the rhetoric you hear from elementary school teachers saying that if we only had some male teachers we could help little boys feel like they are little boys. Some of us say that if you have authentic female teachers in classes the little boys will know they are boys. Sex is used as a weapon and not really to liberate people. There are other things. People have religious hangups. They get in their way. I am referring to G. A. Longo's book, *The Spoiled Priest*. His whole discussion describes how the church wasn't able to answer some of his questions. They kept telling him to have faith. He finally had to give it up.

It seems to me that the issue of overwhelming importance today is who is going to make decisions about whose life. What gives anyone the right to make certain decisions about someone else's life? We have lived in a society where people have really been conditioned to line up to allow other people to make decisions about their lives. If you really study the resolution of the Oedipal complex, Freud's whole thesis, it really seems to me that it ends up that the young person learns that he is supposed to take orders from his parents, right or wrong. So people grow up first with their mothers on their minds, then their supervisors on their minds, then their teachers on their minds, and what happens? They become adult teenagers. They don't become men until they become chairman of a workshop or head of a department. By that time they 'learn how to get everybody else to line up. They haven't learned how to liberate people.

We had a situation at a school in Harlem where the board of education felt that they should decide whether we, a predominantly black community, should have a program commemorating the life of Malcolm X. Many of us were disturbed that there were a large number of people on the board of education who didn't have the emotional or intellectual freedom to understand the meaning of Malcolm X's life to black people. The decision to honor a black person by black people was largely a black decision. Anyone who really respected black people would not get involved in making that decision. Rather, they would get involved in having black people make the best possible decision for themselves. This incident occurred despite the fact that on the day after it was George Washington's birthday, when all the schools in New York City are closed.

I took my son to visit Mt. Vernon several years ago. We had seen the main house. Then we went walking around the grounds and we came to the slave quarters, which were not so labeled, by the way, even though they had Aunt Jemima dolls at the souvenir counter. He asked me what it was. He was a smart kid. He noticed the difference in the decor. I said, "This is the slave quarters. By the way, Lincoln supposedly freed the slaves." He said to me, "Why didn't Washington do it?" He knew about the cherry tree bit and the Potomac River and the fact that George Washington is the father of your country, but he didn't know that George Washington was a slave owner and that he didn't really give up his slaves until he died. I would say any teacher who really respects my kid, whether she's black or white, ought to say to my kid, "David, maybe you should not want to honor George Washington's life, because he was a slave owner. Maybe, if anything, you ought to commemorate his death, because he didn't give up his slaves until he died." What I am saying is that I feel instinctively, instantaneously closer to my Jewish friends who don't buy Volkswagens.

I am also talking about the relationship between people who are in superordinate positions and those who are in subordinate positions, whether people who are in superordinate positions just because they have the power to make certain kinds of decisions really ought to make those decisions, whether they ought to give up the need to make a decision about someone else's life, particularly decisions that should only be made by that person himself. I will say that Senator Eastland would probably say to me and to you that he would not make a decision about my life, with which I would agree. And yet, he is in power to do so in Congress. I frankly don't want him making any decisions about my life. I would be very happy if he would give up his need to make a decision about my life. I really think this is the issue.

I look at what is happening in the black community as the communities are becoming much more controlled by the black community. For instance, at the Harlem school, the moment we got a voice in the school, vandalism went down. Suspensions were stopped because you don't suspend your own kids; no matter what kind of education you get, you don't suspend them. You may send them home but they can always come back because it is their school. We don't have signs up saying, "This is your school," because when the signs were up before, the people never believed them. You don't have to put up signs on your own school saying, "This is your school." We don't have people walking around the hall asking parents, "Can I help you?" when they really mean, "What in the hell are you doing in school?" The parents say, "If it is our school we will keep the outsiders out. We know who they are. This is our community." The affective quality of the school has changed automatically.

Take the issue of the whole move to take over the policy. This is no accident, because the average social worker working on the problem of narcotics addiction will have a policeman sitting in the room, yet every kid in the community knows that the narcotics problem could not thrive without the collusion of the police. The numbers game could not thrive without the collusion of the police. Large numbers of illegal activities are concentrated in the black community while other people benefit from them economically. Don't forget that the people who control the dope racket and control the numbers don't live in our communities, but yet they make very important decisions about our lives. Now the addicts in the community are treating each other. It's a kind of a treatment that most social agencies cannot give because they are outside of the whole thing.

Malcolm describes the way the Muslims were treating addicts. It was a six-step process. The addict really was never cured, but he could achieve a cured state by getting involved in helping another addict off dope. There was a contract between the addict who had been helped and the one he was about to help that kept the addict off it. If you know anything about Alcoholics Anonymous, if you have any friends who are members of it, you will notice they walk around with the telephone numbers of other members of AA so that when they feel like they've got to have a drink they call up another member of the AA. They may sit up all night together drinking coffee. Both of them know they are helping each other when they are drinking that coffee. I have a friend who was called by another friend. The other guy almost convinced him to go back on drinks, so he called up still another guy and the three of them sat up. That was a contract to make sure he stayed off it. What I am talking about is a certain kind of potential understanding people who have suffered the same kinds of problems have for one another, which is not, by the way, a part of the regular treatment program. No community should have to ask anyone to get involved in this kind of process.

REID: Could I stop you right now with a question? You're talking about people in control of their investments. The State of Oklahoma recently passed legislation setting up the ombudsman position officially in that state. Do you believe that there can be such a thing as an ombudsman with state sanction who is, in fact, an advocate for the people? Would such a person have to straighten up spontaneously? Will the person be able to realize the dynamics of the community? This bears directly on public libraries, certainly, and communities, because some professional public services could see themselves appointed as ombudsman, and play an ombudsman role. Certainly people who have information can. But the question first is, can a role like this be effective and be the same role if it is sanctioned by the state, acknowledged by the major society, or does that nullify the role?

WILCOX: It has been my experience that when you are part of the state you are really against the people. For instance, I have noticed a pattern of whites who come into East Harlem and who really get connected with black people. They begin to be maligned by other whites who work in the community. The classic case is Elliott Shapiro, the principal of P.S. 100 in Harlem, who really merited the attention, the affection of the local people. Every year they had a big party for him. If you mentioned his name to any other principals anywhere in the system they talked about him like a dog. In fact, when he became the superintendent on the Lower East Side they insisted that he didn't have enough courses in human relations, even though he had his doctorate. He had to go back and take a course from someone who didn't know anything about human relations.

PARTICIPANT: He was wanted by the community. I don't think enough has been understood about the black condition, by most people who make decisions, for the decision to be made in their best interests. Most of us are conditioned, whether we know it or not, to uphold the system. Most of us are conditioned to want to avoid conflict. Most of us want to be loved. Unless this ombudsman was a very unusual guy, he would end up rationalizing the system in some way.

PARTICIPANT: Are you perhaps saying that this ombudsman, as you are describing him, is then going to be dealing with comparatively small changes, comparatively minor issues that may be important to individuals, rather than the larger issues, at least numerically larger? Aren't we saying that we need to have more local decision to really control the people, and that at the same time, the significant overall societal issues are rapidly moving to a higher abstraction level of decision making? One of your colleagues in New York stated it I think rather convincingly when he said, "You can't solve air pollution in New York by only dealing with the Negro." We apparently now have some grudging acceptance by the national administration that you can't solve welfare by dealing with it at one stage only. Is that what your question was?

WILCOX: I think the people of the local area are concerned about solving air pollution and all these kinds of problems, but we spend so much time trying to get a voice in decisions that we never get a chance to really discuss the decision we are going to make. If the people who were concerned about air pollution on a national basis would get involved in the process of helping people who were suffering from problems, I think they would come up with it. Instead, all kinds of political interests and money get involved in it.

REID: What is your view of the increasing activity which is labeled "participation in decision making at the local level"? For example, aren't the model cities hearings very, very typical of "participation"? Could anybody give us some examples of real earthy processes they have been involved in in which the decision making by the persons most involved was real? In other words, that whatever decision that was made by that group was the de facto decision that influenced what happened, and not a decision that went into the minutes.

PARTICIPANT: Mrs. Reid, since I work in model cities I can tell you that there haven't been any definite decisions. We sit around and talk and try to get our overall participation from the citizens. I've been wondering whether the citizen will really play a significant role in the model cities. I am very doubtful because I haven't seen much participation from the citizens.

PARTICIPANT: I also work in model cities and I have the same attitude. We can talk a lot, but we don't seem to be able to get much past that point.

WILCOX: I think we are moving to a new level of participation. Most of the participation in the past really has been trying to help people to learn how to fit in. The schools want parent participation, but they really want parents to come in and have cake sales or mark up some books for the library. We're saying that there are these divisions of labor and that there are certain decisions that should not be made outside of one's life. For instance, I think it's a democratic inherent right for people to be involved in the education of their kids.

REID: Involved in education means what?

WILCOX: To the degree necessary.

REID: Firing personnel?

WILCOX: Definitely, sure.

REID: How about the flow of money?

WILCOX: We're taxpayers.

BUNDY: But he's your kid. Isn't that a pretty darn superior–subordinate relationship?

WILCOX: What do you mean superior–subordinate?

BUNDY: Well, he's your kid. Therefore you have made decisions for him, but maybe this kid would have a better chance if some parents weren't making the decisions.

WILCOX: Well, I'm against kids' being involved in it.

REID: When you get to the point that a local group can make a decision about its budget or a budget of any given public service, you've had not just a change in decision making; you have had a series of other changes in the social system that are pretty fundamental, before you can even get to that point. Wouldn't that be true?

KAHN: Brandeis University has just published a study of nine pilots in model cities. It describes the engagement and the struggle between the administrator's powers and such citizen representatives exactly as

Dr. Wilcox says. It's still around the issue of how well they make decisions, rather than what decisions are to be made.

REID: And what will happen to those decisions?

WILCOX: Another point. As I looked around the country, I saw that a lot of people have had no experience in learning how to make decisions. My people are trying to impose self-determination on people, but you can't do that.

SEGAL: I think we need to distinguish between having the resources to allow alternatives to decisions versus being stuck and captive. For example, in the suburbs if I really don't like the school system and the decisions made there, I've got alternatives. I've got the resources to pull my kid out and find the proper coddling private school for him. The ghetto people don't have it. It seems to me that often we get trapped into assuming that we in the suburbs may have decision-making power that, in fact, we don't have in terms of the actual body politic. What we have are the resources to save our kids in a way that the ghetto person does not. I think if we keep confusing this we are going to be overlooking what may be one of the critical parts of the problem, helping people to have resources for alternatives.

REID: But the alternative is a cop-out every time because you never deal with the question of being involved. Now, suppose you assume that you want to avoid a cop-out. Then what would you do? In other words, how do you really get down to the fact of decision making, the fact of involvement? Because it might be interesting, just as an intellectual exercise, to discuss our country in terms of small communities, and a little bit bigger communities, and the next bigger size, having something to do with decision making so that they don't have to cop out to seek an alternative.

BUNDY: Could you picture a community that might have four or five choices of where to send their kids to school, all supported by public tax funds based on each school's ability to get people together?

REID: There ought to be competing school systems so that . . .

SEGAL: I have to respond at a gut level. I want to run for the school board of my community after my kids are out. If I don't cop out, as you say, when I have the resources to choose alternatives, it basically means I am making my son pay the consequences. I may improve the system in ten or fifteen years, but by then he is lost. After he is out, then I can devote ten or fifteen years to other kids.

WILCOX: We are making assumptions that people know how to make decisions. I'm saying they don't.

The other part of my thing about imposing self-determination is that most people I know who claim they want to make decisions really are asking the other people on top to approve their decisions, to approve what they want to do. Do you get my point? The model cities is a good example. People are going around asking the city government to approve their plan.

SEGAL: When you get to model cities, education, all of these things, maybe what we are really doing is finding a new kind of ghettoization. You see, if the federal government comes in with model cities, and all these people get involved in decisions about model cities, you are telling them what to decide on. Perhaps first they should be asked, "What is it you think is important enough to engage your decision-making facilities?" I think this is where I see the real tragedy of our society. We are not respected in terms of what decisions are to be made. Instead, there is imposition. You can play all kinds of lovely games with model cities and participation and all that, but how many of these people who want decisions really see that as what they want to be concerned about?

KAHN: I would like to push a bit further on that point. I happen to believe that, increasingly, elementary education is going to be funded on a federal level. Will this cause a prescription of what can be decided? Will this cause the range of opportunities for decision making to narrow?

WILCOX: There has been more money spent on ghettos to keep them in their place. Enough money has been spent to keep them in their place to actually have solved all their problems. That is my own feeling.

REID: Will funds cure the problem of class within the context of the ghetto?

WILCOX: The people that I know across the country who are working in ghettos, the people I consider most effective, wouldn't dare get involved in model cities because no one wants someone else setting their agenda. Anybody in the ghetto who would get involved in model cities really isn't doing anything else, because if you are working in a ghetto there are so many other problems on a day-to-day basis that if you work in there systematically, you would have no time for a big activity.

WASSERMAN: Dr. Wilcox, let's move the discussion to the library setting if we can. Let's ask you to set the agenda. From the implications of what you have said, I would take it that in the present ghetto culture it's more difficult for whites to achieve any degree of success, because they bring with them the whole hangup of the culture and their commitments to it. That is, the institution is a reflection of the culture. Looking at it from your vantage point, what can a library do? What should a library do? How would you set an agenda for the library to be viable, meaningful, and relevant now in the ghettos?

WILCOX: One of the problems in the ghettos is getting literature that is relevant to what people want to read, relevant to their problems. Not only the whole black thing, but just things about the black condition. That's one thing. Second, I don't know of any real effort of libraries to get involved with the community where the community is. Most libraries in ghettos operate the same way they operate in upper middle-class neighborhoods. You wouldn't know that it wasn't an upper middle-class neighborhood if you walked into the library. Third, at least one of the problems I have found in schools is that the people who make recommendations for books for the library often are not the people from poor communities. I don't know of any systematic effort to get people to use the library for any reason except to raise the statistics of the libraries. About ten years ago, I got involved with helping some local librarian check out books. I had people lined up with fifty books that they weren't going to read, so the statistics would look good.

WELBOURNE: Paul, you raised the question about what the library can do. For a black man in the ghetto it's not so much the question of the library's doing anything different than the other institutions. The basic problem is an institutional one. As long as libraries exist, even though they seek to reform themselves, the culture that they have will thwart their own purpose. I don't think libraries left to the people who run them now, or the schools that produce the professionals, will seek their own destruction. It goes against the grain. It is not so much a destruction as a creation of an entirely new thing. The only way you are even going to be is by bringing black people into a creative arena to do something under the name of libraries. It won't look like a library. Don't be surprised when you don't recognize it because that is a sure sign of success, that it's beginning to be creative. I think that it is good to work in a direction of reform, because at least you are not resisting, but the reform only has to open up the system to allow people to be creative

WASSERMAN: Yes, but that is a rationalization for giving the task to others. The universities, presumably, are committed to social change and responsibility. We've got a role to play. Are you saying, in effect, forget it? They've got to do it themselves. Let them redo it.

WELBOURNE: No, that's a rationalization for the given culture to survive itself.

REID: Would it be a fruitful line of pursuit to suppose we could push the "destruct" button and we would no longer have libraries? Let's go then to the issues raised by Mr. Wilcox: what is needed in communities and what we want to have happen in them. How can this professional array of techniques be supportive to what we want to happen there? Let's get back to this business of decision making, playing games about decisions. Isn't so much of the involvement and the farce of decision making a result of the fact that people really do not know the issue that's really at hand and do not have the data? Or is there such a differential in the amount of information that people have that, in fact, people are making a decision about one thing when the matter at hand is really something else? Is this something that a new group of people, a new group wandering in, could perhaps set up and do?

KAHN: There is also a question, "Is there an ability to implement any decision?" People can be allowed to make decisions, but if they don't have resources to put their decisions into effect, what's the difference? You can talk for a long time about decisions, about making them and so forth, but if you don't provide the wherewithal to make any sort of change in existing organizations then the decision is just worthless.

WELBOURNE: That's where institutions get in the way. Institutions and concepts get in the way.

KAHN: If you haven't made a decision, I don't think you have the ability to put one into effect. You don't have the ability to go out and say, "O.K. Contract here. We've got to get this done. We ain't going to decide where the roads and stuff got to go, where people's houses are going to be changed and this sort of thing." You don't have this scope. This has not been provided to you. On this level it seems to me that the idea would be to get the people who are in power, whoever they are or however we have to do it, to actually give $1 billion, not $30,000, because that's what it takes. In the society the way we live now, you talk about big money, you talk about big workers who want to do something big and need the power to buck the other people. You would have to consider this as much as anything else in decision making. What use is your decision going to be after you have made it?

DONOHUE: When you don't have the bucks to implement it yourself, it seems to me the thing to go after is the political and economic power to enforce the decision once it is made. The problem Dr. Wilcox has raised, the power of people, applies to white middle-class suburbs equally.

BUNDY: Yes, but mainly both of you are evading the question Mrs. Reid asked. Price is no object; now what would you do?

WILCOX: I am wondering if anybody in this room heard me. Maybe I am dealing with a group of professionals who feel they have found the truth. When you asked a question about a white guy in a black community, I had a reaction. If you come in to help, what is the relevance of your whiteness? Do you want them to accept you as a white person, or as a person, black or white?

REID: But we don't have humanness in the ghetto either. Consequently, we have to have a beginning point, the racism in the ghettos. We've been well trained in the education of this society to say, "You're a white man. I don't know if I want you here." So the question is somewhat relevant. He is saying, "Aside from this point, let's get down to the nitty gritty of what goes on." Is there anything?

WILCOX: But you have lost my point.

WASSERMAN: Let me state it differently. Let me say that here we are. Our role and our commitment is to prepare people to do useful work in a technical field. I'm saying to you, how can we be helpful? What kind of agenda . . . ?

PARTICIPANT: How can you have an agenda to be human? I can't stand it any longer. How can you teach somebody to be human?

SEGAL: I would say the name "human" is a bit of rhetoric too. I'm talking about delivery, I'm talking about giving something useful to a human being. That is being human too. But first you have to look into what they want. I'm asking.

PARTICIPANT: We have to listen first.

PARTICIPANT: What makes you say they haven't been? This profession has been listening for a hell of a long time. We're not all a bunch of bigots.

SEGAL: When Jim said something before about changing the institution and all this, my reaction is as a crazy-headed clinical psychologist. If I were thrown into a ghetto library or a suburban library or the Library of Congress, what I first might want to do is listen to what people asked of me in terms of services.

REID: Suppose they don't come in.

SEGAL: Then I want to go out and find out what I'm not hearing.

BUNDY: All right. Let me just take that up, because we have listened to people and wants, to some extent, in this profession; but the people always respond to the institution. Librarians will listen, but what the users say to them is in response to an institution they have known. They are not responding to possibilities they have never seen.

WELBOURNE: Can you assume a whole new concept of thinking, when the old way is so much a product of institutions? When you think of institutions, the first thing you think of is domains and not crossing somebody's territory. You put boundaries on what you can do, whether you know it or not, because this is your profession. You feel bounded by certain roles. You are going to work in this framework. The answer may mean going over that line. If the answer means going over that line, and you are thinking in terms of, "I'm not thinking past this line because that's somebody else's . . ."

WILCOX: If this group was in a sensitivity session, you would have to deprogram yourselves. You need a whole different perspective of life, really.

REID: In the context of the profession, not concerning its structures, but concerning what it could become in terms of roles and functions, what it can do? Can it become purely human and listen? As hard as both of those are, can it become human enough to deal with the problem of hunger, the problem of rats? Are there any mundane things that "programmed" people might do to afford this generation that's coming up . . . ?

WILCOX: Not unless you deprogram yourself. Because only you can go out and build another job for yourself. Most of the effort I've seen with poor people doesn't end up helping them. Personally, I will not get involved in any more of these problems where people get rich on the backs of poor people. One of the reasons I am doing full-time consultation now is because I want to be able to make my money somewhere else, so that I don't have an economic relationship with these people. At least two days a week I give full time at no expense to the people I am trying to help.

REID: Do you happen to have any direct contact with the poor people?

WILCOX: Oh, yes.

REID: What are you doing?

WILCOX: Number one, I have learned to listen from them. They educate me.

REID: What do you do with what you learn?

WILCOX: I try to help them do what they want to do.

REID: In what area?

WILCOX: You name it.

REID: Tell us what they say.

WILCOX: In what area? Actually, I haven't had a lot of contact with people about the use of the library. In fact, most of the people I know . . .

REID: You just talk about their human needs and what they want. We can make the interpretations of the kinds of things we need to do to deprogram ourselves . . .

SEGAL: You are programmed to think of the library too. We are thinking in terms of what we can do to be useful to human beings. Forget about the library! You're hung up on libraries! You tell us about circulation. We're not really interested in circulation either. We're trying to be viable for human beings. We're asking, what can human beings whose commitment in life is dealing with information do? How can they be human?

PARTICIPANT: We don't go out and ask them, "What do you want?" We ask ourselves and determine what we think they want, or we ask libraries what they are doing, but we don't go out to the people and say, "Do you want a library?"

WILCOX: I'm being very honest. Let me give you one of my concerns when I meet with people like this. I hope I'm not categorizing you, because maybe I am.

BUNDY: In a way, you are. I'm not saying this is totally inappropriate, because I am getting certain kinds of data from you. Maybe I am reacting to the way you are reacting to me. I'm only human. I'm not asking for brownie points, or asking you to change, or anything. I'm getting certain kinds of radar. Now, you see, when I talk about your getting involved in your own liberation, I'm saying that's one of the things that has to happen for you to be able to understand what I am talking about and to want to use it creatively. When you were talking, I was thinking about what would happen if a guy out of a storefront that I know walked into your library and said, "Listen, we'd like to set up a library in our storefront." I was thinking about all the questions you would put to him, such that he would never come back.

WASSERMAN: Precisely that happened in a major city in the U.S. Exactly that.

WILCOX: My response would be on two levels. Number one, I would try to find a way to help the guy. I would figure out how I could help him set up the library in that storefront. I would try to help him to learn all the skills he needs to know in order to do it. I would work on establishing a relationship with him so we could really talk about what he needs to know and how I can best help him. Then I would think about how to turn that institution around. When my supervisor comes around, I would think about how I could work him over in such a way that he would have nothing to do but go along with me.

WASSERMAN: Let me suggest the dysfunctional consequence of this.

WILCOX: By the way, let me say this. If any of you have libraries in poor black communities and you are viewed as dysfunctional by the system, then you're not doing anything.

WASSERMAN: Let me suggest what the professional problem is, if you're concerned about professionalism.

WILCOX: No, I'm not concerned about professionals, I'm concerned about humanism. I say if you're a professional, you're a human being first.

WASSERMAN: Of course.

WILCOX: No, don't say of course. I say I'm a professional but I say it in the context of trying to be a human being. I don't want to be a professional outside of being human.

WASSERMAN: Let me suggest to you what I mean. If we . . .

WILCOX: You've got a hard exterior, you know that? Why don't we talk about professionalism and humanism, because if we understand that then we can get on a wavelength.

WASSERMAN: What's the point of being comfortable? Let me give an illustration.

WILCOX: When are you going to be tough?
WASSERMAN: I don't want to be tough. You're using definitions. Let me just . . .
WILCOX: Uh, oh! Do you understand my definitions?
WASSERMAN: I understand your definitions.
WILCOX: Play it back to me so I know you understand me.
WASSERMAN: Let me go on with the point before we do that. Do we have to stop there?
BUNDY: Put your spears down!
WILCOX: What makes you think we're fighting? Do you feel any hostility?
WASSERMAN: Do I feel any hostility?
WILCOX: From me?
WASSERMAN: No.
WILCOX: Why did you think we were throwing spears?
BUNDY: Well, I know you were really speaking friendly, but you had spears in your hands.
WILCOX: Did you feel I had a spear in my hand?
WASSERMAN: No. Why did you feel I had a spear in my hand?
BUNDY: I withdraw the spear.
WILCOX: Maybe we're both liars.
WASSERMAN: Maybe we can do useful things, provide information and deliver information that would be very, very valuable and important. We know something about organizing. We know something about what happens when somebody else does it, who is kind of an amateur at the task. We'd be good guys, we'd be helpful, but maybe our energies might best be spent in devising ways and means of using our technical skills to provide better access and more information from more knowledgeable resources. That's all I'm saying.
WILCOX: Does that mean you want to remain professional? You want to always be able to use one of your technical skills?
WASSERMAN: I don't care about that. Maybe all the guy wants you to do is sit and drink a cup of coffee with him.
REID: There is nothing wrong with that, actually. The library can do that or the new thing can do that. Serve coffee, O.K.
WILCOX: You see, we can't even drink a cup of coffee together. That's why I ask you guys about this professionalism. If you are concerned about using technical skills and all this kind of stuff, what you are asking that person to do is to ask you a question where you

can respond with your technical skills. They don't even know those questions.

REID: That's it.

WILCOX: Why should they know those questions?

REID: Preston, how can we deal with that problem, the library and this group of people? You are very comfortable with the two concepts, humanism and professionalism.

WILCOX: Don't separate them. Human professionalism.

WASSERMAN: Yes, professional humanism.

WILCOX: That's one problem: you've been used to thinking in fragmented ways. Card files, index . . .

REID: I don't know anything about those things at all. Sensitivity training will help you if a guy comes in and says "I want to be able to prepare a proposal for an air force study on some sort of munitions thing." But . . .

WILCOX: You ought to be careful about helping those guys. It is interesting you would use that as an example of talking about humanism.

REID: You know why I used that? I used that deliberately because we are at our best there, because society is at its best there.

WILCOX: Well, drop out there.

REID: Okay, now let's look at something else. We do not know how to deal with the nonproblems that people place upon us.

WILCOX: The problems you don't understand.

REID: We don't have anybody pressing us, and we know there is a pressing need. That's our problem, you see, the nonproblem that we confront every day. There is no great pressure upon us to do these things that we know need to be done, but we want to know what they are, where they are, who to do them with. So there are some first steps to take. Some sensitivity training might make us very comfortable and effective. If a guy comes in and wants a cup of coffee, and you have never had coffee in the library before, it doesn't make any difference. You go down to the corner with him and you stroll back. You make coffee and sit back and talk with him. That's easy. Yes, it is.

WILCOX: That's easy. All right, but now what would you be talking about when you're drinking coffee with him?

SEGAL: I guess I am puzzled by your question, in terms of his comment, that they don't know what questions to ask, because it seems to me that one of the traditions we do have . . .

REID: I didn't say that. They weren't asking any.

SEGAL: It seems to me that the tradition the library field ought to look at is a pretty lousy one in terms of the way it's practiced in the United States, but there is a tradition of early education and helping kids to learn to ask questions, helping people to learn to find out how to question. Supervision in social work and in psychology, I think, is geared to helping people to learn to ask questions. Where is that tradition in the library? As far as I know I don't see it in terms of the curricula.

WELBOURNE: I think it goes the other way, though. Again, library education is learning to ask the questions so we can help them to get to work . . .

PARTICIPANT: Sometimes they don't come at all.

WELBOURNE: But these people are communicating all the time, and it's people who don't have to sit there who are the ones asking those questions.

SEGAL: I think the smartest people are people who don't use our services. They know they shouldn't come in; they'll get worked over.

WILCOX: That's because we're not dealing with their human needs; we're dealing with their information needs.

REID: We're not dealing with the informational needs of people in the ghetto. Don't kid yourselves. We don't have libraries out there. We don't have people out there. And they don't believe it can be done.

WILCOX: They have libraries in the ghetto, but they're locked up.

KAHN: There I would differ with Dr. Wilcox. It is barely possible that if you were really dealing with the informational needs of the ghetto they may very well feel their human needs someplace else.

REID: A person who is an orthopedic specialist does not have to worry about the total actualization of a person. All he has to do is make a contribution in the particular area that he can, with the understanding of what a human being is, of what it means, and so on. But he doesn't grow him up; he doesn't develop him; he doesn't actualize for him. This group of people never should believe it can take on the whole person.

WILCOX: I'm not asking you to solve the world's problems.

REID: Or even an individual problem?

WILCOX: I'm making a simple statement that if your library is sitting there and poor people are not using it, there is something irrelevant about your library. If I call a meeting and people don't come, I can't blame all the people who didn't come. There was something wrong about the way I called the meeting also.

SEGAL: Are you saying then that all the people in the city should be concerned with humanism no matter whether it is in the library, the school, social work, or even your local bar?

WILCOX: Definitely. Why not?

BUNDY: People do not typically use information for nonhuman needs. People quite typically use information to satisfy human needs. There is really not this separation.

WILCOX: Oh, no! People who build bombs call themselves human, and I don't! You see, I really don't have a question about your giving information to people who build bombs.

BUNDY: All right. I get you. We're going to sort out whom we are going to help. Is it inconsistent? Maybe we haven't really established a level of understanding.

REID: Is humanism a very important part of society as we now have it? I'll just come out of the chair and be myself, since I haven't been. This society is very, very hep on knowledge and information. I am inclined to think that even if librarians are doing their job or start doing their thing, that that thing is going to evolve into something still using knowledge and information. I base that on my observation of organizations in the ghetto, groups and activities in the black community that are more organized than they ever have been. I am inclined to believe that we are probably not going to do away with the substantial amount of knowledge that has piled up, any more than we are some of the artifacts of our society. I think some of the knowledge we have is like an artifact. Some of it may not be. Associated with this is information flow. Now, should I assume that all of that is antihuman? That is the first thing we have to understand. If that is antihuman, then we cannot possibly ask any intelligent questions.

WILCOX: If libraries were organized right, you would have more books under the title "white institutional racism." In fact, that would probably be your biggest section. Second, there is the fact that poor people are not using the library while they are paying taxes to support the library. There has been no responsible effort on behalf of libraries to develop other ways of reaching them. For instance, why don't you have more tapes? I don't think poor people are antiknowledge, by the way. I just think their kind of knowledge is not the kind of knowledge that fits in with what most people want to consider knowledge.

BUNDY: They say we are giving library service if we put a branch library in this neighborhood. Their standard is not the library's utilization but the library's presence or absence.

WILCOX: That's right. There has been no evaluation. If libraries received money on the basis of how many poor people used them, they wouldn't get money.

REID: When you appeared before the Senate committee, you addressed the question of a national accumulation of data about communities with respect to everything social. By the time you report on everything social, you report on damn near everything. You said this doesn't need to be at the national level; this needs to be at the local level because communities need information about themselves. All right. So when I left the Commission on Civil Rights, the organization I was in, and came here, one of the reasons why I thought it was important to be associated with this profession was that it seemed to me that information about a whole array of things was pretty damn important to poor people. I don't really think I can do very much about their humanism qua individuals, because you see I'm not big enough for that. I just handle myself the best way I can. That's probably as far as I can get. But I think if people have all they need, they will take in their own human problems themselves. I think every individual has this capacity if he's not deprived of what he needs to do it.

The culture that I see the black man evolving on his own is not too different in terms of its use of organization, knowledge, and information, by and large. Maybe the substance differs slightly, but the tremendous thrust of it is so similar in terms of those particulars that it is still useful. Black people are clamoring now about better education for their children. There is no question about it that the paramilitary group really digs this information thing, because they've got all the mechanical things to go along with it and keep it moving fast. Therefore, there is some relevance to considering the questions "What do you need?" "Where do you need it?" "How do you get there?" That's what this profession is all about. Profession is just a rubric to keep from saying a whole lot of things; it is just an umbrella, as you know. All right, we don't give a damn about books. We have long ago forgotten that books are the most important thing going. We know there are all sorts of things—tapes, videotapes, conversation, talking on the telephone, customized service because you know the client, capturing local history, working on the problem of identity. But you see, what we really need is to have people come in to talk with us who rub against the poor, because we don't have this opportunity. We need people to give us insight into the needs, insight which can be addressed by the business of knowledge and the pull of information. We need to maintain local writings. This is what we are about. We need to have anybody who has this kind of experience make input into this kind of . . .

WILCOX: Well, I think there is a whole new body of knowledge developing. For instance, the guys I know in the black community who are really thinking about the nature of society are looking for stuff that shows the interrelationship among bodies of knowledge in one single article. This whole fragmentation, as far as I am concerned, occurs because educated people have become specialists and don't understand anything outside themselves. Also, I am thinking about how the library can become a political instrument in the black community. This whole concept of something being apolitical is for the birds, because nothing is apolitical. How can the library become an institution as it operates in the community, contributes to the community's developing its own autonomy? For instance, I would assert that most institutions like yours that operated in any community, particularly in poor black communities, are very much controlled from outside the community. The effective decisions are not made locally, or, if they are made locally, they are the same decisions that someone would make downtown. So even the life style of the library has nothing to do with the black masses, the physical structure in itself. It is a plan someone had for some other community. It has no relationship to the life style of a particular community. We even thought about having schools that have a classroom on one corner, a classroom on another corner, a classroom over there, and maybe one in a storefront and one in the basement of a church where people go, and so forth, or near the supermarket. This is why I was trying to get you to look at new kinds of definitions, because I don't really think that the same models now are going to serve large numbers of people. And I'm concerned about large numbers of people.

You mentioned social indicators. I happen to think that the social indicators that have been developed so far are by people who don't have the problem they are trying to solve. I'm trying to find a way now, myself, to begin to click, to get people in ghettos clicking data around their own problem. For instance, I'll just give you two examples.

I worked with a group of ex-cons. Two of the men tell that the moment of intervention is the point where a guy commits a second crime. You all know that in this country it is easy for a black guy to get arrested for committing a lesser crime that a white, and he'll serve a longer period of time. Studies have shown this, particularly in the South. So the likelihood of a black guy's going to jail is much higher solely because he is black. If he lives in a poor community, the chances are increased. When I was working on that problem, the ex-cons were telling me that when a guy commits a second crime, that is the best time to intervene. The first time he commits a crime, he thinks it is a mistake. His family is behind him and they think it is a mistake. The parole officer also is on the side of the guy when he comes in for the first time. But the second time his family begins to say, "Oh, he's a black sheep." The guy begins to think, "Maybe I am a criminal," and the parole officer says, "Here comes this guy again!" This is the moment when you can really intervene in his life. The parole system has been set up, spending millions and millions of dollars and never asking local guys about this kind of a question.

The second issue is that there is a parole practice of not allowing ex-cons to relate to each other when they come out of jail. If they are caught with each other they can be sent back to jail. Now, the ex-cons know that they can help each other better because they know each other's problems. They almost have to pay the parole officer off to be left alone. He knows that the ex-cons work together. At any moment he can use that against them to get them back into jail. So they are really at his mercy. Every time they see him they've got to play a game with him. They are accidentally caught with each other and they use me for all kinds of accreditation. I'm embarrassed that they have to use me to accredit what the hell they're doing, helping their own community and so forth. Now, for three months I have been trying to arrange a meeting with the parole officer . . .

REID: Ah, there's a function we never thought of: legitimizing local activities.

WILCOX: Yes, but what I'm trying to get across is that there's a whole new set of social circumstances that a lot of people don't really understand. By the way, I don't think it's an accident that we haven't solved those problems. I don't think people really know how to solve them, even though they walk around acting as though they actually have solved them. For instance, all of you probably act as though you know how to reach the black community if you can get a library in the black community, but they won't come in. That's B.S.! You know that your supervisor will come around and you will start talking about how the people won't come in.

REID: It's not quite like this. Could I tell you . . .

WILCOX: How do you know it's not like that?

REID: Well, because . . .

WILCOX: Why are you people so defensive?

REID: We're not defensive. It's worse than that. In a lot of places the supervisor doesn't ask that question at all, doesn't even think of it.

WILCOX: That means they don't even have anything to say.

REID: That's right. So in some places it isn't like that. It's much worse. In other places there are people sitting down trying to figure out how they went wrong the last time they went out there. In other words, the range is wider. What you said doesn't really get in the full range of the problem. There's the constant missing in some places that really are working on it. Then other places don't even know they're not, and don't care, and of course that's . . .

WILCOX: I would say the thing I am suggesting to you is the way you should work in any library, whether it's being used or not. The big thing has been missed here. When I talk about humanity I am talking about all people. That's why I question you about professionalism. Is a professional someone who is a depository of knowledge? Is it someone who has a vested interest in helping other people to get the skills so he won't need the professional?

BUNDY: I once heard a farmer say, "Libraries are essential when I need information, but will you stop trying to cram it down my throat the rest of the time?" There are institutions that serve functions when we need them, but we don't have to say everybody has to be there all the time.

WILCOX: Well, why don't you get paid according to how many people come in?

KAHN: It's not surprising that you are creating a box for yourself, boxing yourself in. I have no quarrel at all with the notion of Mr.

Wilcox that the information needs of people in the ghetto in many cases are very different. Probably somewhere along the line, we had better consider that there are major information needs for poor white communities, and the middle and upper white communities, that have direct bearing on the institution.

PARTICIPANT: You know that information. You know nothing whatsoever about the ghetto.

KAHN: I would submit to you that first of all we know less about poor white communities in many cases than we know about the poor black. I'm also not so sure we know what we think we know about the upper middle class.

PARTICIPANT: If you think you have no body of knowledge whatsoever, why be in the library business? You know you know something.

KAHN: The definition of what I know is not the subject that concerns the guy out on the street. You know that as well as I. His sole concern is his need to make it for himself, not whether I can make it.

PARTICIPANT: But if the guy out on the street wants to know about himself, and you can't tell him, your lack of knowledge is his direct concern.

SEGAL: I get concerned because I think that you can get very enmeshed in the notion of the content. You have to have the specific facts. What I thought you were implying before is that one of the characteristics of a professional is that he helps other people not to need him anymore. Maybe we don't look at the right question. I include social work struggles in this because they have been process oriented ad nauseam . . . . It seems to me the question I see lying there is does the profession have a process? That doesn't mean professionals have to know black suburban, exurban, poor white communities, but do they have a process that helps move from what people need, to how they begin to find information that is relevant to them?

REID· Oh, but that's generic.

SEGAL: Yes, it's generic, but I think we lose it frequently and get involved with the content.

TAYLOR: I'm sorry. I can't help but think of all those poor people who come into libraries. You con them into it with your process. They've gotten there and you've got nothing to give them. I couldn't care less if you've got the right process, because at the end of that process of conning me into a building, getting me interested in books, those darn books have nothing in them relevant to me, my life, where

I want to go, what I want to do, what I want to be, what I have been . . . .

KAHN: If you get to that point through my process . . .

PARTICIPANT: Then I'm lost, because it's like the social worker in the ghettos who processes us to death. We look around and we haven't got anything. We've finally learned who we are and we find out we're somebodies with nothing because the social worker is running our music programs, the social worker is running our library programs, and the social worker is running our education program, and he doesn't know anything.

KAHN: I can't buy that.

PARTICIPANT: I buy it because I've got all those poor souls in the ghetto walking around, after having been conned by processes, who find out that after five years of processing they have no knowledge.

WILCOX: You're talking about manipulating.

BUNDY: You're talking about education.

WILCOX: I think there's an important distinction here. I think you are talking about manipulating a process. Somebody comes into the library. He wants to get certain kinds of information, and the librarian doesn't have the honesty to say, "Listen, we don't have it but I'll try to help you get it." He says, "Listen, how about reading this? Tolstoi!"

SEGAL: I think the problem has been that they have substituted their choice of programs for helping people . . .

KAHN: And the implication of that is that this other bit is really at least as good and is probably what they ought to read.

PARTICIPANT: Tolstoi is not for me. But are you willing to accept the fact that if someone comes in and you tell him you don't know what he needs, and he goes out, that everything is fine, cool, great?

SEGAL: No, because part of the process ought to be helping him to articulate more of what he is searching for, no matter how he does it. We need to listen and see how we can manage both to get him the information content he wants and to help him learn the process so he can find out for himself next time.

BUNDY: We are also playing games with the school. For example, at Fairmount Heights,* I can remember checking the adult charge-outs.

---

* This refers to the experimental High John Library set up in the Fairmount Heights community. This experimental program is designed "to initiate change in public library service and in library education

One of the most frequently charged out books in Fairmount Heights is *The Grapes of Wrath*. Now, I am assuming that this was a school assignment that somebody made them read. So we're part of a plot.

WILCOX: How many of you know the best-read books in the ghetto?

PARTICIPANT: Why isn't it more important for me to know what's read in my community?

WILCOX: I don't get your question. I get my question. Why is it important for you to know? All right, I'll respond to you. You are trying to find a way to reach the people in the ghetto communities. One thing you might know is what the people read.

PARTICIPANT: I can tell you: "How to Do-It-Yourself." In our area they read a lot about how to do-it-yourself and things where they can help themselves. They do not have too much time for pleasurable reading.

TAYLOR: In Harlem, instead of doing-it-yourself in the house, they've got do-it-yourself history, do-it-yourself painting, do-it-yourself sculpture; you know, they are finding out how to do everything themselves. They don't limit it to the normal do-it-yourself topic. The range of do-it-yourself may be different but the basis is the same. They want to do their thing their way. Technically, I don't live in Harlem anymore, about sixty feet away, so I'll say "them" instead of "me."

WILCOX: Let me ask this. How many of you take recommendations from the community as to what books should be in the library?

PARTICIPANT: This is what I was driving at before. I don't think it is important for me to know what people read on the national scale. That's professional information for me to know. I am much more concerned about what is happening in my neighborhood.

SEGAL: Depending on where your neighborhood is. Maybe what's happening in New York will be happening in your neighborhood next year, or two years from now, and you should be prepared for it. If you wait for them to come in, you won't have the books on the shelves to give them. You need to anticipate them.

WILCOX: If you were political you would be concerned about what is happening nationally.

PARTICIPANT: I didn't say I wasn't concerned; I said I put that information into different categories.

especially in the area of library service to the disadvantaged." *Library Journal*, "High John" (January 1968).

WILCOX: No, I differ with you.

BUNDY: Then you would be a pacemaker. You would decide, wouldn't you, what they needed to be reading?

WILCOX: Actually the best-read books are *The Pimp* as of last year, and *Trick Baby* by Iceberg Slim. They are paperbacks. How many of you make social studies? How many of you go out and stand in front of a bookstore and see what people look for?

NIMER: Who can afford books?

WILCOX: I am asking how many of you make social studies.

NIMER: The people who buy books are not the same people as people who want to use them.

WILCOX: I'm asking you, how many of you make social studies? You tell me that the books that people buy are not books that they read in the library.

PARTICIPANT: In answer to your question about social studies, I can give you a personal example. I spend an awful lot of time in juvenile homes and what have you. I listen to the inmates talking about their reading interests and what they would like in the library there. It's the things they have not had access to. It's the books that are not available because of the censorship processes that avail in the State of Maryland. I would say that *Soul on Ice* is circulated more than any other book in any prison library in Maryland, and yet we aren't allowed to buy it.

WILCOX: You're not allowed to buy *Soul on Ice?*

PARTICIPANT: Not in the state prison. There is a reason for my saying this in my inarticulate way. I really believe, as librarians, or whatever we're supposed to be, getting the information together is not really the problem, because some way or the other the ghetto man is going to get the information that is most relevant to him. If we want to keep on being in the library, I think we have to hear what Mr. Wilcox and Mr. Taylor are saying; I think we have to really listen to what people are asking. There are several things we're really hung up on. For instance, this morning Mr. Wilcox said that a library should serve as a place for ghetto children to express themselves. I guess the library will end up being a museum, an exhibit hall for expression. I am appalled by that. The other thing he believed was that the library should serve as a center for self-preservation, for perpetuation of the community, preservation of the community, but he didn't say anything about the library serving as a center for certain kinds of survival information. I think this is what we should be talking about. Should we be concerned as librarians when a person comes in off the street and asks for information about welfare payments, or how to get rid of rats? What are we prepared to do? I, for one, say maybe the library doesn't have any business doing this. Maybe somebody else could do it better than we.

SEGAL: We're already doing it. In New York State it wasn't the librarians who made sure more people knew about Medicaid and Medicare than the budget people had predicted. Why the libraries weren't involved in informing people about their rights I don't understand. There were a lot of other people, mostly indigenous workers, who made sure people knew the information about Medicaid and Medicare. This can bankrupt the system, because the system banks on the belief that these people won't find out.

BUNDY: Or we could begin to claim to be providing the information and confuse society a little further? We could take too little money and claim to do more than we are doing.

PARTICIPANT: I have a feeling that in one little local area here we just recently started doing what we should have been doing everywhere. Perhaps we don't have people who are constantly writing to say, "See how well we are running our libraries!" Those people are really doing it. They aren't praising or patting themselves on the back because they have gimmicks and gadgets. They are actually concerned about human beings, the people who live near a library.

PARTICIPANT: That brings up a point. Now, relevant to your question, I am interested in finding out what happens once you get a project like High John started. What happens? Does everybody cop out? They watch it, and you watch it. You try to see how it is going to progress, but along the way something happens. It becomes a sticky situation where it may be a risk. I am interested in finding out what happens when you start to do the things that need to be done, what happens in the process. Why can't they follow through?

REID: When you've got something stating you're trying, some things work and some things don't, but when you get this dysfunction you mentioned, pulling and pushing. What happens, then?

WILCOX: What kind of dysfunction?

REID: There's no problem to get something running a little differently from the tradition. How do we secure it so that it keeps on changing, keeps on evolving, and doesn't all of a sudden slip back into its traditional posture? This is a concern. Why does it always have to be a small thing in the context of the traditional?

BUNDY: Well, maybe somebody from Prince Georges County will also ask for the same thing.

PARTICIPANT: I can see working where the main branch of Prince Georges' library could do the same kind of thing. I'm almost sure they're not reaching all the poor people in that area. They might be serving . . .

WILCOX: You see, you are asking the wrong people. You know the answer.

PARTICIPANT: No, I don't.

WILCOX: If it's a library that belongs to the people, you should be asking them that question.

BUNDY: No, no. She is saying the reality of it is the political structure. It is organized on a county basis. It's allowed one library with federal funds to set itself up. It was willing to take it on, but she is saying why aren't they setting up more?

REID: Instead of asking this group, we should be asking the people who live there.

KAHN: I could possibly say that libraries could be out in other poverty communities in Prince Georges County. I could tell other people that it is only a librarian's job and that there is a potential model.

REID: And that at least in that community the people there could be saying to that community, "O.K., how does this shake out, as far as what you need? What else do you want? Where do you want this to go?" Instead of directing it towards the persons within the institution who might then make a decision about High John, try to build up around High John.

PARTICIPANT: I'm sure that in Prince Georges they have people who are not being reached.

SEGAL: I hear a thing that I think is relevant. I have this feeling that part of what everyone is saying is, "How come we're so great on demonstration projects?" Why is it that once we demonstrate something good we don't do a damn thing in terms of generalizing? And if they're too good, we close them down. When will society begin to see that it isn't always upward and onward, and bigger, better, and expanding?

PARTICIPANT: As long as a thing is doing well, everybody is up in the air and watching carefully. It is a great thing, but if you keep watching it one little thing or two little things don't work out. Some-body's backed out. They're not sure of themselves, so they don't move full force ahead.

PARTICIPANT: Yes, but I think there's something else at stake. In this particular case there seems to be developing something about people doing their own thing. It's commitment.

BUNDY: But see, we've had contacts with other parts of Prince Georges County, and we've explained to people about High John. I still don't think it would be a top priority in their community's list of things they wanted. If they did get to decide, I'm not sure they'd choose a library first.

PARTICIPANT: I've got a question about High John. One of the things that has troubled me most about it as an institution is that being a community project and looking at the shelves didn't reflect the com-munity. Maybe I'm wrong, but it doesn't reflect the community as much as I thought it should have. If I were an outside librarian walking through High John and not talking to the staff, but just looking at what's on the shelves, looking at the physical structure, I wouldn't see anything much different from any other library around. I want to bring that point out because it gets back to something else. If I were an outside person who walked through and saw this I would figure, give it a few years and it will blow over. They'll go back to doing their old thing.

REID: Your statement is true. I think there's no question about it. The original collection that went into that went into it because the person thought that book selection is book selection and a good collec-tion is a good collection everywhere and put it there.

PARTICIPANT: It's a lousy collection for black communities.

REID: All right, it was a mistake.

PARTICIPANT: I'll go even further. I know the black community where most of those books came from, the Pennsylvania Avenue branch. I was in that library for a number of years. The collection was lousy there, and it's even lousier in a small city.

PARTICIPANT: Now, I think if we want to solve the problem, the thing is to make High John a black library and then evaluate the reaction to it. Right now it is perpetuating the system. If it doesn't go on, it's because it isn't anything distinctive.

KAHN: There is something wrong with what you are saying. She shouldn't have to make it a library. She should start with the idea that this is something that belongs to the people. Maybe she doesn't even need the books on the shelves. If the people realize that this is a part of their community, they will start coming in and talking about it, asking her for *The Autobiography of Malcolm X*. She'll run down and get it. She won't have to go all the way through . . .

TAYLOR: There is something that bothers me. Let's face it. I'm black. I grew up in Harlem, but damn it, people in Harlem don't know what books they are supposed to read. People in High John don't know what books they are supposed to read. People in this gentleman's community don't know what books they are supposed to read. The fellow from Columbia is right when he said I dictate tastes, because after struggling my way through college and reading books, I know what books my black people should read. If you wait for them to come in and ask for a book, you've got to be wrong. I mean, someone, somewhere, has got to have enough knowledge about black people and black communities, black desires, black necessities to say, "Look, there are thirty books. Put them in your library for those black people to read." You can't wait for them to ask for them if they don't know they exist.

PARTICIPANT: You're contradicting yourself. You just said you would get collections of books and impose them on the community.

PARTICIPANT: I said High John had a collection of white books. I know that an awful lot of people in the United States are capable of picking a good black library. I know that the majority of people working in libraries can't.

WILCOX: But I think you should take it a little further. They can't pick a good collection for anybody because they've not been educated.

KAHN: You really would not have to debate about anybody picking books for anybody, but rather about people having the right to have resources to get what they want. If they don't know what they want, help them to begin to reach for it.

PARTICIPANT: You started talking about humanism, and we get to the point where we start characterizing the people and what people want rather than trying to make it a human library.

REID: She meant black professionalism, which is as antihuman as what you said before.

WILCOX: Were you saying I was antihuman?

BUNDY: Only white professionalism is antihuman.

WILCOX: When he talks about the fact that *Soul on Ice* can't get into the library, he is also saying that the John Birch Society can't get into the library. I say that is anti-intellectualism, because if you really care about people, you would want a book on the KKK in a black library because the kids should know about the racists. I question the humanity of any librarian who prevents any book from coming into the library, or who stays there when they keep books out. Any book. From a dirty book on sex to the Bible.

REID: Putting the KKK in there when I don't want them to read it is professionalism?!

PARTICIPANT: There would be somebody in that community who would want to read it and know what's going on.

WILCOX: Yes, that's right. I'm saying that any librarian who allows any book to be kept out of the library . . .

BUNDY: Sure, but we can't buy them all.

WILCOX: Wait now, I'm not talking about buying them all; I'm saying anybody who agrees or condones by inaction a book's being kept by a library has a question about where he is.

PARTICIPANT: I don't agree to getting all. I'm interested in black people learning about themselves, but I think somewhere along the line somebody or something got hung up. We bring those books; we have them in there. I read them, but how do you get the other people to read them?

TAYLOR: Which books are you talking about?

PARTICIPANT: I'm speaking about black history.

TAYLOR: You go crazy figuring out which books to put in your library. You'll have to read all of them. Most of the books that are written for black people should not be read—even by black people. An awful lot of them are bad. An awful lot of them have misinformation. You've got to read them to find out which ones are correct, which ones had editors who knew what was going on, and which ones were fooling. It takes an awful lot just to be an expert in the black area. O.K., that's fine, but you've got black people who have been goofing up for a long time. No one is saying that when you have a good black library you exclude them. You see, I'm not saying because you have good books for black folk that you exclude the Holy Bible or a book on the KKK or anything else, but what I am concerned with is the actuality that you can get books on white subjects, on international subjects very easily, and you cannot get good black books very easily, which means you have to make it a conscious effort in this time of continued segregation to put black books on the shelves of black community libraries. That's all I'm saying.

PARTICIPANT: I'm eager to see people read. I'm going to get these kids to become aware and be able to identify with their culture.

WILCOX: Did you first estimate that they were sincere?

PARTICIPANT: I have to struggle to get them there to listen.

PARTICIPANT: Did you actually enjoy life and were you actually interested in the book you sold to the kids and did they just dig it? I suggest you get *The Pimp* by Iceberg Slim and give it to them to read.

WILCOX: I was just thinking. I looked up the definition of the word "fuck" in the library recently. I couldn't find it.

PARTICIPANT: I'm very serious and I'm interested in learning something from all of you here.

WILCOX: You really haven't dealt with a lot of issues.

PARTICIPANT: I want somebody to tell me something. I want to be able to hear something positive.

WILCOX: What is something positive?

PARTICIPANT: I really want to be able to go back and do something.

PARTICIPANT: I think there is a danger in that kind of thinking. If you really had dealt with a person telling you that these are the books . . .

PARTICIPANT: . . . then you would be saying, "Tell me something about your library." He says you are in there telling the people what to read.

PARTICIPANT: The most important thing is not what they read.

WILCOX: Let's take a hypothetical case. I'm in your community. I'm on vacation. I live right down the street. I just figured I would come over and read a couple of books. I don't read too well. Can you give me some ideas on some books that I might take to read?

PARTICIPANT: I would have to find out what you are interested in.

WILCOX: Well, I hear a lot of talk about black power. I think I might be interested in that. I might want to read something about Marxism.

PARTICIPANT: Right there I would take you to . . .

WILCOX: Don't take me to it. Are we both learning?

PARTICIPANT: Well, I'm not a librarian, though I work in the library.

WILCOX: You said you wanted to learn, and I came over as a human.

You didn't get into the role. That's where you shooed me off. Because one of the ways to learn about these things is not to have him tell you things or me tell you things but to experience it. See my point? I'm thinking of another situation. I understand, my name is Mr. Jones and . . .

PARTICIPANT: Hello, Mr. Jones.

WILCOX: Hello, how are you? What's your name?

PARTICIPANT: Evelyn Parker.

WILCOX: Evelyn Parker. How long have you been in this library?

PARTICIPANT: Oh, about a year and a half, but all my life in the field.

WILCOX: You live around here?

PARTICIPANT: Right up the street.

WILCOX: We're glad to have you here. I have a club down the street; it's a community association. We used to have a storefront and we had a poverty grant, but the money ran out. We had really wanted to read, but we just stood around and had discussions about what was going on, some of the things that happened to me and so forth. I was wondering if the library has any place for community groups for discussion. We would like to have it on Tuesday night because all the guys work and go on the subway. We'd like to do it, like 3:00 . . .

PARTICIPANT: I have to check the calendar. It seems to be O.K.

WILCOX: How much is it going to cost us?

PARTICIPANT: Nothing at all. I can give you a key.

WILCOX: What time do I have to come by to pick it up?

PARTICIPANT: We close at 6:00.

WILCOX: You close at 6:00. Some of the guys always have a can of beer with them when they come to meetings.

PARTICIPANT: It's O.K., if you put all the cans in the trash.

WILCOX: You have no objection?

PARTICIPANT: None at all.

WILCOX: You still don't get the role.

PARTICIPANT: Everything I am saying I know is not really true in High John. You come to the beer problem. We do offer our services. We have our basement and all, but when I have to get into a role I know there are obstacles. In my mind I know there are obstacles, because things just don't work out that smoothly.

WILCOX: Maybe I was imposing getting you into the role playing.

PARTICIPANT: Yes, because you have to think a certain way. I have to know where you are coming from next. But why did you want me to do that?

WILCOX: Because you were asking questions about what you should do. There's no answer I can give you. You have to be willing to find the answer yourself. One way to find the answer is to experience the situation.

REID: Very good. I'm glad you did that, Preston, because that speaks to the question this lady asked, which was to tell her how to run a library, which we cannot possibly do. Besides, it is very good for us to hear many people speak as we did tonight. It is very good for us to hear people contradict themselves and for people to contradict each other because it is like that. It's difficult. It's complicated and there are many threads and strings. We certainly appreciate your coming, and we thank you very much.

WILCOX: By the way, if you can't say the word "fuck" out loud, you haven't been.

3

DISSIDENT ELEMENTS IN
THE CULTURE

Tuesday Morning, August 12
Chairman: John Berry
Panelists: James Welbourne
Stanley Segal
Edward Taylor

Berry: The topic this morning is "Dissident Elements in the Culture." I don't think there are any particular ground rules, so we'll just let each person say what he wants to say. You are free to say what you want at any point. We'll begin with Jim.

Welbourne: The latest thing on my mind is whether dissident elements exist now in our society. Is it easy to be labeled a dissident in this society simply because of some of the technological phenomena at work over the past thirty years or so? I am wondering about the TV generation, the effect of mass media in producing individuals (I won't say reducing individuals because I think it is a positive force), in turning individuals into spectators, observers, manipulators rather than participants in a society's culture, that have been the predominant case in other generations. When I think about TV and the TV generation, I begin to watch how people who become used to watching the society in a box, viewing it, watching it go about its business, and finding out that by manipulating certain levers they can control that picture, disrupt it at will, change it if they want, and not really affect their own personal situation whatsoever. It's not very hard to make an analogy to the outside when you walk into society and see it, too, operating in a showcase way, all around you.

We may also realize that there are social levers in society that you can manipulate at will that will have similar effects of disruption. If you become comfortable in a role as spectator and are unaware of this affecting you, you may be labeled a dissident without being a dissident in a destructive sense of the word—a dissident by default. One of the mores of society to enforce its own rules is the threat of expulsion from that society, but if you feel yourself outside that society to begin with, if you are only watching it, then those implied threats no longer work. It has never been so much the enforced threat itself as the implied threat which has kept members going along with certain social rules of society. The younger generation, the TV generation, just does not see itself working under these principles. Yet society at large, because it has not changed, still operates under these assumptions. There are no tables; there is no correlation when you make a threat, an implied threat, and it is not heeded. How do you control these potential disrupters? The mechanisms are no longer working.

In an urban technology, such as we have now, the social levers pushed in one place have ramifications throughout many other places. It becomes increasingly important to deal with the elements that might disrupt it. It's hard, because you no longer have a small core of revolutionaries that you can focus on and isolate, concentrating your time only on these. You have a young population who, just in their everyday activities, may become potential disrupters. Anyone could set it off just by doing his thing.

Perhaps this kind of understanding can be used. This concept might be used by the group of revolutionaries if they wanted as a strength, a kind of support they never had before in changing society and in forcing society to listen for the first time. They might become the actors on the screen that the TV generation spectators are watching. These spectators are taking their cues from the actors. They take certain positions and certain stands. Well, the spectators can very easily pick it up and put it into effect without too much soul searching or pressure on the mind. If the actors are listened to, I think some things can be avoided.

I think there are similarities with the student culture. Most administrators and even faculty often ask students, "Don't you see you are about to disrupt the institution that produced you, allowed you to dissent in the first place?" This is meaningless. The student sees buildings. He sees bureaucratic rules. If the buildings and institutions do tumble, he doesn't see that it affects him personally as an individual. He hasn't tied himself up with the existence of that institution. So he is quite willing to see its faults. It's not just a joke. It is not a ploy in the traditional sense where he makes a threat, but he really won't go through with it. Actually he just sees this as a game. I think if we think about this, we won't play poker with the dissident element. We won't be trying to bluff them, believing they are playing a bluffing hand and that they just won't go through with it. I really think there would be no hesitation to pull some of the levers and see the whole thing go. I don't know whether that is a bad thing or not.

BUNDY: Are you saying that the conventional terms are amoral?

WELBOURNE: In conventional terms, I guess they are pretty amoral.

PARTICIPANT: Where does their morality lie?

WELBOURNE: No morality! It's a morality you create as you go along. It's a morality based on the rhetoric of the morality that has always been held by the larger society, only this time it is a morality they want to see played straight down the line.

SEGAL: Isn't there another way of looking at it? I think I always have trouble because we mass lump. I think I can locate at least three different student dissident groups with different aims, trying for different things. All three groups do serve one critical function whether it be moral or amoral—or anything else. This is the confrontation of a stodgy institution that has gone merrily on its way. They are beginning to get the people in part of the university community questioning, looking, and sometimes changing. So I get a little bit unhappy when we get caught on morality-amorality, because it seems to me there is a clear statement to be made, that student dissidents have been a focus for change in the university institution.

BUNDY: I wouldn't argue that.

PARTICIPANT: O.K., I didn't think you would.

TAYLOR: I don't think I agree with you. I think morality is one of the major motivating facts.

SEGAL: But not in terms of getting involved in conventional morality-amorality. The issue is that there is an institution that was long overdue for evaluation and change.

TAYLOR: Yes, but part of the motivating thrust is the question of whether a society is being confronted with the dilemma, "Either put up or shut up," and the putting up or shutting up means to stop giving a moral line when you don't deliver moral results. Perhaps this is where the whole thing got its massive beginnings.

SEGAL: Tell me what you mean, because I'm not clear.

TAYLOR: Well, for instance, the question of the Vietnam war is, in a great many people's minds, a moral question. I think a great deal of the support for the antiwar movement comes out of the notion that this is an amoral act committed by a society that claims a certain morality. That's a case in point. The race question certainly has fantastic moral overtones. The society says, in effect, "All men are created equal," and then proceeds to prove the opposite. I think this is a moral question that has been asked in moral terms. The student dissident, along with many other dissident elements, is saying, "We want the society to take on some morality, to become a moral force rather than just a political one."

PARTICIPANT: You are saying that the dissident element is more moral. That is perfectly clear to me.

TAYLOR: It's downright puritanical.

BERRY: There is a difference between the morality of ultimate aims and goals and morality that people react to when a building is occupied, card catalogs are burned, or whatever behavior is involved as the attempt is made to confront institutions with the gross immorality of the war, civil rights, and lousy education. That may be the immoral business in our society.

TAYLOR: Basically, there is only one thing wrong with student dissidents. Because they go to institutions that refrain from teaching them the actual immoralities of the institutions, and of society, they grasp the general immorality of society—like Vietnam, like the race question—and beat those general moralities to death. There are an awful lot of specifics that they could attack if they knew, but they don't know because most administrations don't tell them. Occasionally they learn a fact or two by rifling files in some college president's office, but generally they are uninformed. If librarians really wanted to do something, they could inform the students about what's going on in society so that they could have some specific immoral facts to confront with all their energy, and so they would stop beating all the old dead horses.

PARTICIPANT: Well, I'm worried about this morality. We seem to act from the beginning as if there were only one morality and that everybody who is a dissident is good. I don't think we can do that.

TAYLOR: Let's say that most dissidents start out good. Some of them get bad. Some of them go bad because they are confronting a bad society and badness generally begets badness.

PARTICIPANT: Are you saying the whole society is bad and all institutions are bad and we have to change everything?

TAYLOR: Yes, I am.

PARTICIPANT: I agree with you.

TAYLOR: Well, it would be awfully nice if you could point out something good in society, but I doubt if you can. You can point out something that, temporarily maybe, for the space of sixty seconds, might not do too much harm.

BERRY: But we do exist in the face of an enormous data bank of immoral acts committed by the society.

PARTICIPANT: Who is to say what is immoral?

BERRY: It's very simple. There is good and bad. It's not a hard judgment to make.

TAYLOR: Well, I mean we could reverse the whole thing and say that society, as it is, is moral and everything else is immoral. This gives us a point of reference. The idea is to decide what is moral. If you believe that society, as it is today, is moral, then everything else is immoral, which means I am going to have to be immoral.

PARTICIPANT: The very fact that we can gather here to discuss these questions shows that there is some morality left in society. It's not all bad.

TAYLOR: Oh, no, no, no. I wouldn't say that at all.

PARTICIPANT: The freedom to discuss it.

TAYLOR: Would you count that a moral good?

PARTICIPANT: I would say so.

BUNDY: It's a social good in itself

PARTICIPANT: If we were completely immoral we wouldn't even allow dissident elements to exist.

TAYLOR: That's not true. I beg to differ, because I come from a society and a group where the freedom to discuss has been used to deter action. It only depends on your point of view whether freedom of discussion is important. The first thing that a city does when it finds out that its black population is getting upset is to get them together in meetings. They will hold meetings ad infinitum and let people discuss everything and draw plans for change. Then they ignore the results. But in the process, three, four, and five years can go by while people are discussing.

SEGAL: Is it the fact that they don't let the masses into the discussion that is immoral?

TAYLOR: I am just pointing out that talking and sitting around the table and getting things off one's chest is not necessarily good in itself.

BUNDY: It's very civilized.

TAYLOR: Who says that we need that kind of civilization when you are going to use this civilized process to destroy and enslave a portion of the population of the United States? That, to me, is uncivilized. I know many faculties that control their students the way the cities control the Negro population. They let them talk. They let them plan. They let them do all sorts of things and they do nothing in the end.

BERRY: You have to counterpoint that. I'm on your side. My experience the past two years at Columbia University is . . .

BUNDY: All psychologists are on your side.

BERRY: Now why would you say that? Columbia has used the notion of discussion this past year as a way of kind of holding back action. But I think the other thing you have to admit also is that the radicals and the dissidents want discussion too. Many of the people who stand up and are the dissenters and the radicals don't want to act either. This discussion gets to be a mutual immorality in your terms, unfortunately.

SEGAL: There's another element. I think you have to agree that there are revolutionary bodies at work in this process. One of the first things that a successful revolution does is to stifle the discussion, and quite rightly so. You cannot, in fact, mount a revolution in the face of endless talk. What happened in SDS, it seems to me, is very important in this very context. At Columbia not many weeks ago they expelled the PL [Progressive Labor party] faction of the Columbia SDS. That act of expulsion was done with great self-righteousness on both sides. It was achieved by as few as 5 votes out of 500 people or 300 people present. Both sides felt they were right in stifling the position of the other. The two factions each said, "We are morally committed to stop you doing what you are doing. It is going to destroy either our movement or our organization." Both did it with great righteousness.

PARTICIPANT: I think that is precisely the reason why it is so difficult to discuss the moral issue. Isn't morality an aspiration? Don't we mix up two different concepts? The society has an aspiration to be better. As human beings, we are not living up to the goals and standards that we set up. Right now, we are comparing the existing morality of the society against the aspirations, but we haven't had the chance to test that other morality yet.

BERRY: I would prefer to throw out morality altogether and just deal with aspirations, with goals. You decide what you want and I decide what I want. Then let's get together and let's find out in which areas we can cooperate to go forward. If we talk about what is moral to you and what is moral to me, we'll still be talking about that next year, not getting anything done. If we deal with that goal, that aspiration, either I like it or I don't, either you like mine or you don't. We fight over it and come to some conclusion and we'll get somewhere.

PARTICIPANT: I think that's precisely the issue that we are facing. We are saying that something ought to be different. We have to agree on that. From there we fight to work out ways to make it better. I think the whole group is interested in making it better.

BERRY: I can quarrel with what you are saying, because it seems to me you always get back to whose definition is better. There's the whole history of the civil rights movement, where many people felt it was better if people didn't have certain rights.

PARTICIPANT: Then we are facing a very difficult issue. On one hand we are talking about individuals independent of each other, and we are not interested in that. We are interested in a group living together. We have to have common goals. We have to have a common morality as a goal.

WELBOURNE: The morality issue revolves around integrity of position. Society always has a cooperation and applied compromise in which, although you have stated goals, you come to the table saying, "All right, I'll agree to look the other way over this, if you'll agree to allow me to have that," which already implies a degree of deception, a hypocrisy. If there really are certain things that you believe in strongly enough, you don't put up with the opposite of it. This is the morality, the integrity of one's position.

Now, if a society depends on just this for its existence, to hold together as a group depends on just this kind of give and take. So long as you don't enforce certain things straight down the line, then society by nature has to have a hypocritical base. The dissident element is ready to let this drop because they are saying, "I believe one way. I'm not saying you can't have your own biases and prejudices too, you know. It's just why do I have to negotiate with you the nonnegotiable demands that are coming up? This is my position and I'm willing to go this route." Now, society says, "We can't tolerate you because society exists in a negotiating kind of a situation."

You see, that's exactly what I'm not going to get into, because once you begin to negotiate, you begin to water down, you begin to make deals, you begin to make compromises, you never get what you started off with, what you wanted. One group of people decides what they want and they believe in it, then they go ahead and do it. If it means another group can't live with them, well all right.

PARTICIPANT: That's nazism; that's fascism. It eliminates the other group.

BERRY: We're at the very basis of the word "radical." You hear the word "radical" used very loosely these days. It seems to me that one way to define "radical" is to say that the demands that a radical movement makes are unmeetable in the context of the institutions in society in which it exists. That's what a radical movement is doing. What John Brown did, in effect, was to say, "There is no way to compromise on this. Therefore, I'm going to kill three men, arbitrarily, and by decision." Yes, it was an arbitrary act. It was an authoritarian act. That's what revolution is. There are elements among this dissident group who are revolutionary. Oddly enough, though, the net result isn't always that different. It's O.K. for the city voters in Long Island to use our social forms to reject the school budget and say, therefore, the school system in that city is not going to be supported. But it's not O.K. when a kid gets up at an SDS meeting and says, "We have taken care of the school question in our district; we burnt the school down." They both did the same thing. One guy did it in radical terms. The other guy did it in reforming terms, we think, or at least we accept that.

TAYLOR: Both of those are in the American tradition. Speaking of nazism and anarchy, the United States was born on anarchy. Our tradition is one of "Take a gun! Take some power and get what you want with that power, with bald-faced power!" You remember, we were basically formed from convicts and rejects and whatnot from Europe. No matter what the U.S. has loved over the years, it is not a passive, mild, sweet, loving nation. We are a nation of anarchists.

When these kids come along today and say, "I'm going to take what I want, I'm going to burn things down. I'm going to strike," they are right in the mainstream of the American tradition. I know, because I have a heritage based on that American anarchy. So when you say that is nazism, no it's Americanism!

PARTICIPANT: I think you're unfair.

TAYLOR: Unfair?

PARTICIPANT: Yes, because it's not anarchy that made us what we are or aren't. You are referring to some historical facts which are not implemented in this sense in the society today.

TAYLOR: They're not?

PARTICIPANT: How could you have a technological society with the anarchy you are referring to?

TAYLOR: Of course you can have it! Right now, instead of telling everyone that they're serfs, we fix it so that it is economically not feasible for the vast majority of Americans ever to earn beyond a certain amount of money. They work for the top 100 families, the top 100 people who own most of the wealth in this country, who control us now by letting us all get together. It seems as though we have a semblance of freedom, when in actuality we are forced to work for the financial and industrial powers of the United States, or else.

PARTICIPANT: You mentioned 100 families. There are 200 million people in this society.

TAYLOR: That's right. This country is run by a few. It is not a free country, no matter how much we mouth about our freedom and our ability to talk. There are only a few places to go. All of those places fit into the economic plan of those 100 families whether you like it or not. We're in Vietnam not because we want to go to Vietnam, but because Vietnam is important to the industrial complex of the United States. And we're there. Period. Regardless of how many peace marches, regardless of how many millions of people in the United States object to it, we have remained in Vietnam. We are pulling out only because we have managed to think of new industrial means to make money. So, we are replacing Vietnam with our Mars, moon effort, et cetera. There are other ways to pour all of the poor slobs into their working cubbyholes to make money once again for the top 100 families in this nation.

PARTICIPANT: On the first day, I asked Mr. Busby if he thought there was a controlling group somewhere in our society that circumscribed what local communities could do. You seem to believe there is. What is the importance of neighborhood activity, working to improve neighborhoods, and other actions in this context, if such a thing exists?

TAYLOR: Well, with regard to neighborhoods, black people are basically interested in how they are going to slave for these 100 families. Let's face it, we're not going to overthrow the 100 with any kind of black revolution at this particular point. It may take us 50 or 100 years to get to that point. Right now, all we are fighting for is a place with the slobs. We don't want to be the lowest slob on the totem pole. We say, "Give us a chance to slave for the $10,000 or $15,000 a year that someone else is slaving for."

PARTICIPANT: I'm damn glad I live in a country where I can be one of the slobs.

WELBOURNE: Well, I'll take it one step further. In the context of management, if you are an authority figure, a recognized leader, you derive your leadership from the people who recognize it. Even though this country is ruled by the elite, it is done through the pervasive mythology that there is no elite and that the people are really ruling themselves. By default, the people allow this to go on under the illusion that at any one time they can change their system and that they just haven't taken the time collectively to do this.

Now, systematically, if you are conscientious enough, you can show that this is a myth. You can show instance after instance of communities wishing to express their interest. You can see how this community expression does not develop into reality and policy. Once people are forced by a confrontation to see where the naked power lies, they can no longer exist under that mythology. Once you begin to destroy this and the belief in the system and its integrity, you begin to expose the power that does exist. Those people who have to pull the strings will now have to become visible in that string pulling. It won't be allowed for the middle management, the middle level, to do it. They would show how powerless they are.

BERRY: Let me try a different tack on what you two are saying. I want to turn it around. I'm not sure I can see the 100 families. It is absolute utter stupidity that gets us caught in many of the binds the culture gets involved in. In a sense it's a lack of intelligence and a lack of really looking at implications of political action and behavior, a lack of really being able to envision the complexities of the current world. Sure there are manipulations somewhere along the line, but I don't think it is that organized. I think for me that is the hope. The Vietnam bit helps all of the military-industrial complex, sure, but there are whole elements of just sheer stupidity that lead us into these things.

TAYLOR: I agree with you. No one is saying the controlling forces in the United States are smart. They are only powerful.

BERRY: But I think if you put "powerful" and "frequently stupid" together, then there is an interesting problem to work with.

TAYLOR: Yes, this brings us to the point where we have a mass; we can drill a hole in it because we have a bit of intelligence. So, fine! We carve out a little niche, but in the end it is only a little niche. Granted, it's a niche that may make some of us comfortable, may make us feel that we can live our lives and probably a few generations of family comfortably with a semblance of freedom, but it is still only a niche in that structure. Occasionally, one of the more powerful elements will come along and shift the whole structure. With that shifting, an awful lot of little people get their positions shifted, too, and there is a great feeling of change, a great feeling of accomplishment, but basically we're the same.

This society will only get somewhere when everyone in it is taken care of. That's what the ultimate should be, where we don't have to worry about people starving in Appalachia, or Harlem, or Bedford-Stuyvesant, or India. We have enough right now to take care of the entire world without any haggling, without anything, any kind of competition whatsoever going on. Yet, in spite of all this, we're caught up in constant confrontation, competition, and starving—ridiculous kinds of human deprivation at a time of the greatest possibility for humanity there has ever been.

PARTICIPANT·   I can understand your idea of having the people on the bottom move up just to the level with the rest of us slobs, but I would like to know whom you see as being the ultimate controlling factors. Frankly, I don't want to be. I don't think that most people I know would want to be. Also, I don't think pure democracy, where everybody is a controlling factor, is going to work. Even Plato didn't see this. So who is going to be controlling your ultimate world? If it's the people, do you really think that when they get power to control they will be less capable of being corrupted?

WELBOURNE: That's not important.

TAYLOR: The people don't run anything. The people who are interested in power eventually run things. Sometimes they come from the bottom; sometimes they're already on top. But only those interested in control do control. The majority of people are just interested in living. All they want is the next meal, the next house, the next car, what have you, so they can live their lives comfortably.

PARTICIPANT: But who would you put in power then?

TAYLOR: I wouldn't, and can't, put anyone in power. I have nothing to do with the power structure as it exists at this particular point. When I do, then I'll worry about those decisions. Right now, I am only worried about shifting around the relationship of the slobs.

PARTICIPANT: I think that's the problem we are facing. We all agree with you. We all share the same idea. What we are interested in is finding methods to achieve those ideas. Repeating over and over the same thing, that all of us agree with, will lead us nowhere.

SEGAL: What are we after here? Do we want an exposition of what all of us think dissident elements are? Or are we trying to arrive at the answer to this lady's question, which is, "who should be in power in terms of this institute?" It seems to me we ought to explore a little further what dissidence represents in this society, and what the range of dissidence is.

REID: I would describe the following as a dissident group. When Charles Evers was elected mayor, unfortunately there was a time lag between his election and the time he took office. There was enough time for what I would describe as a dissident group to arrange somehow for the city to be $8,000 in debt when he became mayor. He actually has no employees. He cannot run the city. That is what is happening. While the federal government is trying to decide whether it will bail out the city, private groups are making contributions of $250, $500, to try to prove that they disagree with the dissident element.

You can get a city in debt very easily by overobligating. It can be done very, very quickly. If the city is overobligated then the new mayor has no employees. As a matter of fact, in that city all of the city employees are volunteering. That's the only way there is a government. This is an illustration of Ed's point of anarchy in the midst of organization, which is your point. A city is an organization. The officials of that city could act through the channels of organization in an anarchistic way to achieve an anarchistic outcome. I would call this a dissident element in the face of the fact that there were the sanctions, national sanctions, formal and informal, against Negroes' having a right to vote. But the Negroes finally did get the right to vote. There was a black mayor (inevitably, because of the population, eventually there would be), but there was an element which was very much against that. I'm inclined to say that this is a dissident element.

SEGAL: This is illustrative, but I don't think it's always that subtle. It's very simple. There are all kinds of dissident elements. There is a subway union in New York that put the city on its knees because it dissented from what the city was willing to pay the workers. A teachers' union in New York is a dissident element that was able to bring a school system, in part at least, to its knees over very, very specious questions, in my opinion.

PARTICIPANT: In fact, more than bringing it to its knees. There is a teacher element in New York City that keeps the school system from teaching. Period.

SEGAL: So you can say, yes, the UAW represents a major dissident element in this culture.

PARTICIPANT: Except no one calls them dissidents. They call them, you know, the honorable, the marvelous, the sublime.

PARTICIPANT: This gentleman made the statement earlier that all dissidence was good.

PARTICIPANT: He didn't mean to say it.

PARTICIPANT: Perhaps you need to clarify this, because this confused me. We had a statement made earlier in this institute that not all change is good, that not all change is progress. Some change takes you backwards. All right, now you are saying, I assume, that dissident elements are elements that want change. Now are we to assume that . . .

BERRY: But this is what you have to sort out! Take Ann's example and the New York teacher's union, some of the others you talked about; I have trouble calling them dissidents mainly because it seems to me that they are not change-oriented; they are status quo–oriented. In the New York City school strike, many of us felt the union really was stopping the thing. It was an antichange. It was keep-things-as-they-are orientation. This is very much the way the Mississippi situation sounds. They wanted to keep it as it was in the power structure.

SEGAL: I don't think dissidence is always for change. Dissidence very

often takes the form of dragging heels for the status quo or something
that preceded it.

PARTICIPANT: Then perhaps what Mr. Taylor meant was dissidence
for change.

TAYLOR: Our interpretation of dissidence or humanity or a lot of
other things changes with the conversation. In the context of that
moment, I meant one thing. But now that we have, in effect, reversed
the interpretation of dissidence, what I stated then is no longer true.
That's why I wanted to get away from generalities and down to specifics.
If you reinterpret dissidence, my previous remark is no longer valid,
as you pointed out.

WELBOURNE: Let's go back. I would say that your previous definition,
without reinterpretation, ought to be valid. To begin with, society
takes a stand. We can presume some things are good. Do you mean
that dissidence that takes this form, therefore, is good? We have to
take an objective stand. Everyone has his own prejudice and bias.
The problem is how to direct it. I may see your case as a prejudice
because it doesn't reflect mine. It's a point of view so far as you're
concerned. My point of view you may see as a prejudice. Therefore,
if you are really talking about a democracy and the will of the people,
you find the will of the people also includes very bigoted, oppressive
attitudes. Yet you say, "Well, I didn't mean *that* will of the people."
You see what I mean? You are beginning to reinterpret as an individual
what is meant by freedom to have an opinion.

Until you can be comfortable with the idea that someone may exploit
the attitude to your detriment, and both you and they have to accept
these consequences, you don't have anything but hypocrisy. That's democracy, basically. Now if you are saying you want to live in a controlled aristocracy, where you recognize the fact that you live in an
oligarchy because society has to be established with a ruling class and
a poor, then say it. Don't feel uncomfortable about it. Say it! This
is the way you have to do it to organize things.

PARTICIPANT: I have a question that might help me in understanding
a little bit. You're the executive director in the Harlem Cultural Council. This Council is funded to some extent, isn't it?

TAYLOR: We get money.

PARTICIPANT: And you have some staffing, right? There are some
people?

TAYLOR: Some, yes.

PARTICIPANT: And you have some programs, don't you?

TAYLOR: Yes.

PARTICIPANT: Now, suppose a group of people got together and decided they didn't like the money you were getting.

TAYLOR: Oh, that's happened quite a few times.

PARTICIPANT: How do you regard these people?

TAYLOR: How do I regard them? I don't think of them as dissidents. Some of them I thought of as complete asses. Others I thought of as opportunists who just wanted their particular cut of the pie. A few I thought of as being extremely misguided because they hadn't taken the time to look at the facts. All of them I dealt with in as harsh an autocratic manner as you could possibly dream of. Because in my cause of advancing black culture, I'm tough. I'm tough because that's the kind of world we live in. You do not accomplish anything by being nice, by smiling, by compromising. You have to face the fact that when people rise up against you and you believe you're right, you have to stick with your beliefs.

That means when I fight, I fight with every possible weapon I can fight with. That means if it's Tom Hoving at the Metropolitan Museum with his exhibit, "Harlem On My Mind,"* I will kill his political career if I have to. And I did. If it's Doris Freedman, the head of the New York City Department of Cultural Affairs, I'm going after her job. That's the way I fight. Why? Because she is willing to offer $50,000 to someone to take me out of the Harlem Cultural Council. They don't play clean, so I don't play clean. It's a dirty

---

* "Harlem on My Mind," a Metropolitan Musem of Art multimedia exhibit tracing the history of Harlem from 1900–1968, created controversy even before it opened. According to *The New York Times* (January 17, 1969), thirty-five blacks picketed the press review, protesting the exhibit, and vandals defaced ten paintings in the museum's European gallery. Senior art editor at the *Times,* John Canaday, refused to review the collection of 600 photos, blowups, slides plus video tapes, and recordings, because "apparently" it had "no Art." Mayor John Lindsay of New York charged that the introduction to the exhibits catalog was racist because of its anti-Semitic content and should be withdrawn. Hoving denied the charges and asked viewers to make up their own minds. As tensions between the Jewish and black communities grew, the exhibit drew huge crowds. Eventually the museum withdrew the catalog, bowing to pressure from Lindsay, Jewish organizations, and other political leaders. At stake was $3 million in city aid to the museum.

world. It's black and white in this particular instance because I represent a black cultural council.

PARTICIPANT: Who wants to change the situation in this case?

TAYLOR: In this particular case, I want to change the situation, and they want to change my situation because I have caused so much change. Two years ago when I became the director of the Harlem Cultural Council, I had spent approximately sixteen years in white, western European culture in downtown New York, essentially with white people. I spent very, very little time in the black community. I was a believer in humanity. I was a believer that you do things for the greater good, that we should all get together and discuss. Unfortunately, I got fascinated by blackness and I want back to Harlem to work. I started working with my people. In working with my people and facing their everyday problems, I began to find out that there was a group of people on the other side that I could not trust at any time, anywhere, in any way, that they would do anything to kill me and my people and any advance that my people could make.

I have watched my telephones being tapped. I have watched detectives being put on me. Why? Because all I wanted to do was to say that black culture was worthy and that people should study it and that it should be given a chance. Now that may sound ridiculous to you, but that's the way life is. Just by saying that Alexander Pushkin was a great black man or that Beethoven had black blood, I am considered a hyper-radical. If people want to buy me out and try to destroy me, to get something on me or to throw me in jail, then I'm going to have to deal with them in the same rotten, old, dirty terms, which means I go for the jugular vein of whoever it is that's on the other side of the table at that particular point. They say the best defense is an offense. The Harlem Cultural Council is alive today because my stance is always offensive, in both senses of the word.

PARTICIPANT: Do you trust us?

TAYLOR: I never automatically trust anyone. I trust you after you have proven to me that you are worthy of trust and only then. Then I trust you with 50 percent of my ability to trust. I always will watch you.

PARTICIPANT: I should use the same tactic toward you.

TAYLOR: I think you have to survive however you have learned to survive. I have learned that this is the only way I can survive in advancing black culture.

PARTICIPANT: How can we communicate?

TAYLOR: I talk to anyone. I communicate with anyone. I never say that I won't talk, that I won't negotiate. I have walked into situations where people have threatened my life.

PARTICIPANT: We don't.

TAYLOR: No you don't, but I have been where people have said, "You cannot walk down the street on a particular day because someone is going to get you." And I say, "Well, I have to walk down the street that day because I have to negotiate points *a*, *b*, and *c*. And if I don't walk down the street, points *a*, *b*, and *c* won't be negotiated." So I walk. If they choose to fight, I fight. If they choose to talk, I talk. If they choose to negotiate, maybe we'll get somewhere. But I never, ever, sit behind and say, "I can't go out today. Someone's threatening my life."

PARTICIPANT: But I think one of the questions that we are facing is, "Can we walk together?"

TAYLOR: I just told you. If you want to get somewhere, if you want to discuss, if you want to negotiate, I'll negotiate with you at any time. I don't have to like anyone to negotiate with them. I don't have to like Doris Freedman at the Office of Cultural Affairs in New York or John Corey at the New York Public Library. Liking and disliking is beside the point. All I want them to do is to respect the fact that I represent a group of people who are capable of slitting their throats if they don't negotiate, which means that they have to respect my power.

PARTICIPANT: What about yesterday's concept of humanism?

TAYLOR: There's no humanism in this world. No, no! You talked about humanism. I didn't talk about humanism. The only humanism in this world is being able to build up enough power on your side for someone to respect your arguments in a negotiation.

PARTICIPANT: I've been sympathizing here with the terrible problems all of us have with education. We see them. We read about them. Can you make the transition at some time in the future, from a society in which you have to deal with other men in the way you have described, to something else?

TAYLOR: Well, basically, I believe that when we solve the black–white problem, there will be the problem of earthlings versus moon men, men versus women, or something. These prejudices and factions will always exist. At this particular point I'm forced to deal with the black–

white problem. I'm not so altruistic as to believe that when I solve that, the problems of the world are solved. All that I am doing is, somehow or other, making sure that I, my children, my relatives, and their descendants can live as black people in the world, and live well. When the new problem comes, someone is going to have to take sides. Someone is going to have to negotiate those problems. I don't believe basically that man has proven in his history that he is capable of living without prejudice, without exploitation, without confrontation, without fighting.

SEGAL: I think you said something very true for the whole concept of dissidence, not just the black problem. It seems to me that this is one of the sets of learnings that you eventually have to come to within the culture. You can't make the assumption of trust and reason, particularly when you get involved in power and its exercise and the superior–inferior relationships; you constantly have to take his stance. I hear him and I shrink from realizing this is basically what we have done, and this is what we have communicated to the dissident groups. This is what we have communicated to our university students.

If you don't take the building at Berkeley, you're not going to get any reasonable reaction to what you are saying. If you don't storm Columbia, you're not going to get it. If you don't agitate, if you don't begin taking stands in the black community, you're not going to get it, because you can't make this assumption of trust and reason. The whole thing operates on "What's the minimum to cool it?" We have a whole educational system in New York City where, as far as I can tell, the function of the school people in the schools, especially in the ghetto, is cooling it, not trying to understand what these people have a reasonable right to expect. So that gives you your viewpoint and I hate it when I hear it.

TAYLOR: The actuality is that I hate it too.

SEGAL: I suspect one of the real problems with dissidence is sorting out what you really hate from the person. I think we frequently can turn toward hating the person or persons who are confronting the society with its own basic teaching of "Don't trust nobody!"

PARTICIPANT: Aren't you overstating the issue by assuming that there is a hate in everybody, in all the issues? I have difficulty finding that hate in myself. I may hate other things; I'm not perfect; but in this particular respect I don't find the hate.

BUNDY: Well, could we look at the other side of dissidence? Let me take something I can understand a little better. A faculty member has power. He also has problems, by virtue of the fact that he has power, so he must listen to an adolescent, undergraduate student in order to prove that he really, literally, *will* listen to the student. But there is no real communication because they are not equals. This is his dilemma.

PARTICIPANT: Which is the problem of the society!

WELBOURNE: I don't think Ed Taylor's response was a dissident response, though. It was in the best tradition stating a demand, indicating a power base, recognizing the other by default and saying, "Here we are, mutual opposites. Let's sit down and make it a negotiation."

Society can work on this basis, because once you achieve a power base and you are recognized, like unions, then you do come in and you have a voice. You join the power structure and the power elite. A true dissident response, I would say, would be one that ignores that whole network and says the very vehicle of a conference automatically co-opts you into listening and responding because you have come this far; you have said, "If you make a given response I will also make a given response." You have committed yourself to that level, but you have already said, "There is something about the institution itself that forces one to compromise that I am against." You can't go into it.

WASSERMAN: It seems to me it is a question of the zone of the possible. When you talk about dissidence, in the true sense that you speak of it now, you're imposing conditions that are intolerable to the existing structure. You're saying, "Either get with me, buddy, or we burn you out!"

WELBOURNE: No, not even that much. Because you're not saying, "Get with me." You're saying, "I don't think you can." But that's no reason why I shouldn't try to do it. If others see my point of view and want to do it, too, in your organization, okay.

WASSERMAN: If you push it to the limit and don't negotiate, then the only two alternatives are concession or destruction. I'm differentiating you from Taylor. He's saying, "I'm talking. I've got a point of view and I'll slit your throat if we can't concede something to each other and make a bargain." That's different from saying, "Look, Jack, you don't come with me, we kill you. Let's not talk about anything. You do what I say or you're dead." That's a different situation!

BERRY: Yes, the trouble is that these two situations cause one to build into the other. This is what happened at Columbia, really, a long time ago. It's been beyond that phase for a long time. SDS really didn't want to do anything except build sufficient observable power to have strength from which to negotiate. It is very interesting the extent to which they have stuck with that initial program, which was to escalate student dissent to such a level that it became a national problem. That certainly is a goal they have achieved. And it worked.

It has had some interesting effects. A dissident governor of California, by virtue of relating to that confrontation, has taken power and has said, in effect, "I now have control over the University of the State of California, in all of its manifestations." This is a very serious thing, in my opinion. It is a result of this kind of confrontation. In any case, what they wanted to do was escalate their position to the point where the President of the United States said, "Student dissent in this society is a major national problem." Then they would have power. They would have something with which to negotiate. And then the whole mechanism of cooling it begins.

This is what college administrations and faculties and student groups are about doing now, a lot of it anyway. There will be more confrontations but, in effect, the "cooling it" philosophy is at work. As anybody who is on a college faculty today knows, if a student wants to see the president he probably gets there faster than a great many members of the faculty. This is a simple matter. This is part of the program and it has worked.

REID: Is this really a new form of the frontier way of handling society in which we live?

TAYLOR: I said before that it's in the great American tradition, and it really is.

REID: This is the program. This is the exercise one now goes through in order to achieve whatever changes the person or the group sees need to be changed. This is the format.

TAYLOR: I was once a student. I was once a student leader at a time when student dissidence wasn't quite the national thing that it is now. I am curious about your statement on teacher–student relationships. I steadfastly refuse to teach because of what happened to me as a student leader. I cannot stand teachers. I cannot stand going to schools. Once I got that bachelor's degree, I swore I was never going to set foot in an institution again. In my lecture series at NYU, I start out by telling people, "I'm not a teacher. I don't want to be a teacher. This is just an extension of the Harlem Cultural Council. It just happens to be in a college classroom."

I feel, basically, that teachers shouldn't be called teachers. They should think of themselves as something else. I have taught privately and I love the private teaching circumstance. It's basically on a one-to-one level. The thing that I use is teaching by private students is a complete respect for their individuality and for their person, which I don't believe ever really exists in classrooms.

BUNDY: Many of us teaching right now never want to see another student who is present because it is a required course. We don't like the relationship any more. What you people are not yet discussing, and it's the opposite of dissidence, is the great apathy, the indifference, the buying your degree by sitting there and giving it back, and that's the majority. Some of us who are worried about that said, "Okay, the dissidence will be good," but then the dissidence sounded to me like I still want a father and mother.

BERRY: What? Where did it sound like that?

BUNDY: For example, let me take Jim Welbourne and me. Now we have a friendship, so I disagree with Jim because I disagree with him. Before, I had to be polite to him because he was a student and I had to hear his point of view. Now I can say, "I don't like your point of view."

BERRY: But I don't see Jim or the students of this school here mounting a barricade, so I don't know that you can say that student dissidence exists here. Jim represents it in a sense, certainly, but I still don't understand what you mean when you say we are still looking for the mother and father.

BUNDY: I think students take advantage of the fact that we want to lean over backwards, some of us, to listen to their point of view, so they don't really engage in an equal exchange with us. We are always forced to keep our gloves on. I have a feeling that if I took my gloves off with the students they would respect it more.

BERRY: They have never had the gloves taken off in many of these confrontations and I think they've come out bloodied. They weren't looking for daddy.

TAYLOR: I don't think that teachers are always going to be as careful as you have been. Eighteen years ago when I was in high school, I was a student leader and everything was fine. The teachers backed the student organization, as long as the student organization did not have anything to say about the teachers' particular area of control. It just so happens that the teachers took a point of view that was opposite to the students' and what happened at that point was that the students said, "No, we will not support the teachers." The teachers said, "Well, who are you not to support us, or to tell us what to do, or anything of the sort?" which was a complete negation of our humanity as students.

BUNDY: And I say the students negate our humanity as faculty members.

PARTICIPANT: But why shouldn't they, if you're willing to be pushed over? If you're willing to be pushed, why shouldn't students push as hard as they can? If they were willing to be pushed, by God, we as teachers would push as hard as we could.

BUNDY: Right; this is the dilemma, in part, of the liberal faculty members. This is where the dissidents are headed. They're not headed for the real reactionary faculty member. They handle him with kid gloves because he fought them and they know it. They head for the liberals.

TAYLOR: I guess I have the reputation for being a militant liberal, and that means that you just don't take any crap, but it does mean that you spend an awful lot of time understanding that individual in the audience of a classroom. Some of my students and I go at it tooth and nail privately.

PARTICIPANT: That's the learning situation.

TAYLOR: That's right; you're right. The thing is that I never tell them that they automatically have to accept what I say. I say, "Now I'm a voice teacher. If you do *a* and *b* you're going to get *c*." They say, "I don't believe it!" Then I have to proceed from my teaching capacity to prove to them, in spite of themselves, that *a* and *b* lead to *c* and that they should not get hung up in doing *a* and *b* because *c* is bad. When I solve that, I have solved the major vocal problem and I go on to the next vocal problem. Sometimes we have confrontations and the student gets stubborn. He won't exercise. He won't respond. Then I have to break it all down and try to build it up again, but we love each other. My students and I do love each other, white and black students. I do teach white students still. That's the only way it can possibly be.

When I was in school the last time (I made the mistake of taking a few education courses at City College), no one listened. I had an interrupted college education. I came back from the army to go to college. I couldn't stand the place because there was no intelligent dialogue in the classroom. There was an individual up there who regurgitated a lot of formulas, regardless of any implications the formulas might have. If any students disagreed with any implication of the formula, they got lower grades, or they were shunted aside, or they became horrible elements in the classroom that had to be controlled, and no teaching, as such, occurred. I am interested in teachers' teaching, and in their not being controlled by the student; there should be mutual respect between the teacher and the student.

SEGAL: Mary Lee started out using the faculty member–student illustration to say that mutual respect frequently is lacking. It is necessary to have mutual respect between you and your students, and this can get to be a very messy problem.

Let me go off a minute on something else. One of the things I begin to feel as I listen to us, this morning, is a critical notion of dissent. Whether it be oriented toward change or not, I feel that with the increasing voices of dissent we can listen more carefully and look at what needs to be done.

I think it's fun to get involved in the dynamics of dissent, what's underlying it, who is really controlling what. Still, it seems to me that maybe the constructive element of it is seeing that people begin reacting. What does the whole society begin seeing? Then there is the problem of what to do about it. I get very frustrated by the fact that I think we *see*, but we don't *attend to,* the messages of dissent. How do we begin getting more people to attend to the messages of dissent?

BUNDY: Well, the first message, to me (I don't know about the rest of you), is that word about survival. After that, we'll talk about other things. Do any of you feel that way?

TAYLOR: There are a lot of questions in this discussion for libraries. Should libraries teach methods of revolution, effective methods of dissent? Should a library be a center of dissent? These are questions I would like to ask you as librarians. Suppose you were a librarian in the midst of the community that was very much engaged in being active in the whole dissenting process. What would your function be? What would you see your function as a librarian to be? Would you decide that you were going to editorialize and maintain the traditional library? Or would you stock all of the books on revolution and all of the pamphlets and left-wing publications, all of what dissenters feel they need to know and learn to engage actively in their dissent? How would you handle your library?

PARTICIPANT: Those things should be in the library in the first place. They shouldn't have to be brought in.

BUNDY: Everything should be in the library.

TAYLOR: It's obvious that everything that should be in the library is not going to be there when you need it.

SEGAL: I don't want them to be super-libraries. Every time I go to the library I don't want to find they're teaching revolution or dissent. I very much want them to be able to make available to me a whole spectrum of things without their values getting into what's right and what's wrong, what's good or what's bad. I want them to listen to me and help me with my problem.

BERRY: The library should be the magnifying glass of the social question. This means, obviously, that there have to be priorities. A major question for a library in Harlem is what the priority is. It's pretty clear, I think. It suggests that some of the things that you might want there, as a consumer of that library's services, wouldn't be there because they had decided that they were going to magnify the questions that relate to that neighborhood or place.

PARTICIPANT: That's why we are delving into library roles—to provide the circumstances to outsiders of the specific community library.

PARTICIPANT: Suppose you are in a library in a neighborhood that has a dissident element. You're serving the entire neighborhood. Assuming that you then have materials available for the dissident group, you also need to have materials available for the rest of the community. Obviously you are not serving this one group; you are serving the entire neighborhood. Would the dissident element respect the prerogatives of the rest of the neighborhood for it to be their library also?

TAYLOR: Yes, but now, once again, if you put the right librarian there, he or she will get both elements in that library. If you put the wrong one there, the dissidents will burn the place down. With that comes the whole problem of who is going to be the librarian within this particular hypothetical community.

For a case in point, go back to the Harlem Cultural Council. I have an administrative associate who works for me, who is both a performer and a teacher. When she was teaching, being an Afro-American, she frequently grabbed kids, slammed them up against the wall, slapped them, told them to sit down and listen. A few young white teachers fresh out of college were teaching at the same school. They were having disciplinary problems and asked her how she controlled the class. Not thinking, she forgot that she grew up here in Washington. As a matter of fact, she forgot that she was black, that the students were black, and that the teacher asking the question was white. She said, "Well, I do thus and so." The teacher made the mistake, of course, of trying to do exactly the same thing with the students, and she was beaten up.

She had to realize the fact that she could not do the same thing. I can go into Harlem, and I have, and people have gotten tough and threatened to fight. They have taken a stance, and I hit them. Don't you do it! Don't you dare do it! If I happen to hit someone who messes up around the jazzmobile, the dancemobile, I can do it, because of my color and because of where I grew up and what I know about them and what they know about me, but if you did it there would be a riot. You would be lynched on that Harlem street. You just have to face facts. I couldn't do it if I were teaching in Little Italy or Germantown or Chinatown.

You have to understand how much you can do and how much you can't do, where your power is and where it isn't. Now, I wouldn't dare go over to what was formerly the Irish east side of New York and try to pull that. I know many black people who had to form groups of six people and fight their way to school when they lived on the edge of the Irish east side. They had to group again and fight their way back. That's life! Sometimes you have it and sometimes you don't. You have to know when and where you can do what. With your library you have to know who it is that you can put into that position of authority and what he can do.

PARTICIPANT: Dr. Segal, I would like to go back to something you said a minute ago. You said, "How do we get them to see the message of the dissidents?" Do you mean by "them," people who aren't dissidents?

SEGAL: The base society.

PARTICIPANT: I was wondering, isn't it a fact that people see poverty? They know that it's there. They know that the schools in the inner city are bad. It's not a matter of knowledge. You mean more than just that when you say, "See the message," but what more is there?

SEGAL: I guess I mean looking and not seeing, hearing and not listening. It seems to me that this is the framework for concern. It's not just awareness; it's somehow being more in touch, more in tune, more understanding, so that the message moves you to consider at least what actions the society has to take. The fact that dissidence is so rife in the society almost says conflict and confrontation look like the only mechanisms we have for getting people to really see and really hear at this point. That's a tragedy.

PARTICIPANT: Let me ask this of Dr. Wasserman. I think it might get us back on the track talking about libraries. This is a hypothetical question. If you were a librarian on a campus that was basically antidissident, and yet you as a librarian were prodissident, how would you rationalize yourself in this situation? How would you handle yourself in light of what was going on, on campus?

WASSERMAN: It's hard for me to hypothesize a situation in which I am not, but I think the situation in which I am is a reasonable analogy to what you are talking about. In a sense, what you have is someone with an administrative role within the establishment who identifies the fact that if he stays with the establishment structure and provides no option of alternatives, then he is simply reinforcing the existing structure. Institutionally, it makes no sense, and professionally, in terms of the goals and aspirations of librarianship, it makes no sense, as you are trading off in the middle. I'm sure that Ed Taylor has this problem, even though he sounds as if he makes all these judgments unilaterally. There must be somebody there with whom he must deal.

In effect, I have the need to rationalize what I do with a superordinate structure above me, not always making them privy to why, or what for, or how, or when, but keeping my peace there, so that I can use resources to achieve ends toward which I am as committed as Ed Taylor is to his. At the same time, I am concerned with having impact on our field and the culture for which our business exists. I must listen to all sorts of suggestions, but I can't take them whole. I can't deal with students who want to turn things upside down, but I've got to negotiate. If I am effective in my role I will anticipate dissent. I will encourage dialogue to forestall the need for confrontation.

PARTICIPANT: Could you envision yourself as an arbiter between the two groups?

WASSERMAN: I think this is one of the responsibilities. It is necessary
to explain to the institution what is going on and to identify a kind
of strategy for survival of one's professional school within the structure,
to serve as a prototype for survival of the institution. Because if it
wants to survive, it must be responsive. If this can be done in a
model sense in one professional school setting, then there may be
the capacity for the institution to do the same. Now, take it out of
this context. If it can be done in a professional context in one institution, it can perhaps also be conceived of in other institutions where
the same processes are ongoing and in other technical disciplines.
BUNDY: There is something I have observed, being another player
in the same situation, which is now dissimilar to some libraries. Wasserman says, "Absolutely no, the students will not do such and such,"
and Welbourne says, "O.K., then absolutely we will do such and such."
I get confused and think they both mean it and later they reach an
agreement. As long as I was naive about it, I was terribly upset. This
is a level of sophistication we don't have in most libraries to solve
our internal quarrels. We are really like game players in a very sophisticated time.
SEGAL: There's a convention in the society that you never ask for
what you really want. You always ask for more. I'm sure you get
involved in this all the time. When I have to submit a budget to
the college for my department next year, I'm not going to say what
I really need is one more faculty member and this kind of equipment.
I say I need five faculty members and this much equipment, because
I know the game. The game is that everybody asks for a multiple
of what they really want and hopes they end up with what they really
want. It's this kind of thing. The student dissidents never, ever make
a statement of what they want without somewhere writing into it
that it is nonnegotiable. By now, nonnegotiable doesn't mean it, you
see. So we know, in a way. Some day we are going to find out there
really are some nonnegotiables and then both sides may be in terrible
trouble.
WASSERMAN: You have identified the strategy of nonnegotiability.
There are times when dissident elements don't want to negotiate. They
want the issue to be enlarged. They want it cast against the broader
canvas. They don't want negotiability. Now, that's essentially at the
level of the university. I suppose that's what the college presidents
worry about these days. That's why they are running around having

meetings, meeting with everybody they can collar in order to have a meeting.

TAYLOR: The problem with the student dissidents is that whenever they say that something is nonnegotiable they need to be able to back it up. SDS represents a small portion of the student body. When they say a point is nonnegotiable, they cannot really back it up from the student point of view. When you say something is nonnegotiable, you mean that everyone behind you, or everyone you represent, is not going to give on that point. Unfortunately, many of the student dissidents say nonnegotiable without having the power to back it up. Many times we in the community say it, but that is exactly what we mean and we do back it up, to a man. That point we just don't talk about!

WELBOURNE: I think that if a student dissident, any kind of dissident, says nonnegotiable and bases it on actions of some uncommitted following, then he is being naive. If you're saying that we personally, this band, these three students are going to disrupt, we are committed to this, and that's nonnegotiable. You don't have to worry about what 97 percent of the others are going to do. This administration is dealing with these three who are going to do something, and they have to be committed to do something. I think this is where you find the radical and the revolutions, because that is what they're going to do. The administration gets uptight, and they go to the other 97 percent and say, "What can we do? I really want to be relevant to you people. I can't talk to that group because they're out of it." Well, maybe for that 97 percent something can be done to ease their condition, but that doesn't say anything about the three who said they would disrupt the meeting, if that's what they said. If this is part of their program, that it is the destruction of institutions, then you're in a nonnegotiable situation literally.

WASSERMAN: Yes, but it is the assumption of numbers, isn't it, Jim? That is, if you've got three people, you can manipulate them out of the way easily.

WELBOURNE: It's hard in this culture, though, because it is so tied together. Organizational societies are geared on schedules, on times, on events. When they go out of kilter in one area, it throws things out of kilter on a much larger perspective, so you see that three people can have ramifications throughout.

TAYLOR: As a matter of fact, if you try to deal with the three that way, you may give them the power they didn't have in the first place. They made that point nonnegotiable to force you to act in such a way as to bring the students behind the three. They didn't have this before.

SEGAL: But there is an issue in what you're saying about the three and whether they can disrupt. This is the whole issue of the other groups you are talking about in the university, the other student groups who are not behind the disruption. If I'm generous I would say they are caught in not knowing how to behave when confronted with dissident groups. If I'm not generous, I would say they are irresponsible in the face of something that is disrupting something supposedly they want. It seems to me the issue is what responsibilities both sides take in a confrontation. Do they just delegate it to Big Daddy up there who is the dean or the president? This interaction, or lack of it, makes small groups of dissidents much more powerful than their numbers would lead you to believe.

BUNDY: It could be worse. We're not in civil war. When a student tells you he is going to blow up a building, he is trying to communicate. In civil war he will blow up the building.

SEGAL: That's right, that's absolutely right.

BUNDY: Well, that shows it could be worse.

SEGAL: My suspicion, Mary Lee, is that if you go back on all of the major student upheavals, and if you look at some places that haven't had them, one of the real differences is whether people picked up the messages and started doing something about it. At Columbia there was a large amount of communication; a number of attempts were made to get the administration moving. Every attempt was met with blankness, no response, negative responses. Finally there was no way out. Berkeley had the same thing when it started. There had been attempts to get some response.

WASSERMAN: Well, let's look at dissidence positively. Institutions don't make concessions, unless there is pressure at pressure points. It's very, very difficult, indeed frequently impossible, or seems to be impossible, on the part of those who hold power, to be otherwise or do otherwise. So, in a sense, if there is anything that might be conceived of as enlightened administration, frequently it's stimulated and given the equipment it needs to pursue a path of enlightenment via the channel that begins as dissidence.

SEGAL: Does that suggest that you advocate the institution going out and inciting dissidence over itself?

WASSERMAN: Not precisely that, but to recognize it and to see it as a useful mechanism in its own behalf, as a built-in change mechanism.

BUNDY: John, you answer this. I spoke to a gentleman from Harvard about the fact that we were recruiting black students in the library school. We discussed whether we could have some way the black students could be together if they wanted to be. He said whatever you do, don't give it to them. Make them demand. They must demand. So, in other words, it is not that easily solved. An enlightened administration just can't give it to them. It's more complex.

BERRY: Well, let's face it. All of this is like learning to know someone. Each school will have its own particular set of personalities. There's no real formula, no formula that gets down to handle each little situation. You really have to play that by ear. The general thing is to be responsive, to be sensitive. From there sensitivity means to go whichever way you have to in order to make the situation work out well for all concerned.

BUNDY: But in reality, we don't want you to give us anything.

BERRY: Some students will accept whatever you give them. We were discussing the black students at Hunter College last night, and Dr. Segal said it isn't the black students who are creating a fury. Well, if you were dealing with those black students at Hunter College, you should actually program an upheaval in their lives. They're all too bourgeois and too system oriented to do anything correctly. They have to be shaken out of their complacency with the system.

WASSERMAN: Now you're talking about library education, for the most part, because it's that kind of culture.

BERRY: You can shake them up without inciting a revolution. I agree that an administration should shake up a student if he is complacently bourgeois, but you don't have to do it as an administrative revolutionary. That bothers me.

SEGAL: One of the stances we are beginning to take at Hunter is to begin having a lot of the student personnel staff ask all students, but particularly the nonactive black students, what led him to their choice and their decision. Not to foment revolution, but rather to help them look at this as a decision they ought to make about themselves, rather than just letting it happen. I think it can be done without inciting, but by really helping people do what education should help them do—to explore not only content but themselves and their own decision making about themselves.

PARTICIPANT: We have talked about the dissidents. I'm not too worried about them because they're loud enough and they know what they want, but I am worried about these people you say we should incite. Should we really? They seem to be happy. They don't bother anyone. They probably made a decision that they liked the school.

SEGAL: I think they pay prices in their own life. I think anybody who is in a situation where the major society confronts them with a set of values and things changing, if they don't actively decide and come to grips with themselves and their own decision, they are in a very vulnerable position.

PARTICIPANT: How can you tell whether anyone made a decision or whether they didn't even think about it?

SEGAL: One of the things I think you can do in an educational institution is to raise questions and hear responses. If you begin to raise questions with people and listen to what they're saying, you can begin to tell how thoughtful they have been about it. You can tell what the constraints are and the restraints and barriers that have stopped them from making decisions for themselves, what things have facilitated them. And I think you don't have to approach people with "Have you made a decision?" but rather through a dialogue: "Where do you stand in this?" Again, I get as concerned about the college girl, in terms of her decision making about family, career, et cetera, as I do about the black student. It seems to me that here is another area where the society can screw you up pretty badly, if you don't know and haven't thought through "What do you really want?" If you react instead to the kind of Uncle Tom stereotype if you're black or the feminine women stereotype if you happen to be a woman, and don't think through where you stand, education has failed you. The extent to which many educational institutions avoid this side of it is one of their worse crimes toward their students.

PARTICIPANT: It sounds almost as though you wanted to pressure these people into making some kind of a decision.

TAYLOR: Thinking, thinking! The idea is that anyone who goes to school is a vegetable who sits down and absorbs whatever comes from the teacher without questioning, without realizing somewhere along the line what the basis of knowledge, of thought, of decision is. This kind of student is not really a competent human being.

PARTICIPANT: But not making a decision is very often actually making a decision. I don't want to make a decision.

SEGAL: If the student can state, "I don't want to make a decision because I have looked at the alternatives, and I don't know where I stand. I don't know what's going to be best for me," that's a decision, I would agree. But I have a feeling there is a whole business of being swept along and not knowing why the hell they're here anyway and who they are. I don't think we help kids to come to grips with themselves.

PARTICIPANT: I think the educational system as we know it does exactly that for the most part. I think the educational system really has the responsibility to show us what the alternatives are. I could really relate to what Stan said about women. Frankly, that's why I'm a librarian.

PARTICIPANT: I'm still worried about the fact that the aggressive like to make decisions and like to impose their ideas on those who won't or don't make decisions. You have to choose between these two alternatives.

BERRY: That's another question. When you talk about people trying to push others into a decision, that's coercion, but when you're trying to force people at least to think about alternatives or options . . .

SEGAL: There are as many alternatives for decision making as there are people. If you take the spectrum of family marriage through career woman, this is a big, big spectrum, and a woman, if she thinks about it, can find the place that's best for her, not that's best for me, man, who says, "I want you in the home," but for you, woman, who makes some decisions about where you want to be in this combination. It is the same for the black student. There's a whole range. He doesn't have to be Ed's militant. He equally well doesn't have to be the server of the establishment. It isn't a dichotomy. It's a continuous spectrum of possibilities.

BUNDY: To give you an example, Jim and I asked one black student recently if he would like to be separate. He said, "When it's to my advantage I want to be black. When it's not, I don't."

PARTICIPANT: There are two schools in library reference work. One school is to tell the person where the material is. The other school is to go with him and find the solution for him. Can we follow up your distinction by saying that our function is only to direct the user to the material without finding the answer for him? Or should we take the other way? This is one of the major debates going around in the reference section.

SEGAL: Preston Wilcox said something last night that I found beautiful because I happen to think the same way on it. That is, I see the role of the professional as dealing with his clientele so that they no longer need him. Now in that context, when the professional does something for somebody rather than helping him to learn the process of doing, he's not serving his clientele maximally. Someone ought to get out of an interaction with a professional . . .

PARTICIPANT: I disagree 100 percent.

SEGAL: There's a difference between psychiatry and technical proficiency.

PARTICIPANT: The only kind of help where you do your best by getting them off your back is the help you give as a therapist.

BERRY: There is no value in a person's receiving information from an institution about the processes. What in the hell does he care?

BUNDY: Who the hell cares whether you can use the *Reader's Guide?* That is the problem.

PARTICIPANT: You go to a lawyer for professional opinions. You go to librarians because they are specialists in their area, too.

PARTICIPANT: If you teach them the process, you will have a much better educated clientele, who will come to you with much more sophisticated problems.

TAYLOR: Let's face it, it's a fallacy that you go to a lawyer for legal services. That's crap! A lawyer gives you exactly what you ask him for. If you ask him nothing, you generally get nothing out of a lawyer. Most people in business who depend on lawyers or accounttants to run their case or their books find out eventually that they never get their cases won and that their books aren't well kept. Professionals aren't, by themselves, a panacea in any area.

PARTICIPANT: Do you have to be a lawyer to go to a lawyer, or be a doctor to go to a doctor?

PARTICIPANT: I'm going to tell you something. Today, if you know something about your problems, you get them solved. If you know nothing, you get the run-around.

WELBOURNE: You're making it too narrow. In the process of serving someone you should allow him to understand how this process has developed. Let them see it's not some mysterious thing that you pull out saying, "Here it is! Look at me, the big librarian!" You show him that there is a process of thinking. You begin to educate that person. He's not going to displace you. He's going to use you effectively the next time around.

BUNDY: That's fine, but that's not the only form of control we've got to have around the professional. I should be able to pick up the phone and ask somebody a fact, without having to go down and share an experience with him.

TAYLOR: Sometimes it takes three days to find the correct phone number to get that fact. It's not always that simple.

BUNDY: I'm not worried that he's going to take away my function, whatever that is.

WELBOURNE: The reference function is a process of question-and-answer negotiation. Do you assume that the first question that comes out of a person's mouth is his question? Of course you don't. You shouldn't. You should refine his question through a process of negotiation, and this person should not be talked down to in the process. He should be able to feel that there is a communication, a working together toward the mutual solving of his problem. He should begin to expect this, not to appreciate an answer when it is given, but to expect this communication. This is the role of a librarian. The question negotiation comes first and the service is an end result.

BUNDY: Of course that's true, but the point is if I went into the counseling department wanting a copy of the college catalog, do they put me under therapy? Sometimes I only want a copy of the college catalog.

WELBOURNE: Then elucidate that. If you said, "All I want is the college catalog," all right then, you've got it. A lot of people want more.

TAYLOR: The reverse happens many times. The black student will walk into a college asking for a catalog when he really wants to know which one of the various schools in the college he should go to, which one would possibly offer him a scholarship. He has a million questions that are in his mind behind that request for a catalog. If you just give him a catalog without thinking, without exploring or pulling, that student is lost.

WASSERMAN: That's not only true of a black student; that's true of most people who come into a setting where they are uncomfortable about the artifacts that are there. Many people who will come into libraries, white or black, react that way, and the diagnostic process of an intelligent person who plays this role is to do precisely what you say. Find out what the guy wants.

BERRY: There's a difference between diagnosis and process.

WELBOURNE: There is, in a way, John. There is a white, middle-class hangup about being independent about finding information. I found it to exist in higher education. Over and over again I found the attitude that says, "If you're going to read or lecture to me what's in a book, I'd rather be off by myself and read it."

REID: Jim, you're generalizing from an academic experience to the broader world.

WELBOURNE: Not yet, I'm not.

REID: Just a minute. Let's take the business world of the white middle class and upper. The business world doesn't pride itself on being independent. It damn well hires people to do their stuff for them. This is where I disagree with Stan. The more you know about what a service will do, the more you exploit it in your own behalf. You do not have a hangup of being independent. You want to use it, use it, use it, and use it. The academic world may give its brownie points on being independent, but an awful lot of the payoff in the world outside of academia is gotten by manipulating a whole array of talents, one of which is this particular one here. And, if you do not translate this to working with the under class, the black man, where are you going to put it? You have to begin where the person is, in terms of his needs for this service, and help him to need more of it, because the more of it he needs, and uses, the more mobile he is, the more alternatives he has. So I think maybe your analogy isn't applicable in this particular area, because this profession asks for exploitation as it relates to the black man, the under class.

WELBOURNE: I agree exactly with what you say, Ann. I think that the status quo of educational librarianship proceeds from an assumption that people will come in, and if you don't get in their way by trying to be helpful but make available to them what they need, you have done your job. It is a result of middle-class independence. If they are "educated," they can negotiate an institution. Indeed, librarians can get in their way at some point by being too helpful. This is programmed into our instruction and brings us to where we are now. We set up a library and assume people operate on our values too. If we do our job and build a good collection and then stand there ready and responsive to operate, people will come in and use us as they see fit.

But if there are people who value a verbal exchange more than they do an independent connection with a dead book or a dead artifact or a machine, and we're standing there being a dead machine, nothing is going to happen. We've got to have an understanding, an awareness, of the fact that in their priority set what comes from you first is more valuable, and then they will take what you give. If they have communicated with you and trust you, then what you recommend as a book or something of this sort will be trusted. But you just don't opt out and say, "Now you pick and choose among yourselves." That's not appreciated. Yet, in academia, you make the assumption that this should be appreciated by all people, or else they're not scholarly, they're not self-sufficient, and these are things that are valued by a society.

BUNDY: This is an interesting question. For instance, the typical undergraduate goes to the university library and he has to struggle, believe me, to get anything. Well, maybe his struggling should make him more wanting or striving, but it seems to make him give up.

SEGAL: Well, I think there is an alternative. An undergraduate struggles because he doesn't know what the system is. For example, every once in a while you look back at your own experiences and feel guilty about things. For a while I ran the orientation program at Buffalo and now, as I think back, one of the stupidities of my life is that I didn't help these kids to become oriented toward the university's library. I didn't get the people from the library to come in and show the new students around, help them to feel that the library was a place where they could be comfortable and that librarians were people they could ask questions of. So, what happens? Kids wander around the library. When they have wandered around for three-quarters of an hour, and nobody has said, "Hey, what do you want?" they walk out, and that's it! There is a way of orienting them to the institution, helping them to know what's behind the scenes of it, what it means, what the intricacies are of such idiotic things as, "I'm sorry. That's at the bindery!" What does that mean?

BUNDY: I heard a student group give an orientation at the University of Maryland library the other day. I followed them for a while. They said things like, "Here are the copy machines. This means you don't have to go to class—you can copy someone else's notes." That was how they had been able to explain this library.

TAYLOR: That's an important fact for a student. Everyone should know that. Between last night and today I have been disturbed about this whole question of what libraries and librarians are supposed to do and to be. What is the underpinning of a library? When I talk about music and art and dance, I know where I'm coming from, but when I talk about libraries, *my* feelings are entirely different from what I feel *your* feelings are. Basically, libraries are books and reading. I wonder why libraries are so divorced from the reading process. As librarians you don't help people understand what's inside the books. I can't understand why, as librarians in a library system, you haven't begun to concern yourselves with reading and the understanding of the inside of the books. If my business were dealing with hundreds of thousands of books every day, I would really have to be concerned with reading.

PARTICIPANT: Well, we make a distinction between education and library science. What you are referring to is probably the function of the teacher.

TAYLOR: Why should the education be in the classrooms and the books in the library?

PARTICIPANT: Maybe we're asking the wrong question.

PARTICIPANT: We're on the right question. We need to pursue this. Perhaps there's some need for dissidence here.

TAYLOR: Last night Preston Wilcox said, "Give them *The Pimp* by Iceberg Slim." He said that because they would read that book. That, for me, was important for the library. You should give someone something that's going to hook him on reading, something that is the logical jumping-off point for another book. *The Pimp* by Iceberg Slim gets into the whole question of dope in society. Maybe the next book . . .

WASSERMAN: We bet on that 100 years ago but it didn't work. That's precisely what people said about the public libraries 150 years ago in England when it all started.

TAYLOR: Wait a minute. Was the premise wrong, or only the approach to the premise?

WASSERMAN: No, I don't think the premise is wrong. It's a good premise, but that's not the only thing we need to do. One thing we're very interested in doing is finding other informational alternatives to books. Now that's a library function, and a responsibility, too. What you're talking about is reasonable and highly relevant.

We need to do that more than we've done; that is, we need subject understanding. If we're dealing with artifacts and we don't know what's in them, then we're just handservants. We're just picking things up and carting them away. If we are to introduce intelligence into the process, we need more people in libraries who know their subject. If a guy comes into a medical library and wants to know something, he should be able to say, "Look, here's my problem. Is there something in this repository that will solve it for me?" That's not the same as coming in and saying, "Give me such and such. Do you have it?" "No, we don't have it, but we'll borrow it from somebody."

If we're professionalizing, we must get into the substantive questions. In the public library—and I think we're concerned in this discussion now with that—there's more than the books. There's the problem of delivering information to the people for whom information is important. It doesn't come in that container. We would like it to, but it doesn't.

TAYLOR: Yes, I want to get into that. Let's face it: you can get most any answer you want from a book somewhere. Now, why are you so concerned with other information sources when you have not completely solved the problem of getting the information out of your present information sources to the people? Why aren't you capitalizing on the information you have to the point of getting it across to someone? You're going to another information source when you still haven't created the proper stimuli.

WASSERMAN: I think you can do what you're talking about simultaneously with worrying about helping people problem-solve for themselves.

PARTICIPANT: Libraries don't deal with books. They deal with knowledge. They deal with the background of our society, of all society. Reading is part of it, but it's not all of it.

WASSERMAN: If you stuck to your book analogy, for example, you might rule out the whole business of lending record collections in libraries. You wouldn't want to do that.

TAYLOR: I wouldn't rule them out. What I'm trying to say is, it's very possible for libraries to get caught up in having closed-circuit TV sets, microfilms, records, et cetera, and they still haven't gotten anyone in to get this information out. I'm saying if you have completely mastered the process of disseminating the information in your books, then you can worry about records and microfilm, et cetera, but you still have the basic problem of creating an interplay between people and the informational function.

PARTICIPANT: Because this is a how-and-why conference, rather than a what conference, let me ask you a question. Now let's say I am an eight-year-old third grader. I go to school in Harlem. All day long, I learn readin', writin', and 'rithmetic. I learn that when I grow up I'm going to be a middle-class businessman on Madison Avenue. One day you come to my school. You give a talk on the value of black culture in America. You shoot my whole learning process all to hell. Now, I ask myself, how am I going to become conscious of black culture, and what it means to me? Why should I even bother about it? How are you going to tell that to an eight-year-old boy?

TAYLOR: O.K., you want me to tell you how I have been telling it to him? I normally don't lecture to eight-year-olds. I perform for them. The Afro-American Singing Theater does a show which on the surface seems almost irrelevant, namely, "Down in the Valley" by Kurt Weill. Black? No! Except that this show has a twist that involves black participation in the opening up of the West. In seeing Kurt Weill's "Down in the Valley," and in talking to the performers, the children find out that the ninth and tenth cavalries were black, that one-third of the personnel on cattle drives during the great days of the cattle drives were black. When they find that out, they find out that somebody wrote a book *Negro Cowboy* and that there's a little pocket book edition. They find out something all of a sudden that's different from what they knew before.

We tell them about "Stagecoach Mary" and "Deadwood Dick." They go to the library looking for information on Deadwood Dick. They go to the library. We know because after we perform in the schools, the library near that school has to come up with their copies of *Negro Cowboy* in the little pocket book so the children can read about Deadwood Dick and the ninth and tenth cavalries and Stagecoach Mary. You see, that's how we do it.

WASSERMAN: There is one thing in what you said that concerns me a little bit. I don't think what you're doing takes away this kid's dream of Madison Avenue.

TAYLOR: Sometimes it does. Sometimes we do exactly that.

WASSERMAN: But it also allows him to move toward that dream as a complete human being, and to think he has possibilities and chances for it.

TAYLOR: I am disturbed because we got away from libraries. I'm not a librarian, but let's talk about libraries anyway. What I just told you is important for libraries. Now, I don't believe that any library complex should be exclusive of performing and/or display facilities. I believe that every library should have a photographic or art display area, that it should have a lecture hall that serves as a concert hall, that serves as a theater, so that then you can invite in the Alvin Ailey Dance Company to perform in that theater in your library complex. After that, John Martin's book on the dance should be one of the most checked-out items, or the autobiography of Kathryn Dunham, or the life of Eartha Kitt, or what have you; all of these books should become important, hard-to-get items the week after because of the stimulation of those performances. A library functioning properly today should be exploiting other manners of presentation to get people into books just as "Down in the Valley" creates a rush for *Negro Cowboy* and the desire to get information on Deadwood Dick and the ninth and tenth cavalries.

PARTICIPANT: But it's not just to get people into books. It's part of it.

TAYLOR: Well, books are always something greater than just books.

PARTICIPANT: This is more sophisticated. What you are talking about is the custodian of the collection. We were interested in that in the nineteenth century. What we are trying to do now is to teach, to expose the user to the vast knowledge, and teach the user how to encounter, how to correlate, how to relate different parts for his own need. This is much more obvious at the university library than at the public library or the community library, but this process has to start somewhere. It's not only to provide the book that the person is asking for; it is to expose the person to the situation in which he can start choosing on his own, starting with the book he asked for and finding out how to use that book. Knowledge is the relation. Knowledge is not a given book or a given item. It's the act, and that's what we are interested in. We are not concerned about circulating a book twenty-five times, because that's not an objective any more.

TAYLOR: Why shouldn't you be concerned? I am very much concerned about the circulation of *Negro Cowboy* or *The Autobiography of Malcolm X*. I am very much concerned about how much that book is read. It's not automatic. No one is asking for it. I'd love for him to have the automatic problem of the over-circulation of certain books. You don't have the problem, because you have not created any stimulus for the problem.

PARTICIPANT: No, but we want to stimulate the problem in different ways, not by exposing the user to one book that you think is a good one. We want to start with that book and let the user develop a way of getting out of the library what he needs,

TAYLOR: But each thing that happens in it creates and opens up a new area. If they see Alvin Ailey one week, they move to your books of dance. The next week they see an exhibition of Charles White, and they start going through your art book sources, and the week after that they hear a concert of Leontyne Price, and they start digging into sources that way. They learn the process of finding out how to supplement their life with what you have at a library and how to dig and to expand. That's all accomplished. You don't think one concert, or one photographic exhibit, or one art exhibit, or one anything, is going to be the end of the library's programming for a year. The idea is to have a continuing . . .

PARTICIPANT: That's exactly what I'm trying to say! We are accustomed to this concept of library measure, which is difficult to measure in terms of statistics. We counted circulation in the nineteenth century and we are doing it today, but we are doing it for different reasons. We have the highest statistics today, not because we just handed the books out but because we created the interest. We created it by an educational process not unlike the teacher in the classroom situation. Because of this, we consider ourselves a profession, and we want to separate. It is why we feel we have definite objectives which are unique to our own training.

REID: May I make one point that I think is pertinent to this part of the trade, and we just don't know it? I had fallen into the trap of thinking that circulation wasn't important at all. But it occurs to me that in a given neighborhood, a given community, there might be some key books, key points of information, key questions. If we are not providing some interaction between those certain key things and people, we're probably not doing much at all. Maybe there are five or six books in Harlem or in Fairmount Heights. They may be different books or some of them may overlap. If there is not a continual disappearance of that book off the shelf, maybe there is room for concern.

BUNDY: We studied circulation in Fairmount Heights and it did not reveal readership. The books disappeared. They were paperbacks and they disappeared.

PARTICIPANT: The whole concept of open stock destroys the validity of the statistics as the measure of the use of the library.

BUNDY: One of our students went to High John when he was in our program. Maybe because he was black he was more frank, but he asked me the question all the library students would like to ask: "What was I supposed to do? If I was supposed to answer their questions, I didn't know what their questions were. If I was supposed to sell the books, I never read the books. There I stood."

WELBOURNE: Well, let me ask both Annie Reid and Ed Taylor something, because they do come out of other disciplines. Even in your most idealized situation where a library is performing as you would like it to, would you exchange what you are doing now to be a librarian?

TAYLOR: Actually, the funny thing is that in the kind of library I envision, I would be very excited to participate. Why? Because if I were running a library (and we're planning a library like this), it would be part of a total cultural concept. When something happened, that happening would always be supplemented by what was available on the library shelves. It should be almost automatic that when someone goes to a lecture, or to a concert, or to a play, or to a dance, they know what is available to them to follow up. They should be able to glance at the bulletin board going by and see covers of the books that they know they are going to have to read after listening to that lecture.

WELBOURNE: But Ed, don't you think of libraries as something you would like to use? Don't you wish libraries were efficient so that you could use them properly by telling the people whom you perform before, "I know the library has it." The library doesn't really have to get involved if it just did its role of stock building. If you had an idea that the right collection was there, you could refer to it. You see, you're still being the creative person yourself.

TAYLOR: I'm not saying that the librarian has to put on the show.

WELBOURNE: You don't want the librarian to put on the show?

TAYLOR: By "put on the show," I mean librarians don't have to be competent dancers or what not; all they have to do is to be able to do more than stamp out books. They should be able to know that when the Alvin Ailey Dance Company comes in, maybe they will push five books that first time. When the Rod Rogers Dance Company comes in, they've got to push five more books. It's a tremendous job to know which books to put out, at what time, in conjunction with what goes on.

The whole problem is if a librarian doesn't know what's in the stacks, what's in the books, and how those books relate to the various events, and I know most librarians don't know that, they put out the most ridiculous things imaginable as suggestions. It's important to know which book to recommend first, because if you put the wrong five books out, there won't be any follow-up. If you put the right ones, there will be.

PARTICIPANT: Who are we to decide? I thought that maybe I could make the decision, but it's not always that way.

TAYLOR: When it comes to book programming, at the Harlem Cultural Council people ask me when I am putting on a show, what books I recommend. Many times I tell them, "Well, I'm sorry, I'm very busy now. I'll have to get back to you in an hour." Then I call up Jean Hudson of the Schonburg collection and I say, "Jean, look, this person called me about so-and-so. Now I only know such-and-such a book. Is it any good? Is the information correct? What would you suggest?" And Jean Hudson of the Schonburg collection says, "Well, so-and-so books are really good. Why don't you recommend those?" Then I call them back and say, "Read these!" But I had to go to someone with a broad base of knowledge who knew all the books, who knew what was good or bad.

PARTICIPANT: How could you accept her point of view?

TAYLOR: Her business is books and my business is not books. My business is general culture, so I went to an expert on books. Now if she led me wrong, next time I would have to go to someone else.

PARTICIPANT: How would you know she led you wrong unless you had a chance to read those books?

TAYLOR: Because people come back and give me answers. They say, "You recommended so-and-so book to me, and it was a dud. No one liked it."

REID: I was asked a question earlier, and I didn't have a chance to answer. Jim asked me if I would be a librarian and I want to answer that question. Yes! With just two provisions. One, that you give me a chance to find out a little bit more about learning first. That's the thing I want to do now. The second provision is that I would want to run it with private money, because I really want to run it the way I want to run it. Then I would do all sorts of things.

BUNDY: There's another role for librarians. Suppose I'm in a community and I conceive of my objective as expanding people's cultural appreciation, knowledge, et cetera; then when you perform, you're working for me, in a sense. You're one of my books. I may send people to see you. I may send them to a library. I'm sort of running the show.

WELBOURNE: Take that one step further, Mary Lee. Evelyn Parker, one of our participants in this institute, is an excellent dancer. She's creative. Why should she need to have an Alvin Ailey Company come in to stimulate people? Let's use people who have talents already, music and things. Let it be part of the librarian's requirements that he be part of his own resources, just as much as the books.

TAYLOR: This is one of the basic fallacies of community-type thinking. Most communities say, "We have a dancer. We have an artist. We have a singer. We want to use ours." And they're wrong. You know why they're wrong? There is no inherent competition between Alvin Ailey and Evelyn. They supplement each other. There is no conflict. The community people have been deprived of self-expression for so long that many of them get uptight when outside professionals are brought in. The trick is to use the outside professional as the stimulus for the same kind of activity within the community. When that's done, the dancer in the community will eventually say, "Well, next year, we've got to have Rod Rogers and Eleo Pomare and the Louis Johnson troupes." She will know that when they come in, she will be more respected because of her dance involvement than she ever was when she was just a dancer in the community all by herself, and no one realized what dance was all about.

SEGAL: I have a feeling we're copping out in a way. We start out looking at dissidence in the culture. Now, in that context, if you begin asking me questions about the librarian dissidents, I don't want to get involved with this stuff. I want to ask these people a question. It seems to me the dissidents are saying, "This society has got to change." What I want to know is, damn it, do you librarians want to change your libraries?

REID: And one reason I want to run my library privately is that I want to act as a dissident element.

SEGAL: You are saying, "I don't want these conditions, so I can change it." I know you and Mary Lee, Paul, are terribly concerned about this. But when we talk about books, and the use of books, and modifications of certain techniques, I'm lost. When I walk into libraries, they're still the same as when I was five. I discovered lovely people there who helped me to learn. Now they've died and I don't know who is there any more. But it seems to me that while the dissidents are screaming about the society, the library, like other professions, is not responding.

TAYLOR: Now, here's where we get caught up. You said our discussion disturbed you because it was a cop-out, when actually what I was discussing is a changed library. Yes, a changed library. That is, for me it's not a cop-out. It's very much to the point. I mentioned a library performing complex, because there are only a very few of them in existence. Very few librarians have ever thought about the interrelationships of general cultural programming to what's on their shelves.

Most libraries have been so esoteric about the whole business that they haven't convinced anyone that there was a relationship. What I am talking about now is what is actually happening within dissident elements in major cities and smaller cities across the country right now. Books and performers, lecturers and readings and what not are all violently interrelated. The reason the East Winds Cafe, and those other places, are stimulating reading is because there is no difference between the poet's performing his poetry and getting a copy, and going home with those poems. People don't feel this separation of performance and the document.

SEGAL: Let me go to what I am more concerned about with the library. It seems to me that there is a complex world where things happen which affect us. I want to know what's going on in this complex Washington world and New York State world and New York City world, in terms of legislation, proposed legislation, past legislation, and how it affects me. I don't see the library at this point helping me very much with this, in telling me, in informing me, in helping me to come to grips with that information. Now, I know in the ghetto this is one of the things that a lot of the civil rights groups have made it their business to do. I want to know why libraries aren't doing this more. You must plan to start doing something like this.

PARTICIPANT: Survival information.

SEGAL: Not just survival. To know what comes out, how the complexities of the culture can begin to be communicated to the people in the community.

WASSERMAN: I don't think these functions are opposed.

TAYLOR: That's what I was going to say. He poses it as a conflict, and there is no conflict.

WASSERMAN: I think libraries are closer to this, traditionally, but the practice of librarianship has never, never reached this ideal. You're in the mainstream of the American public library ideology. It's been one of the myths, the slogans of the culture, that that's what a library does. You ask a librarian.

TAYLOR: But they don't do it. It's like democracy in America. We all talk about it and there isn't any. What we're saying at this point is stop talking about the cultural interrelation and get involved in it. We have a project we call the North Manhattan Project emanating from here in Washington. It's being run in New York. The North Manhattan Project is based on this whole idea of performances and displays, exhibitions of various types of books in the library. It's a federal project. It's a public library project. And the thing is, it works. It works very, very well, but no one else is doing it.

BERRY: What do you mean by "very, very well," in the case of the North Manhattan Project? Is it in terms of this book-pushing concept?

PARTICIPANT: Have you really pushed a lot of books?

TAYLOR: Yes.

PARTICIPANT: How many?

REID: In what area?

TAYLOR: If you have cultural programming, the kinds of books that are going to come out are those kinds of books. Dr. Segal's program is a completely different one in the area of survival which should be running at the same time.

WASSERMAN: Let's put it a different way. I think your point is well taken. We're not doing what you outlined, although it's part of our folklore that we do do that. We do it with other interests in the culture, interestingly enough. We do it for the business interests. We match up with them. We don't do that very well either, but at least we have made that commitment. We put business collections in the downtown area. We buy the books and make these available. We interlock with business, but we don't with some other elements of the culture.

4

SHIFTING PHILOSOPHICAL
PERSPECTIVES IN
PUBLIC EDUCATION

TUESDAY AFTERNOON, AUGUST 12
LECTURER: WILLIAM M. BIRENBAUM
PANELISTS: PAUL WASSERMAN
ANNIE REID
MARY LEE BUNDY

BIRENBAUM: I approach my subject this afternoon with some trepidation, especially after sitting through the morning session.

I'm reminded of a story about a long-standing animosity, a deep-rooted hostility between distinguished American men of letters—Henry James and Samuel Clemens. Part of their careers overlapped when they both tried to make a living on the public lecture circuit. Of course, Henry James was very different from Samuel Clemens. He was very well-read, for one thing. He was a very proper man, one who dressed impeccably, who spoke with great aplomb. Sam Clemens had a lecture to give when he was on the European circuit. He had checked into a small pension in a city in the south of France. Right above where he was to sign in was written in beautiful, elaborate script: "Henry James and valet." Samuel Clemens immediately picked up the pen and signed: "Samuel Clemens and valise." The innkeeper looked at him and said, "I understand the valet, but what is a valise?" Clemens said, "Any fool knows that valise is the feminine of valet."

The moral of this story is that I approach this group without a valet, but with a battered valise, ready to make a rapid retreat. I know the one thing I should not do is say anything about your declared area of expertise, that is, your preferred knowledgeability about the ignorance in your field. Instead, I should confine my remarks to fields about which I can declare a superior position with regard to possessing ignorance. I will be inclined to do that, though there may be linkages between what I have to say and what bothers you, if anything really bothers you.

In the United States, in the educational field, there have been only three or four significant territories staked out. They are very significant. During the Constitutional Convention, when the subject of education arose, the entire debate consumed less than an hour. The question about who should control it, and how it should be rigged, was reduced to only one sentence in Madison's notes on the Constitutional Convention. The conclusion was that education should be locally controlled and that it was not an appropriate matter for elaboration in the Constitution, which itself was meant to be a detailing of relationships between national and local sovereignty. The assumption was, at that time, that lower education, which was essentially church based, was capable of being governed by a combination of laymen and experts, with the laymen in the ascendant role growing out of a particular, local, geographic definition of jurisdiction. Community control at the local level was almost assumed to be the appropriate way to rig it politically.

Thomas Jefferson, at a later time, added a second great idea to the American outlook upon this business. He related the education of large numbers of common people to the capacity of those people to govern themselves within a republican system. The format of the University of Virginia was based on the assumption that if the people were to govern themselves they had to be fairly well educated in order to pull it off. This was a unique idea, linking political power directly to the education of a broader mass.

The third significant contribution came from Horace Mann, with the idea of universal public education. In that idea, a linkage was formed between the achievement of education for all and the achievement of a certain economic equality throughout the American society. The Morrill Act, setting up the land-grant colleges, really extended this main conception of a relationship between economic survival and equality to the higher level of education in the country.

None of these ideas, of course, has worked out perfectly. The question of community control has become confounded by the urbanization of the country. The question of the capacity of the people to govern themselves politically has become confounded by a combination of the technology and the urbanization and, therefore, growing complexity, of the political problems. The question of education as a force for economic survival has become terribly complicated by the nature of the technology and what one has to know to survive economically, and by the sheer quantity of knowledge involved in economic survival.

As a matter of fact, I think it can be concluded that what has happened in the area of knowledge production in the span of American history has been to create a kind of equalization of ignorance on a grand scale. This has set up significant challenges to all three of these premises: first, that laymen can govern educational systems best; second, that education can equip people for political participation within the democratic ideal; and third, that education can really lead to economic survival while at the same time creating a capacity for political participation in this kind of a society. Now I suppose every society, every country, at every time in history feels that it has unique problems which are very acute, but my experience in my profession leads me to believe that America now faces a series of extraordinarily acute and unique problems.

As I listened to the discussion this morning, at moments I felt that librarians were defining themselves and their part of the institutional systems to encompass the whole of what universities traditionally were thought to do, or ought to do. I felt kind of sorry for librarians' taking on such a mission, because I feel that people like myself who are college presidents, or teachers of graduate students, confront problems that are so horrible and which we cannot solve that it would be extraordinary if you could. Even I am reluctant to take on the fatality of these problems. I really marvel at your boldness in wanting to.

There is a certain amount of self-flagellation involved in any new profession. There is a tendency, I think, on the part of professions that are unsure of themselves to outdo more established, prestigious professions in behavior that they think leads to prestige and status. It's like young institutions. I remember when I came to Wayne State University in Detroit. It had just become a state university, and its model was the University of Michigan. Here was this vibrant, young, brawling, half-baked institution in the middle of Detroit, attempting to imitate what was going on at Ann Arbor, which was a dying thing, an archaic model—doing it in the name of being respectable.

Librarians, who fought so hard to be members of the faculty and who have fought so hard to achieve a certain kind of professional status, like other parts of the academic civil service which are new —deans of students, adult educators, et cetera—sometimes tend to excesses in imitating what they consider to be legitimate models, which in turn, therefore, would legitimatize their own existence. On the other hand, they do hold a very central and key position in the academic bureaucracy, and tend, therefore, sometimes to take more credit than is their due.

My point is that librarians are in a terribly upset and sick situation mainly because the institutions of which they are a part are terribly upset and sick. They are terribly upset and sick because the society of which they are a part has its own peculiar upsetness and sickness at this time. Therefore, you should not be especially upset by the fact that you are upset. One aspect of your sickness should not be that you are upset because you are sick. Naturally you are sick. The most you can do, it seems to me, is come to grips, for your own purposes, in day-to-day operations, ·with the base causes of your illness, which is all that people in my position are trying to do.

In this kind of a society, it is almost a badge of honor to have been fired. That's not normal. It isn't only in our professional roles where this kind of a feeling overcomes us. Those of you who speak of your difficulties as professional librarians are people like myself who may discuss their difficulties as professional presidents of colleges. These days we have to examine also our personal lives, our other roles in the society, and the degrees to which there are relationships between our performances as fathers, as citizens at large, as laymen operating in several aspects of the society's operation, in addition to our professional role, in order to understand more completely and honestly our shortcomings in our professional roles.

I have my own explanation of the illness in terms of the particular institution of which we are a part in American society: namely, academic. I can explain this to you very briefly, which I will do, and then throw the floor open to discussion.

There are several paradoxes that are involved. I can almost put them on the board in short form. There is a paradox between thought and the institutionalization of thought in terms of educational systems on the one hand and action or behavior on the other. On the behavior-action side, two grand developments have occurred since this country started which are action systems. One is technology, and the other is the concept of democracy. Opposed to this, on the educational system side, are the lower school organizations that we have created and the higher ones that we have created which have so deeply ingrained a kind of resistance against anything that implies action or behavioral responsibility. The larger society is democratic in its thrust and utterly dependent upon the technology for its economic being.

If we go back to the origin of the American academic system, the European models, this development makes great sense. These models were addressed to the training of very restricted elites to run the society. When the University of Chicago, my alma mater, suspended the greatest number of students suspended by any university in the country last spring, it was perfectly natural for one of the senior professors in that system to say that if a university is thought about as being democratic in its organization, then it will cease to be a great center of scholarship and academic learning. That is perfectly natural, put in the terms of this model.

It is perfectly natural for people like Sidney Hook, under current stresses, to be parading around the country saying that the demands of the dissident students, white and black, bear upon this half of the picture and if they are acquiesced to, if we get involved in the action or the behavioral demands of the dissident students and super-impose them upon this conventional structure, the result will be the politicalization of this in a manner that will subvert any potentiality for continued scholarship as we have known it in the western university system.

These are the kinds of acute issues or paradoxes between thought and action, between the technology and the democratic impulses of the country that have been built into these organizational systems. These paradoxes can be refined somewhat and made more pointed. For example, under the technology part, one can point out the truth —that the way technology has developed leads toward greater and greater centralization of control, on the one hand, of varying systems; but on the other hand, the effect of the technology, if one can come to grips with the centralization of control of overall systems, is to enhance the opportunity for individual choice.

This is a terrible paradox which you can illustrate any number of ways. For example, in the publishing field, the technology has utterly encouraged the centralization of publication of newspapers in our great cities, but has at the same time decimated other aspects of the mass media by breaking down the magazine field into a large variety of outlets and enhancing the number of opportunities for what people have to pick, particularly from the growing underground class. Translating this into the technology of computer recall, on the one hand, the systems allow for greater centralization of what is to be recorded or programmed but, on the other hand, as a consequence of that, allow for greater opportunity and variety in what can be recalled. These kinds of tensions and dilemmas that are building to our present situation are very confounding and confusing as we attempt to restructure the institutional systems in which we find ourselves a part.

Unfortunately, I have found that the great issues of our time—race, democracy, greater egalitarianism, the impact of the technology—tend to take the form of very specific, bread-and-butter situations forcing people to choose between small aspects of self-interest and participation in the grand issues. For example, the primary issue among my library staff is the reduction of their present work week to thirty hours. They have achieved faculty status. Their pay, their tenuring opportunities, and all the rest are the same as everybody else's, but obviously they don't teach within the framework of nine- or twelve-hour teaching loads. Some adjustment must be made of their working hour situations. Some relationship must be made between their working hour situation and that of those who teach in classrooms in terms of nine- or twelve-hour loads per week. Their demand is for a reduction from the thirty-five-hour work week to a thirty-hour work week.

This demand arises within the context of a limited budget for two fiscal periods ahead. They are aware of this and they know that if a decision is made to reduce their working load from thirty-five to thirty hours, with an outer limit now set on the number of dollars available so that no new librarians can be added and no new personnel hired, that a certain service–delivery gap will be created by the reduction of teaching hours. They also know at the same time that I'm on a campus which is obligated, as a result of other policy decision making, to receive more blacks and Puerto Ricans next fall than any other unit of City University. They also know that this is a campus where not only can this new minority group population coming in basically not read and write well, but the preponderant white student population cannot read and write well.

So you say to them, "How do you feel about the big issues?" The response is, "Well, we're terribly concerned about the big issues. We're dedicated, loyal workers and terribly upset about the big issues, but we want the thirty-hour work week and we want it now!"

In those departments of my college that are still on twelve-hour teaching loads, there is a very arbitrary unionized demand to conform to nine hours within the next sixty days. If we go on nine hours within the next sixty days, there is only one way that can be achieved, given the budget. That is to increase class sizes that are now in the low forties up to the low or mid-fifties.

WASSERMAN: Aren't you making an assumption that this is irrevocable? That is, you are suggesting, in effect, if I understand the implications of what you are saying, that by making this choice, they are taking an arbitrary stand. Ergo, this posture is an evil stand because it then negates the capacity of the institution to behave effectively in terms of its ultimate objectives.

BIRENBAUM: No, I'm not quite saying that. What I meant to say was that the attitudes on the part of those who frame these options is, "That's somebody else's problem." The attitude of the one in charge has to be that there is something wrong with the institutional rigging that frames the options in quite this manner. That is something that it does not help to talk about in the abstract, because the decision making has to be real, concrete, and generally immediate. Therefore, the options, the choices that have to be made right now, are not the kinds of choices that you can discuss in a chapter of a book abstractly. They are the kinds of choices whole systems have to make now.

I can give you another example of this on a somewhat grander, but equally immediate and even more far-reaching scale. Disruptions occurred recently at City College. The black students at City and the people of Harlem had always said that the thing that was wrong with City College, situated on the periphery of Harlem where it has been for almost a century, was that City College kept the blacks out. The academic year 1967/68 ended with a student body that was over 80 percent Jewish, that was less than 5 percent black and Puerto Rican, and with a faculty that corresponded to these ethnic descriptions. City College has a wall around it. On the south campus the wall has a gate. The ironic thing that happened in the City College disruption was that the black students got up early and captured the gate before the regular establishment arrived to go to work, and locked them out. That was the ironic thing.

Well, one of the demands that came out of that situation from the black students amounted to what has been characterized as a "quota system." The leaders of the Board of Higher Education of the City of New York, the leaders of the AAUP in New York, the leaders of the collegium, the leaders of the teaching unions of New York, are against quotas. The reasons they are against quotas in American society is that they are for integration. Being for integration is one thing in the abstract. To write a chapter in a book about being for integration is one thing. To act as if you were acting in an integrated society, defending the way it is, is another.

In the City College case, the power elements of the situation acted as if City College had been integrated as a part of an integrated university, City University, as part of an integrated city, New York, as a part of an integrated country, the United States. Throughout, the ideals and operating principles upon which power was transacted were on the basis of a chapter in the book, the abstraction rather than the reality which was City College and the way it actually was.

As a result of this sort of thing, naturally, those who possess the power reached an antiquota conclusion. The conclusion was that quotas were unacceptable because they are un-American. They will subvert an integrated society, which we have; therefore, we will go into an open admissions basis which is more pro-American. Everybody has equal access! Everybody can get in! Equal opportunity is what open admissions means. The only trouble with that conclusion is that it creates a new $50-million-per-annum operating gap in the budget.

This raises the political question of how you get an extra $50 million. There is only one way it can be gotten in the State of New York at this time, and that is to charge tuition in a free-tuition university. It turns out, because of the politics of the situation and the ideological rigidities of the situation, that the very constricting power constituency that argues against quotas because it is for integration, from the same liberal-based ideology must argue for free tuition. This means that the economic muscle which might give meaning to an open admissions policy as a counterpoint to a quota system, precludes that the economic muscle is not there. This is where the thing now is hung up, which means that there will be greater disruption. It's inevitable that in this situation there will be greater disruption.

I think these are the kinds of hangups that we've gotten ourselves into throughout the university system, and it would be extraordinary if the library part of it did not come to reflect in an extraordinarily intense way many of these hangups. What I am saying is that the commitments of the academic system, given our inheritance, are basically conservative. They look mainly toward the past and the conservation of it. They are essentially repetitive rather than creative in nature. They are essentially elitist rather than popularist in character. They are naturals for having walls with gates in them built around them. It takes a layman like a stupid newspaper reporter on *The New York Times* to cook up an adjective like "prison" to put before the description of City College's walls as he wrote his story about the locking of the gate, the capture and locking of the gate. The gate was captured by the black students in the prisonlike wall of City College.

A case can be made that academic libraries, particularly, have been sort of prisons for books. Certainly this would account in a ready fashion for the security emphasis of the main floors, architecturally, in such things. Success in the measurement of the flow of product in such institutions has been a demonstration of how many things did not go out illegally, legality being defined by the securitylike atmosphere built into the main floor of the building. You are confronted with new clienteles who are challenging your definition of legality. This is a real problem. It's like the problem you have with the challenge to the conventional legal meetings of due process.

The Grayson Kirks, the Abrams at Brandeis, the Hayakawas, and the others are shouting about the maintenance and preservation of due process in higher education and the abuse of due process by the students. Due process means the showing up of faculty and protection of faculty democracy, the preservation of academic freedom. Faculty democracy, in my university with 11,000 full-time faculty members, means that a little more than one-third possess the vote. Those who have tenure at City University possess the vote, at least until September 1 of this year, when all that will be changed.

Generally in American higher education, those in the upper ranks with tenure possess the vote on personnel, on budget, on curriculum. That's faculty democracy. On my own campus, the two-thirds who teach full time without tenure have no vote, and I have to confront them at a time when my students are rushing in saying, "Give us the vote on the curriculum committee, on the personnel committee, on the budget committee!" How can you give students a vote on these committees when two-thirds of those who teach for you don't have the vote? Those who have the vote really determine the meaning of academic freedom as that term has traditionally been applied to faculty on our campuses. Some due process!

Everybody is screaming about black studies. You look at the universities as to who is making the decisions about the new black curriculum, particularly in the social sciences, particularly in history and political science. What percent of the voting faculties are nonwhite? Well, at City University with its 11,000 full-time faculty members, as an example, less than 1 percent of those enfranchised to vote on the subject matter areas are nonwhite. From the black student's point of view, that's some due process!

It was like the decentralization issue in the New York school system when Albert Shanker and the union were yelling, "Due process!" while Rhody McCoy and the Ocean Hill–Brownsville people were yelling, "Due process!" The union people meant that if there is a basketball game in progress in keeping with AAU rules of basketball and there is a referee on the floor administering those rules, that referee ought to be respected in his administration of the rules. As I understand it, it turned out what the Ocean Hill–Brownsville people finally were saying was that the AAU rules are no longer fair. It's the rules of the game that are under investigation and reconsideration here.

You have your classification systems in the libraries. They are, in a sense, the epitome of the classification systems used in the universities as a whole. Knowledge is in such turmoil, the reconsideration of these issues of due process and integration and segregation are so deep, that university classification systems are being challenged, and fundamentally. If they are being challenged, naturally the ones that you use are going to be in deep trouble. Well, I think there is this kind of joint problem that we endure together that is the base of the thing.

In conclusion, I would say this: what I got out of the morning discussion was not so much a confusion or disagreement about how you do things, but a considerable amount of no understanding about what it is you really want to do. The intensity of your discussion seemed to reveal that you people were upset about that. Well, on the one hand, you should be. On the other hand, you should put it in perspective. The university system of which you are a part doesn't know what to do.

WASSERMAN: But in part, the function of knowing what to do is a function of the capacity of those who perform within it to figure it out for themselves. To the extent that one group within the university can conceive of its own aspirations, and its own potential, and its own contribution, within the framework and structure of higher education, this helps that ship adrift find its way to the harbor. So we can't abdicate our responsibility and say, "It's your problem." It's our problem, too. And it's our problem to the extent that we focus and address our attention to our piece of the action.

BIRENBAUM: I agree, except that this means, to me, that you should not overemphasize your own hangups, your own built-in hangups: the sex imbalance in the profession, for one thing, the relative newness of faculty status in the profession, and one other complication which is sort of unique to you, which is that you, more than almost any other part of the whole, are a front line for an enactment of the technology issue. You can be a department of history and get along just fine these days without really coming to grips with that. You won't be a very good department of history but you can get along that way. I don't think you can be a library and get along that way, now.

WASSERMAN: Well, the technology is one of the confusions on the part of people like you who see our solution in technological terms when it is not a technical problem. It's a problem of intelligence. It's a problem of clientele response. You use technology if it's relevant, but it's not a matter of technology and plugging it in, because technology has no answers for us. Technology serves us when we exploit it effectively.

I think there are a lot of people who play administrative roles in academia who have sort of a mystical notion that if only those people could plug it into the machines our problems would be resolved. We would save all those books. You would save nothing! The machines don't do anything for us that we can't program. Before we figure out what the program is, we need to know what we're there for and calculate a strategy for response to clienteles. I think there is a lot of confusion in academia about the technology and how important it is for librarianship. It may be important but it is not a high priority as a first order of business. I think there is gross confusion about this.

BIRENBAUM: Certainly, the basic question is what do you want to do. I don't think, in your business, given the way it is and what you have to deal with, that you can ignore the technology to a lesser extent than most parts of academia.

WASSERMAN: No, but don't you see, the technology becomes a snare and a delusion, just as that's the first priority you suggested to us. When you think about a library, you say, "Look, you can't dismiss this." I'm telling you, if we address ourselves to that question, we're confusing our perspectives as to priority. That's an implement.

BIRENBAUM: On this point, Mr. Wasserman, we may disagree. There is a key relationship between the question "What do you really want to do?" and the technology. If you fail to address yourself effectively to the question "What do you really want to do?" in the case of what you people have to do, the technology will confront you anyway. Under those circumstances, you have a peculiar problem.

WASSERMAN: Isn't that the history of some experiments that people have taken the technology and ignored the kinds of questions you're asking?

BIRENBAUM: I'm not saying the technology is going to solve your problem.

WASSERMAN: I think you are being accurate. For example, the Georgia Tech school, which is strictly technologically oriented, doesn't ask these questions. When you say intelligence and consumer, I think, "What does he mean?" Can you spell it out more than those two phrases?

BIRENBAUM: Ed Taylor talked about it this morning. He suggested that he would like some people to know what it's all about, so that if a library is to do something, it has to have someone who is knowledgeable. I don't think we can exactly say this is relevant for an academic, as much as having some substantive understanding of what it is a clientele uses or needs so as to marshal resources wherever they come from for that purpose.

WASSERMAN: That's intelligence brought to bear on library functions.

BIRENBAUM: There are two ways of looking at what you are saying. One is the reason the substantive knowledge and intelligence aren't there is that the people who come into the field just don't have it.

On the other side of it is that the training institutions have not confronted themselves with the relevant substantive knowledge and their growth of intelligence.

WASSERMAN: There are other reasons. There is the reason that librarianship hasn't put a premium on subject knowledge, and librarians have not seen this as a value for themselves. There is the reason that administrators have not wanted to pay for the preparation of substantive people to play library roles. They wanted card filers, and they've got them.

These are choices we must make. We need our own ethos. No one else can give them to us. I guess my argument is that I think we need to overextend librarianship. We've underextended librarianship. We haven't reached far enough. We've been too complacent about our contribution in terms of what it has been. It's not good enough. Just as the university's contribution to the culture has not been enough, our contribution in our professional product has not been enough. We must calculate a strategy for making it otherwise. We don't do it when we ask for fewer hours, and we don't do it when we ask for faculty status. We do it when we calculate our perspectives.

BIRENBAUM: On the other hand, I think you have to be realistic. You can't ask students going into this field to be what senior, highly revered, extraordinarily well-paid faculty members are not. You cannot ask future librarians to be whole men and whole women in academic situations where hardly anybody in the faculty is, where if you add a whole faculty up, you're lucky if you have a whole man or a whole woman. You just can't do that. That's unrealistic. You get into the kind of hangups here that you tend to get into when you talk about teacher training and what the new teacher should embody.

WASSERMAN: I think you're right. I think it is a matter of degree. You see, we're at one end of the continuum where the stereotype of librarianship, as perceived by those who view it, is of someone who knows very, very little about many, many things. Between that and your ideal academic is a wide continuum. In a number of discrete areas, perhaps, we need more intense knowledgeability of some of that continuum.

BUNDY: May I say it another way? As a teacher and a librarian, I got out of teaching once and I'm thinking of doing it again because I don't think the classroom is the place to be. I don't see why we can't have more people wanting out of the classroom and into what were libraries and can become something else.

BIRENBAUM: But why do people think the classroom is not a place to be? I mean, what about the classroom?

REID: May I address the whole school? Could we get off higher education and into the schools? Probably the worst thing that has happened to people who thought that schools were going well was to have so clearly documented, recently, that schools made people different. The Coleman report, of all the things that schools do wrong and of all the regressions that had to regress over again, came out with the finding that there wasn't one single school variable that accounted for any kind of educational area.

That's really a rather solid condemnation of schools. The variable, the one thing that seemed to vary as educational achievements vary, even using traditional educational achievement measures, was the family of the students. This means that the school sort of provides a place for persons to go from nine to three to get in out of the rain. It provides routines and exercises. Persons who are not never get to be.

PARTICIPANT: I think the most interesting thing that has come out this morning is that the people who are not librarians comment on what librarians are and comment about what their idea of a librarian is. We have argued with that concept and said, "That is not what we are" or "That is not what we want to be," but the people who have said what we are don't listen. It is an interesting paradox that the nonlibrarians who have commented have all stated their conceptions of a librarian or a library, and we have immediately disagreed, saying, "But that's not what we are at all" or "That's not what we can be." It seems to me there is a big gap here between listening and hearing.

REID: Persons who are not in the library business can only reach conclusions based on the manifest behavior that they observe.

PARTICIPANT: I'm not too sure that isn't what it is.

REID: Why? That is what it is.

WASSERMAN: The question, ultimately, that we're considering together is what can it be? What can we make it? How can we adapt it otherwise? We know what it is! We know it's not worth a damn most of the time! All we have to do is walk into a library and ask for something, or try to get someone to listen to us while we ask for something, or be evaded or avoided, ignored by people whom we encounter in the university in a library. We know this is so, but if we know it is so, and we're comfortable with it, we're talking about nothing. If we're concerned with the field, we're concerned with adapting it to make it otherwise, to make for a different perception on the part of those who do encounter it.

PARTICIPANT: What strikes me is the fact that people can comment on what a library should be and we say, "We already do that." Second, if we're so hung up on how to adapt the thing to a completely foreign field, we're ignoring the things that are built into the library profession that people expect of us. We're saying, "We don't want to do that. That's not our thing."

BUNDY: Well, of course, you're right, but on the other hand, if Ed gives us a simple way out, I don't think we can afford to take it.

WASSERMAN: I think this participant is saying something. I hear her saying, "You talked yesterday about the importance of listening to the clientele and helping them to undertand." She is saying, "You've got examples here of where some of your clientele have said some things about the library, and you're not listening." You may hear, you may see, but I think your response, Mary Lee, is not to let us feel satisfied that you heard it.

BUNDY: No, no! I think what she's saying and what you're saying is just because you tell me your view of the library, I don't have to buy your view of the library.

WASSERMAN: You have to help me get a view of the library as you see it.

BIRENBAUM: It seems to me there is an impossible situation brewing here. The guys who are training people, like some of these, have to face facts at some point along with the rest of us. There was a presumption in the past that the academic place was a community, that the parts of it that claimed varying expertise collaborated in the input to what you are. You don't know, you can't expect to know, it cannot be expected that you know the latest developments in every discipline and, therefore, the latest composite of purchases for the stacks that you want to undertake. Unfortunately, the academic community is no longer a community. We know that. Faculties within departments don't communicate with each other, let alone across the departmental lines. The specialties have proceeded to a point where, within a given department, there are breakdowns of communication about what is relevant and what is not. On the other hand, my publisher tells me that last year there were in excess of 26,000 new titles published in the United States alone commercially—in the United States alone, and we're second to the United Kingdom in the number of new titles that come out in English. This is extraordinary. How could you possibly know?

BUNDY: We now have studies which show some things you don't know about yourself and your reading interests and what you're likely to ask for. We're getting much better predictability.

REID: What difference does it make? To get away from one aspect of your technology part, what difference does it make that schools exist or universities exist? Do they exist for only negative purposes? In other words, at the lower level, schools do not exist for any special purpose. It would seem that upper middle-class kids teach themselves. Just by reading about bringing people together, they learn in spite of teachers. Teachers need not even be there. The studies really show that it doesn't make an awful lot of difference what happens. These kids get to be what they get to be. They're already programmed and they're programmed from home through the culture. All right, now, what difference does it make when they get to the university? Does it only have a negative influence?

BIRENBAUM: Well, of course, I have a bias about this. Getting into the university now has a negative influence, primarily. That's part of the tragedy, but it only continues the negative influence of lower school systems.

REID: Right! And libraries are really part of that culture.

BIRENBAUM: Of course.

REID: This gets to the point of what we ought to do, what we want to do.

BIRENBAUM: Which underscores the significance of what I understood Ed Taylor to be saying this morning. Ed was trying to say that there were other centers of input now, particularly on the urban scene, that are perhaps more significant than the traditional centers of input upon which academic libraries have relied. This has implications all along the line, from the acquisition procedure and program to the choice among the technological options confronting you, to the architecture, to the way you memorialize it, build it, and program the people through it. If you choose a different input base, if you refer to a different configuration of talents regarding that base, you have a different set of decisions about the technology, about how you build it, about where you put it, about the programming of it. That's what I understood Ed to be saying, essentially, using the arts as an example, but one could use other bases.

REID: Ed was saying that everybody thought his ideas were old hat. But the point is that if Ed went to the trouble of telling you the great thing he had discovered, he had not seen it as old hat. Some of the things that we really feel are the essence of this profession really have a legitimate base in reality. There are effective things to do and people think they are going on, but if people keep thinking of them as new ideas, they are not going on.

BIRENBAUM: But it is not that complicated. In a great city like New York, on Forty-second Street and Fifth Avenue, there is a library which is perhaps superior to any other collection of that kind in the city of New York, including Columbia's and certainly New York University's. On the other hand, if you look at New York University, Columbia, and Long Island University, and all the rest, plus the technical libraries available in New York, for example, the best libraries available to those engaged in pure research in the field of economics are not academically institutionalized in New York City. They are elsewhere in New York City, other than on academic bases. Now, what I understood Ed to be saying in part, and Ed, you have to get in here at some point if we're misinterpreting you, was that it is now possible to look at New York City as a whole resource area.

The thing that has hung up the university in its relationship with Forty-second Street and Fifth Avenue is purely institutional systems, budgeting techniques, managing techniques. For graduate students in any of the great universities in New York to have the kind of access to the material they really need, rigid institutional, bureaucratic, managerial systems that have been more than five decades in the manufacture stand in the way. It's a big thing when Columbia can make a deal with Forty-second Street and Fifth Avenue, for a certain number of its graduate students to have access to a certain thing in that building. It's a big deal! Well, now, what I'm saying is that technology is such, the impulse of the people is such, the issues are such, that New York as a talent resource reservoir must begin to be looked at as a whole. New systems employing the best of technology, new managerial approaches, have to be invented to plumb out of the whole of this territory the best resources, whatever the problem is.

The same thing has happened with universities. Here comes a stupid, ignorant freshman imbued with all the imagery of American higher education. He is going to college to learn. He gets there, and immediately he is segregated, not once, but five or six times. He is compartmentalized, departmentalized in five or six basic ways from the first day of freshman classes on. Freshmen are separated from sophomores. Undergraduates are separated from graduates. Whites are separated from blacks. Liberal arts are separated from vocational or applied science curricula. Commuting students are separated from residential students. By the time they get through chopping up that freshman into little pieces through the managerial technological systems we've adopted, he has no more access to Forty-second Street and Fifth Avenue than he has to the moon.

REID: The first thing that happens to him is not all of that, but the fact that he is alienated, and made aware of the fact that he is an alien.

BIRENBAUM: The young people are alienated. All this does is give them new reasons.

REID: The minute he rubs up against that managerial system, as an individual he's through!

BIRENBAUM: That's right! That's why, in the black communities of a city like New York, experience seems to indicate that the majority of the students who have dropped out of the secondary schools are better off than those who stayed in them, at least within the last half-decade. This is not a platitude. There is at least enough evidence to support this proposition to make it debatable, legitimately.

When I see what we do with some of the people we take into our colleges in the city now, I sometimes wonder if they should be put there, given the way the colleges are. If you really care about this and you're in a position like I'm in, you are inclined to find yourself being really honest only as a leader of the disruptions. Indeed, only if you lead the disruptions are you at all honest in the possession of whatever power you come to possess in a position like I have—only if you're a leader, only if you can defend your leadership as a disrupter. Now, this is a very peculiar situation to be in if you're part of an establishment. It is a very strange, perverse situation.

PARTICIPANT: Isn't it true that when you get to the level where you might be disruptive, like the Council of College Presidents and that kind of thing, you get the same kind of sorting out very quickly. The senior colleges, the community colleges, all of that . . .

BIRENBAUM: That's true, except that people like Ed know, and others in the room also know, who are on the front lines, that the ultimate power centers in these systems are now in a state of chaos and confusion. They are so off-balance that people like Ed and me can get by with an awful lot these days.

REID: Capitalize on the cool-it period, as long as someone else is escalating.

BIRENBAUM: As long as we can keep it disruptive! Now, you people are not noted for your disruptive qualities, and this is a problem. It's both a curiosity and a problem. You're not noted for your disruptiveness, even . . .

BUNDY: Well, then stop keeping us that way! Let me tell you what I started to say earlier. You still want a supply depot, and that's passive. It will never disrupt anything. It will give you what you want. Eventually it will become efficient in doing it. But let this institution take on some point and purpose by finding a client group, and it will defy you and any other institution that wants to stop that particular client from learning something, because he goes to, or lives in, or was born at a particular place. Let us break the boundaries in our way with our client groups. Let us not be servants of your systems again.

BIRENBAUM: O.K. I'm with you. Why not?

BUNDY: This is a problem in all New York State planning. It's a depot service. When you talk to the users at the other end, the user wasn't involved in planning and acquiring the TWX at Albany. They don't know their clients. They don't know how many engineers there are. They don't know how many scientists there are. They don't know their clients. Only in the special library, can they say that a certain ten people, at least, have a specific interest. They can work out systems for those clients.

BIRENBAUM: O.K., but I come back to the basic question. What do you really want to do? I've got the newest campus in the system. Mine is two years old and it's brand new. It was built before I got there. It's the most audio-visual, communications oriented thing. I've got TV in every room. I can plug something in at my desk and talk to all 10,000 students at once. But the point is that there is nothing to put on it. The problem of putting together with a team, a talent pool, something creative that you might have some vague idea you might want to put on it immediately puts you in mortal combat with the ongoing system, because the going system segments everything in such a way that you cannot.

I've reached a basic decision as a college president. I have this whole thing. Once you get a part of it, you have all this drive to get more. You get one system. Somebody says, "For another $100,000 you can make it ten times better." There's this constant drive to perfect the system. I have made the decision that (a) I need a counter-college within the college, and (b) to have access to a technology communications system is to have access to the most potent weaponry system in our society now. Therefore, you build the counter-college on the basis of that technology. What I am doing now is identifying some subversives outside of the course, outside of the credit structure, giving them access to the film-producing equipment, the TVs, the computers, and all that stuff and saying, "Go ahead!"

BUNDY: Did you give this job to the librarians? Are they involved, or did you just leave . . .

BIRENBAUM: There are a few who are involved, but as it turned out, the library was not much different from any other department. That is to say, you find a few oddballs among the librarians, like you do among mathematicians. Finally, I suspect it has nothing to do with their being mathematicians or librarians. If they are oddballs and specially trained through the Ph.D. level in math, their knowledge in math has a bearing on it, but that isn't why they are oddballs.

BUNDY: You say we aren't disruptive. You know it's all very nice to have these books, but some children can't read. What if we said, "O.K., the school has failed. Screw you! We'll teach these kids to read." Now we're being disruptive to the local school system. Some public libraries are doing this. Now, do you see the need for an institution that could be flexible right now, relate itself to learning, but not defining terms and not worrying too much about it, acting maybe more on hunch and instinct, filling gaps, stepping in?

BIRENBAUM: But let me tell you something about this emphasis on reading. I don't see that as the basic problem. Reading is, itself, a technology. The capacity to read involves technology. It's the motivation to learn that is critical. Some people can be motivated best through other media, initially, like film, like music, like dance, like numbers.

You know, a most amazing thing happened, that I really shouldn't say in public. The governing mechanism of City University that deals with the board is the group of sixteen presidents who meet regularly for a full day every few weeks under the chairmanship of the chancellor. They sit around and they make policy. Then that goes to the board, and generally, the board rubber-stamps it. There are some students who do very poorly in the first two years of high school who suddenly during the last two years of high school become very smart. They receive an earned high school average that is less than the official threshold required to get into City College this year, which is 86. If you don't have an 86 earned high school average, you can't get into this college. Well, these guys, because they're bad the first two years and good the last two, end up with an overall average less than 86. My faculty thinks we should interview some of these students and admit them. We made another discovery that is absolutely sensational. We learned that there were high school students who got very poor grades in social sciences and very high grades in math and science. When the grades were averaged, it didn't come out to 86. Then there was a third discovery. There were some kids who graduated from high school with earned high school averages of 72 who then got drafted and went to Vietnam and fought a war for two to four years. When they returned at the ripe old age of twenty-two or twenty-four, they showed a learning capacity that is sensational. Something happened to them in Vietnam, or Fort Dix, or Fort Benning that changed their learning capacity. But they don't have an 86 earned high school average. My group feels they ought to be in.

Well, in City University, there is a pecking order. Brooklyn College has been on top the last few years. It takes almost an 88 earned high school average to get into Brooklyn College. This is a function, in part, of the number of seats available versus the number of applicants. City College, traditionally, was number one. It has dropped to number three in recent years, with Hunter College on Park Avenue occupying number two spot. There is a real competition among the sixteen for who is number one, who is number two, who is number three. We are supposed to accept 900 new freshmen next fall through central admissions on an 86 earned high school average base. As a result of my faculty's amazing discoveries about the varying learning rates of students, they are asking permission to take 250 students whom they will admit on the basis of interview, leaving a balance of 650 who will be admitted on an 86 earned high school average. Well, the other college presidents went up in smoke. If you subtract 250 from 900, what will that do to this figure regarding the remaining 650? It will push it up. We will suddenly move from number three or number four position to number two or number one position in the pecking order. They voted not to permit this.

Now, my point is this: we are hung up. We have gotten hung up within the terrains of these systems, some of which are technologically imposed, some of which are the result of tradition within our profession and our institution. If there is anything which is irrelevant today to American higher education, it's German university traditions, or English, or French, or Italian. If there is anybody in worse trouble than we, it's they, with their great traditions.

If we could take a fresh look at the realities of what we confront as we feel them.

BUNDY: I feel black right now. You began by saying, "Don't aspire to do too much like other overaspiring people. Be realistic. Face all these limitations." You've just convinced me the school system is so bad we couldn't do worse. I'm prepared to take it up. Now, you kick me back.

BIRENBAUM: If you really meant that, the first thing you would do, it seems to me, is stop thinking about yourselves as librarians. Your educational programs prepare you to do this thing in our society. You own conception of yourselves after you become institutionalized reinforces it. You might stop thinking in terms of security, and bureaucratic and managerial systems that have evolved to this point, and instead begin to think about substantive problems of the technology, the bureaucracy, and the learning situation.

REID: The order is bad. The order is terrible. First, we will start thinking about the social conditions of man and the actualization processes of man.

BIRENBAUM: I'll buy that!

REID: But you have to say that. You really have to say that. You have to keep telling us.

BUNDY: The minute we get society, we get organizations; then we get institutions.

REID: You have to start thinking about the nature of man.

BIRENBAUM: You have to start thinking about what you were talking about before—learning.

REID: All right. That's in a context. You just can't start thinking about technology first.

BIRENBAUM: I would just settle for a fresh look at the myths, like the one about the library being the center of the campus, the heart of the campus. I don't know of any library that really is the heart of the campus.

BUNDY: I can conceive of an intelligence center with a lot of technology and a lot of people who understand people who would be mostly not in the center but out with people, coming back in for resources and supplies. This could replace your university. This may be the university of the future. I don't think we're in competition. Certain kinds of people will create it.

REID: This group ought to have a great sense of freedom by now, freedom from leadership.

BUNDY: They can't get a word in edgewise to have their freedom.

REID: Freedom from leadership that can't be constrained by any thoughts.

PARTICIPANT: I think the crux of the issue is that suddenly we're starting to realize that education is really done on an individual basis. One of the greatest trends in current education is individualized instruction or individualized teaching techniques. This is going to create a demand for some sort of resolution between the educational establishment and the library establishment. Suddenly the teachers will recognize that they can't give instruction to 500 students at one sitting, that they're going to have to send these students off somewhere to do the learning themselves. This is where libraries come in. I don't think we're going to have competing school programs.

BIRENBAUM: Do you remember the study out of Harvard that looked at all this stuff? I forget who did it, but what they came up with was that new ideas come in and then get used in traditional ways, or they don't get used at all. There is no evidence yet that any of the individualized learning innovations have really done a thing. It's another promise.

BUNDY: You know, I just had another thought. We're going to think of ourselves as aspiring people, we librarians. You're way ahead of us. You're talking big words. Let us just try something for a while.

BIRENBAUM: Yes, try something. Even a declaration and a taking of position upon issues other than the issues you normally take positions on would be extremely helpful at the present juncture. For example, there are faculty leaders in the social sciences, as well as in the arts and other fields, who are now parading around the universities taking credit for what they are doing in the field of black studies. The truth of the matter is that there are very few academic libraries in the United States that have been properly tooled up with materials that are supporting even the half-baked programs that they are coming forward with in these subject areas.

I would welcome, indeed, I have pleaded with my chief librarian, my director of libraries, to come out with an independent proclamation of his own about the fraudulence of the tuning up of the library in these fields as compared with the declarations of the faculty element of the institution about what they intend to do curricularly in these fields. Now, in my university as a whole, if the librarians in all sixteen units would stand up and say that City University's pretentions in this field are absurd, given what they're doing in the library to back it up, it would be very helpful.

BUNDY: Are you prepared to have most of the universities in this country lose their accreditation because we stand up and say we haven't got the collections to back up the programs?

BIRENBAUM: What makes you think the accrediting societies are impregnable these days? The accrediting societies are indeed troubled, too. They are a part of all this. I'll give you another example.

There is a firm that came to me in New York and showed me an extraordinary thing. They would come into my library, take a wall, and put a bunch of slots in this wall, about so big. Over each slot they would put a label. For example, on one wall, they would have Shakespeare and then there would be three slots. One would be labeled *Macbeth,* one would be *Hamlet,* and one would be *Midsummer Night's Dream.* This company was prepared to put on a central recording device the best Shakespearian actors for a particular play. The library issues to the student a blank cassette of the appropriate tape blank. When he comes into the library, he drops his cassette in the slot, comes back after two or three hours or however long it takes to record it, and he receives a recording of the best of the contemporary, English-speaking world's dramatists recording that play on the cassette.

This company has other crazy ideas—like they take the book *African Genesis* and find somebody who thinks the author's anthropological ideas are crazy. Then they record them both in a debate on the ideas of the book. The student comes in. He drops the thing in the slot.

He comes back, takes it home, and listens to it. They could do this for any number of fields.

BUNDY: I think that's a good idea. Our accreditation standards for community colleges require 30,000 volumes for the first so many students. Recently I visited one. They had achieved the standards of building, space, number of volumes, everything. No one was using that library and the underground student paper so informed us in great detail. The students were prepared to lose their accreditation.

BIRENBAUM: In New York State, it's 50,000. In New York State, it is written into the law that no college can even petition for Board of Regents recognition unless it can show that number of books. We asked the commissioner of education, at that time, Jim Allen, which 50,000 volumes? He said, "According to the law, it can be 50,000 copies of Book *A*."

BUNDY: But the point is, that college president had built a four-story building, and when the committee told him he needed a lot more things, I think the guy was ready to shoot himself. He could understand the building. He could put volumes in the library, librarians with library degrees, and he could build his building, but to fathom the purpose of the library in his institution was beyond him and beyond his librarians.

REID: The first thing we ought to do is expose the accreditation standards. We need to become human beings with clear outlines so that people know what we stand for.

BIRENBAUM: The librarian was interested, but the faculty committee that backstops all of this kind of major decision making was extremely wary of it, for the obvious reasons. This would really torpedo a good part of the rationale behind the students' getting their three credit hours per fifteen weeks. That's a real challenge.

TAYLOR: They should come to my lecture course at New York University, because that's exactly what I would like to do. I teach that if you can get a film to do it, or a tape to do it, or anything else . . .

BUNDY: I know a librarian who did it that way. She said, "Look, the best faculty and the best minds in the country certainly aren't here, but we've got them, or we've got access to them. Don't limit yourself to a third-rate education because you're here." And it's true. The faculty didn't particularly like it. Are you saying there is a natural opposition in the faculty, if we begin to make some of these moves, or will it be with the administration?

BIRENBAUM: What I'm saying is, don't put that in place of a faculty. Use this idea in order to free faculty to really educate.

BUNDY: I don't care whether they do it or not.

BIRENBAUM: Well, I care. As a president of a college, after I get through the budget battle out of which the library department gets its share, whatever it is, I generally can little understand the qualitative implications of the share allocator. Second, most faculty people with whom you deal are not encouraged by the present rigging to take an overall view of the consequences of their input. Third, the student clients, who are the main consumers, are hardly consulted at all. They go to the library like they go to a corner drugstore with a doctor's prescription, and you know to carry a prescription from a doctor's office to the pharmacist is not a creative act.

Then there's the community and the growing relationship in education at all levels, including the collegiate, between the cultural environment of the community and the learning enterprise, whether we're talking about Columbia or my two-year community college. Put into this their concern about it, their utilization capacity of it in relationship to their own youth. The youth of that community or their own is practically nil. Now, it seems to me, out of this situation a whole complex of issues emerges about which someone ought to take a stand. The president won't, because he's got too many problems and he doesn't want more issues. The faculty won't, because they're interested only in self-interest, their narrow, non-overall point of view. The students won't, because they're processed, carrying it from the doctor's office to the corner drugstore; that's their mission in life. The community won't, because they're not invited. I just feel that you're passing up good opportunities to be constructively disruptive at a time when, if we need anything, it's disruption.

BUNDY: You've done more than the militants did to make me feel good and disruptive.

REID: But you can't be disruptive! A system can't be disruptive! Organizations aren't disruptive. Individual people do things that are disruptive. One thing that has made students so terribly impatient with the world of academia is that they can't find anybody, any clear person, to push against through their dissidence. They have been trying. Maybe if the professor won't be anything at all, when he gets upright and throws me out, I'll discover that at last I've made him a human being.

I'm inclined to think that this is one thing that's got to happen in higher education or all the rest of it is going to go down the drain. Students are going to insist upon climbing out of this alienation, nonhuman, nonentity bag. They just don't want it. I think it also goes out into the community. This same thing applies to the public library, to persons who are out there in the communities. They want people. They want to know where people stand on issues. Librarians are going to have to be known for what they care about, what point of view they have.

BUNDY: Would it be appropriate to have a college president hear from Jim Welbourne? This morning, he was going to explain his idea of an information service to the dissident elements on the campus and get a reaction from the students. You were going to do it this morning. What happened?

WELBOURNE: I now have the first input anyhow. I received a request from one of the SDS members on the campus. We have been talking about the fact that the college library does not serve part of the student population. One part that they totally ignore is the campus activists. The SDS, the student left, probably abhors the library the most because they consider it the establishment, and the primary aim of the SDS is to get information to disrupt the establishment. They are part of the clientele. Someone needs to have an information service geared to their needs. Someone needs to exploit the bureaucracy and enlist the undergraduate libraries and the other library facilities on campus in their behalf. I was trying to get this as a role that the student members of the Library School Students' Association might play on their behalf. Now they're beginning to take us up on it, asking for aid in doing some research for a pamphlet on the racist institutions of education in the Maryland area, in the Maryland educational higher system. I asked them to list the kind of questions, the date they needed answers by, and what sort of things they would like to have access to.

BUNDY: Did they swear you to secrecy, not to tell their questions?

WELBOURNE: It took about two months of talking and just being among the students for them to present this question. I think that implies they don't have to swear me to secrecy. I'm going to do something for them. I am currently writing a proposal to set up an information service for student activists. It's a hypothetical situation that might turn into a reality. It would take into consideration the kinds of things this particular kind of group would need to know, the kinds of literature, the kinds of index language and terminology that reflect the way they look at the world, and not the way we decide to classify the world in terms of establishment, disruption, that sort of thing. The idea is to set up a service that would be responsive. It's in the thought stage. I'm for group action. Once you start doing something, you'll create the thing you were thinking about. You should write a proposal by looking at it in retrospect. You should go right to the problems, the shortcomings. You'll learn.

BIRENBAUM: That's right, but I don't want to be unrealistic about this disruptive function, Jim. By encouraging disruption from the base of your profession, I did not mean to imply that you must do the superhuman task of becoming the whole man. That's almost too much. I would not see your disruption taking the form of providing answers for the community you serve. It would be just very, very many points ahead if you could frame a few incisive questions.

BUNDY: He was giving you an action program. Part of his action program is some of the questions he can answer.

BIRENBAUM: You don't want to get trapped into the bag of saying, "We have the answers." Because you won't have the answers. But you sure can ask some questions from a privileged position.

REID: Framing some questions can be a very, very highly political matter, really.

BIRENBAUM: Right! Disruptive!

REID: It really can. For example, we could ask, "Do you know the value of the land in this neighborhood?" Or, "Have you looked at the plan recently for land use?" People come by and try to buy your house and land for $20,000. You only paid $6,000 a long time ago, and realize it will probably be worth $150,000 by the time they put in the high-rise and the plaza there. So the library could say, "Have you taken a look at the land use plan recently? Here it is!" and spell it out and show it to people. That's a highly political act, particularly if you really bring people in to talk about it, and you involve the people who are really in this thing.

PARTICIPANT: But, Annie, are you saying that it's a political act, avoid it, or a political act, do it?

REID: I'm saying do it.

PARTICIPANT: That's a library custom that we referred to this morning when we were talking about the ancillary activity to stimulate library use. When you invite a lecturer who is an expert on a particular problem, you have posed the question and gotten the members of the community interested. You won't be called to task for having done it, because you've brought someone in from the outside to do it.

BUNDY: We only wanted to get more books used.

PARTICIPANT: Were you actually asked this question?

REID: It's a question that happens around libraries all the time. They know it, but they don't tell anybody.

PARTICIPANT: If you're asked the question, it's nonpolitical.

REID: It's political. You're not going to be asked the question. Persons who are losing their lands that way do not know this, but libraries every day and all over this country are sitting right in the midst of hot land that is changing hands.

PARTICIPANT: But you need to be more than political; you need to be intuitive. You need to decide what kinds of things you need.

REID: In addition to being involved in information, there is also a highly political function, and libraries need to get into it. We need to think it through and bring in the people needed to help, but we need to do it.

BIRENBAUM: When you say political, I get the feeling that this is where a lot of librarians back off.

REID: Right. That's not just information; that's being political. Know it and do it.

BIRENBAUM: One result of the planning group that Preston Wilcox and I were part of in the Bed-Stuy college was the conclusion that all books issued to freshman students entering that college simultaneously ought to be put in the hands of the adults with whom those freshmen lived at home. The college was budgeted so that that could happen. Well, it followed from that, if you were going to put them in the hands of the parents, the aunts, the grandparents, or whoever young people lived with, that you have to do something with the books with those people. This had planning implications for the library design. The library was the only really effective physical resource in the plan that could be used as the developmental point for all this. Out of this came a program development, some of which had to do with discussion and editorializing, but a great deal had to do with the engagement of other kinds of audiovisual presentations and live presentations pursuant to the works.

When we talked at length with the people in the community, the adults, we found out what is so true of white middle-class people with regard to books: namely, that there are people who never read books, but who are very eager to possess them, not even to read them eventually, but just to own them. This is a phenomenon we're all familiar with. People buy books like mad which they never intend to read. They want them either to fill out shelves, to have them on tables, or just to have them around. In this kind of community, satisfying that impulse to possess is a tremendous breakthrough. There are virtually no outlets to satisfy that impulse in such a community.

For the youth of the community, going to this college was a natural bridge. Now, on the basis of that bridge, if you could move toward educational programs for the adults with whom those younger people were associated at home about the same subject matter of the curriculum, not necessarily in the same form, or even at the same levels, you've already done something which has a very direct bearing on your potential with the freshmen in your college. It seemed to us it was worth exploring, at least.

PARTICIPANT: I want to make a couple points of information on this. One point is that in West Virginia, there is beginning a program called "Knowledge," which is a political use of information sponsored by the Office of Educational Opportunity to provide information to poor people about some of the issues that they themselves have to know about in order to confront state legislatures and groups like that. It really has two wings of information—a service wing and a community organization wing—but it has not yet really gotten off the ground, and that is about all the details I have on it.

Second, concerning Mr. Birenbaum's comment about a counter-university, I think this is going to be a fairly common occurrence. One of the things I'm involved in at Syracuse now is consulting with the student government, which has at its disposal about a quarter of a million dollars to spend as it wants, due to some pressuring and getting $5 from every student as part of the student fee. They are in a position to set up a free university. They are better organized and able to get information out of students, any student on campus, within two hours. This is basically what they're going to do, and they're going to set up their free university on top of the existing institution, probably with the permission of the establishment because this is one of the ways to induce change in a very entrenched liberal arts college.

The question I would really like to ask Mr. Birenbaum is, in giving this kind of analysis of the situation, what are the ideas? What are the kinds of things you're trying to bring about? What are your goals as far as change goes?

BIRENBAUM: I have an answer for that, but it's a very transitory and immediate answer. We have a top priority at the moment. It bears upon the humanities and the social sciences, because I think the problem to which we are addressing ourselves is less acute in the sciences, and for a very interesting reason. The top priority which we have framed for ourselves is to relate in a continuing fashion the organization of learning processes with the opportunities for action opportunities, pursuant to the learning processes in the social sciences and the humanities. This is the immediate defined target.

BUNDY: What do you mean by that? Field work?

BIRENBAUM: I'll move over to the sciences to give the example. I'll describe two situations in medical sciences. The medical-biological life sciences are now where the action is, and they are very, very interesting. I attended the first day of second-semester registration for new freshmen at one of the great medical colleges of the South, Medical College of Virginia at Richmond. Two thousand students, heart transplants, kidney transplants, the whole bit. The IBM machine ground out course cards for these freshmen, each of whom received his four or five freshman course cards plus an extra IBM card which told him where to go on the second day of freshman status to meet his first patient.

The students met each patient where the patient was, where the stink was, where the dirt was, where the corruption and the bureaucracy work—in the hospital, in the ward, in the clinic. They met the patient. They were with patients from that point on. Not third year, first year! Not second week of first year, first week!

Now, couple that with a second point that goes with it. Carnegie has a study on the education of educators under the direction of Charles Silberman. It parallels Clark Kerr's, to some extent. It will be published this fall. I've seen the advanced text, and Silberman says, generally, that American higher education looks pretty dreary. There were a few spots he saw, both geographic- and subject-matter-wise, that looked interesting. One was what was going on in medical education. Surprise, surprise! He attributed this to two reasons. First, the state of the knowledge is such that things are happening that the technicians and experts can no longer handle within the terms of the disciplines and the classifications. There is the question of when is one dead, when do you transplant? the question of tampering with the genetic code further: should you do it or shouldn't you do it? If you do do it, what are the consequences of doing it? These questions spill over into philosophy, into aesthetics, into theology, and into many other things. The top dogs in the medical life science business, apparently as a result of political pressures coming at them from other professions in the community, have been compelled to move out into other disciplines for help in working out answers. That's one wholesome thing that has happened.

The other thing is that the state of the knowledge is such that none of the discrete institutional forms for practicing this knowledge can now remain discrete. In the colleges, in order to teach medicine now, it is imperative to have access to hospitals and clinics where the patients are. In the hospitals, where therapy is given, no longer can you have a first-class hospital without an on-premises series of research operations. No great metropolitan hospital is worth its salt without its own teaching components and programs for upgrading the professionals working there, as well as for integrating students who are entering the profession. Consequently, among the college research center, the hospital, and the clinic, the lines are now blurred. The managerial systems are blurred. The deployment of talent is taking a completely different form. This is resulting in a new kind of vitality.

In my shop, there are low-prestige programs, career programs that we put the blacks into, such things as the two-year terminal programs to prepare them for jobs in electrical engineering, civil engineering, or how to be a nurse's aide and how to enter the field of fire science, and things like that. This is where my best teaching is going on. The reason the best teaching is going on is that after the first week of school, the nature of these programs, which are too short, requires the teachers to get the students out of the classrooms and into the labs. I have freshmen coming in after one or two weeks who are actually having dead cat cadavers put in front of them and are given a knife. They have to cut into them. They're walking into these magnificently equipped rooms with all kinds of electric engines and machines. They actually have to plug something in, and take something in their hands, and do something.

At the same time, I've got my high-class, liberal arts transfer students walking into introductory philosophy classes, getting lectures on aesthetics. They study architecture, for example, in New York City, but they can't even tell you where the Seagram's Building is. If you took them into the lobby of the Seagram's Building and said, "Look!" they wouldn't know what they were seeing. Yet they're taking brilliant lectures, passing tests with A, B, and C grades and being stamped with three credit hours in the philosophy of aesthetics in architecture.

Our top priority now is to find situations in the city where people are working in history, in political science. I've got kids in political science courses studying the structure of the government of the United States at a high level of proficiency, who can't even run an effective student government. This is incredible! I've got kids in there studying the history of the world who can't tell you that Staten Island was the last place north of the Mason-Dixon line to abolish slavery. They can't tell you where it happened, who acted in it, why it happened, and what the implications are of it, pursuant to its happening.

We're trying out learning relationships with nonacademic talent pools in other great, nonacademic resource centers. I've got problems. For example, if you want experts in art history, in my opinion, with but three exceptions you do not find them in universities. You go to the great museums, to the curator staffs, or to the galleries. There isn't a decent university theater operation in New York, and in my opinion, there never will be, for an obvious reason. You would be mad if you invested a lot of money in a university theater in New York. From an academic base in New York, you do other things with theater. I've got problems because I'm insisting that whatever talent we employ, wherever we find it, that talent must enjoy the same status as those back in the home base who teach. This includes decisions regarding the curriculum, regarding voting on personnel, regarding the whole works.

This is really taking on the establishment at the gut level. But if we can break through here and really get some learning resources together for breakthrough, we're going to do it. We've already got the first thing set up. It's in the easiest front, the sciences. At my little place, we have originated the first programmed address to black veterans returning from Vietnam. We're staging it at Fort Dix and on campus. We're taking the six months normal waiting period when GIs sit at Fort Dix, waiting to be discharged, from the time they get back from Vietnam to the time they get back into the world. We will give them a preparatory course. If they go through it, they can get into college without any questions asked, high school diploma or no high school diploma; whatever happened in the past, they get in.

As a result of this, the people at Fort Dix and the Department of Defense came to us and said, "We feel that all the training we're giving people to be medics for certain levels of professional technical work in hospitals and in the medical profession is being utterly wasted. Why don't you take our medics, many of whom are not high school graduates, why don't you take them after we get through with them in Vietnam, after four years or two years of practical experience, and do whatever else you have to do with them to put them into certain key areas of professional work?" We said, "Great!" The only problem was we didn't have any of the stuff. The only places that had the stuff were the great hospitals in my area. So we went to the great hospitals where there were great surgeons and other doctors and said, "Be a part of our faculty. Define your operating room as a classroom of my place. We'll give credits, give you accreditation." Well, the faculty in the sciences went up in smoke.

But we won. We're going to try it this September. We're going to give the degree. Those doctors, with their Ph.D.'s, their M.D.'s, and their surgical or their psychiatric experience and training, will be members of my faculty with full status. The kids will get a certain number of credit hours in the hospitals under their supervision.

Life is going to be more and more of this. The kind of central resource which you represent professionally has to get in tune with this in the sciences, in the arts, in the social sciences. If you're out in the sticks in Waterloo, Iowa, I admit you've got a problem, but I don't think the schools out in Waterloo, Iowa, are going to be the cutting edges of this development in our society. I think, not by choice, but by survival necessity, the Columbias will be. The Staten Islands will be. Probably the saddest catastrophies of what's happening will be the Cornells that grew big and famous and qualitative on the wrong base. The bases that were once right are now irretrievably wrong. Unless the Ann Arbors can reach out to the Detroits and connect, unless the Ithacas and the Cornells can find a way of doing New York or Buffalo or Albany right, they are lost causes. In the case of Cornell, which I think is a classic case, I'm afraid it's declining. It's an institution that does not have a future.

PARTICIPANT: It seems to me that what you suggest by your answer is the combined thought and action-behavior parts of the model.

BIRENBAUM: That's right. The reasons for the separation are historical. The reasons are no longer relevant. Aristotle remains relevant.

Aristotle said, "What we have to learn to do, we learn best by doing." This no longer is a matter of ideology, in my opinion. It's a matter dictated by the state of the knowledge. You can read about the dance, but at some point, if you're serious about it, you must do it. You can read about politics, but you must take into account the kind of students we're raising in this country, from both the black neighborhoods of the city and the suburban middle-class white neighborhoods of the metropolitan regions. They're going to insist on doing, whether the present faculties want them to or not.

The difficulty is that my faculty, the senior, tenured faculty on my campus, did a little survey. Less than 10 percent of them are under fifty. They are wonderful, liberal, decent men, products of the trade-union fight in the late 1930s, products of the Hitler war, the kind who will vote for JFK with enthusiasm, but they are utterly out of touch with the new issues and the moods regarding these issues. Bridging that gap is the challenge.

WASSERMAN: To translate your model into our terms poses problems for us educationally in preparing people for this field, because you speak of the great institutions which can be great learning possibilities. We don't have great prototypes into which we can merge our students.

PARTICIPANT: Why isn't the University of Maryland library a great prototype?

BUNDY: I would rather take on the Brooklyn Public Library.

BIRENBAUM: But, Paul, one of the things that happened in clinical psychology after the war, with the impetus of the Veterans Administration support for a lot of training, was that with the trainees going into installations and the faculty behind them coming in, they brought about changes.

WASSERMAN: You take a bad scene, and make it a learning experience?

BIRENBAUM: It's a method of learning. For example, written into the VA training program were certain kinds of relationships of consultants from the university and the installations. This spread from the VA places to other internship settings. So I think that, in a funny way, the insistence on internships, and the university and students coming in, did something to affect the practice.

WASSERMAN: I'm sure the two are very much intermeshed into one. I suppose we find good rationalizations for not taking it on. It's easy to stay in your own back yard.

BIRENBAUM: If psychology hadn't had the federal funding, it might never have gotten on.

REID: You know, Mary Lee, I wonder why you prefer to go to Brooklyn, or Harlem, rather than tackle the University of Maryland library? It could be any number of other places, but it seems to me that this school should really do it here.

BUNDY: Interestingly enough, we have a history of this in library education. As we grew up and went into the university, typically, the head of the university library was also the head of the library school. There was an uneasy partnership and they shifted out. Now, in fact, you can't get accredited if one man is playing both roles. The library schools thought they came off the worse. The library staff got the prestige from the library school, and the library school never felt they got that much. You're saying times are changing; maybe we should move in that direction.

REID: No! All of that does not explain why you don't want to take it on.

PARTICIPANT: Throw out the accrediting agencies. Who said they knew what they were talking about in the first place?

BIRENBAUM: Do you know what happened to Middle States last week? The most beautiful thing! There was a two-year college out in the Middle West somewhere, Missouri, named Mary Webster. They ran their college for profit. Middle States refused to accredit it, and they got sued by this college as a restraint of trade. It was brought up in a federal district court in Chicago and the college won the first round. Now it will go to appeal. The point is that everybody knows that the accreditating association is a transitory group of established faculty committees.

REID: They are responsive to the political situation.

BIRENBAUM: And to the establishment.

REID: Well, that's the political climate.

BUNDY: You all find something to say intimating that I really wasn't giving an answer to your question. There are 30,000 students at the University of Maryland, right?

REID: Yes, and you teach some of them in this profession.

BUNDY: So my first reaction would be we don't have the manpower now to take on the 30,000, plus the educational function.

REID: But that's what they say out in the public library. "Gee, all those blacks out there and none of them can read."

BUNDY: I want to know what I've got going for me to make it.
PARTICIPANT: You've got 30,000 students and a library.
BUNDY: Let's forget the library. I would be willing to take the 30,000 students, I think, before the library. All libraries are functioning in 1940 terms. This one is not much worse than others.
PARTICIPANT: Change them!
BUNDY: If you really want to get serious, I've got to start fresh over in the student union and the communications center.
PARTICIPANT: Then go out and do it. Put in new books and rehire people. Those are all excuses.
BUNDY: All right, I'll toy with the idea, but I don't think I would start with that building, or those books, or those people.
BIRENBAUM: They can't blow it by building their offices around it.
PARTICIPANT: Those are simple logistical problems which can be solved if you want to solve them.
BIRENBAUM: I think you're oversimplifying the problem.
PARTICIPANT: No, I'm not oversimplifying it. Logistics is like World War II when you had to move all the troops and build planes and bombs. If you have to do it, you do it.
BIRENBAUM: If you have the resources to muster. You need the resources to muster. You can go out and try to sell your case. That's the way you fight wars. We haven't even got consensus that there is room for change, you see.
PARTICIPANT: Organize SDS! They're looking for a legitimate problem. Tell them that you want to take over the library. Give them all of the information to picket and destroy all the collections at the University of Maryland so that you can have a library school.
BIRENBAUM: I'm working within the establishment, not outside of it.
BUNDY: Well, I feel a little freer. I'll talk to you later.
PARTICIPANT: You don't have to do it. Sit back and say, "SDS is getting on me. They want this. What am I to do?" You don't have to do it; just see that it gets done. Then when the administration of this university wants to know what to do, they're going to come to you because it's a library problem. You have a solution. Pull it out of your back pocket and say, "There!"
PARTICIPANT: What is so wrong with this library?
BUNDY: It's a 1940 library, like most of our university libraries. It's bogged down with its commitment to collections, getting books on shelves. It's unable to know the 30,000 students. It hasn't got

the manpower, the resources, or the understanding of the issues, and what it means for change.

PARTICIPANT: Do your students have any connection with it at all?

REID: Actually, it would be very helpful if the students refused to come until the university committed itself to doing something about the library. Then the dean would be helpless. He would have to talk to the vice president and say, "What in the world am I going to do?" There would be no students in SLIS [School of Library and Information Services]. No students would come.

BUNDY: I don't think I would do it that way. At the student union, the students have set up a communications center. Right now it's political. They want to get some communication with the administration. They want to be able to get their transcripts in less than two months. Why not leave that library alone? Let it continue doing just what it is doing, and get a corps of people over in the union doing some other things, like what Jim was talking about.

REID: Because you need a bigger place. You need those books and . . .

BUNDY: I don't need those books. I don't know whether I need the staff. I don't need that building, I don't think.

PARTICIPANT: You just very straightforwardly and quickly talked about changing the system, to our friend over here. Now when you're confronted with the possibility of changing, you're finding all sorts of cop-outs.

BUNDY: I'm willing to take on the student and his information need. You made me realize I just don't want to take on the institution.

PARTICIPANT: Let the students take on the institution.

PARTICIPANT: The University of Maryland library added 175,000 volumes last year. Is that responsive? They spent $1.179 million for books and materials. They have about eighty-nine professional staff members. It would appear to me that they're doing their thing, as set forth by the administration. Any student is free to walk in. They are open about 100 hours a week, which is pretty good. I don't see anything greatly wrong with that.

PARTICIPANT: May I say something as a former student of the University of Maryland? I take exception to your statement that students are able to do whatever they want. I think this library is totally unresponsive to the student. They are so means-oriented that if you dare ask for them to bend a rule, they don't care what your reasons are, or who you are, or why you want it; they do not bend the rules. They are very classic in running their little library.

PARTICIPANT: Do they restrict the number of books you can take out?

PARTICIPANT: I don't know if they do or not. Let me give you this as a personal example. Maybe this is very minor, but on two occasions that I recall I had need to use materials and was refused. Once during semester break, I couldn't do it because, of course, they had no way of knowing that I was going to come back the next semester. I might keep the book and not bring it back. Another time I was doing some research for one of the professors who was on the school's library staff, and I was not really classified. I wasn't a faculty member and I wasn't a student, so I was sort of in limbo.

PARTICIPANT: I'm getting tired of sitting here and hearing all these generalizations about how bad the world is, and how bad the library is, and how bad library education is. Nobody is even challenging it. When I go over to the University of Maryland library and see a library with more than a million volumes, with thousands and thousands of journals, that is open a hundred hours a week, which has comfortable chairs, good lighting, and anything that I would expect to find in a library, I just don't see what the problem is.

BIRENBAUM: Its measure is the function of its capacity to be responsive.

PARTICIPANT: I'm a student right now. I worked as a staff member for the past four years while I was doing undergraduate work and while I was in the library school. I think it is an important issue that you raise because as a potential institution it's very valuable. The library school virtually ignores that potential resource. That is misusing funds by just having the appearance of a library, and having none of the commitments to do what we're taught in classes ought to be done. The library school sits on the top two floors of the building, virtually ignoring the lower half. It doesn't tell its students how to begin to criticize constructively that failure to use those resources.

One thing that happens is the library begins to encourage student workers who go to the library school to be professionals, to take jobs in various departments within that library. This is happening in a number of departments right now. Because these students are considered professional, they can criticize what goes on from certain standpoints.

BUNDY: All right, Jim, you've attacked the library school. You worked for four years. What was your great impact on it?

WELBOURNE: It doesn't matter what happened four years ago. I'm talking about right now. You begin to start having a research program by tying up things that are going on in your class with things that are wrong with the library, and you get students to work on this. If they are not allowed to work on this bureaucratically, because the directorship of the library doesn't like it, take it outside. Tell the students they are not getting their library services which they are paying for, because they do pay for them.

BUNDY: If I were the librarian there and some student wanted me to help him get his transcript, how could I help him?

PARTICIPANT: Send him to the registrar's office.

BUNDY: He couldn't get it there.

BIRENBAUM: I want to be clear about your point. I want to be clear that at no point did I mean anything I said to be critical of the University of Maryland library, as you have described it.

PARTICIPANT: I'm not talking about you.

BIRENBAUM: My criticism is of the University of Maryland.

BUNDY: But this gentleman put us in a very exciting world of university change. It didn't have to be the Maryland library. But if we can't say that the University of Maryland library isn't up to the times, we can't say it about any of our libraries, so I guess we have to say it. We didn't want to.

BIRENBAUM: This comes back to the question we began with. No one can say that the American armed force in Vietnam is not up with the time. It is one of the most highly perfected. The seats are soft. There are a million volumes over there. The whole thing is running as well as any armed force can run. What more do you want by way of a modern armed library than our force in Vietnam?

You are asking, "Why doesn't the University of Maryland library serve a really significant educational function?" The answer to that has nothing to do with the library or the army. It has to do with the University of Maryland, with the question with which we began: "What do we want to do?"

BUNDY: If we became a catalytic force, then we would have to deal with the whole university. I can see it coming now.

REID: The first thing you might have to do is convince this man that what you really want to do is to look at the measures that he's using to serve individual human beings. People learn in terms of individual action. In order for a library to be effective at all, it has to do something about individual actions in connection with learning.

PARTICIPANT: I went over to the Maryland library yesterday. I walked up to a desk and asked the librarian for a certain document. He very quickly identified the document and said, "I'll run up and get it." He didn't know me from Adam. He ran up to the next floor and returned in one minute with the document, and I found the information I wanted.

PARTICIPANT: In answer to Dr. Birenbaum's question, "What do we want to do?" I would like to convert part of library education to the education of a private practitioner, someone who would have the flexibility to get into the situation where he is needed, to merge his conscience with the conscience of the other members of his team, who is not burdened with the terrible shell of bricks and mortar; not only that, but someone who is also able to get out of the situation, a consultant. You don't need a librarian there all the time, any more than you need a doctor at home twenty-four hours a day. Your mother can take care of you. The doctor makes his diagnosis and tells you what to do. He sets up the situation, so that help is retrieved, and someone else can take over. The librarian consultant could size up the situation, evaluate it, make recommendations, and set things up. There are normal routines that can be carried out without him.

PARTICIPANT: A doctor is called in in an identifiable crisis, however. The librarian, as you pointed out, has to spend his time first identifying certain crises.

REID: That can mean different roles. I can see what's being described here as being a possibility in a different context from what I talked about last. It is a different set of roles.

PARTICIPANT: I'm not saying every librarian should be like that.

REID: Right, but it's a useful concept.

BIRENBAUM: My position is that when a modern college or university seriously invites a student to learn, it is a crisis situation. Consequently, if such a student, pursuant to such an invitation, really goes to a library, his is a crisis that's altogether comparable to what happens when someone sick runs out for a doctor. You have created essentially antilearning situations here.

The only thing about the library is, it really is central. It may not be the heart, but it certainly is the key to the whole thing. Though it may not be able to generate answers in and of itself, it is in a very strategic position to raise critical questions and to wed the power of its centrality to these questions so that they have force. The next time I go around and have a chance to hire library leadership, I've learned how terribly critical it is to find in that kind of leadership not technical competence and experience first, but courage and intelligence in light of the issues, on the assumption that if you have that, you can find the technical competence needed.

I don't have half the competence technically needed to run my college, but I have a staff. I have my own resources where I can find them when they are needed generally. That's not my problem. My problem is one of courage, or the lack of it, and perception, sensitivity to what is important and what is not. I know when I'm being sandbagged. I know when my headquarters is boxing me in. I know when I decide to fight them and when I don't. That is to say, I know the compromises I make and I live with those.

Let me come back to the meaning of a point that Paul made at the outset, that the technology and the technical competence can become a crutch. It's there whether you think about it or not. It's there, and it is a terrible complication for your profession, because it has such a direct bearing. Whether you like it or not, whether you use it wisely or not, it's there. It can really become a crutch. Look at the ads in *The New York Times* for librarians. What do they ask for? Or the ones who are seeking jobs; what do they advertise about themselves? Generally, all the wrong things.

WELBOURNE: Because they are expected to.

BIRENBAUM: All right.

WELBOURNE: That's the way they get jobs.

BIRENBAUM: That's the way they got jobs.

BUNDY: As you talk to college presidents, they're talking more like this and less like . . .

REID: Well, why don't we see ads like that for them, then?

BIRENBAUM: Because presidents don't put ads in the paper.

WELBOURNE: Because the education of the professional does not train him in terms of those values. The education of a professional, whether it be in library school, social work, or any of these new professions, is primarily directed to training for the technical skills that are fairly automatic. Incidences of leadership, of change agentry, of when to fight and when to turn the other cheek—these are issues that are not taught in professional education except in a very few special places.

BIRENBAUM: He bothers me, though. I'm going to sign off, Paul. I want to say one thing by way of signing off, because he bothers me. I said it in the beginning and I'll say it again now. I could not presume to really talk about your business except from the very nonexpert perception of it I have, and therefore I did not mean to be especially critical of what you do. I'm critical of something very different. I guess I'm making the point again that you're in a boat that is leaking badly along with a lot of other people.

I have another thing to say, which is that the dean of students is obsolete. I have said this to hundreds of deans of students with the most extraordinary consequences. I can prove I was once a dean of students. I've never been a librarian. I really know that deans of students are obsolete. Everything in their quiver full of arrows is wrong. Everything is wrong from educational psychology to counseling and guidance to their version of financial aid to extra curriculum. The whole thing is absolutely obsolete. As a profession, I guess they are about the same age or a little younger than you.

WASSERMAN: Oh, we go back to the Stone Age.

BIRENBAUM: But in five decades, they've had it. They were born and they're dying in five decades.

PARTICIPANT: College presidents are rapidly becoming dispensable.

BIRENBAUM: I wouldn't say they're becoming dispensable. I'd just say that they are dispensed with greater rapidity.

WASSERMAN: I think that that's the best note on which to end this thing.

5

RESPONSES FROM THE ESTABLISHMENT: MODELS AND CUES FROM OTHER FIELDS (PART ONE)

WEDNESDAY AFTERNOON, AUGUST 13
CHAIRMAN: MARY LEE BUNDY
PANELISTS: SIDNEY GALLER
                    JONATHAN FREEDMAN

BUNDY: In regard to the timekeeping, we thought we might proceed by starting with Dr. Galler. We will let him talk, and then you can respond to him. Then Mr. Freedman can speak and you can respond to him, rather than waiting until both have finished. After the break we might turn it into a general discussion and ask, "From looking at these two separate areas, is there anything we can say generally about how institutions are responding on a positive basis to the kinds of problems that we have been discussing for two days?"
GALLER: I always feel at a disadvantage in leading off. I would much rather wait for somebody to start and then determine my strategy. Let me be very candid with you. I am neither a museologist, nor am I a librarian, and I certainly am not a sociologist. If I had to call myself something, I suppose I would call myself a WASP—"a Washington administrator, scientist, provocateur"—a member of the establishment, representing the establishment, upholding the establishment, and at the same time trying to provoke the establishment into actions that in my view, and the view of others, are progressive and relevant.

If I had to choose a title or theme for my discussion today, I think it would be something like this: "A Museum as a Special Participant in the New Dialectic in Social Relevancy." But before doing that, we first have to make up our minds just what a museum is. A museum means many things to many individuals. You must forgive me, but at this point I cannot resist trying to make my point with a kind of corny tale.

This is the little vignette about the young physician fresh out of residency who decided he had worked hard for so long that now he was going to take a little vacation. He took a trip up to the mountains and found a place near a small lake. It was so beautiful that every morning he would take a walk by the small lake and watch the sun rise. One morning he took a stroll. As he was passing the lake, he suddenly heard a call for help. He looked down on the lake and, sure enough, someone was drowning. And so he did what any self-respecting physician would do: he swam out, dragged this person halfway up on shore, and started administering artificial respiration by the old method. He pressed once on the rib cage and a stream of water came out of this chap's mouth. He pressed again. Another stream of water came out. He did it once more, and a third stream came forth. By this time he was getting very frustrated and alarmed. At that moment another young man came walking by. He stopped for a moment, looked, and clucked disapprovingly. The young physician at that moment was extremely frustrated. He looked up and said, "Sir, are you trying to tell me how to administer artificial respiration? I want you to know that I am a physician." The second chap said, "Oh no, I am not trying to tell you how to administer artificial respiration. I happen to be a hydraulics engineer. I just wanted to point out to you that if you don't pull this man all the way up on shore, you will pump that lake dry." Now I suppose if there's a moral, it is that there is always more than one way of looking at a given situation, a given facility, a given organization, or indeed, the establishment.

What is a museum? Well, let's be very mundane about it and skim the dictionary definition. The second edition of Webster's new twentieth century dictionary describes a museum as a place for a study: a building or a room for preserving and exhibiting rare and interesting, or typical, specimens of works of art, science, invention, or objects of natural history. Fairly prosaic, and I suspect a definition that is consistent with the view of a museum that most of us have had. But I would like to try to approach an operational definition of a museum, especially in relation to societal problems. I will back into this by quoting from, of all things, Genesis.

And God said, Let us make man in our image, after our likeness; and let him have dominion over the fish of the sea, and over the fowl of the air, and over the cattle, and over all the earth, and over every creeping thing that creepeth upon the earth.

So God created man in his own image, in the image of God created he him; male and female created he them.

And God blessed them, and God said unto them, Be fruitful, and multiply, and replenish the earth, and subdue it; and have dominion over the fish of the sea, and over the fowl of the air, and over every living thing that moveth upon the earth.

If one translates this injunction into a contemporary operational setting, we can say that a museum is a special library, a total documentation center, that through the acquisition of collections and ancillary information, and through the production of fundamental knowledge through collection oriented research, a museum, in effect, is a standard, a yardstick for assessing the effectiveness of man's dominion over his earth. The collections, both in the natural sciences and in the arts, represent three-dimensional modalities or forms of information that can be brought together, correlated, and synthesized. This enables us to view an ecological or environmental situation at various points in time, or to view a cultural or sociological situation in a given place at a given time.

And so, I look upon a museum as a kind of special library that can be mobilized to participate in the characterization and solution of societal problems. In my view, the most exciting thing that has happened in museums in many a year is the fact that museum administrators, directors, scholars, have suddenly recognized that the museum does represent this highly mobilizable source, and that, indeed, there is a relevance of museums, a relationship of museums, to societal problems, to contemporary society. They have recognized that part of the underlying responsibility of museum scientists and scholars is to bring to bear the resources of the museum to help out in dealing with society's problems.

How do we do this? There are at least three ways: research, collections, and public education. Research is important, whether it is scientific research that deals with the biology, the ecology, the geographic distribution of living organisms in relation to the environment, or whether it is scholarly research that examines history for clues to the nature and the substance of certain kinds of societal problems that confront us today.

Second, there are collections. By collections, I mean not only objects per se, not only objects for public exhibit, but objects with the collateral information that has been collected about them. In addition, I include the man-machine mechanisms for pulling together, synthesizing, translating, and interpreting knowledge gained from the collections in relation to contemporary problems. In this category, we should not overlook a unique potential that museums have (and I stress that it is a potential): they can incorporate a form of systems analysis and attempt to apply stochastic, mathematical model making to problems. It should even be possible to inject enough information into a model to be able to project the cultural and physical ecology in given areas and predict if certain situations should or should not occur. This is way out, but I predict that it will come to pass.

The third way that museums can become active participants is through what I call instant public education. My learned colleagues shudder when I use this phraseology. My definition of the phrase encompasses the development of educational techniques that will convey information to the public, not only about objects, but about sociological and physical ecological systems. I call it instant education because as a layman, not as a professional pettifog, but as an observer of how people relate to exhibits, I see that first and foremost it is a visual relationship. If it is properly portrayed, the people then begin to read the information that is attached to the exhibits. So it is possible, almost in terms of subliminal perception, to give the viewer a kind of electric charge, a pulse, a certain orientation, a feeling that will then perhaps provide or initiate the momentum for becoming more interested, going to other sources, and learning more. So public education in relation to museums has a marvelous opportunity for feedback from the viewer, for developing at least two-way dialogues, and maybe even more.

Let me tell you what I mean. How many opportunities are presented to the average person living in the average community to tell the community planners, the power structure, the community developers, what kind of life he would like to live, and in what environment he would like to be located, and what sorts of needs he really has?

There are very few occasions, very few indeed. It should be possible for museums to develop computerized and deliberately provocative situations utilizing objects and whatever resources are available that will ask the viewer, "Is this the kind of cultural and physical environment that you wish to live in? If not, tell us how you would like to live, under what circumstances." Of course, there would have to be directions for pushing the right buttons; the response would be in the form of three-dimensional displays, actually putting together units so that the viewer then has an opportunity to get a first-order view of what he thinks he wants, how he feels he would like to live, and under what circumstances.

I could go on and on, but maybe I have finished my soft-shoe routine at this point.

PARTICIPANT: What would you do, sir, if after all this, people did not come to visit your museum?

GALLER: That's a provocative question. We have already tried to do something about it. There are some people who never come to a museum. The solution is to bring the museum to them, not the kind of museum that is on the mall, but the kind of museum that they have had a role in designing and shaping and can relate to.

PARTICIPANT: Do you consider it the responsibility of the museum keeper to go out and sell his museum to the community? Is it the social worker's responsibility or the sociologist's responsibility?

GALLER: I really can't answer that, because we each have evolved roles for ourselves over the years. The curator, the professional curator, has evolved his role and skills. He is very good in his role. He may also be a person who feels a very deep sense of social responsibility, and therefore he may be prepared to make his skills available to fulfill his responsibility. Whether he may do this directly, or whether there needs to be some intervention—a middleman, a sociologist, whatever it takes to apply those skills—to relate them, I can't say.

PARTICIPANT: I notice that the telephone directory lists a neighborhood museum in Washington. Could you tell us something about that?

GALLER: The Anacostia museum. This is what I mean when I said we have already done something about this. We have brought a museum to the people who, under ordinary circumstances, have not in the past, for whatever reasons, come to museums.

PARTICIPANT: What does it contain? Since you said it is related, how do you find out what they need?

GALLER: Well, I better not say much about that for a couple of reasons. The most obvious one is that I don't know enough about it. It is an innovation that the secretary of the Smithsonian Institution felt was needed, an experiment that we have tried. I would say that in every way, except possibly financially, it has proven to be successful in the sense that it is accomplishing what it set out to accomplish: namely, to become a part of the community ecology, to fill a place, a sociologically valuable, culturally important niche in the community. When you get down to the tactics of doing this, I really can't speak on it.

PARTICIPANT: I have another question. Is this third thing you mentioned, the three-dimensional thing, is this operational?

GALLER: Not yet, no.

PARTICIPANT: If it becomes operational, will this be only in the Smithsonian headquarters? If so, you would get response only from the kind of people who would come to a museum already. Or will this go into outlying areas also?

GALLER: Let me distort that question slightly by saying that it is our hope that most of what we do in the way of innovation is not merely for the benefit of the public that comes to the Smithsonian, but serves as a model or a demonstration for other museums, in other parts of the country, to examine and adapt to their own special interests and communities.

PARTICIPANT: But that's just a geographical thing. There is a very small proportion of people who would go to the museum anywhere. If you are going to judge what kind of environment people want . . .

GALLER: I see your point. We have plans for extending these communication tentacles out into the communities. I think that here is where perhaps we, a museum—in this case, the Smithsonian—has to decide where its legitimate contributions, investments, need to be, and where we begin to go beyond our own ability to contribute.

PARTICIPANT: In the museum in Anacostia, you are really portraying African culture, so you are relating to people who are already used to going to museums. I can see where you can go a little further . . .

GALLER: Excuse me. May I interrupt to ask you one question? Are you referring to the Anacostia neighborhood museum?

PARTICIPANT: Is this the Frederick Douglass Museum?

GALLER: No, it is not the Frederick Douglass Museum. The Anacostia neighborhood museum is not, has not been designed, to meet the needs of the museum conscious community.

PARTICIPANT: At the Frederick Douglass Museum it is all black, but we are still not reaching the people who aren't already museum oriented.

GALLER: The Anacostia museum does. Indeed it does! We know, based on our experience and our observations, that the location was right. It is located in a community that has not been museum conscious. I wish there was some mechanism for determining whether we are ringing the bell, hitting the target, in the exhibits that are evolving down there. We do recognize that those exhibits are the product of inputs from the community, things that they would like to see, or have, or play with. It's different from the ordinary museum in another way. There are exhibits that are feelies, touchies, smellies, well, not really smellies yet, but where the viewer becomes a participant, picks it up, plays with it, does things with it, and learns something about it.

PARTICIPANT: You have described for us how you present these museums to the people. Would you follow that up by giving us the tools or techniques you use to evaluate how successful you are? I'm not talking about this neighborhood thing. I'm talking about the museum itself.

GALLER: There are the conventional tools for evaluating. There are questionnaires where you ask people what they like or what they don't like, and cards for offering them an opportunity to indicate what it is that they think we should have or to offer criticisms. It is quite possible that our exhibit people and our academic people have more to present in these kinds of things, but, in general, I would say the evaluation approach is both conventional and, in my view, unsatisfactory.

PARTICIPANT: That's what I wanted to understand.

PARTICIPANT: Let's follow this up one step further. How do you go about presenting your case to whoever is funding this museum?

GALLER: When you say "presenting your case," do you mean justifying the need for support of a museum? We have different constituencies, and different peer groups, and different segments of what I call the financial power structure that serve to support the museum, the Smithsonian Institution. I am sure that what I am about to say is totally unfamiliar to everyone here. You tailor your justification, hopefully, to relate to the interests of the sponsor, whether it be Congress or whether it be a private foundation.

BUNDY: I think we're all wondering if you are a model for librarianship. With due respect to the museum field, I think it's an excellent example of a static, long-standing institution that I never thought could change. I thought it collected objects and we went in and looked at them. In your definition of the institution, you are reaching for what we have also been reaching for this week, a shift from static to active. We are using the term "mobilize." Some of the specific aspects you mention are directly parallel to librarianship. For instance, you seem to be keeping your objects. One of the issues in librarianship is, "Do we have to throw out the books in order to serve in new roles?"

GALLER: Let me hasten to add that that is one of the issues in museums also.

BUNDY: Politically, do you feel the need to sell the object to your constituents even though you have new objectives? Do the people who fund you accept this evolving role of the Smithsonian?

GALLER: They are in the process. Perhaps I should point out that, in my opinion, there is no basic incompatibility between viewing objects and viewing problems. If a view of a problem becomes the objective, then the strategy for presenting objects becomes very different from presenting objects merely as testimonials to a given kind of scholarship or research. The strategy is different in the sense that you now cross disciplinary boundaries, you develop a synthetic strategy where your exhibits are coordinated to present a problem, not a testimonial to a field.

BUNDY: As you picked up these problem approaches, did you find new alliances, new support? And where were they?

GALLER: Yes. Very much so. For example, at the federal level, in Congress, I think it is fair to say that our appropriation subcommittees have been quite taken with the approach that the secretary is following in developing these social relevancies. They appreciated the new views of problems and not merely views of objects. There is a response from the establishment. Certainly I can say, without fear of contradiction, that this has developed interests from the private sector, from groups who had not in the past considered museums as a socially relevant resource, but who are now beginning to reappraise their thinking. Timidly, in some cases conservatively, because they are not sure what the ultimate is going to be, they are willing to take a gamble, whereas in the past they didn't even consider museums in the category of socially important facilities and organizations.

PARTICIPANT: As a beautiful example of this, let me plug a competing institution, the Museum of Natural History in New York. For many years it had the same old stale exhibits. If you went there as a kid, you could go back as an adult and find everything exactly in its place. Very recently, however, there is a marvelous exhibit there called "Will Man Survive?" It represents a lot of things. They took a big entry hall, a glamorous old Teddy Roosevelt facade, and they built the exhibit within that facade. You enter and go upstairs. There are different-sized rooms. They have used the environment of this special little facility to make a point. It is striking. It comes down to what you are saying. You come away really having a sense of what the problem is. You have been bombarded with the problem from all sides, using a number of different media.

GALLER: Or at least you have been bombarded with what we think is the problem. Let me say that all is not peaches. What we have going for us—and I'm speaking not just of the Smithsonian; I'm speaking of museums that are conscious of the new role that they must play—we have goodwill going for us and motivation, but remember, we are in the early stages of a period of transition. If you examine the museum population, if you examine the ecology of the museum, if you please, you discover only a few places, only a few cases, only a few instances, where non-object-oriented, non-museum-related people are beginning to come into the picture, beginning to interact and help to redefine or enlarge the definition of what is a problem.

So, let's face it, museologists and object oriented scholars are, first and foremost, museologists and object oriented scholars. They may be rank amateurs in assessing the true nature of a contemporary, socially significant problem. It is a period of early social experimentation, amateurish experimentation. This is changing slowly. I think there is a direct relationship between the rate of change and the availability of financial resources. There are opportunities for change in a museum that do not exist (well, they exist, but they are not as accessible) in a university community. The typical university is structured along departmental or disciplinary lines, and heaven help us if we try to cross these boundaries. A museum like the Smithsonian serves as a kind of forum where we can bring groups of specialists together who share common interests, and who have a kind of provocateur approach to life, to help define the form and substance, or redefine the form and substance, of a problem.

Ultimately, I feel that museums will reach their optimum level of value when they incorporate persons who are not merely interested in the information conveyed from objects along structured lines, but are interested in using objects, and other forms of documentation, to illustrate a problem and a solution. For example, if we take the broad panorama, the need to maintain and enhance the quality of man's environment, the need to abate environmental degradation, if we take this and examine it today, we find that it is a very ill-defined problem area that, at this point in time, is presented through the eyes of the scientist, primarily the ecologist, who thinks of it in problem-solving terms along the lines of his experience, his background, his resources. We need to bring the scientists together with the power structure—by the power structure, I mean the financial community, the industrial community, the political sectors of the community—because you cannot define environmental pollution simply in terms of a scientific or technical problem.

There are economic and social pressures and stimuli that produce this problem, and today there is no real neutral forum for bringing them together. These sectors are becoming alienated. All you have to do is pick up the papers and read about thermal pollution in the Chesapeake Bay and the nuclear power plant at Calvert Cliffs. The good guys are the conservation oriented persons, the scientists. The bad guys are the politico, the engineers, and the utilities. They are at loggerheads, and the irony is that each one of these sectors is truly interested in solving a problem; however, they have such divergent approaches and are under such different kinds of pressures that they cannot solve this problem on their own. They cannot communicate unless they are placed in a neutral forum. Museums, as kind of crypto-universities without the panoply of departments, can provide that kind of a forum.

PARTICIPANT: Do you have priorities for service to children, younger adults? What is your philosophy on this?

GALLER: I really can't dwell on this detail because, as a nonoperating administrator, I am afraid that I am far removed from that sort of thing. We have an Office of Academic Programs where these things are considered and priorities set. Of course, there are channels for communication interaction between a program and the exhibits office. But I really can't tell you how our specialists go about establishing their priorities in terms of age groups, socioeconomic strata, or what have you.

PARTICIPANT: Dr. Galler, we have been here for two days listening, in the context of libraries, trying to determine for ourselves just how libraries can be responsive to the community. The community, as you mentioned, in which there are power blocs. One bloc, perhaps, that wasn't definitely pinpointed was the community. Do you see a role for the community in determining the content of a museum or the programs of a museum? If so, how? How is it going to come about? Or is it coming about?

GALLER: Well, in answer to the first part, absolutely! We do not want passive audiences; we want community participants. How it comes about, how you develop this communication and feedback, I mentioned one way. There surely must be many ways, undiscovered or available, but not adapted so far; I can't say. But I can say it must occur, if museums are to be places where communities can view themselves in terms of their problems and their aspirations.

PARTICIPANT: Can I extend that and ask you how you view the kind of confrontation that took place in New York at the Metropolitan prior to and during the exhibit (see p. 121)? Is this good or bad, do you think?

GALLER: I can't answer that in any expert way. I am not trying to evade your question. I saw the confrontation. I can't say that I liked it, but I thought it was very important. I thought it was important in the sense that this was a view of life from a sector of the community that needed to be discerned. It might not have been an accurate view, but that's unimportant. It was a view.

PARTICIPANT: Excuse me. Are you saying that you don't have any voice at all?

GALLER: I don't have any voice in what?

PARTICIPANT: As far as getting a change.

GALLER: I certainly hadn't intended to say that. But, in response to that specific question, my view of this confrontation . . .

PARTICIPANT: I would like to take it away from the exhibit. Just the confrontation itself: was this a good thing to have happen? I often feel that it's good that attention is finally called to the library when there is confrontation on a college campus concerning a library.

GALLER: I'll try and answer this if you promise me that you will consider this only as my personal and very inexpert opinion unrelated to my role in a museum. I firmly believe that confrontations are useful if we are prepared to follow up and benefit from those confrontations.

Confrontations without follow-ups are sources of frustration. That's Sid Galler's personal view.

PARTICIPANT: Let me reconstruct the question so that we may discuss it in another way. If museums are the honorable monuments of the past from which we can reconstruct tests to suggest the future development of the society, these suggestions could be many different things, because people do not see each development of the society in the same way. Someone thinks that we should destroy everything that we have and build anew; someone will say that we should change everything. From the museum administrator's point of view, in that model situation where we are reconstructing the past and suggesting by that reconstruction a future, should we represent all the possible views—the dissident view, the controlling view, and all the shades in between? Should we present everything so that as museum directors we are neutral? Should we try to present all the views on the subject of the future development of society?

GALLER: I'll respond, but I warn you that I detect the loaded words that you have used. First of all, I don't view museums as monuments of the past. I view museums as special libraries, as special centers of documentation of past events that represent a knowledge resource for constructing models for assessing contemporary and future society, and its problems. I think museums should indeed receive the points of view from all sectors of the community. When you say neutral . . . let me just skip that word for a moment. I would say that the museum's responsibility would not be completely fulfilled by merely receiving the views of all sectors of the community and displaying those views. I think the museum must somehow or other develop a means, or strategy, some mechanism for showing the relationships of these views, the interactions, the causes and effects of these views, and in some way or another synthesize these views so that the community collectively is given a whole series of options, a whole bunch of mirrors of itself in its different dimensions, with its different aspects, and has an opportunity to react, to feed information back into the system.

BUNDY: Let us see if we can now draw some generalizations. Let's take that dormant sector of society, the university, and particularly professional education, and talk about it.

FREEDMAN: One parallel between what Dr. Galler says and what I will say is that one can view a professional school in professional education as like a museum in terms of trying to bring change to it, to start looking at reconceptualizing in one way or another, to come to a position of making it relevant for what is happening in the society today.

Let me say a couple of things about who I am. I am a sociologist. That word came up frequently in one context or another, when I was teaching on the faculty of a school of social work. I teach in part because I am what I would call an action sociologist, an applied sociologist, much more than an academic sociologist. I am much more interested in social problems than social theory. You will see this bias come out in what I am about to say.

Social work education traditionally has been very cut and dried. There is a Council on Social Work Education, a national body, that pretty much determines what the curriculum should be through accreditation and curriculum guidelines. When a student comes in for a two-year program, he is placed in an agency, an established agency usually, although some schools of social work have gotten away from this. He is supervised in his placement by someone who has experience and has a master's degree in social work. Unlike most professions, the master's degree is really the union card, so after completion of the master's a lot of people go out and take on supervisory positions immediately. There is a phenomenal shortage of social workers. For example, all the graduates of all the schools in New York State could be used by one institution, one agency, in New York State for the next ten years, and there would still be job shortages. So there is a terrific need to produce more social workers and what we might call better social workers.

One of the interesting things that has happened in the last few years is that this cut and dried approach to social work education is breaking down. Our school is about to be accredited. We find that now, as opposed to the last time we were accredited, the committee on reaccreditation is looking desperately for new ideas and approaches. Almost every school now has been given a license to innovate in one way or another. So this is indeed a change. What we are doing at Syracuse is reconceptualizing what the education should look like. We are very much in the middle of this. I will share with you some of the ideas of what we're after.

To begin with, one of the things we find about social workers is that often they leave school and go into some sort of agency; they sometimes become what you might call a tool of the agency, petty bureaucrats doing a lot of form-filling-out or working fairly routinely and taking the position that the agency is always right. A few social workers, on the other hand, take a position very much on the side of the client. These are what are sometimes known as social-action social workers. They have a habit of not lasting too long in any one agency. Thus we have these two positions of social workers. What we are trying to do is to develop a third position where the continuum between agency and client develops into a triangle. The third part of the triangle would be the worker as a fairly autonomous person making decisions. This would give the worker some leadership characteristics, an ability to mediate between the agency and the client.

The difficulty is, of course, that most of the people involved in social work education are not really in a position to do this. They have placed themselves along this continuum. The educators come from practice into education. Very few people go into social work education as educators. Some people get tired of practice and come into education that way. In a way it is part of a vicious circle, which I think is also very true of librarianship and a lot of the other professions. In order to bring about change, you have to find teachers who are going to be able to teach the kind of change you want to bring about. If people have been trained in traditional ways and have then done traditional practice for many years, they are not apt to teach change. There are not enough innovative kinds of teachers around to build slots in any kind of educational change position.

One of the solutions (and I think basically this is the way our team has handled this) is to select young people. Most of the people on our faculty are assistant professor or less. Most of them are in their late twenties or early thirties. Most of them are working on a doctorate. They are much more able to understand what I think might be called the consistent state of disequilibrium that the school is placed in in order to bring about change. So there is nothing very static. There are many changes being made. At this point the curriculum has been changed from the very rigid kind, where you know pretty much exactly what you are taking for the next two years, to a position in which every student will have at least one elective anywhere in the university per semester. This is an intermediate form. I will tell you where we are going with this in a few minutes.

We have done away with the thesis which has always been one of the stupidest busy-work projects that social work students do. We have replaced this with what I call independent study, which allows a student to work with a professor on a project that they agree about. It is not subject to the rules and regulations of our rather stodgy graduate school. This project might be a movie, for example. Last year we just started some of this. We found one student who followed an elderly woman as she made up her mind to move from a tenement into public housing. He did a film tape presentation. I think we will be getting a lot more of these kinds of things. Two of my students have already approached me about doing a reader called *Social Work Through Literature,* including the writing of some original material. So the range and the possibilities of this independent study can become a lot greater than the traditional thesis. That is one kind of thing.

Where are we going with this? I think this is going to be a temporary kind of curriculum for either a year or two. With the help of something we have in Syracuse called the Center for Instructual Communication, a very high-powered educational operation, we are moving to what we term a kind of core module approach. We are going to try to determine what people should have as a basic core knowledge—attitudes, behaviors, and so on—and try to give that to everyone. Then we will allow students to choose from a series of modules, to make their own choice in terms of their own career interests. A module might take anywhere from a few hours to master to a much longer period of time. It would be on a specific kind of topic. We are going to do this within a context of social problems. Again, we are not far enough along with this so I can say, "All right, here is a particular module! This is what it looks like." But we are seeing the basic curriculum as social problem oriented.

One of the important things is the whole issue of leadership. If you are going to train people around social problems, they are going to have to speak out on that problem. They do not get examples from their faculty in this regard. For example, when Nixon's latest welfare proposal came out, not one faculty member or the faculty as a whole spoke out on it or even was asked to speak out on it. It seems to me that this, of course, is a very specific issue in social work. For example, the newspapers did man-on-the-street interviews. There is the whole question of getting the faculty in a position so that they will start developing and demonstrating role models around the kind of leadership that we want our students to follow.

There are a couple of other areas that become important. Like other forms of professional education, we end up teaching a knowledge base of one kind or another without teaching the behaviors that the person is going to exhibit in the field, without really putting the person through situations, the kinds of situations where we want him to function. We are talking now about the ways that we can simulate this kind of education and this kind of practice where it doesn't exist now. The school, for example, has its own agency in which it places students. It is a disaster area, because there is no real educational program in that agency. I think there will be more and more moving away from the traditional agency on the grounds that these are not the models of practice we are training people for.

Maybe we can put people in other kinds of situations. Sometimes on the level of policy and planning, which is now becoming an issue, there is a terrific need for social planners to be trained. This seems to be a kind of vacuum area in terms of formal education. The problem is that this is a very tricky thing to train for, but it is something we are trying to consider in what we are developing. I would say, on the whole, that the approach that we are trying to take now towards education builds in some of the relevant issues and tries to get away from what has been standard. The result of this is still too early to tell. Some of it is in practice; some of it is on the drawing board; but I think the implications for this kind of movement to other professions is rather important. One other aspect of this is to give cross-professional courses. There is no reason, for example, why what I teach in my school, which is called social science concepts, could not be taught to architects, lawyers, librarians. As a matter of fact, there has been an attempt at various times of library students to take this course.

BUNDY: The attempt was to get in it, or to get out of it?

FREEDMAN: To get in! It didn't work out. There is no way. Each professional school becomes a bastion unto itself. It's very hard to cross over.

BUNDY: What we do is to joint-number our courses.

FREEDMAN: I don't think we have any joint numbers, or very few. I think I will stop there and see if there are any questions.

PARTICIPANT: Dr. Galler, and especially Mr. Freedman, the first thing that I noticed is that you expect librarians to become interested in social work; but I don't see too many social workers becoming particularly interested in librarianship. When was the last time you, or anybody in your office, went to a library board of trustees meeting?

FREEDMAN: I haven't been to one, but, you see, there is more than one way of looking at it. I'm glad I don't go to library boards of trustees meetings. One of the things I am doing, incidentally, is helping to plan a library for the inner city. I am doing this by other means. I am not doing this through the system, per se. I am doing this directly with some of the youths in the community. This is one of their interests.

PARTICIPANT: How many social workers are doing this? That is the question, not what you are doing.

FREEDMAN: Not many social workers.

GALLER: May I comment on that? I think that is a very good point. It hops back to the point that this gentleman made: that is, will the curator do this, that, or the other. My frustration is that we are all trained to do our thing in a certain modality, when in point of fact, the problem cannot be solved from that modality. Let me extend for a moment, with your permission, what you have just mentioned in relation to museums as problem-solving resources. We have to remember that in spite of our desire to be responsive, we can only be responsive in terms of our own backgrounds. We only know how to do our thing in a certain way.

While it is true that there is a new, fresh breeze blowing into museums, some museums at least, I honestly believe there will have to be a new kind of museum with a new kind of museologist. I use the term museologist not to describe the actions and responsibilities of the establishment, but to describe the person who will share the responsibility of using this new kind of museum in a new kind of modality. We are going to have to be exposed to an entirely different set of academic and experiential stimuli. Not merely a scholar, a historian, an artist, and invertebrate zoologist, this museologist is going to have to be specially trained to look at a museum not as a repository of objects for scholarship, but as a transducer and a transceiver connecting the community to the museum, and giving the community both a view of itself and an opportunity to say something about that view.

BUNDY: Don't knock what he is saying! We have tried for four years at Maryland to bring behavioral scientists to the faculty of the library school. We don't want social scientists who couldn't cut it in their discipline. How much is the discipline of sociology producing people who want applied sociology?

FREEDMAN: That's a good question! Let me combine that question with another comment. One of the things you hear when people from a variety of fields speak is that you might go home from this conference with the idea that the traditional institutions of this society—schools, libraries, museums, social work—are in a great deal of trouble. In many cases they are not meeting the needs of one community or another. They have remained standpat for too long. The old rituals and routines no longer suffice. An institution that continues in the old way can become vestigial.

One of the things that has happened to a lot of professions is an attempt to change the method of education. Not every institution, not every museum, not every school is trying this, but around the country today you can pick out a number of institutions where some rather innovative attempts are being made. I would classify these institutions as vanguard institutions. These attempts, on the whole, seem to go across traditional disciplinary boundaries. The new museum director could be a new kind of social worker in a different form of institution, or a librarian. The model for a museum could be the model of the new library. When you see these institutions, we might raise the question, "Is this a library? Is this a museum? Is this a community center?" It's a new kind of institution, basically, that is trying, in one way or another, to meet the needs of its surrounding community, or at least some of the needs. When it comes down to the educational process, I think what you will find is that there is a common body of knowledge that trains people in these disciplines for this kind of activity. I think what will happen at certain places, again not everywhere, will be to start bringing in expert faculty to teach cross-professionally.

BUNDY: In these plans, is there someone who understands information dissemination? Is this built into most of these?

FREEDMAN: It always comes up as an issue. It depends on the program. What they say about social workers they really say about librarians, too. In order for most social workers to work in any kind of program like this, you have to spend a year retraining them. They have been educated wrongly. There are now splits in a number of academic disciplines—psychology, certainly, sociology—which I know quite well because I am involved on one side of the split. There are the old-fashioned academics, and what is called variously the radical caucus, the insurgent sociologist, the radical sociologist.

There are a number of different groups, which have now been organized into an East Coast chapter and a West Coast chapter. What they are concerned with is the real applied sociology. They are about to hold a counter-convention. If you really want to have fun, go to San Francisco in the last week in August. There are going to be two conventions—the straight convention and the cool convention. The cool convention is going to have little theater, picketing, and all sorts of things. This is beginning to happen.

One of the difficulties is that a lot of the people who are involved in this movement have terrific difficulty in getting jobs. The traditional sociology department looks down, and always has, at anyone who mucks around in applied work of any kind. He is considered the bottom of the barrel. Note, I am not in the sociology department, and I don't have that difficulty. I know of three cases where my friends in sociology departments were thrown out on the grounds that they were too active. One friend of mine got paid off for a year on the grounds of exciting students too much. He had a different view of the world, and his department chairman said, "We don't need that kind of sociologist around here." There is going to be a lot more of this. The discipline is under a lot of pressure now.

PARTICIPANT: I am curious. Earlier, you pointed out that one of the traditional things that you were breaking away from was working in an agency. Yesterday Jim Welbourne brought up how library students were being encouraged to get involved in library work part-time. I am curious as to why this agency work would not be successful.

FREEDMAN: Most agencies are still doing things the way they did them in 1940.

GALLER: Why are they still doing them the way they did them in 1940?

PARTICIPANT: It seems that the innovative person, if he got into this 1940 situation and the agency knew he was trained to be a professional in that field, might be in a very good position to help bring about innovations within the system. Why should he deliberately cut himself off?

PARTICIPANT: What do you mean by "a very good position"? He would be where the problem is, that's true.

PARTICIPANT: Jim pointed out that in the library, for instance, the librarians don't consider him just another student worker. They know he is training to be a librarian. Therefore, they listen to the new ideas he brings from the library school because they realize he is training to be a professional librarian.

BUNDY: Stop right there, and let Jim answer.

WELBOURNE: I was telling the students we're placing in a library situation that they must communicate to the professionals with whom they are working, that they are, indeed, professionals in training and that their views should be heard. Too often I have seen students with some very good ideas who did not speak because they were just students. They should say, "We are in the graduate professional school. We are learning criticisms and new ideas in the field." They have a right to speak, and they should challenge the professionals at that level. Students who are going out to work must communicate their own future status while they are on the job.

BUNDY: Perhaps the student or beginning professional is in a position to effect change in the agency, but what about the client?

PARTICIPANT: In connection with that, will you clarify something for me? Are you talking about added dimensions to the profession, or do you reject everything that was done up to now and want to refute the whole thing? I get the feeling that in most cases, you feel we have to add another dimension to what we are doing, and that dimension will affect what we are doing up to now. It is not turning completely away from what was done up to now and starting anew, am I right?

FREEDMAN: I think you are right. The traditional agency use of students in social work is as free labor. Students get their training by helping with the case load or something like that. If the student goes into the agency in a new way, he may get involved in agency planning. Maybe he doesn't go to one agency. One of the things we are talking about, and have done something about, is to have agency-free units. This means taking a social problem like mental retardation and placing students in all the mental retardation facilities that are available. These students then come together and talk about the similarities and differences that they are finding.

One of the things that happened in a unit of this kind was that the students saw a critical need for $100. They felt they could do one hell of a job with $100. They wrote a proposal and we were able to get them the $100. With this minimal sum in the world of proposals, they did six or seven little programs. It went very well and they learned much more that way than if they were just there taking care of an individual kid's problem or something to this effect.

BUNDY: You are an administrator, aren't you? Recently I read somewhere that some of the young social workers were changing the system, because instead of getting people off welfare they decided to put them on welfare. As I understand it, this is disruptive of the entire system. What if young student librarians came in and had this effect? It seems to me that you as an administrator, having to keep a whole system going, will almost inevitably face problems.

FREEDMAN: I don't think in terms of disruption; they are there to assist. I think good ideas can come from the lowliest page in your library, and they should be listened to. I don't think in terms of confrontation and disruption.

BUNDY: Let me put it in a different way. We all know disruption in reference work. If you do a good job you get more patrons; if you do an effective job with an exhibit more people come in, so you can very quickly overload the library.

FREEDMAN: Then you would have the ideal opportunity to go to the administration of the university and say, "Look, the people really dig this thing. You have to have some new reference libraries." Most administrators that I know of will give you this, if you prove the need for it.

PARTICIPANT: The problem here is that you are comparing two opposing things. In one situation a loading up is undesirable; in another situation a loading up is very desirable. There are undesirable factors from the point of view of every organization, which may not really be undesirable from the point of view of society as a whole. There would probably be some kind of undesirable effect that a student librarian could exert on his library which would upset his administrator—perhaps not collecting fines, not asking for identification, not checking outgoing books.

GALLER: May I comment? In my opinion, most of the units that make up the establishment, especially agencies, both private and public, are mission-oriented and not problem-oriented. Everything that they do and all of the resources that they gather are justified in terms of missions, rather than in terms of problem identification and solving.

Why do I make this distinction? It is not only possible, but indeed it does happen that in a mission-oriented unit of the establishment, the perpetuation of the organization is encouraged. Change is not an important factor because the mission remains the same, and missions are eternal. Once the experimentation is complete and a reasonably effective, reasonably efficient organization has been tooled up, that is the way it remains. It has demonstrated that it is effective in fulfilling its mission. Problem orientation inherently requires an ability to change organization and reallocate resources with a response time that is far shorter than in a mission-oriented unit.

To put this in a slightly different way, one reason why I think that we are not being very effective in discerning and solving societal problems is because, in my view, the ideal unit of an organization to serve as a springboard in attacking these problems would have to have several inherent characteristics. It would have to be self-organizing, it would have to have an ability for self-learning, and it would have to have the characteristic of self-correction. These three taken together would provide the mobility and minimize the kind of vested interests that develop in fixed organizations that are designed to meet missions. Only in the evolution of the problem-oriented units can you hope to evolve problem-oriented people, whose social value and social acceptability by their peers are not based on whether they are applied or basic. They are given the kinds of training, the kinds of experience, the kinds of exposure that will permit them to be flexible. As long as we are trying to solve problems from structured, vested interests, mission-oriented, relatively immobile springboards, the opportunities for an evolutionary change will not really exist.

FREEDMAN: I think the reality at the moment is that you have perhaps some problem-oriented people in mission-oriented institutions.

GALLER: Right.

PARTICIPANT: But are the two mutually exclusive? I don't see why. A reference department, for instance, or a university library, is mission-oriented. I define this mission as serving the faculty and the students of that institution. However, if it is sensitive to the problems of the students and faculty, why can't it constitute itself at the same time as a problem-oriented group within the structure that it has? I don't see why the two have to be in conflict.

GALLER: I'm not saying it is impossible to do what you suggest. I am saying it becomes very difficult to do it, by virtue of the fact that in gathering the resources and obtaining the approval of those who are responsible for resources, invariably you are justifying your need for resources to solve problems to peer groups that are not problem oriented but are mission oriented.

BUNDY: Try an example I heard recently of a university library that is trying to work with a group that is bringing in people who have been disadvantaged. They don't meet some of the ordinary requirements of the institution, and the library is trying to work with this group. It has very few resources to work with; it doesn't have a collection. The institution isn't willing to give much time. One of the main things this group said they faced was that they were becoming alienated from the librarians. They were identifying now with the other people trying to solve the problem. They were unable to reach understandings that would have been required to get them the resources to help with the problem.

PARTICIPANT: The administrator in that case should have looked at his priorities and said, "Now in this situation we are going to have to let this go, and fit some of the money into this problem area."

BUNDY: One of the problems that happens with us is sort of parallel. The minute you design some programs to help some incoming people, some special group, the programs become things you should do for everybody.

PARTICIPANT: Are we a mission-oriented group? We all learned in library school, at least I did, that most of our situations are pragmatic and change from one day to another. With that learning experience, it seems to me rather hard to be what one would call mission-oriented.

BUNDY: Dr. Galler is raising another question where we may not have a sense of mission. Our commitments may be to the collections or to the maintenance of the system by which we keep them.

GALLER: My view is, they are missions. I dare you to go to a curator of insects and say you want a chunk of his collections to be used in a way that is completely unrelated to his field of scholarship. See what his response would be.

PARTICIPANT: When I look at the Smithsonian and think about changing it, I would start from the very root. I can't see where extensions help, places like the Anacostia extension of the Smithsonian. This gives only certain people a chance to look. If I had anything to do with your museum, I would change from the very beginning. I would take out some of the things that were not as important.

I would want to be in a perspective where everybody could see, not just a segment of people.

GALLER: You are just rephrasing more eloquently what I said a few minutes ago. We need to evolve new kinds of museums. These museums should be problem-oriented.

PARTICIPANT: Explain what you mean by problem-oriented.

GALLER: I mean they would be designed to provide communities with insights, views, and opportunities to participate in the two-way communication process, to gain perspectives on how changes occur and should occur. Museums today, even the most innovative ones, are not designed to do that. This experiment that we are talking about, Anacostia, is just that. In order to retool a museum that has had a mission to serve as a monument to the past and to serve selected communities, there are two possibilities: one, the community of scholars behind the scenes; and the other, the public community through exhibits. Why? I can tell you why.

PARTICIPANT: I know why we are here. I am saying that the change has to come about before any of these organizations can do anything.

GALLER: I am saying that given the choice, I would rather buy a new automobile than try to retool my old tin lizzie. It would take a major investment in time and effort to try to reorient people who have major stakes in their past experiences and who have made their reputations within the bounds of disciplines. That's an impossible situation.

FREEDMAN: If I were a problem solver in a mission-oriented place, I would (1) lose my job, and (2) lose my friends and colleagues. I think that this is a problem that always comes up, and I will talk a little bit about it. What becomes important is really who your references are. Who are the people who are really important to you in terms of what you are doing? One of the things we hope to do concerning the social work model that I was talking about is to create a group of people who will go out into the immediate community in which the school operates, but whose reference group will be their fellow students. They will be committed to some sort of change position.

One of the nice things about professional schools is that there is a turnover every two years. The people you get out into the field get out there quickly. They are put into positions of responsibility rather quickly. Usually what happens to them is that they become supervisors taking the agency position. They can talk a good game of change, if you go and visit them as I do occasionally, but they say it is too early. A lot of people go to school because of commitments from a welfare department, or something like that. They have to pay this back by working so many years. Their usual response is, "Well, when I get done with my commitment, then I will be a free man. Then I will be able to go out and do something." One of our educational problems is to build in behaviors that will allow students to act as change agents while they are in school, and then give them an opportunity and a reference group of other people doing the same kind of thing, when they go out to supervisory positions. I think there can be parallels with librarianship.

PARTICIPANT: When you get your students from practitioners, those who have already had some experience in the field, you are not going to succeed in training change agents. No matter how acquiescent they are in the classroom, this is part of the game they have learned in the bureaucracy. I was bibliographed in the school of social work, and I can see that difference in the older and the younger. The older were just conning you. They knew what they wanted. They wanted that union card. They wanted to get out into the agency, get more power. They wanted to get along more peacefully and comfortably.

FREEDMAN: We are a private university. We do not necessarily have to take everyone who applies. There are two state-supported schools in upstate New York. We might become much more selective about our admissions. The important criteria may not be age, particularly, but dimensions of creativity, directions relating to the kind of person the applicant is. Some of our older students happen to be extremely creative as problem solvers.

BUNDY: This brings up something you said in the very beginning that forms a good parallel to librarianship. You mentioned the tremendous shortage of social workers. In librarianship, we are beginning to wonder if there really is a tremendous shortage, or if it may not be an artificial monopoly created by the library schools that say, "Without this credential, you can't do certain things." Perhaps many things could be done by people without this credential.

FREEDMAN: There is a beautiful parallel here. Because of the shortage, a lot of agencies take people who have baccalaureates in any field. If you don't know what to do, you become a case worker for a welfare department. The school has now started to look at what we call the continuum of education: at one end the paraprofessional, someone who does not even have a college degree; at the other end, someone who has a doctoral degree. Starting this year we are sending out people with a bachelor's degree in social service through a rather exciting undergraduate program. This raises interesting problems.

PARTICIPANT: It sounds like a step backward to me, certifying people for social work when they have had only one year. The master's degree is a two-year program.

FREEDMAN: This would be a four-year program. You can specify in terms of manpower what you think the baccalaureate-level person is capable of doing, which would not conflict with the master's-level person. What happens now to them is they become middle management types. Most of the front line work, so to speak, because of the shortage, is really handled by people with baccalaureates anyway. We are trying to deal a little bit more realistically with the manpower shortage. The strange thing that is happening is that as people designed courses for this undergraduate program, they found that they could teach pretty much the same thing on an undergraduate level that they were teaching on the master's level. Now the problem becomes: if the undergraduate program is really your old master's program, what should your master's program be?

PARTICIPANT: It puts the pressure on in all kinds of ways.

BUNDY: At Maryland, we have not yet had a meeting of interests. There are some people from the field who would very much like to see this, but we haven't even had the confrontation. We are having it now. To me the most promising thing is the challenge to professional education at the master's level to evolve whole new programs. The worry is that we might be asked to run the undergraduate school. A good question, I think, is how much does a professional school commit itself to the whole continuum?

FREEDMAN: I think this has to be a very conscious consideration of the school.

PARTICIPANT: Well, what are you doing? Are you running the undergraduate program? Not you personally—the school of social work.

FREEDMAN: The school of social work, after not doing it for many years, has just taken over the undergraduate program.

BUNDY: Well, yesterday we were advised to take over the university. Now we add the undergraduate program.

PARTICIPANT: I just don't see how a graduate school and the graduate faculty can be dedicated to graduate education and, at the same time, run an undergraduate program. The aims are different. I don't see it as a continuum.

FREEDMAN: What we have found is that we have recruited different faculty. I am the only one who is teaching on both levels. I am not, you know, a strict professional. I think the graduate program can give a kind of expertise to an undergraduate program that it would not be able to get in any other way.

PARTICIPANT: Years ago in the teaching profession, the trend was to a fifth-year program. In California, it is exclusively fifth-year even for elementary teachers. In library science long ago, in 1947, we started giving up the bachelor's undergraduate program.

BUNDY: One of the realities of it is the existence of it. There are over 300 institutions in the United States turning out people in undergraduate programs who are functioning in professional capacities. This is the undergraduate education program.

PARTICIPANT: They are not accredited by our professional associations.

BUNDY: Well, that's exactly the point.

PARTICIPANT: I don't even interview those people for positions in my library.

BUNDY: Mr. Freedman has given us another parallel in the accreditation association. I was involved recently in a meeting of the deans of library schools talking about the possibility of shifting our accreditation from the ALA to the Association of American Library Schools and inviting the participation of ALA, ASIS [American Society for Information Science], SLA [Special Libraries Association], and other interested groups. One of the key questions that came up, of course, is "Why do we need to do it?" People in schools that now have information science programs said the accreditation association isn't welcoming the kinds of changes we are trying to make. The response from the ALA was, "We have standards that don't preclude your making innovations." This is not enough.

PARTICIPANT: The association you are talking about, the Association of American Library Schools, had accreditation. They had that function from 1914 to 1921 and they muffed it. It became a mutual admiration society. They didn't do the job, so it was taken over by the ALA. This is just a matter of history.

BUNDY: As a matter of fact, I think your facts are wrong. The committee on accreditation had it. I don't believe your facts are right.

PARTICIPANT: They are right.

BUNDY: Let's ask Ralph.

BLASINGAME: It is not right. The Board of Education for Librarianship had an accredited library school starting in 1926 or so, but this was a library association not an association of library . . .

PARTICIPANT: That's what I am talking about. Before that time, there was the Association of American Library Schools. When [Charles C.] Williamson made his survey [Training for Library Service, 1923], the schools that he surveyed were those accredited by themselves as a group.

BLASINGAME: You are implying that a change took place when that survey was made, and that since 1924, somehow some magic device has been supplied which really develops schools whose curricula are suited to the present time. To say that they are better than they were before is to say nothing at all. In the years I have been in librarianship, I don't see any great change in the curriculum.

PARTICIPANT: Well, I say that the profession, which has to use the product, should have something to say about the product. If it is turned back to the schools to accredit themselves, they are not responsive to the profession.

BLASINGAME: He is implying that in the system that exists now there is responsiveness. I would challenge that!

PARTICIPANT: The CLA [Canadian Library Association] is made up of members . . .

BLASINGAME: I don't care what it is made up of. I am saying there is no responsiveness. It doesn't matter who is in it. Just look at the results.

BUNDY: It gives those of us in library education an out. We say, "We put in what they wanted, although we know better." Let us give the library schools of this country, the educators, not the deans, the responsibility for library education and then let's see what they do with it. At present, there is a little game, and it ends up nobody is responsible.

FREEDMAN: This is the basic difference with social work. The accrediting group there is the Council on Social Work Education, which is made up of educators. They accredit both undergraduate and graduate programs. The NASW, the National Association of Social Workers, is the practitioner group. The two are quite separate.

PARTICIPANT: There are professional groups where the accrediting is done by the schools. I think our system is better; the accrediting is done by a professional association rather than by the schools. This is one man's opinion, but it has some validity. I think the change that was made, from the schools' accrediting of themselves in 1924, was a good change.

BLASINGAME: Where is your evidence?

PARTICIPANT: Librarianship has come along very rapidly in the last few years.

BLASINGAME: I absolutely deny that. After looking at literally hundreds of libraries . . .

PARTICIPANT: You deny that library education has improved since the new standards . . .

BLASINGAME: I deny that it has improved since 1947, when I got my first case study.

PARTICIPANT: Speaking as a fairly recent graduate, 1965, even if it has improved since 1924, well, if that's improvement you can have it.

BLASINGAME: Wouldn't it be wise for us to admit that institutions have achieved a kind of internal equilibrium? They have achieved a kind of equilibrium with the environments in which they operate. These equilibrium situations show up in the ideas that are given preference, in the way resources are allocated, in the acceptability of the individual within the institution of the society. As a matter of fact, as a consequence you can say that in the bureaucracy generally, social work, librarianship, museums, et cetera, have to a degree solidified, hardened, in the way they are willing to allocate resources. Change is a challenge, however it occurs and wherever it occurs. The individual who attempts change is going to run into exactly this kind of attitude, that things are just dandy the way they are. So as a consequence, within the whole structure we have very powerful forces at work which limit the function of the bureaucracy.

BUNDY: Jonathan is proposing that professional education lead rather than follow the field of practice. I would like to ask Mr. Galler if this is now what is being done at the Smithsonian. This doesn't take away your right as a member of the profession to have a point of view or hire or not hire a graduate. Still, some schools in this field should be willing to stand up, cross all these imaginary or real boundaries we have talked about, and say, "This is what we are doing. Give us a chance! And then evaluate us!"

PARTICIPANT: Within the present structure, I don't think that the accrediting agent, CLA, is going to stop you.

BUNDY: All right. I will give you an example. The most interesting and exciting work going on in curriculum development right now is going on through a subcommittee of the American Society for Information Science. Some of the most interesting developmental work taking place in curriculum planning in the library field is going on with people interested in undergraduate programs. This is not being brought within a framework. So over here we are in danger of having schools of information science. Over there we are in danger of having undergraduate programs. There is no interesting work going on in curriculum development in library education proper.

It really shouldn't matter who accredits us. We should just get together and do it. But if you go to a meeting of the Association of American Library Schools, by definition, only the faculty of accredited library schools are there. Some of the most innovative thinkers in the whole information spectrum are not there. We are denied access to them. Interestingly enough, they don't want us. You are seeing the splitup of a field. You are seeing the possibility that in the library schools we might be a cohesive force. If your point of view were pursued vigorously, there would be an information profession, but you and I wouldn't be in it.

GALLER: I'm not sure if this is a comment or a question from a person who is not a professional librarian. It seems to me this dialogue exemplifies the opinion that I expressed earlier about the difference between mission orientation and problem orientation. My interpretation of your view is that the method of accrediting is fulfilling its mission. It is producing products designed to fulfill the "librarian" mission. Your point, I believe, is that it is not solving contemporary problems, that the mode is not sufficiently flexible to readjust and mobilize resources around problem-oriented targets rather than straight, classic, traditional fulfillment of missions.

PARTICIPANT: That is an evaluation of my point of view. He speaks as a library educator. I speak as a library director, so naturally we see things from different points of view. I am using the product of his school, of accredited library schools, and I am very happy with it. He doesn't seem to be happy with his product.

BLASINGAME: I spent some twenty years in administration, yet I hadn't been out of administration for six months before I was "accused" of being a library educator. My point is that institutions are museum-oriented bureaucracies. As I look at others, the same thing is true.

I was an administrator for a considerable period of time and an innovator with a certain degree of success. Then I stepped into the academic world and kind of back through the situation. What I see is a bureaucracy with lots of pieces that you can point to as mission oriented. One would be accreditation; another would be admission of students who tend to be practice oriented. The pressures of the field on the school tend to make us stay the same. Do you want a cataloger? Do you want a reference librarian? Do you want this, that, or the other thing? As a result of my whole experience, and after all only six years have been in library education, I am beginning to feel very strongly that as long as practice dominates teaching (and it thoroughly dominates teaching) we are not going to get anywhere.

GALLER: There seems to be a close parallel in medical education as well. The product is certainly fulfilling the mission reasonably well, but is not really designed to cope with the whole series of concentric circles that make up the total problem.

FREEDMAN: There is another element to this. We are in the midst of a period of rapid technological and rapid social change. One of the difficulties becomes (at least in social work, and I think it is also true of some of the new technology in library science) that if you are going to educate people for practice, you cannot really say that the practice of today will be the practice of tomorrow. You would be much wiser to educate people in a manner that allows them to roll with the times—the ability to find out, the ability to put information together, the ability to keep up with the times and the trends.

One of the formulations at our school is that we don't know what the practice that we are educating for will look like. It could be the same. In certain places it probably will be the same as it has always been. But there could be a very good chance that it will be quite different. We are not really going to want to bring in people every five years for retraining. We would rather educate them once and have them be able to do this for themselves. I think this raises a realm of issues for the accreditation process in library science.

PARTICIPANT: This is a matter of selection. It would seem to me that if the library schools emphasize selection, they could choose the sort of person who can, even if he is educated to practice, change with the times, keep up with his profession. If they select a high type, and I think our standards of admission are pretty good in library schools . . .

BUNDY: Do I have to keep telling you you are wrong?

PARTICIPANT: What do you mean by "pretty high," "pretty good"?

BLASINGAME: The measures which you have suggested do not correlate with the steps in developing innovative spirit. Absolutely not!
Indeed, one might say that a B average in a second-rate college really
insures that that person isn't about to try anything new.

FREEDMAN: And you run into another problem. What do you do
with people in your field who have no professional training and don't
even have a baccalaureate, who are out there doing the job as well,
if not better, than someone with all this training? What are the ways
that you give that kind of person legitimacy?

GALLER: Implicit in this dialogue is not just problem versus mission
orientation but libraries-as-satellites-of-user's-institutions versus librar-
ies-as-kind-of-retailers-of-problem-solutions. Now, I can see where a
library that is built and structured to provide services to a certain
kind of institution like a university might be, if not a slave, at least
a captive of the total university establishment, and would be forced
to appraise its role and allocate its resources to meet the demands
by the university group. And depending on the mix of people, the
mix of users in the university, that library might be innovative or
might, in fact, be quite traditional. Whereas, I also sense here that
you are searching for a role for the library and the librarian as a
kind of retailer, a direct relationship to a public, on a problem-solving
basis. If my sense of this discussion is accurate, then I can recognize
how the kind of product that is suitable for your kind of library
would be completely unsuitable for what you may be thinking of.

BLASINGAME: Every study of academic libraries or the use of academic
libraries that we've gotten over a very long period of time says the
same thing over and over again—that the library serves extremely
few people within the college context. Most of the people who come
to it use it as their book room. Period! This situation has existed
for a long time, and yet, if you read the accrediting manual, you
find no mention of measures of effectiveness in terms of how many
people really use the library and what they use it for. You find measures
of how many volumes they have, which is absolutely meaningless.
You find measures of how many square feet of space, how many
dollars go into it in terms of percent of the total, how many staff
are hired, et cetera, et cetera. This situation is self-perpetuating because
we have been taught in the university that that is the way to measure

things. We have done it because we can do it, and do it without extending ourselves, except to build larger and larger empires.

PARTICIPANT: I happen to be involved in law librarianship. People have been admitted to law school just from a high school. Some of them have not even finished high school, and they have done beautiful jobs as lawyers. I am European and I am very much for traditional higher education, but there are individuals who can perform just as well without it. I don't know if we can have the same thing in librarianship, because we have guilds, you know.

PARTICIPANT: Could we change the subject? I'm not ever going to have a chance to get as good an answer to this question again, so I am going to ask it now, because we are talking about the establishment. I have come here this whole week just to find out what the establishment is. Would somebody define it for me?

BUNDY: In the particular session today, responses from the establishment mean responses from the traditional institutions, like professional education, like the Smithsonian. During the week the establishment has meant us: that is, people who exist in the traditional bureaucracies.

PARTICIPANT: I think that word is thrown around rather loosely. Jim Welbourne called his Congress for Change in an establishment situation in order to bring change within the establishment. It seems to me that when changes occur, they will become the establishment. In other words, we have been throwing the word around so loosely, I am confused by just what it means. Is it white middle-class America? Is it Madison Avenue? Is it the guy who works from 9:00 to 5:00 and lives in Silver Spring and owns two cars? What is it? Who is it?

PARTICIPANT: Does it have to be defined?

PARTICIPANT: Yes.

PARTICIPANT: Why?

PARTICIPANT: Well, in the sense of the title of today's session, it is as Mary Lee described; it is a shorthand term that we customarily use.

BUNDY: Let me try it another way. Maybe the establishment in librarianship means those institutions, local, national, et cetera, that are at the moment controlling decision making in our profession. This would include the American Library Association. This definition says those who control the power are the establishment.

FREEDMAN: It's like many words. It is something that is used about other people when it can equally well apply to oneself.

PARTICIPANT: In the context of our profession, what does it mean to be establishment within the library?

BLASINGAME: If you regard the institution, any institution, as having achieved a state of internal equilibrium, and then having achieved also a state of equilibrium with its immediate environment, whatever it is, then I think we would have to say that every person within the organization is a member of the establishment in one degree or another. You can pick out the people who are articulate in the present state of things and say that they are the establishment but, as a matter of fact, it is much more pervasive. It is hard to tell where it begins and ends.

PARTICIPANT: Let's try a functional definition. The establishment could be defined as those who control the services and the products of a society.

BUNDY: For all practical purposes I have severed my connections with the American Library Association. They may represent the views of 20,000 people, but they don't necessarily represent the views of the profession. They are simply organized to say they do. So I refuse to say I left the profession by saying I no longer belong to the American Library Association. This is an antiestablishment view. This is not an establishment view of my position.

FREEDMAN: Yes. But you would still be seen as a full professor in a library school.

GALLER: I think it's awfully important that there be a full response to your question, because we use the word "establishment" more and more as a term of opprobrium. Perhaps the view that we take of this very ill-defined something runs the risk of overlooking the positive contributions that could come from what we call the establishment. It's not all black; it's not all white. It may be more rigid than it should be. It may have different priorities, different targets from what we think it should have. It may be allocating resources that in our view are not designed to meet the high-priority problems.

PARTICIPANT: You sound very much like my friend here did just a moment ago when he was disputed.

GALLER: Except for one thing. I am not passing a judgment as to whether it's good or bad. I am saying that before we decide that we want to dump it because its useless, let's make sure that we know what it is, and whether there is anything that is salvageable that can be turned in the direction that we feel needs . . .

BUNDY: Another thing is that the people involved in sort of anti-establishment movements are organizing. I have a point of view I now want to relate to people. I would like to have some common objectives. I think we are very sensitive to the problems of bureaucracy. I think we are prepared to say this organization will go out of business once it has achieved certain objectives, but I wish I knew more about how to do it. If you set up a institution parallel to the American Library Association, one of your objectives should be to go out of business after you change the American Library Association. These are suicide missions, sort of.

PARTICIPANT: I am amused that in this context I am being regarded as a friend of the establishment and playing a conservative role. When I worked for Russell Shank at Berkeley, I was considered antiestablishment in those circles. This is the first time in my life I have ever been cast in the role of an establishment person or a conservative. I think this man and I would agree that although we are in the establishment and defend it, we likewise are aware that there are changes needed.

GALLER: I will agree, except for the phrase "defending it." I'm not defending it. I am looking at it in a very objective and hopefully scientific way to try to see whether it is the most suitable mechanism for reaching problem-oriented goals. If it isn't, why isn't it? What can be done to salvage, or change, or improve, or adapt it? If nothing, then let's all agree to junk it. I come back to the point that this gentleman made. I suppose those who are antiestablishment from their own establishment, if there are enough of them to rally together with a common purpose and a common objective, may create a very suitable establishment.

PARTICIPANT: But there is no such thing as an ad hoc establishment. It would become just as hidebound and as unresponsive to change as the ALA appears to be to some people.

BUNDY: We don't know yet. Some of these new groups in this profession haven't had an opportunity to show us. It seems to me it is one of those things that Jim Welbourne had on his mind in the Congress for Change. It came out as a movement instead of an organization. I'm not sure I understand the difference between movements and organizations.

GALLER: Well, I understand the difference. I think a movement can produce a confrontation without a solution, whereas an organization can provide a mechanism for a solution to a confrontation.

FREEDMAN: Movements have a tendency to come up as a response to problems, and organizations in response to missions.

PARTICIPANT: John Wesley started the Methodist society as a movement, but it became a organization parallel to the Church of England. It became an establishment very quickly.

FREEDMAN: This is one of the tendencies. Saul Alinsky, the noted organizer, has said on occasion that organizations should have time bomb mechanisms so that they will go out of business within three to five years. If they are working on a problem, they will have done whatever it is they were going to do in that time.

GALLER: I don't think it needs to be that way.

BUNDY: I was on an ad hoc committee to recruit people into librarianship. The first round is over, but now that we have recruited them, we had better worry about educating them. We have decided to go on.

PARTICIPANT: And you try to set up new ideas. Now you want to find out how to produce a booklet and all of this for recruiting . . .

BUNDY: Let me give some of the reasons for it. The reasons for it are the satisfactions you get out of working with a group of people who share the same mission, who want to solve the same problem. In the practice of librarianship we have really been deprived of the sense of going at an objective and solving it. If I ever went back to practice I would have to have that. Somehow I would have to have one little part of that library where there were four or five of us working on something, even if the whole library weren't organized that way; I couldn't go back to practice without it. One of the real problems is not that we will organize and become a bureaucracy, but that without legitimacy we can't find each other and keep up our communications. If we can only get to one association meeting a year, we must meet when the ALA meets. There are more strikes against us on a geographical basis nationally because of the difficulty of finding people who feel the same and who want to solve the problem. I don't think the danger is bureaucracy at this stage; the danger is lack of coordination and communication.

FREEDMAN: Also, education for problem solving is quite different from education to have a niche in an organization.

BLASINGAME: Let me point out that I am much too realistic to talk about dumping the establishment. My plea is for understanding of what it is and how it operates. Until we understand it, we are never going to get to the point where we can bring ourselves to depart from mission-training operations.

BUNDY: The thing I keep saying is, it's nice to have young people come into the profession change oriented. Now, I am at the stage in life where some of my friends are deans of library schools. They all seemed like reasonable people when I was in the doctoral program with them. Now they have taken on so much commitment that no stimulus whatsoever would shift the leadership of this profession.

GALLER: Perhaps we will never be able to define the establishment in a way that will satisfy all of us. Perhaps another approach is not to try to define the establishment as such, but to agree on a set of criteria that have to be considered in order to produce solutions to problems, and then compare the existing apparatus with those criteria and see if, indeed, that apparatus is suitable.

PARTICIPANT: Those who are able to decide the criteria would be the establishment, those who are in a position to decide if we are going to try to maintain this organization and bring it back to equilibrium, if it still has possibilities, or to junk it, if it doesn't.

BUNDY: Let's give Dr. Galler a chance with his criteria. Maybe he was going to give us some. Were you?

GALLER: I was going to look at the situation from the standpoint of a biologist and see what some of these essential criteria are. Number one, they have to be adaptive, a high degree of adaptability.

BUNDY: What has to be adaptive?

GALLER: Whatever mechanisms exist. Number two, they have to be self-organizing in order to be adaptive. Number three, they have to have the ability of self-recognition in order to be adaptive. Number four, they have to be self-corrective in order to reduce errors and improve their efficiency for coping with problems.

BUNDY: All right. Now let me ask you this. As some of the reformers in the library profession challenge the national association, the response from those who control power is that until they see positive programs of action there is no basis for change. Yet this is implicit in their asking for change in leadership. Are these criteria you are bringing up?

PARTICIPANT: From the biological point of view, you are forgetting one thing. They have to have the ability to duplicate themselves. Otherwise they will be extinct.

GALLER: To duplicate, but not to replicate. I am sorry. I withdraw that. To replicate, but not to duplicate. It's a fine but important distinction. You have to be able to replicate in the sense of producing other mechanisms that have the same degree of adaptability but with the potential for improvement.

BUNDY: What happens if you leave out replication? It isn't going to die, is it?

GALLER: When we think of the establishment, the organizations exist to solve problems. Do they meet the criteria needed to solve problems? If they do, are there enough of these organizations in existence to meet the demands for problem solving? If not, we should be prepared to replicate the organizations. And, of course, we have to be prepared to replicate the units of the organization, the human resources.

PARTICIPANT: If it is self-adapting, it will be changing constantly, getting feedback, making corrections.

PARTICIPANT: It might be well to remember that in the living organism you have the capacity for making mistakes. It is through making mistakes in the production of the next generation that we get change. We tend to attribute will to the change in the living organism, whereas it is probably totally a matter of chance. I don't know much about biology, but I understand that every living thing has a genetic system. By virtue of the fact that it has to be repeated many hundreds of thousands of times, there are changes. Some of these changes, which we might regard as mistakes, turn out to be better adapted to the environment than others. Most of the mutants die off because they are less well adapted. A few of them survive and create changes within an organization. Human organizations have no such inbuilt devices for random change. Whether we should look for mechanisms for random change or mechanisms for planned change I feel is a good question.

GALLER: I don't want to strain the analogy with the biological organism. Forgetting for a moment about random change, if there is a mechanism for recognizing and correcting mistakes, self-recognition, which means self-improvement, coupled with the potential for adaptiveness, will enable the apparatus to recognize and respond to changing problems.

BUNDY: I'm going to stop us now and thank these gentlemen very much.

6

RESPONSES FROM THE ESTABLISHMENT: MODELS AND CUES FROM OTHER FIELDS (PART TWO)

WEDNESDAY EVENING, AUGUST 13

LECTURER: REV. GENO BARONI

BUNDY: I briefly told Father Baroni where we were and tried to give him a role within our structure, but we are perfectly agreeable to your going in any direction you like. He has two or three things that interest him very much that, it seems to me, would interest us, so why don't I just let Father Baroni talk.

BARONI: We were just talking here about structures and what seems to be happening. I work in a free-lance kind of area. I am very interested in social change, especially social change of a large, middle-class consensus group, which makes up the American society. I believe that our urban crisis, for example, is not down the street where I live, which is Fourteenth and B Streets downtown. I don't believe that the urban problem is there. I don't believe the urban crisis is there. I believe the urban problem is in our educated, middle-class, newly arrived elite. I believe that religion and education are responsible for creating this middle-class consensus group. I don't know about religion. I just dropped off a nun who is marrying a priest friend of mine in a couple of weeks.

When we look at our own structures, especially if you are trying to be on the cutting edge and trying to change and reform structure,

234

it seems to me that some of our institutions are falling apart. I am talking about church institutions. Some of them are falling apart with a divine significance. I would have to say the human institutions of the church are falling apart with a divine significance. I think that is very healthy, because that makes us face up to things.

I really believe that the rapid urbanization of our society, and the decline of the relevance of the major faiths create for us what we call a secular city, a polarized city, or a pluralistic city. I also believe that the bad housing, the overcrowding, the despair, the loneliness, the frustration, the political disenfranchisement, all these things, are forces at work stifling the development of human life, spawning misery in that marvelous achievement of man that is supposed to be known as a city. You just have to take a look at Washington to see where we are and where we have to go.

Take our metropolitan complex, Washington, D.C. Of course, we have our beltway, and it should have done a lot of nice things. At the time of Lincoln, the Washington metropolitan area had a 25 percent black population. Today, 100 years later, the Washington metropolitan area still has only a 25 percent black population. So what's happened? The city is 72 percent black. Ninety-six percent of the school children are black in the city. This is higher than any other city in the country. What about the suburbs, which are 96 percent white? The District line is like the red wall of Berlin—a symbol of separation, discrimination, and everything else.

I think we are developing a fantastic culture gap between the new middle class and the new poor. This culture gap has some fantastic characteristics, economic characteristics. Millions of people moved out of the city to suburbia during World War II. They moved out in the typically middle-class affluent way to share the productivity. They moved out to their little mini-meadows. Millions of people moved out; millions of people moved in.

So who was left in the city? The aged, the technologically unemployed, those who picked cotton or peaches in the South and came North to find themselves as the "manchild in the so-called promised land" that Claude Brown talks about. Left behind in the city are the people who have been products of the southern rural school system, unprepared and unable now to cope with modern urban life, and trapped in a ghetto which is morally, economically, and sociologically perpetrated by what I call the white middle-class consensus group.

So we have the economic gap. We have the racial gap. We have the social gap. If you want to go to Bethesda, or Chevy Chase, Maryland, or Falls Church, Virginia, you go on the beltway, which is called the "Negro bypass."

We have fantastic economic, social, racial, physical separations in our society, in our culture. I was taught in the public and the private school systems about the same thing. I was taught that we had to make it. I was taught you cannot be a coal miner like your old man who just came off the boat from Italy. You can't be a snotty-nosed Italian or a snotty-nosed Irish. You've got to be somebody. You've got to be something. We had the competitive American kind of thing. I call it the *Readers' Digest* mentality. This *Reader's Digest* mentality of making it as an individual—be something, be somebody—is different with a kid at Fourteenth and Swan. "Willie Smith," you say, "throw out the slings and arrows of misfortune. You are going to grow up. Study hard and you are going to be somebody." He looks around Fourteenth and Swan, and says, "Be what?"

We were brainwashed with this tremendous ethic and the tremendous educational system. What did it make us? It made each of us into an individualized, departmentalized individual who cares only about himself. In a typically American individualistic way, we have this fantastic migration to suburbia to share in what an affluent gross national product can provide.

Religion only baptized that. Religion said, "All you have to do is save your own soul. Worry about your own skin, your own soul." We have this materialistic thing, this religious thing. Put them together and we have this departmentalized, individualistic product of our educational, religious system. This person is a great individual. Everybody now in the suburbs looks very much the same—Protestants, Catholics, Jews. Everybody dresses nice. Everybody looks nice. Everybody smells nice. When it comes to the question of urban crisis or social change, they are S.O.B.'s. They are really bad, very, very bad.

It is that large, middle-class American consensus group that is the issue, that is the problem. I am in one of those institutions where many of these people belong. What has happened? All our structure, every cotton-picking, Catholic order in this community started out teaching kids who were poor. They were starting hospitals for poor people. But they moved up with the snotty-nosed Italians and Irish. Now all our people are newly arrived, modest middle class. They are part of the large American middle class. That is the consensus group. The people here are not responsible for the problems here.

Blacks are so right. But I can go beyond the blacks. The Italians have a better word. Some of my relatives are in the Mafia. The Italians say "cosa nostra," which means, "Do your own thing. Do our thing!" I worked with some black contractors in several housing programs. This black contractor was absolutely floored that some other black guy was hustling for protection money to watch his buildings or else they wouldn't get finished, they wouldn't be there. I said, "Well, the Mafia has been doing that for years."

The problems are the cities, like Washington. One-third of the people live below the poverty line, in Washington, where the mortality rate is 70 percent. This means that blacks have died at a rate 70 percent higher than whites. This means that at this time this year, there should be 2,500 more blacks living than there were last year, if they had died at the same rate as whites.

Go beyond mortality to morbidity. Look at the fantastic consequences of city life, the violence that is done. People say to me, "What are you going to do about riots, violence?" Where does the violence come from? The violence comes from the structures of welfare, of housing, of employment, of health. These things do violence to life. All the Job Corps in the world are not going to save the kids who are being scared and crippled by the violence of life. And the violence of life comes from these structures in the institutions. I have seen ten-year-old twins with T.B. I have seen kids at Children's Hospital with their fingers bitten off by rats. I have found in my garbage can a blood-stained pillow case with a full-term, newborn, but dead, child in it.

Who knows the humiliation? In the old Hebrew scripture, there was a word for murder, but the same word meant humiliation. Murder kills the body. We see red. It is against the law and all that. Humiliation is worse than murder. It doesn't kill the body. Humiliation kills the spirit. It kills the soul. Millions of people are born who are going to be destroyed by the violence of life, scarred and crippled by the violence of life.

For example, a mother recently was on the street outside the Women's Bureau. We have 148 agencies in the city who are supposed to work for the poor. What happens? There is a great dichotomy between their good intentions and their ability to deliver. Here was a mother, disoriented. The children had to go to Junior Village. The mother went to the psychiatric ward of the hospital. The mother died three days later, twenty-nine years old, five children. I don't know what she died of medically. She really died of a broken mind and a broken heart. What happened to her husband? What happened to her children? This is the violence of life. The issue is: who killed Mary Ethridge? Senator Byrd and the welfare system? the D.C. school system? the housing system? These are the structures of society. They aren't meeting needs. They aren't responding to human needs. Why aren't they responding to human needs? Because Congress and the middle-class status quo are not responding to human needs.

Last year we had the riots. I still have trailer trucks full of clothes. We got canned goods for the Poor People's Campaign. I opened up some of these cans. They are unmarked cans. Open them up and you get artichoke hearts, pimentos, all junk that somebody was trying to get rid of. Give it to the poor! This individualistic, paternal, rural, individualistic, compartmentalized mentality! This individualistic mentality responds to poverty in an individualistic way.

It never passes Christmas Eve that some good, middle-class doctor calls up. He is already celebrating. He has had a few drinks. He says, "Look, I have two station wagons loaded and I am going to help some family. Just give me the address." There is a tremendous guilt also in this new middle class. This doctor was taught by his grandmother that you can't have Christmas unless you help somebody. We have a compartmentalized subconscience and an individualistic conscience, but there is no social conscience that carries over to the economic, the social, the political, and the international spheres.

So this group here, the educated, middle-class elite, the large consensus group of the American society, where most people are, has no social conscience. You go to a synagogue, Baptist church, Lutheran church, Catholic church. You say Mary Brown has five children; her husband is destroyed; her kids are being scarred and crippled; she needs this and she needs that; and people respond beautifully. Americans are very generous as individuals. You can get all the second-hand underwear you want to help Mary Brown. But you talk to them about Mary Brown who has to go to court and charge her husband with nonsupport, kick the husband and father out of the house to get a meager minimum below $75, a thing which nobody can live on; even Radcliffe girls couldn't live on these budgets. This is what the system of welfare does to the individual. You talk to the same group that gave us ten times the clothing and all this second-hand underwear for an individual. You talk to them about changing the welfare system. What does the middle-class consensus group respond with? "Oh, those people! They are illegitimate, immoral, lazy, no good so-and-so's." What are they responding as? They are responding as Social Darwinists. They are hostile. They are resentful. They are fearful of any program of social change that will change the health, the welfare, the housing, the employment structures of our society.

We watch Congress here because we are a colony. We don't have the right to vote. What was Congress doing that morning? Dirksen was up there talking about praying in the school. I couldn't give a damn if people pray in the school or don't pray in the school. I went to a white Protestant public school. I was one of three Catholics. Kids used to ask me when I was teaching school, why didn't I get married? I said, "Well, there were three Catholics in my public school. Two of them got married, and I didn't have any choice." Every teacher I had was a white Sunday school teacher who was shoving the Bible down our throats, making us sing songs, making us read Bibles. I had to go to the Baptist church for baccalaureate or else I wouldn't have graduated. Here I am a Catholic with a neurotic guilt complex developing already. But now, talking about change, we are singing those same hymns now in the Catholic church. I know them all. "Righteous Is Our God" by Martin Luther. We used to think Martin Luther was the second devil. Things do change, for the wrong reasons.

What happens, and what has happened, is that our newly arrived middle class are scared to death, are hostile, resentful of programs of social change. You can talk to the Irish. In our structure the Irish are the worst. The blacks and the Irish are going to get together some day. It's like Detroit. You take the blacks and the Poles and you've got 75 percent of the city. So we are trying to develop a Polish caucus to agree to what they want, so they can meet the black caucus and come out agreeing on a few things. But what happens to the Irish? The Irish are scared to death of the Protestant public school system. What are they afraid of? It's very familiar now. I get the same rhetoric. They are afraid of their culture. They are afraid of their identity. They are afraid of losing this. They are afraid of losing that. So their teachers weren't educated. Some of them couldn't even speak English. Italians and Irish teachers started their own school systems to protect themselves against an alien, foreign culture. They didn't want to be brainwashed. We are getting the same thing now from the black community. So we have a whole network of schools that are going broke.

I am proposing that we just transfer them over into the community. Let them run their own school! Let them do their own thing. I have worked with economic development and tried to get money for new guys to go into business and so forth. There is no equity in the ghetto. Two small guys are in business and they are crying the blues. Why? Because the people in their neighborhood still think that the white man's ice is better than the black man's ice. That's how destructive our kind of system has been.

What have we been taught in our whole structure? I used to teach *Silas Marner*. That's about the worst thing you could teach. I wish librarians would burn it. What do *Silas Marner* and *Ivanhoe*, and so forth, have to do with kids who are supposed to face the real world? That's what the curriculum calls for. Instead of giving kids Alan Paton, or Malcolm X, or other real stuff, you have to fight the system all the time. What I am saying in all this is, and this is the issue, how do we reach them? We are white. We have our options. The blacks are going to do their own thing. If they want to buy a carload of ice, and want to do it their own way, that is their privilege. We've goofed up plenty, so let them make their own mistakes. They will get themselves together.

My experience has been that you can take kids from the poorest black school and put them in the fanciest white suburban school. The black kids demolish the white kids. They just demolish them, because the black kids have been in the movement, and the white kids don't know what it is all about. They come up in this suburban hothouse, where everything looks the same and smells the same. They just get shattered. We are reaping the harvest now of this kind of an individualistic thing that we have talked of, competitive, materialistic, and so on.

If we ended the war tomorrow, this big group of people here, the American consensus group, would not take our $30 billion out of Vietnam and do what we have to do, because the scandal of affluence is that we have tolerated millions of people living in our midst without hope—some because of race, some because of poverty, and some because of both. We've got the money, the technology, the science, the know-how, the resources, to put every man, woman, and child in this country on their feet and to begin to do it around the world. Why don't we do it? Because this large, educated, middle-class elite doesn't have the will, the heart, the soul, the guts, or whatever you want to call it. It is not a technical thing. It is really not a technical thing.

If this group, going back to Congress the day they were voting about praying in the school—the same senators, and I counted them, who voted to have praying in the school, trying to put it back in—they were the same senators, the same day, who voted against extending the school lunch program for poor kids. The same senators who wanted the praying in the schools were the ones who were saying, "We don't want to expand the urban teacher corps. We don't want to expand anything." The same ones! That was the day I remembered because here was this little kid who was running home with his so-called surplus food. Food that we don't want, so we give it to the poor people. This little kid is running home with this surplus food for his brothers and sisters to share and gets hit by a ten-ton truck at U Street. The same people will always say, "Well, what can we do?"

Over here in northern Virginia you have an area, a congressional district, where there is an average of one-and-a-half college graduates per family, not bad products of the system. Who do they send to Congress? Broyhill! He does more damage to us in the city and to the poor in the city than any 10,000 people. All the second-hand underwear in the world isn't enough. I remember when the Georgetown kids used to come down into the ghettos in the old days wearing their Goldwater buttons. They wanted to do something for poor kids. It was a tutoring rage then. These kids said, "Gee, these little kids are smart. Too bad they didn't inherit department stores."

The Georgetown kids still want to come down and help. I think that's good. So where should they go? They should take their know-how, their ingenuity, their time, their energy. They should go over here and organize this white community and stay out of the black one. They should organize the white community and send somebody to Congress who is going to make some changes in the structure, like in health and welfare, employment, schools, libraries, and so on. That's what we should do but we're too lazy, especially the liberals. They are too lazy to organize and do the dirty work and all the leg work it takes.

What did they do in suburban Maryland this year? They sent us Hogan, who is going to be another Broyhill. Another Broyhill! In

1966, we got "one man–one vote," so I said, "Hooray!" I wasn't worried about the Eastlands or the Stennises. I was worried about those congressmen from the Eastern Shore, up in the rural area, where they send a congressman to town with 20,000 people, while the suburbs are sending a congressman to town with 350,000 people. So the suburbs got extra congressmen, and I said, "Hooray!" These extra twenty new suburbanite congressmen came to town from the educated middle class. Eighteen out of twenty of those new congressmen who came to town in 1966 voted wrong on every single issue affecting the city.

So the issue is how do we now reach, reeducate, retrain? How do we create, not an individualized, compartmentalized, narrow person? What's happening to people who are afraid of freedom and of openness? This happens in the church, as well as in democracy. When people are afraid of openness and freedom, what's their option as an answer to urban problems? Fascism! I hear them. "Shoot the looters! Put the National Guard out there! Shoot to kill, those people, these people, them people." The whole thing is fear, tremendous fear because of a lack of being free or open. There's a natural tendency to lock up. Fascism is an option. Put the bars around the city and lock it up.

BUNDY: Put them in concentration camps.

BARONI: That's fascism, right! The other options are militant legal social change or chaos or violence. There was an instance I remember during the riots. This was in Detroit, Twelfth Street in Detroit. They had a special documentary all night to explain the riot. Everybody was watching television. The streets were burning. They had scenes of burning and looting and so forth. Then they had the everlasting commercial. What was the first commercial? Fly Pan Am to Paris! Have dinner at Maxim's! Charge it! . . . Back to the riot! What do these people want? Why do we have riots? After more documentary, a second commercial. What was it? The good-looking, all-American guy, with the good-looking, all-American chick, driving his Mustang down to the beach, throwing out a blanket, bringing out those six-packs, lighting up his 100-centimeter cigarette. The good life! . . . Back to the riot! We learned more about the riots from the commercials. The next commercial was what? Honest to God, the next commercial was a guy driving home in a station wagon to the little pad in the mini-meadow with the wife with the everlasting barbecue thing out, making the hamburgers. She jumps off the roof and lights up his 101-centimeter cigarette. . . . Then back to the riots!

So you wonder why the sixteen-year-old kid who's in the Neighborhood Youth Corps program with his first $42, takes his check, looks at it, puts it in his pocket, walks down the street. Then begins to look for it, puts it in another pocket, keeps looking to make sure he has it, and wonders what he should do with it. Should he buy his mother a new dress? She hasn't had one for three years. Or does he go down and buy a $40 pair of Italian shoes? What does this come from?

I am only throwing these things out. This is the greatest challenge we have, and the greatest responsibility we have. Otherwise the only options are chaos, violence, or fascism, or some tremendous legal militant social change. Because what are the young kids saying? What are the first-generation kids, who come out of the middle-class suburbs and onto college campuses, saying? Coming out of the black movement, what are these kids saying? These kids have a crisis of faith in two things. Democracy! They have a crisis of faith in democracy. They don't think it will work. I was with a bunch of kids who just said, "The hell with it! You are the ambulance service. You are going around picking up the pieces for the establishment. Let it collapse! What are you going to do as an alternative? The hell with it. Let it collapse! It's not working. It's not going to work."

They say the same thing about the church. "The church is really dope. It is hung up with the status quo. It won't help create change." We talk about priests leaving. Why do they leave? Some have got hangups. But celibacy isn't the thing either. Not all of it! Some people turn to a personal relationship after they get tired of fighting the system. We worked with some Protestants who brought back seventy-five guys from Korea, Protestant missionaries. They brought back seventy-five Protestant missionaries. They trained them for one year for a "new missions" field in the suburbs. After one year, forty of the seventy-five wanted to go back to Korea. It's not easy.

We need models. We need work. We have never had a white movement. We've got to take a look at our ethnic thing. The first-generation Italian was screwed up. I took my genuine Italian salami to school. It smelled of garlic and all that. The teacher beat me up and told me to switch it with some kid who had cheap American Safeway bologna. We never had a pot to cook in. We ate the snails, the gizzard, the tripe, all the things which you now have to go to a fancy restaurant to get. But the ethnic groups don't understand. All the cops who live in Chevy Chase or Hillcrest Heights, like the coal miner's son from Pennsylvania, don't understand that they might have been materially poor, but they had a culture. They had a tradition. They had a history. They had a family life. They were culturally and historically complete. They were not forced to come here. Family life was not destroyed. My father with three bottles of wine is related to Garibaldi. With the fourth bottle, he is related to da Vinci, and my father can't even read. He's got a pride of culture, of identity, of stability, of skills. The ethnic groups don't understand this. We never taught it; we never learned it. They say, "We made it. Why can't they make it?"

So we have to look again back to the ethnic thing and figure out how to reach this new middle class. Now the middle-class Italian, the shoemaker's son, has become a gynecologist, a nurse, or a teacher. Now they all call me up and want to know if I have any old Caruso records. They want to try to prove their identity. They want to learn a word of Italian. They are looking for a piece of Italian furniture, something related to their culture, their identity. We have got to take a look at all these things.

I don't know where this fits in with what you are talking about. I just know that I was a librarian; I was a teacher. I'll be damned if I was going to teach *Silas Marner*. I looked at the kids. The first thing I made them do was write down on a piece of paper all the books they had read, whether it was Mickey Mouse or Spiro Angew's watch, anything they had read.

You have got to pray for Nixon, because I was on a program with the Vice President the other day, and he was absolutely out of it about the urban scene. You know what he said to five hundred mayors and county executives about the urban crisis?—and this is the truth. I know because I was sitting right there. He said, "What you all have to do is get together. Learn how to buy your gasoline wholesale from one neighborhood to another. Get a computer so you can make your payroll out cheaper." That was his solution to the urban crisis. That was the depth of it. At the same time, people out here in this neighborhood are always saying, "Too bad you live in the city! Too bad about those people. Too bad we don't have their problems. Too bad we can't do anything about it. Too bad, too bad!"

Something is wrong. The problem is not down there because the blacks are going to do their cosa nostra, their thing. Two things can happen. We can get a black Hitler, maybe, or we can get a white Hitler. We might get a combination of both, or we might get something else. I don't know what we are going to get, but I think we are going to get what we deserve.

BUNDY: The gentleman from the Civil Service Commission who spoke to us earlier said to me at the coffee break, "Please don't go to the ghetto! Please go to the suburbs!" I think you have said it for us in more detail.

PARTICIPANT: Would you comment for us briefly on Nixon's welfare recommendation?

BARONI: Yes. Well, I should talk about Protestants, because I think the churches get the preachers they deserve—Catholics and Protestants. I won't speak about the rabbis. One night after the riots, one rabbi called all the businessmen together. It was a Friday night, of course. He was going to have a special service. He called me up and said, "You had better come out here. We might have another crucifixion. These guys are going to nail me to a cross."

Nixon sounded very much like the Protestant ethic thing. "We've got to help people so they can work. If they can work, let's make them work." He just doesn't have the style or class. There is a good thing there. There is a departure, a change. It's specious, but somebody has made a breakthrough. Maybe it's not done right. It's not enough, but there is a basic change of structure hinted and implied. Consider the welfare system we have now. I have never met a mother who wanted to be on welfare. I have seen this dependency thing destroy people. You wonder where the self-hate comes from. It comes from that kind of a system. That has really got to go. How it will work out mathematically I don't know, but it is a departure.

Everything else in our system right now, everything we do, even in the church, must change. Now we do everything in English. A few old ladies want everything back in Latin. With kids who have had 3,000 hours of television before they hit first grade you can't do a repetitive worship. I don't see how teen-agers can sit still in school after they have had this fantastic learning experience. I have seen some fantastic teachers teaching the toughest kids, though. I have seen learning processes happening. Yet I have seen the law-and-order teachers fail, both black and white, because the black teachers who are now the principals came through the white system. They are still trying to use this system to teach black kids.

There are some changes. They gang up on some teachers. I know a librarian who got kicked out of a local high school because he tried to change the system. He got kicked out by a black because everybody in the school had to comply. But why? Because the black teachers had become the law-and-order teachers, also. "Shut up and sit down! Learn or else." Whereas, I saw three teachers take kids who wouldn't go to school—the classroom looked like chaos, but they introduced them to Romeo and Juliet. With a little briefing, a little bit of lingo to understand what it was about, they put those kids on an old bus, took them to see Zeffirelli's "Romeo and Juliet." Then they took the bus to MacDonald's parking lot. Everybody had hamburgers. They stayed there for a whole day with a bunch of kids that couldn't sit still in anybody's class. Those kids wanted to go back to school and discuss the thing. All the other teachers thought these three teachers were nuts.

The great problem, I believe, is we have new gifts coming up. We have new gifts, new spirit. I think we will be prompted. People are prompted to try and change. I also believe we need the new gifts to meet new needs. I think our structures and our institutions get in the way. We have to develop new structures to make these changes. And what happens? The individual gets so frustrated that he gives up. He runs in to the principal and the principal beats him down. We don't know how to organize. We don't know how to organize changes.

BUNDY: Could we take your institution, the Catholic church, and talk about change within, or about you as an example of change? How many others of you are there? What have you seen happening in the last few years? Or am I shifting too far away from the urban scene too fast?

BARONI: The church is in the same trouble as the democratic system. Sometimes we do the right thing for the wrong reason. We make a change but do it for the wrong reason. It is too late. There is a dread fear of openness. Yet, at the same time, here is our democratic system 175 years old, and it is getting stale. It's getting stale. Unless we can regenerate, revitalize, it is going to go. That's where I agree with the kids. It is going to go.

WELBOURNE: You said earlier in your speech, and I have to agree, that the problem, as far as the democratic society is concerned, is in the institutions. We are doing a service, even sitting here, by trying to seek constructive reforms from within, and doing it in a bureaucratic manner. And the people for whom we are supposed to be doing it say, "Let it go! Let it go!" We are going to work on a new site or on a demolished site and build a new structure, but the old building is getting in the way of the new one.

BARONI: There is a real gap there. This is what we call the 1963 hero reentry era of the white clergyman into the ghetto. I don't know where teachers and librarians are in this area. But we have this hero reentry thing. Some kid comes from Hopkins, the suburb of Hopkins, outside of Minneapolis. He comes down to the ghetto. In an individual way, I could sit around and see seventeen families a day, or however many you could see in a day. The welfare check-writing machine doesn't work except on Tuesday. Therefore, Tuesday is the first of the month. If it's Friday, give somebody some second-hand clothes, a food order, some food stamps to carry them over, stretch the system. You can do that, on the one hand. On the other hand, you can go out and change the system. Raise the minimum wage, and tens of thousands of people wouldn't have to come around begging for seconds to make ends meet. They would work out their own thing. That was the problem with the Moynihan report a couple of years ago. That was why it was very much misunderstood. If you raise the wage, if you change the minimum wage thing, you can affect the 45,000 people in Washington on welfare.

There are an equal number of people, working people, making less than $3,000 a year. There are 90,000 people working in Washington who are underemployed, who could be doing better and who should be doing better. Add up those 45,000 and the other 45,000 and 90,000 and put little brackets around it. Throw in another 75,000 who are over sixty-five. They all equal what? Unhappy people! People living without hope!

At the same time, we need to begin to revitalize our cities. I mess around with housing. What do you do with a man who is eighty-five years of age, who has lived in the same house for thirty-six years? He has paid rent. All he's got are boxes full of rent receipts. Then he gets a thirty-day notice to move out. He could have bought that house three times. Why didn't he buy it? Because credit wasn't given by the savings and loan companies to black men. What did that do to him as a man? What did that do to his children, his whole family structure?

How do you create economic development in a place? It's like a sheet of ice with a puck. There is no equity. A man has to have an equity. A man has to have a piece of the action. A man has to have a share. What all people want is to have a say over the things that affect their life, to have a piece of it. I don't know what my problem is. If we ever got hold of the system, if we ever got hold of that defense budget, for example, . . .

The kids did a lot with the peace thing. Gene McCarthy might be a screwball, but he served as a process. He knocked Johnson out of the picture. The war thing grew out of a handful of kooky preachers and kids. There's a tremendous antiwar feeling. If we could only build up in the middle-class consensus group an idea of what to do with that $30 billion budget, we could produce. We need 26 million new housing units in the next ten years. Multiply that times $20,000 per house, and you will see where we could spend the $30 billion. We need 600,000 units of low-income housing each year for the next ten years. What did we do last year? Altogether we made 141,000 units in the whole country.

WELBOURNE: Father, I can't argue with your motivation or your goals, except I think it produces what we called earlier in the week the "model city syndrome." Once you have identified what has to be done, where you want to go, then the system almost dictates the method by which you do it. If you are going to cheat me, the system tells you how to do it. Because the structure in which these changes are to occur dictates it, it takes the form of study group committees. These are time consuming. Part of the problem is how to get those three or four houses on the block. There is the process of talking about it, planning for it, how to go about it, where is the money coming from . . .

BARONI: I agree with you. But you know what the problem is? I would go all the way with you, except I have one problem. What happens when you get a group of dissidents together? I went to a commune for supper the other day. I have a good stomach, so when the cats were walking over the dishes before the meal, it didn't bother me. Here was a bunch of rebel kids all living together, boys and girls, young men and young women, all living together in this house.

They even had their own school. They had their own teachers, five teachers. They had a little elementary school; now they have a high school for about fifty or seventy-five kids. But I never saw a group that was more autocratic! The same group that wants due process in things that affect their lives, they were just like Hitler, bossing around.

We have the same problem in the church. As soon as you join a rebel group, an underground group, some Messiah type, some tough type, makes all decisions. He bosses everybody around. We've seen it in the civil rights movement. We've seen it inside the church. We have seen it in the underground. The same people say, "Democracy doesn't work." When they put together their thing, we still have that old human thing of "I give the orders. I make the decisions. You do it or else you get out." I saw a kid that I taught in school the other day, and I said, "Hi, Ed." He said, "I am Colonel Major Hakeom." I had to snap to, and he just went, "Boom, boom, boom, boom." And I said, "Well, don't I have a say about that?" "Nope. I made the decision, I am Major Blank, and my outfit is named so and so, and we do methadone. We know how to solve the drug problem." I said, "Well, if I get the money, can't the people who are going to give some of the money have a say in how you run the thing?" "Nope." O.K. He ran his organization like the paramilitary, the same problem we have with the police departments.

I am wondering, taking human contacts, if there is something in between. I agree with you that my problem is, I believe, in an evolutionary change. I am just wondering if it can happen good enough and fast enough. In our society, we don't have any excuse. I don't know what they do in South America or India or China. If you get a bowl of rice in China every day I guess you are well off Take Manhattan Auto, which is down on Seventh and Rhode Island. The Georgetown kids used to drive up there with their old Jaguars. What was the first place that was bombed out in the ghetto? It was the imported car Jaguar place. They had just built a $1 million new shop down there. That place was the first place to go. It is fantastic, the resentment and hostility.

PARTICIPANT: Father, would you comment on ways in which this newly arrived, middle-class, suburban white American can be reached? BARONI: Yes. Last year we tried a program on 1,600 people. We were looking for models. I hate traditional research, but there ought to be some action research. We took a city, an area with twenty-five churches in it. We started from the city line, where people were scared to death of changing. It was an area where people were afraid of new people moving in, competing for their street life, their school life, their social life, and all that junk. I saw a neighborhood where there were ten or fifteen signs saying, "This home is armed." We took twenty-five churches and collected twenty-five key people from each one into a group of four hundred, or whatever. We took fifty-nine trainers and trained them. We put these people in a big auditorium, gymnasium, in tables of eight with a moderator. We had a thing on the psychology of prejudice, a dialogue with psychiatrists. We went through the whole thing, a lot of things. They wanted to talk. I agree with Nixon in one sense. Our suburban middle class are, in a sense, fed up to here with taxes and all that. They feel powerless. So these people wanted to talk. The first couple of weeks, nobody was prejudiced, until we had the riot; then it blew its top. We took those people through an eight-week program and enlarged the group. Then we sent them back and said, "What are you going to do in your neighborhood? We don't want you in the ghetto. What are you going to do in your neighborhood?" They went through the same thing then with the Protestant and Jewish groups in their neighborhood. Some of them did all right and some of them didn't. Some of them came up with eleven problems—drugs, delinquency, zoning, housing, et cetera. Out of that, some very interesting things developed. One guy switched his whole career.

We are trying to put together a proposition for a television series. We would get the Lions' Club, whatever they are good for, the Rotary Club, and all those kinds of groups, and church groups, because we have reached all those people, and at 7:00 Tuesday night we would have this program. You invite ten people to your house, and everyone watches this thing. Afterwards everyone sits around and discusses it for an hour or so. Couldn't we reach 100,000 or 500,000 people using the media? What happens now? You see a good program on television, you drink your beer, and go to bed. The next day, you say, "Did you see that program?" "Yeah, we discussed it a little." "No, I didn't see it." There are no dynamics of discussing. I don't know if we can do it in a mass kind of way, setting up structures like this. This is a program we are trying to sell to the Ford Foundation. NIMER: If you are committed enough to want to invite these ten people, the ten people you know are also presumably as committed as you, how are you going to reach out to the people you don't know?

BUNDY: You don't have to invite ten people like yourself.

BARONI: The people who said they were committed were very shallow about it when you really got down to it. They weren't really that committed.

NIMER: I don't even mean committed in that strong a sense, but if you are a little concerned . . .

BARONI: Concerned, yes, but on election day they didn't go out and vote for the right guy. Some of them didn't even go out and vote. They didn't go out and say, "We are going to get ourselves a candidate" and make the phone calls and have the coffee things and organize, and get all the women going. Sure, you've got a few like that, but the rank and file feel powerless, frustrated. Still, they have got to work, get organized. An individual response doesn't solve a social problem. It's like throwing one Alka Seltzer into the ocean and thinking it will alkalize it. It just goes "fizz." Then you are all shot.

NIMER: Your social lines are parallel to yourself. You can't reach around, up, and down. How are you going to influence anybody else?

BARONI: I don't know if you teach school or not. I found out that I couldn't train people just by the classroom. I believe that action follows teaching, by way of experience, too. I think we need to get human involvement. You have to observe. You've got to judge. You've got to act, but there has to be some dynamics in this stuff. You can give a talk in the suburbs, and bring out Mr. Liberal, and all the liberals will pour out.

During the Poor People's Campaign, we had sixty support groups in the suburbs, people who made sandwiches and goodies for the poor people coming through. Sixty little support groups, all the old rebels that got married and settled down came out to work. All the little old groups came out, all the war resisters, Catholic workers or whatever, Lutheran, Episcopal, Jewish, all the old radicals who had gotten in labor movements and stuff. They all came out of the woodwork and formed these little committees in the suburbs and made cookies. The work of organizing and sensing isn't being done. There is no real movement.

NIMER: Well, I think we are saying the same thing.

BARONI: Only the good people will come. But I am saying those "good people," sort of in quotes, those "good people" only go so far. I go over to northern Virginia. Everytime I say anything about Broyhill, I get my neck cut by good people. Why? Because they say to me, "You know why we vote for Broyhill?" And I say, "Why?" "Because if you don't get the *Washington Post* delivered in the morning, you don't call the *Washington Post,* you call Congressman Broyhill's office. He gets it for you quicker. If you didn't get your military raise, if you didn't get your social security check for your grandmother, call Broyhill."

Maybe self-interest is the thing. I have brothers and sisters who live in the suburbs of Pittsburgh, and they are moving out. I have some brothers and sisters who are moving out of Washington. If they keep moving, they are going to meet in some place like Hagerstown and form a new city. They won't face up to it. When we get together for dinner, it is a fight. It's a screaming fight. You can't get to them morally, sometimes. The only way you can get to them is through self-interest.

PARTICIPANT: O.K. How can you?

BUNDY: Wait just a minute. There is the Catholic conscience, which as you pointed out has been an individual and not a social conscience. Can you use this sense of conscience and translate it into social terms for Catholics?

BARONI: That's what happened to the young liberal Catholic who is all of a sudden wallowing in guilt, because he moved to McLean, or some other place. All of a sudden, wallowing in his guilt, he brings my friend Father Groppi to town. He has a big lecture. This happened to Groppi in seventeen different cities. They say, "What we want you to do, after we have a little business meeting, is to perform. Beat the hell out of them!" These are all young liberals in their thirties. All of a sudden, racism is in. Let's hang the old racism on the church, the structure, the institution, to get it off our back. Get it off my back!

BUNDY: Let me just explore a little more. Suppose you get in the pulpit, and you say to your parishioners, "That is what you need." And you tell them.

BARONI: You can't do it that way.

BUNDY: Why not?

BARONI: You know what is happening to the church structure? We're not getting any money now in the collections. You know why? Because we have two groups of people in the church. One says, "I'll be damned if I'm going to give the church anything, because they are doing nothing." The other group says, "I'll be damned if I'm going to give the church anything, because they're going to give it to some white or some black poor slob." As a result, you get nothing from both groups.

BUNDY: What does he do if you tell him he is going to hell?

BARONI: That doesn't work anymore. There are 300 black Baptists in the city. They work with the bread-and-butter people about the by-and-by and the hereafter, and so on. The kids aren't going to buy it! It's not going to work with the kids. I saw a kid who never heard of Marx. He came up to me and said, "Religion is nothing but dope." What library had he been in?

PARTICIPANT: I would like to get back to the question that was asked before. I work in a white middle-class community. I have this frustration. If self-interest is the only way . . .

BARONI: I don't know. I say, "Use anything." Saul Alinsky taught me that you never talk to clergymen about theology. You always talk about money, economics. If you want this neighborhood to go, then just sit on your rear end. You'll go from 5,000 people to nothing. If you want to get organized and develop a community organization, develop some power, and try to stabilize the community, let things slow down and happen a little more gradually. Put up some cash. Otherwise, you will be wiped out.

PARTICIPANT: My problem is even more specific, because I work with children. I've kind of given up on the adults. I can't fight that kind of thing right now. I figure with the children, there's a chance.

BARONI: Let's examine those kids. What happens to those kids? I taught them, too. When I meet some of the kids I taught, they wear the pajama top, the beads, and so on. They have given up on the system. Why? They say, "Because we learned how bad it was." You are caught in the same thing that he brought up before. Everybody's got a thermostat up to here. They go over the brink both ways.

I still believe that people can be changed. I didn't speak any English until the third grade. I had a third grade teacher who made a believer out of me. I went to a one-room school, read every cotton-picking book. The only thing I knew how to do was read. Nobody else in my family was a reader or is a reader. That third-grade teacher had more influence on me than any other teacher I had in twenty-three years of education. But still we have to get organized.

PARTICIPANT: I learned, many years ago, that in a particular audience, you reach only those who hear what they want to hear. You have to be talking about what they want to hear. The biggest problem is what can we do in our urban community. I have worked a little bit in suburban communities with people with whom I grew up, lived with all my life. You can put them in a classroom situation, develop a program, and stick it in front of them. You can find some very, very interesting talk, very, very interesting revelations coming out of these people. Yet the minute they step out of the door and go into their own homes, they seem to have forgotten everything they said.

BARONI: What does that say, then? Millions of people go to church. They come outside, and nothing happens.

PARTICIPANT: Right. When you try to go to your own people, your own element, your own area, and try to promote change, to get an idea across, it may be fine, in a given situation. There seems to come a time in every party when it's time to talk about Vietnam. You can really get into a good talk at a party. Or you can sit in a room like this, and it's the same thing. You get very, very good discussion. I can go to meetings, like the Stony Brook Improvement Foundation, which is great. All good urban communities have that. I can talk to these people and get some responses, but the only way I could ever get them to think, once they leave that room, is by telling them, "You may not agree with what I am saying, but I will teach your children to believe me, when I am a teacher." I tell them just that.

BARONI: How did you get concerned? What was the process through which you became concerned? If it happens to you, why can't that happen to someone else?

PARTICIPANT: That's the point. Why is it me among a group of about twenty, that I grew up with? I have stayed close to the group I grew up with all my life. Why is it mostly just me constantly harping on them about everything from grapes to Vietnam? Why is it me telling them that they're not doing anything?

BARONI: Well, why is it you?

PARTICIPANT: Maybe it's not. Maybe I'm the biggest hypocrite of them all. How we can get them to at least think?

BUNDY: Father Baroni is saying, "If we can figure out how we produced you then we could produce more."

BARONI: "I am part of all that I have met," you know.

PARTICIPANT: I don't know. Maybe I didn't like my religion when

I first became accustomed to it. I got expelled from Hebrew school. Maybe that helped me along the line. I don't really know how I got to think the way I do.

BARONI: According to the guy next to you, you might really be a conservative square.

PARTICIPANT: Quite possibly. That's beside the point, or maybe it is the point. What I am saying is that in the communication process, and this is what you are talking about . . .

BARONI: Not just communication. I've seen ten working-class families become a social action unit, coming from all the ethnic stereotypes, all the conservatives, the lower middle group, and so on. I have seen them become a group. I have seen them work on each other.

WASSERMAN: Let me ask a nasty question, or put it in nasty terms. What you are talking to us about is political action, really. You are not working within any establishment. That's really the problem we are confronting. That is, we're in an institution, an organization that doesn't seem to be relevant. Our problem in our convention here is to figure out how to make it relevant. That's the issue.

BARONI: But I am in an institution. I'm in an authoritarian structure.

WASSERMAN: Yes, but you're outside it.

BARONI: No, I'm in an office. I have to report . . .

WASSERMAN: But are you changing that institution? You are changing your role in it. Now you function as one individual, but that's not the impact of your institution. You're functioning outside of it.

BARONI: Well, some of that is true, but I also went from a nothing budget several years ago to a budget of $700,000. Where did I get the $700,000? Out of the institution. Why? Because I sold the institution.

WASSERMAN: But couldn't you be functioning out of any institution?

BARONI: No. I am trying to make the institution work for me. I have an office. I have the Office of Urban Affairs, archdiocese of Washington. I have $148,000 in economic development, $75,000 in community organizations, all these things which the structure would have said, "No, no, no," if I told them what it meant plain out and straight. I wouldn't. I had to go the other way. I had to talk to people until I got sick on the damn thing.

I set up a meeting with some people in the community, with some of the committee. They sat in this little room and it was kind of chilly. Here was the church structure, here was the neighborhood.

The church structure immediately began telling the people of the neighborhood all the things the church did for them. "We do this. We do that. We give away this and we give away that. We've got the infant home, and we give away this, and we give away that." Pretty soon some lady said, "Bullshit!" Then there was communication. Dialogue! I had the memo all ready by the time they got back to their desks the next day. I was supposed to be at that meeting but I had the flu that day. If I had been, they would have bounced it off me. The next day, I had a memo suggesting we put $25,000 into a group that wanted to have some self-determination.

It worked the same way with IFCO. IFCO is the Interreligious Foundation for Community Organization. A group of Protestants and Catholics set up IFCO. IFCO became a funnel for getting church money, through a nonprofit corporation, to give to a group that wants a little self-determination without any strings attached. A church couldn't do it directly. We had to create a foundation in the middle. What happened? IFCO set up the Black Economic Development Conference in Detroit, out of which came Forman and his manifesto, so IFCO now is caught with its pants down.

BUNDY: What's your motive? Do you want to convert people to Catholicism?

BARONI: Oh no. I haven't baptized anybody in ages. I believe we have to celebrate the presence of the Lord. I believe in celebrating life and humanity, and so on. I believe in serving. God loved the world. I'm not afraid of the world. I believe in the world. I believe in working with anybody of goodwill for the common good.

I didn't always think that way. I wasn't trained that way. Most of my training came backwards, secondhand. I learned very little in the structure of classrooms, theologians, and teachers. They never helped me. They may have turned me off. I learned myself from reading this paper, and that paper, and this book, and that book, and meeting this person, and that person, in the human dynamics of things. That's where I learned—outside. That's why I say that the learning and teaching situations in the classrooms may not be it.

BUNDY: Is what you are doing the mission of the Catholic church?

BARONI: I would say the mission of the Catholic church is to develop theologically, to find out "Who is urban man?" and "What is urban life?" and "What does it mean to people to live as human beings?" I don't care what your gospel is, or my gospel. It makes no difference to me. I can't preach a gospel I'm supposed to live, or a creed I'm supposed to believe. I can't preach it, I can't believe it, unless I'm willing to work for a decent education, employment, housing, and even some of the luxuries without which life is no longer human.

WASSERMAN: Father, what do you see as the impact of your work, and the work of somebody like Groppi on the church?

BARONI: Groppi is an individual. He won't work for the structure. Yet Groppi is the most conservative guy. He used to go around reading his prayer book. Groppi is a conservative reactionary. He is still eating his Italian salami sandwiches, except every once in a while he blows as an individual. He won't work for the structure. Now he realizes he is white, and he can no longer take this role in the black community. He knows that. He has gotten out with his rangers. He has a different role.

Today I was with a group of black guys. I got an appointment for them with the Federal Housing Administration so they could form a black construction company. Whether they can make it or not, I don't know, but I am willing to gamble. They couldn't get in the damn place, so I called up Romney's secretary. I said, "These guys should have a meeting." I say, "The Catholic church will back it up." So we lost a few thousand bucks.

PARTICIPANT: You do this as an individual. You squeeze some money out of the church. But what impact do you have on the church? What have you done to make other people in the church act in the same way?

BARONI: I am the chairman of the National Urban Task Force for the United States Catholic church. We are trying to develop an urban strategy, an urban policy, an urban concern. We are trying to take the liquid assets of the church and see what can be done in economic development. In Milwaukee, we are trying to take fourteen Catholic schools and translate them from Catholic schools to community schools forming a separate corporation. The church gave that school to the community for fifty years for a buck a year. The church said, "All right, we'll phase out gradually. We'll kick in the $25,000 subsidy this year. Next year it will be $10,000 then $5,000, and then you are on your own. You can hire the nuns if you want to hire them. If they can't teach, and they're no good as librarians, don't hire them. If they want to teach religion, they can teach it on Saturday or some other time."

We can become nonprofit sponsors with a little bit of seed money out of an institution that has some longevity. I can go to a two-bit group and I can put up the $10,000 in order to get $3 million out of the system, and then make 100 different church groups around the country do the same thing.

I was up on the Hill today working and lobbying. Remember Senator Russell? He looked up in that old gallery and said, "I don't know what all these preachers and rabbis got to do with civil rights." We had 10,000 telegrams from Sioux City, Davenport, Des Moines. We tried to create a network. Of course, the congressmen are catching on. A Protestant guy went up to testify for the farm workers, and Vinegar Ben Mizell, who used to be a baseball player from South Carolina, said, "I read the Bible too. Who do all you represent?" He said to the Protestant guy, "How many people?" The guy said, "I guess I am representing . . ." "Who did you clear your statement with?" A Jewish guy got up then, and Mizell said, "Who do you speak for, all the Jews? Who do you represent? How many people? Who did you clear your statement with?" A Catholic guy got up in front of McCarthy, the big B.S.er from Texas. With a real Texas drawl, this Catholic said, "I want you all to know that I speak for God. I want you all to know that I haven't cleared my statement, either." And he said, "If I get my statement cleared, you'll read about it in the *Washington Post.*"

It only takes 2 percent to make the system change. It really only takes 2 percent. Three or four of us have gotten several million dollars out of the Catholic church, and we couldn't even look in at the bishop's structure. We met together for three weeks to plan our strategy for getting on their agenda. Then I put on my collar, used my Italian blood, negotiated, took some militant's thing and reworded it, put a few words of Jesus and theology in it, made it a rationale. This was the thing to do. We've got to make the American people do it, because it is the thing to do.

BUNDY: You spoke about a meeting you didn't go to. It was a confrontation. Sometimes I think people like us get kind of conceited. We've had a set of experiences that make us more aware or more sensitive. We become the interpreters with our friends. Maybe our friends ought to have the same experiences.

BARONI: Yes, but we've got to organize. We cannot let it go to happenstance, necessarily. I was in a library where we were trying to work on the police. I'm scared to death of the police. Some of my friends are cops, just like some of my best friends live in the suburbs. The police structure in San Francisco resembles the Mafia. Really, you ought to learn from the Mafia. In San Francisco, they had a testimonial dinner for the riot squad. The mayor was there. A Protestant minister gave the benediction. Some Catholic priest gave a prayer about law and order, and how the law-and-order people stand for morality and, therefore, the police are morality and law and order. All of this was horrifying. We got rid of the chief of police there, but it wasn't easy. The militants were raising hell on the outside. We were going in the back door, pushing on the other side.

We always cleared the agendas. The agendas were always cleared. They were always checked on. The militants were screaming and yelling, and we were going in and saying, "You got to do this and you got to do that," not because of the militants, but because of this and because of that. So what happened? We had a meeting in the library for the police officers. They were a paramilitary outfit. They were not professionals. There are 29,000 police departments in the country, and they have about 29,000 different ways of doing things. That's where the FBI has really failed. But the policemen were there. Some of the policemen even had their dogs with them. We had a guy give a pious brotherhood talk to the policemen. He talked about brotherhood and humanity. All the walls were covered with pictures and drawings and banners and things. There were banners about policemen. There was a banner about a honky cop. There was a police dog biting a kid. There was a white cop in the black community. There was this or that epithet, and the different kinds of language you hear in certain schools. All these things were around the walls. The policemen didn't even hear the guy who was talking. Before the meeting was over, they were saying, "What about these pictures?" We had a whole thing going with the police.

Sometimes you use different media. You have the confrontation sometimes. You have already picked up two guys, three guys, four guys. You started to work on them and you put them down and say, "O.K., good community relations equals what? Good law enforcement! Law and order, yeah, but no law and order without justice!" Let's put all the pieces together. Let's make the clichés work. This is what you have to do. You have to do this all the time.

I used to drive the librarians nuts. I wanted this book and that book, but they weren't on the approved list. I'd say, "Buy it and send the bill in anyway." What books? I said, "I want a reading list of books. I want to know what books there are I can use, because this kid here is at this age." "Why don't you read this? Why don't you read that?" You just peddle things. The same things happened to me by accident. I read all these books and found out later, when I finally went to a Catholic school, they were all in the index. That was when we had an index.

PARTICIPANT: Father, how do you survive within your institution? Aren't they getting mad at you? How do you manage to . . .

BARONI: I'm in my second diocese. I was kicked out of Pennsylvania. I came to Washington in October of 1960, and John Kennedy was elected in November. I had no status, no standing. I just walked the streets. I was a coal miner, local-yokel hick. Yet within the Catholic church structure I became an urban affairs expert. I looked around at all the universities because I didn't know what I was going to do. I was going to go back to school. Well, the bishop died. I got some good doctor to write me a letter, so I didn't have to go back to Altoona, because I got stuck in a situation there. There was no university where you could get a program in urban affairs at that time. There wasn't a course anywhere in 1960. There wasn't a program.

I gave Moynihan six months. He has lasted six months with Nixon, past six months. Why? He's either nuts or something, but he is still there trying. A few strokes here and a few strokes there may affect millions of people. I have great respect for people's tolerance. But you go so far and you can't got any further.

I also realize that we use our wits, our energy, our talents, and our gifts. You can go after things. You can find people, organize people, and put pieces together, and not have to do just the picking up of the pieces. We've got to prepare for the transition. We've got to help form a nucleus of new structures. When the old structures collapse . . . They are collapsing, you know. Somebody has got to do a little thinking about it and be ready. So we have the revolution. Well, what are we going to have in its place?

PARTICIPANT: We had a small disaster that developed out of a project amendment meeting in St. Ignatius Church in Oxon Hill, if you recall that.

BARONI: No, but I can just imagine.

PARTICIPANT: I attended all of the meetings and managed to get our local library involved by passing out brochures and things like that. I wound up on a committee. The committees were supposed to respond to this sort of thing in the community. We looked around to see what to do. We decided a Negro history course would be fun. It looked real good. We found a guy to teach it. I got the room in the library, and we wondered if 200 seats would do. We got a good man to lecture. We gave a seven-week course, seven lectures once a week. The most that attended any meeting was twenty-four. It has been publicized.

BARONI: Maybe we don't know how to train leaders. Maybe we have to learn something from politicians, too. This is a criticism we get all the time. "You should stay in the pulpit and preach about spiritual things, and about the Bible, and stop getting involved in economic and social things." My rationale is that every economic, every social, and every political problem is a moral problem. The question of justice, the question of right and wrong can't be divorced. Every human interest is mine. I don't care if you are a teacher, a librarian, or what; you've got to relate. The world is too little now not to be able to relate to the Cuban peasants, the Japanese coal miner, the Biafran kid. We've got to find teachers who can help the young people see.

That's the little argument going on now between Cleaver and Stokely Carmichael about the humanity bit. How do we get away from this? Young kids see it. They see dropping napalm bombs on Vietnamese children as just as bad as killing their brothers and sisters. They really think it is crazy, because they were raised on the television one-world concept. They relate very quickly. They just don't understand why we don't have that mentality. We've got to move in that concept of "If I'm hurt you're hurt. If you're hurt, I'm hurt. If you can't be what you ought to be, then I can't be what I should be." And it comes. Whatever the language is, you see it.

I visited some communes in Toronto. I'm interested in the commune thing, new communities, so I went to Toronto last Saturday night. It was very interesting. I visited three. They were all working with Marshall McLuhan and the media thing. I was lost with some of the jargon. These were all professional, educated, thirty-to-forty-year-olds trying to create something—a community. I think you have this thing here for some reason.

BUNDY: It just occurred to me it is a one-shot deal. What he is trying to tell us is that you've come here, you've talked about it, you've made yourself feel good like you went to church, and now we will all go home. Isn't that what you were trying to tell us?

BARONI: That's why I hate to do this.

PARTICIPANT: What about self-government for the District? Shall we all go home and start lobbying our congressmen?

BARONI: That won't solve everything, but you can start by doing that. Right now, Congress is blackmailing the District by saying if you build this bridge and this freeway, then we'll let you do a subway. The people don't have a say. It's a colony. This is the last colony in North America.

Of all the kids I taught, 15 years later, there are only 15 of them that I know where they stand on every single issue. We didn't have the grape issue when I was teaching. The grape thing wasn't on. I missed a meeting one time, and was elected chairman of the Don't Buy Grape Committee, until the free press came in. They wouldn't work for a coalition instructor. The free press said, "We're going to go out and pour blood on grapes." So go pour blood on grapes. But you can't work that with a coalition group of organizations, because you've got to go back to the organization and get a statement, pass the rhetoric, and move the organization. But if you ever move that organization, if you ever move 500 women or 5,000 women, they buy, or don't buy, more grapes than 5 kids. That is the group you've got to get, the housewives. So you've got to work in the women's this and the women's that.

PARTICIPANT: Can I say something? Politics is my bag. I live in California, so I am very far removed from Washington. I don't know what's happening here. Some very bright man in California passed a bill that librarians, foreign librarians, can work for only a year in a state library. That's it. The law librarian happened to be a foreigner. That's me. We marched to the Capitol and tried to explain that the work needed to be done. We asked, "Is there a mistake?" They said, "No. If someone passed the bill, there was a good reason." We said, "May we know what the reason is?" It took three or four days. We talked to a consultant, and then the assistant to the consultant. You never got up to the man. I happened to live in a house where one of the senators goes swimming. I happened to talk with him. I explained that there were five or six foreign librarians who are going to be out of a job the first of September. What happened? They took out this provision of one year. So five or six librarians and I had a job. It seems to me this is a lobbying, if somebody is interested.

BARONI: I will tell you how a neighborhood I know got a new library. It was in a poor section of town. They never put in any new librarians or any new books. It was neglected. The new library was always being put in next year's budget. So, some teachers got organized. They went to the nuns, and the nuns sent in eighth-grade kids with shopping bags. The librarian there must have been a terror; I understand some of them are. The kids just took out all the books they could carry. The next day another school sent in all their students. They just kept hauling books back and forth, and just dumping them—fifty, sixty, a hundred shopping bags full of books. After they got ten schools to go to the library, they called the television and the press. But they first had written a letter to the mayor and the city council, to the budget bureau. They did all the proper things so that they were on record.

You have to be on record. You have to write a letter and state your complaint. They did all that. They got organized. And they got a library in that year's budget. They got a new library, some money for new books. That was a question of organization. The library there was not serving the community. Somebody made it a community issue. Around the issue of the library they not only got a new library, which is one benefit, but there was another benefit. The other benefit was they organized the community. They organized the community around the library. Some people said, "That stupid library! That stupid thing!" but other people put priority on the library, and they got the library. Things happen not by accident.

BUNDY: We have people in the library field who are doing this. They're out in poverty areas. They are responding to the conditions they see. We don't see them too much at meetings, because they are busy doing other things. In professional education, we're asking the question, "How can we be more supportive of our front lines?" What might we do in our professional roles? What can we give them?

BARONI: We've got the same problem in the church. How do you get the newly arrived middle class to respond? They are operating on a two-bit penny theology that used to work by telling them to go to hell. Now we've got to get up a new rationale with a theologist base that makes them respond to today's problems. A bunch of urban guys were in a meeting last week. We talked about program development. We talked about goals. We talked about priorities, and we talked about policy, and how to change goals and policies. I think it was the same words you have used. We went through all of that. We were going to do some research, some training, and some program development. Then we said, "We've got to develop a theology, we've got to go to the professionals because they're not involved out there. We've got to get the professionals."

The professionals have to come into it, to help develop, to do some thinking, provide a rationale. You've got to put all of this together. If you're going to develop a theological base that moves people out there, somebody's got to be thinking who knows the problem. Somebody has to be able to put together the thinking, know what makes people tick, and develop a rationale for the working stiff who doesn't have time. He is too busy in a busy library. He doesn't have the time to do it. But he needs that support. We don't get any support from our theologians. They don't know urban man. They don't know what urban life is all about. They don't know we live in a metropolitan city. They are still talking about some poor guy shooting a deer on some Frenchman's ranch. That's the theological issue in the theology book. They haven't caught up with the modern urban structure, and what it does to man, right and wrong. Who is man and what makes life?

BUNDY: That's what I was getting at. If there is a parallel between the seminaries and the library schools, is there another role the professional school . . .

BARONI: The worst libraries in the world are the seminary libraries. All the old books people don't want, they sell to the seminary libraries. The older they are . . .

BUNDY: How about your locked cases?

BARONI: They have them down in the basement, sealed. Unprinted pieces.

BUNDY: Are the priests in the seminaries speaking out to the Catholic hierarchy?

BARONI: No. We have the same problem. We can use research the same way. Everybody says, "Why doesn't the bishop do this?" Just say, why doesn't the superintendent do it? Why doesn't the chief librarian do it?

BUNDY: Yes, but your seminaries are under the bishop. Ours are not under . . .

BARONI: It's the people. You've got to come up from the bottom. It's the will of the people. If a guy is the administrator, the bishop, or whoever, who is the church? It is not the bishop; it is the people. Who is the government? It's not the president. We work it top down and bottom up, but it has to come this way, too. You've got to get organized. It's the bishop, it's the pope. It's people! Theology is created out of the context of society, but it's in the mill. If librarians got organized, they could get anything they wanted.

BUNDY: What's been the effect of black priests in the Catholic church?

BARONI: We don't have enough. Anybody who is a black priest now is sure to become a bishop. Who wants to be a bishop?

PARTICIPANT: Why do you always talk about the new middle class? What about the old one?

BARONI: What do you mean by that?

PARTICIPANT: You say the new middle class created a problem. Maybe because I am new myself, I don't know where you draw the line.

BARONI: Well, for the first time now, we have a middle class which makes up the majority group of the American people. Before, you had a middle class like you have in other countries. The upper class was quite small, and maybe you had a middle class and maybe you didn't. But now in our country, which is the big consensus group? It's the middle class. A lot of it is new, second generation, and so on.

PARTICIPANT: Do you mean to imply that this new middle class is not part of the old one?

BARONI: No. I throw them all together. We were an urban church. We had an urban base and everybody was poor. You know how I talk to the old Irish pastors and the old middle class in a church? I say, "When the Irish and the Italians were organizing General Motors and Ford, they weren't singing 'We Shall Overcome.' When they were organizing the coal mines in Pennsylvania and the steel mills in Pittsburgh, it wasn't nonviolent, either." I dig up all these history books about how many people the Molly Maguires dumped in the river. It has been a violent nation. Take history and see what has happened, what has been done. I have to speak to these old-timers. They didn't sing "We Shall Overcome"; they were singing the Polish hymns. They were singing hymns, old things, when they were organizing the Ford plant. They were meeting in church basements. The old Irish pastors, some of them had the Molly Maguires meet in St. Patrick's Church in Scranton. They had their secret meetings downstairs. The pastor was part of it.

PARTICIPANT: Actually they ruptured the morals and the ethics of the old middle class.

BARONI: A lot of it is class. People who are modest middle class are very threatened by competition. Street life, school life, neighborhood life, housing, jobs, et cetera—these things are what give people security. What does a modest middle-class man own? He doesn't own General Motors. He might have a house with a mortgage on it. That might be the essence of his equity. He worked hard for it. He is scared of losing it. What you have to talk to those people about is not "Somebody is going to take away your house and your equity," but "Let's make it big enough and share it big enough, so that you don't have to be threatened. She gets her share, and you get your share. Let's make it big enough for everyone."

PARTICIPANT: Suppose the bishop put you in a white middle-class suburb the next time. There you are.

BARONI: I've been there.

PARTICIPANT: How do you make these people give up . . .

BARONI: I don't beat old ladies over the head. I let them light their little candles. I go to see them in the hospital and take care of them and preach nice sermons when they die. Then they say, "I don't know what he's doing, but that Father Baroni's a nice man. He came to see my husband in the hospital three times before he died and he took care of him. I don't know what he is doing out there, but whatever he is doing, he is O.K. He's my man." You've got to cover your flank. You do the same thing with your principals.

PARTICIPANT: You get done what you want.

BARONI: Sure. Everybody says, "He is so shy, so inhibited, so timid." I don't believe they're talking about the same person. The problem with us is every conversation is a confrontation. You don't get much; you don't get anywhere with principals and school boards. Let somebody else do that and then you be ready. When their backs are up against the wall, you come up with a program and you're set. You say, "Well, here's what we ought to do." Everybody's got different gifts, different talents. I really think we could make the system work, but not enough people are working at making it work. The thing that scares me is that a lot of people have given up on it, especially some of our young kids.

WELBOURNE: Let me also comment on your sound advice on organizing. Organizing means pulling together people to do something, coordinating, being attuned to what is going on out there, what you can use, what you can benefit from. You are really saying that you are not really seeking to duplicate the confrontation group. You have your own version.

BARONI: I went to meetings with black guys. In the meeting I wouldn't talk to them. They wouldn't recognize me. They wouldn't even admit they knew me, but I knew what their agenda was. They knew what our agenda was and there was coalition. For example, we get the Poles together in Detroit, have them sit down and say what they want. They really think out what they want. Then we put these two groups together. I'll bet there are a few issues on which they say, "O.K., you support me and I'll support you. We'll do this and we'll do that." Because they've got some common interests. They are bound to have some common interest in there somewhere. I saw LeRoi Jones do that in Newark. As long as the money was on the table, he stayed with the next guy to get his share. He just wouldn't leave until they figured out how to divide the pot.

BUNDY: The thing to do is to keep playing a role. It may be a new role.

BARONI: Sometimes I articulate things, but I haven't thought them out.

BUNDY: Then you have to find if you are going to be comfortable in new roles. You have to find your reference group. Who is your reference group?

BARONI: A reference group is five or six librarians who believe in the same thing. You've got to come together once in a while to give yourselves support when you go back to Timbuktu. It's pretty lonely out there. But somewhere you know there is a gal from California, a gal from someplace else, who is thinking the same way you do, so you just go on. You've got to have that. You know that somebody else is working on it over here, and over here. Sometimes you've got to get together and exchange ideas; then you pick up another one, and another one. Out this far on the cutting edge, it's always very lonely, very lonely. The same with the organizer.

That's the thing we had with Carmichael, a great charismatic type of guy, but damn it, Stokely, you don't know how to organize. There was no follow-through in developing an organization. Some guys have to be the steersmen. Somebody has to do the organizing. The organizer is not the leader. There are people who know how to organize. They get Mrs. So-and-so out there bitching about the library, the toughest, meanest, mud-slinging person. They give her all the information. How many old books they've got, and so on, what they need. They are supplying her the fuel; she is throwing the bricks.

You can be a little program. This is how you build a new library. You just have to have them all ready. Forman has opened up a lot of doors for us. He won't get a nickel of it. Somebody else will. Some of these churches have meetings around the clock. They were scared. I visited the Interfaith Church Center at Riverside Drive in New York, where all the Protestants and Episcopalians were. Forman was running out into the street looking for the Lutherans this time. He thought he was going to be historic. He had his hammer and his nails. He was going to nail the things on the door. And it was a plastic door. He had to go back to the librarian and borrow some scotch tape.

In the meantime, the people inside were sitting there at a meeting, all these pious people saying, "Gee, isn't this terrible, this rhetoric and this language." But they were pushing. They were still saying, "Yeah, we ought to do this and we ought to do that." They were getting as much as they could get as far as making progress. They said, "Yeah, you can't go along with that rhetoric, that Marxist-Mao thing. Some of the programs are right, so we've got to do them this way." That was a little different from what they were doing. The problem with our society is we are going so fast but it is not half fast enough. It's happening in a lot of structures. I've seen it with teachers; I don't know about librarians, but I know at least two dozen terrific urban teachers who quit this year. One year with the system, and they've had it. They just say, "The hell with it!" That's what is distressing, too. If they would hang in, they could eventually . . .

Because who's the villain? Every superintendent of schools is the villain these days. Sooner or later somebody is going to say, "All right, do what you are supposed to do with those libraries. Here's the money go and do it." Who is going to be ready?

BUNDY: That's the question: who's going to be ready?

BARONI: That's where the professionals have to be in tune.

BUNDY: I would suspect we are the most unready professionals. If someone handed us the money at the moment, we wouldn't know what to do.

BARONI: I go to bookstores now instead of libraries, but it's more expensive.

BUNDY: We all do.

BARONI: I call the library. "Oh, we don't have that book yet." I got all my papers written by library people so I am very grateful.

PARTICIPANT: I want to comment on the superintendents of schools being villains. The superintendent of schools at Berkeley, when he spoke to us this summer, said, "When you go in any school and ask the principal why they're not changing, they say, 'Well the teachers won't change.' You ask the teachers why they're not changing and they say, 'The principals won't let us.' " This is the game.

BARONI: Yet, I have seen three or four teachers turn a whole school around. It has happened.

PARTICIPANT: Sacramento State had something like that. They turned the whole thing upside down. They fired the dean or the president. The academic senate turned the whole thing upside down.

BARONI: It can be done. It is the same with the church. I believe that many of our human institutions are falling apart. In a church sense, I believe they are falling apart with some divine significance. How you put that in a secular sense, I don't know. Change is just a dirty word, irrelevant. You don't serve. You don't serve the community; you don't serve the kids; you don't serve people. I am the only reader out of my whole family. I was at the right time, at the right place. Somebody gave me the right book. Why did I become a reader and why didn't my brothers and sisters? Why aren't they readers? They don't read anything.

7

THE PUBLISHING INDUSTRY
IN TRANSITION

THURSDAY MORNING, AUGUST 14
LECTURER: DAN LACY
PANELISTS: PAUL WASSERMAN
MARY LEE BUNDY

WASSERMAN: Our two discussion leaders this morning are Dan Lacy and David Goldberg. We arbitrarily divided the morning between the two. We thought we would ask Dan Lacy to talk with us and then react to the things that we would like to discuss with him for the first half of the session. Then in the second half of the morning, Dave Goldberg will be center stage. Dan, will you start us?

LACY: Thank you, Paul. In talking about publishing and transition, I thought it would be useful to spend some time looking at the rather radical changes in the size and scale and structure of the ownership and management of the publishing industry in this country, and at least open up for discussion the implications of these changes for the output and the social responsiveness of publishing.

Twenty years ago, a large publishing house was one that did $2.5 million of business a year; one that did $5 million was a giant. There was hardly a publishing house in the country at that time that was publicly held or whose shares could be traded on a stock exchange. Most of them, in fact, were personally or family owned and were managed by the men who owned them. Most houses, indeed, were dominated by one man who personally chose the books to be published and gave personal attention to their editing, design, manufacture, and promotion, and with whom at least the principal authors of the house had close, personal contact. Only about 10,000 books a year were published, and publishers' receipts from their sales were on the order of $500 million a year, or less than that—probably $400 million. Today a number of book publishing houses sell more than $100 million a year. The industry produces about 40,000 books a year, and its annual volume of business is on the order of $2.5 billion, or about five times what it was, even more than five times what it was, twenty years ago. Most larger publishing houses and many smaller ones are public corporations actively traded on the stock exchange and equipped with all the panoply of modern corporations. Many are parts of giant corporations, whose center of interest is quite other than books. Corporations like RCA, CBS, IBM, Raytheon, Xerox, and Litton Industries include in their vast domains large book publishing enterprises.

The specialized and impersonal character of modern corporate management has become characteristic of larger publishing houses. The lines between book publishing and other communications industries have become blurred. Magazine and newspaper publishers have become major factors in book publishing, as are broadcasting and electronics companies. Book publishers, in turn, have become very active in film production and distribution, broadcasting, correspondence instruction, the design and sale of educational tests and laboratory equipment. It's not only that one can buy a book from NBC or go to a major league baseball game played by employees of CBS; one can also buy a saxophone from Crowell-Collier-Macmillan or a gerbil or a guppy from McGraw-Hill. Indeed, the publishing of a generation ago is hardly to be recognized as a progenitor of today's complex and sprawling industry.

Why and how did these changes occur? What are the factors that have revolutionized and continue to transform publishing? How have these developments affected the social role and responsiveness of publishing and what will its foreseeable future be like? Well, the factors of change have been many—economic, cultural, technological, managerial. But the first and the most dynamic factor is the population explosion that followed World War II. These figures are by now trite, but they are worth recalling. During the 1930s and the war years, there were, on the average, about 2.5 million births a year in the United States. Following the war, there was an immediate increase to 3.5 million and soon to well over 4 million a year. By the early 1950s, this flood of children had begun to enter school, producing an immediate 40 to 50 percent increase in the enrollment of each grade as it was reached by the 1946 and 1947 cohorts. Meanwhile there was a substantial increase in the proportion of youths of high school age who actually attended school, and a revolutionary increase in the proportion of those who went on to college or other post–high school education. Before World War II, fewer than one in twelve went beyond high school. Now, nearly half do.

By the early 1960s when the first of the postwar generation reached high school, and by the latter years of the decade, when they were in college, the confluence of the population wave and the changing proportion of enrollments' produced fantastic rates of growth, not a 40 percent increase, but a doubling of high school enrollments and more than a 600 percent increase in college students. The total enrollment in schools and colleges last year was nearly 60 million as compared with less than 30 million in the immediate prewar years.

The increased demand for educational materials, however, outran the increases in enrollment. The quality of schools improved. The greater affluence of the country afforded better support. Millions moved from poorer southern to wealthier northern and western states, and from rural areas to cities. As a result, our children moved from schools that often had few textbooks, no school library, and almost no audio-visual materials, to areas in which they were much more abundantly supplied with educational materials. The same thing happened with movements from large core cities into suburbs, which generally meant moving the children from poorly supplied to well-supplied schools. Migration alone did as much as any other factor to increase the supply of books per student.

Another factor was the growing conviction that the schools must be greatly improved and that this improvement required, among other things, more abundant and higher-quality textbooks, school libraries, films, tapes, and audiovisual materials. This conviction was embodied in the National Defense Education Act of 1958, which provided federal funds for, among other things, library books, audiovisual materials, and other new media for instruction. The educational views underlying this act were general in the profession and were reflected in state and local appropriations as well.

The explosive growth of college enrollments brought an even more rapid rise in the demand for college textbooks and materials for college and university library collections. Hundreds of new colleges were established and hundreds of others increased enormously in size, setting up an almost endless demand for books. The demand was increased by changes in curriculum and teaching methods that involved new areas of study and a great increase in the breadth of reading and independent study. But the increased amount of books was by no means entirely from formal educational institutions.

Public libraries grew very rapidly also, increasing their annual book purchases from what now seems almost a negligible figure in the 1930s to about $43 million ten years ago, to well over $100 million a year now. Their growth was also fostered by federal funds, beginning with the Federal Library Services Act. All of these library and educational book purchases received an enormous stimulus from the federal legislation of 1965, the Elementary and Secondary Education Act, the Higher Education Act, and expansions of the Library Services and Construction Act and the National Defense Education Act. These measures produced, in 1966, funds probably on the order of $350 million for library acquisitions. Though federal funds have subsequently been drastically cut, that bonanza year produced lasting commitments. Among other things, many hundreds, indeed probably some thousands, of elementary schools for the first time established libraries, to the continuing support of which they were thereafter committed.

Because of the burst of growth in educational and library materials, it has often escaped attention that there were equal or greater increases in the individual purchase of books. This was due to many causes—a higher level of education, affluence, better marketing methods through book clubs and paperbound channels, a lively interest in public affairs, a generally more serious concern with culture, a higher proportion of jobs or professions that required extensive reading. In general, the production and sale of trade books through these various channels has increased at almost the same pace as educational materials. As a result of all of these factors, the development of the book industry turned out to be very different from what it was thought likely to be fifteen years or so ago.

It was in 1954, I believe, that the Graduate Library School at the University of Chicago devoted its summer conference to the future of the book. They concluded that there really wasn't much future for it, that television would supplant it as a medium of entertainment and recreation, the computer as a reference tool, and television and other audiovisual materials as an educational instrument. But, in fact, book sales increased from $665 million in the year of that conference at the University of Chicago to well over $2.5 billion last year, contrasted with annual book sales during the 1930s of something like $100 million a year. This is a startling cultural fact. It has also had enormous financial and economic consequences for the industry that had been little studied, and it's these I mostly want to talk about.

In contrast to magazine publishing or broadcasting, book publishing requires a very large investment of working capital in relation to sales revenue. Let me point out as an aside here that one can enter book publishing and achieve a national distribution of books with a much smaller investment than would be required for a small broadcaster or newspaper publisher. But for any given level of size in terms of revenue, book publishing requires a good deal higher investment than most of the other media of communication. Authors draw large advances that may be outstanding for years. Inventory must be paid for and is often held for years. Many customers of book publishers are, alas, very slow to pay, so that one-quarter or more of a publisher's annual sales revenue will be outstanding at any given time as accounts receivable.

As a result of these and other factors, one may take it as a rough rule of thumb that each million dollars of annual sales requires an investment of something on the order of $1 million in working capital. Hence, the increase in book sales in the last twenty years has required the new investment of at least $2 billion in the publishing industry. Such a sum could not possibly come from the industry itself. If every dollar of post-tax profits of book publishers was plowed back into the industry, it woudn't begin to produce the needed capital. It had to come from outside the industry. The resources of this capital and the ways it was drawn into publishing have been the principal factors in producing the new and emerging shape of publishing.

There have been three principal sources of outside capital. One has been the general public, through subscription to public offerings of stock and debentures. Another has been magazine and newspaper publishing, and the third has been the electronic industries. Each of these has had its own particular effect on book publishing. Public stock quotation has been the most widely used method of drawing outside capital into book publishing. Publishing companies, even the largest, have traditionally been privately held with no revelation of their financial affairs and no accountability of their management to investors. Outside equity investment was not needed nor would it have been welcomed.

Not until publishing became a glamor industry, exciting the interest of Wall Street, would it have been possible successfully to issue stock to the public. Within the last decade, however, numerous firms such as Houghton-Mifflin; Ginn; Random House; Harper & Row; John Wiley & Sons; Grosset & Dunlap; Pocket Books; Simon & Schuster; Scott, Foresman; Harcourt, Brace, & World; and Crowell-Collier-Macmillan have joined the few previously public companies, such as McGraw-Hill and Prentice-Hall. Relatively few companies of any size and importance remain wholly private, notably Encyclopedia Britannica, Doubleday, Viking, and Scribner's.

Magazine entry into book publishing is, of course, nothing new. In the past, firms like Scribner's, Harper's, and Little, Brown had long published, or been associated with, magazines. Publishers of technical magazines had, in turn, expanded into the publishing of books based on, or related to, the content of their magazines. McGraw-Hill is the largest of the latter, but other firms like Reinhold and Simmons-Bordman had initiated similar undertakings. The rapid expansion of magazines into book publishing in recent years came, in part, as in the past, because the editorial content of magazines could be adapted and reused in book form so that economies of editorial effort could be achieved. A more important reason is that the subscription list of a number of magazines proved to be excellent mailing lists to use in mail sales of books whose editorial appeal resembled that of the magazines themselves. The relatively small working capital demands of magazines, whose subscriptions are paid for in advance and whose advertising revenues come in promptly, made them an excellent source of cash for financing the growth of book publishing.

A magazine-generated cash flow indeed provided most of the capital resources for the extraordinary growth of the McGraw-Hill Book Company from 1948 sales of around $10 million to 1968 sales of over $150 million. Readers' Digest developed a very large book club business. Time-Life founded a very successful book operation based both on its editorial and picture resources and its subscription list. A number of paperbound lines grew from magazine companies, including Dell Books and Popular Books, making use, in this case, of their newsstand distribution facilities. *The New York Times,* the *Wall Street Journal,* and, more notably, the *Los Angeles Times-Mirror* have added book publishing to their newspaper empires.

The most dramatic changes, however, have come not from public subscription, or from magazine entry into book publishing, but from the entry of electronic and communications companies into the book field. I have mentioned some of those who have bought book publishing companies, but let me repeat them: RCA, CBS, Raytheon, IBM, General Electric, Xerox, Litton Industries, Intrex. More recently, general conglomerates have entered the field as well.

These different sources of capital have had different kinds of impact on the book publishing industry. Going public has brought new capital into publishing, but rarely new management. When a previously privately owned publisher has offered stock to the public, the original management has almost always retained a controlling interest. No radical redirection of publishing objectives and practices has occurred. Nevertheless, there are inevitable changes.

The management of a public company, even though it may own more than half the stock, is no longer responsible only to itself. The managers are minority stockholders to whom the directors are in a position of trust. They must report annually to the stockholders and the public. They must submit to questioning by the financial press and by stock analysts. The daily quotations on the stock market constitute a gratifying, or embarrassing, visible score-keeping of public confidence in their stewardship. All publishers, including the owners of entirely personally owned or family held companies have always, of necessity, been avidly profit seeking, but the management of a public company not only must seek profits, but must justify its day-to-day decisions to itself, its stockholders, and the public under the conventional criteria of the business community.

Until recently, turning to the magazine aspects of it, with the major exception of McGraw-Hill and Crowell-Collier, magazine publishers entering book publishing have largely confined themselves to using their existing editorial resources to produce material to market by mail to their subscribers or through their newsstand distribution channels. McGraw-Hill, indeed, began with such an emphasis but soon expanded into general book publishing. Crowell-Collier, after having established itself in the subscription book field, abandoned magazine publishing entirely, but by purchasing Macmillan became a major factor in general book publishing. By further acquisitions, it has become an enormous and exceptionally diverse producer and distributor of educational materials and services. More recently, Time-Life, which had built up a very large book business closely related to its magazine business, has bought Silver-Burdett and Little, Brown and a number of European publishers and has become one of the largest general book publishers. Readers' Digest, which began in the book business by establishing a book club intended primarily for its subscribers and distributing condensed books similar to the magazine in content, has now, through the purchase of Funk & Wagnalls, also become a general book publisher.

Somewhat similar has been the pattern of newspaper entry into publishing. The activities of *The New York Times* and the *Wall Street Journal* have been closely related to their newspaper services, but the *Los Angeles Times-Mirror,* by buying New American Library, World Publishing Company, Matthew Bender (law book publishers), and Harry Abrams, has become a very diverse book publisher indeed. The impact of magazine publishing or book publishing has been, principally, to create a much larger role for the series of books designed and created to be sold by subscription, engineered, so to speak, like the magazine itself, for a particular market. When magazine publishers have entered general publishing, or bought general publishers, there has been little evidence of important change in editorial concept or practice. Magazine editing and book editing have major differences, but their similarities are sufficient to permit compatible unions.

Much more dramatic has been the recent entry of the electronic and communications technology companies into book publishing. This has been stimulated by three factors: technological developments that promise an important educational potential for the computers, a variety of other devices for the transmission and display of energies, and an outpouring of federal funds in aid of education.

It was, in particular, the idea of educational innovation that excited the electronic companies about a potential new market. There were excited visions of embodying the informational content developed by educators and textbook publishers into new formats of the electronic world and using the marketing channels of publishers to place these marvelously effective new products in the schools. It was hoped that this would have a genuinely revolutionary effect on American education, and also be an exceptionally prosperous business venture. The entry of the new technological forces into the industry hence had quite a different effect from that of the entry of new capital from general investors or from magazine and newspaper publishers. This latter investment from the electronic companies was made not only for profit, but with the deliberate intention of creating new kinds of products and altering the substance of publishing itself.

On the whole, however, I think it would be fair to say that the changes resulting from the marriage of print and electronics have been less than had been anticipated. The revolutionary new products to be born of this marriage have proved to be easier to envision than to create. Costs have proved to be very high, and the intellectual problem of devising teaching strategies and materials that can take advantage of a new technology has been extremely formidable. It is easier to say that a computer can measure a child's current knowledge and aptitude, discern experimentally his learning habits, select from a reservoir of resources the particular array of learning experiences that would lead him most effectively to this goal, than it is to present those to him by cathode ray tube display in a sequence and at a pace adapted to his individual needs.

Such a service is indeed well within the technological capacity of a properly instructed computer. But the problem is how to instruct a computer to do what we don't know how to do ourselves. More ambitious projects, as those of the General Learning Corporation, which is a joint subsidiary of Time-Life and General Electric, have been curtailed. The electronic companies have been learning that the production of rather conventional books may be the most profitable way to use their newly acquired publishing subsidiaries.

If the imaginative electronic developments have been slow in coming, publishing has expanded far beyond books to deal extensively with more conventional nonprint media. Films, film strips, slides, tapes, records, transparencies, science kits, computer programs, educational tests, even planetariums, are among the products regularly produced and sold by publishers and constitute a major part of the business of many very large houses. McGraw-Hill, as a matter of fact, now sells to elementary and high schools more nonbook materials than it does book materials.

What have been the consequences of the rapid growth in the size of the industry, the scale of its units, and the diversifying of its products and the sources of its funds and management? One consequence has been an obvious change in the nature and orientation of management. It has necessarily become more impersonal and professional. Professional financial experts, accountants, personnel specialists, warehousing and shipping experts, planners and public relations men have key roles in management. As publishing companies have become parts of large conglomerates, or have themselves become conglomerate enterprises, generalized skill in the management of human and financial resources has tended to replace specialized skills in publishing itself as the principal requisite for executive position.

Financial criteria, as the one set of common denominators running throughout a large enterprise, have necessarily become more important as the basis of decisions. How, except by a comparison of prospective returns on investment, can a CBS decide where to use a given quantum of capital in improving the Yankees, going into new areas of television programming, or expanding the working capital of Holt, Rinehart & Winston? How else can Crowell-Collier-Macmillan decide between a new encyclopedia and entry into new areas in college textbook publishing? This emphasis on financial criteria filters down to the level of decision on individual titles and may join or even predominate over editorial criteria.

Another consequence of the changes described above has been an increasing control over the sources and the markets of materials published. The traditional, and somewhat romantic, view of the publishing function considered it as a sort of broker between writers and readers. The publisher accepted what authors might write and offered it to the public through a chain of wholesale and retail dealers. In this tradition, he controlled neither the creation of the books he published nor their marketing to the final consumer. He was highly vulnerable to fluctuations of tastes, to the availability of adequate retail outlets, and to the flow of suitable manuscripts, with regard to all of which he had a somewhat passive role. But such unpredictability is intolerable to large enterprises which, as Professor Galbraith has pointed out in *The New Industrial State,* must be able to plan the application of capital in human resources, and hence to be able to control, or predict, both the availability of raw materials and the markets for products.

Hence the principal growth in publishing has come in areas in which the publisher can plan and supervise the creation, or, in the case of book clubs and paperbounds, the selection of books for a particular market, and can market those books himself to the ultimate consumer. Probably 80 percent, certainly 75 percent, of the dollar volume of all publishing today consists of textbooks, encyclopedias, audiovisual materials, subscription series, reference books, and the like, designed or created by the publisher, or by authors commissioned by him, to meet the needs of a specific market, or the book club and paperback selections made from the general range of trade titles with aptness for a particular market equally in mind. Probably an equal proportion of books are sold directly or indirectly to the public, to the ultimate consumer—the adopting school or college, the library, the book club member, the encyclopedia buyer in his home, a subscriber by mail. The primary function of publishing is perhaps no longer to issue and find a market for books brought to the publisher by an author, but rather to create, or supervise the creation of, works to fit the precise specification of markets already known to exist.

These trends in publishing have aroused a substantial concern that creative literature, and publishing oriented toward it, may be smothered under the vast mechanisms of the industry. I have, myself, shared some of these apprehensions. On the whole, however, I've been rather reassured by developments as they have actually come. Most of the publishers with a major stake in the educational, and especially in the college market, have realized that it is important in their interests, even their narrowest commercial interests, to sustain a high level of quality and of social and literary concern in their general publishing. Crowell-Collier-Macmillan, for example, remains a major publisher of poetry. McGraw-Hill has asserted a vigorous role in the publishing of bold and controversial books of young and unknown East European authors. Broadcasting ownership has not dampened the editorial sparkle of a Holt or a Random House.

Indeed, the greater availability of capital freed the larger houses for bolder and more imaginative ventures. Moreover, however large the major publishing corporations may loom, they by no means preempt publishing. Such personally owned and managed houses as Viking; Scribner's; Farrar, Straus; and Atheneum are engaged in vigorous and successful traditional trade publishing. Though such publishing is a smaller percentage of the total than in the past, it has never, in absolute terms, been so large or so successful.

A special development assuring further protection against the suffocation of talent and learning under the ponderous march of the giants has been the extraordinary growth of university presses. Though a small portion, still, of the industry as measured in dollars, university presses now assume a substantial percentage of all the titles published annually in this country. This assures an opportunity for the specialized work of scholarship to find an audience, but beyond that, poetry and belles lettres, fleeing the cost of commercial publishing, have often found a home in the university press.

The publishing world, taken as a whole, remains highly varied, flexible, and adaptive. No serious social need is likely to remain long unfilled. When you look to the future, my guess is that we do not face an era of such drastic change as in the immediate past. The present corporate structure of the industry gives ample resources for growth for an indefinite period. The decade ahead will probably be one of consolidating and improving this structure and the corresponding management practices, rather than introducing further radical alterations. Indeed, I suspect that experience will demonstrate that publishing is more successful and more profitable if it is allowed to follow its idiosyncratic patterns without too close confinement in the patterns of general corporate management, and that there will, in consequence, be something of a swing back toward more traditional publishing.

One factor that may produce further changes, however, is the emergence of a number of technological developments that make it more economical to produce copies of text one at a time on order. The essence of publishing has been the publisher's willingness to gamble on the demand for a book, investing in the substantial cost of setting type, making plates, running off an edition, and profiting then by the economies of the mass production of copies if the book was, indeed, in demand.

Under some of the newer technologies, if the text is embodied not in type or a printing plate but in negative micro-reproduction or on a duplicating machine master or computer memory core, individual copies can be produced to order more cheaply than before. Moreover, telefacsimile and computer data transmission facilities make it possible to produce such copies at a great distance from a single, centrally located master. There has been considerable speculation that this technique would radically change or even eliminate the traditional publishing function, but I think this is most unlikely.

Publishing to order, by the reproduction of individual copies, is of course no new or radical development. Probably even today, more book-length works are produced in this way, on custom-to-order, than by printing, as a result of the University Microfilms service of disseminating unpublished doctoral theses. Such a technique can, indeed, in special circumstances, replace conventional printing. A generation or two ago many universities required the publication of doctoral theses in printed form. None now do. I have no doubt at all that this technique of dissemination will grow and that tens of thousands, if not hundreds of thousands or millions of works, including out-of-print books, journals, and unpublished reports, will be brought under such bibliographical control that copies can be relatively quickly and inexpensively obtained, as is now the case with otherwise unpublished theses. But I suspect that this development will be devoted almost entirely to giving access to works for which the demand cannot sustain conventional publishing.

I think it is worth remembering that book publishing, as we have known it, serves efficiently only one very small sector of the whole communication spectrum. The sector that the conventional book publishing serves is the dissemination to an audience of some thousands an extensive work of at least moderately enduring importance, which is not under urgent demand as to time, and for which the audience is, or may be, widely dispersed in both space and time. The vastly important new communications technologies serve wide areas of the spectrum to the right and left of this segment, but none, realistically, promise to improve on publishing's performance of its narrow job. If there is a potential demand for, say, 5,000 copies of a work scattered widely over space and time, none of the new technologies, when all costs are included, can approach the efficiency of conventional printing.

Technology, indeed, is offering as much to conventional publishing as to its alternatives. The use of the computer in composition, when coupled with character generation by cathode ray tube and other concomitant technological developments in printing, offers the hope of substantial cost reduction that will enable publishing to serve efficiently levels of demand now below the margin of practicality. On balance, within the present sphere of publishing, technological progress is likely, within the near future, to bring improvements but not, I suspect, radical changes.

If one conclusion emerges from this hasty overview of this transitional era in publishing, it is that publishing is highly responsive to demand, that demand is increasingly expressed in the purchasing policies of institutional customers, of colleges, schools, libraries, and governmental agencies. The great increase in the number and diversity of curriculum-oriented children's books, the profusion of serious works on international relations, the multiethnic emphasis of textbooks, the enormous increase in the production of audiovisual materials, the new attention to materials for the marginally literate adult are all examples of response to demands that have been expressed through such institutions.

If one questions, hence, whether the highly organized publishing industry that is emerging will continue to offer a channel for the new poet, the untried novelist, the writer of integrity but of limited audience, perhaps the best answer will be found in the acquisition policies of libraries. For this is the channel through which, increasingly, society chooses to express its informational and cultural demands in the field of books. It is to this expression of demand that publishing more and more will closely respond.

WASSERMAN: Mr. Lacy has given us a whole range of ideas, issues, perspectives to respond to.

PARTICIPANT: I have a question for Mr. Lacy. If publishing is so rosy, then how do you explain the decline in reading?

LACY: There hasn't been any decline in reading. There is far more reading today than any time in the past.

PARTICIPANT: I disagree. As a public librarian, I think that if you look at the statistics, you will see that despite the fact that public libraries throughout the United States have increased their book acquisition programs enormously, they are experiencing serious declines. As far as the other avenues for people to acquire books, I think there has been an increase in sales of books, but I question whether people are really seriously reading these materials. I keep coming across collections where someone suddenly died and the books were given to a library and no one had ever read the vast quantity of materials that they had bought. It just seems as if this is an acquisitive society, and no one ever bothers to take advantage of the resources they acquire.

LACY: I suspect that the decline in library circulation that's been fairly noticeable in public library circulation around the country is largely due to two factors. One has been the very substantial improvement in college and school libraries over the last few years, which has taken off the public libraries the fairly enormous load of supporting student use. This has been a not altogether unwelcome cause of a reduction in circulation. I suspect the other has been very largely the increase in the purchase of books as opposed to borrowing them from libraries.

There is a fairly close correlation, an inverse correlation, between library circulation and prosperity regularly in the country. There was a very high level of library use in the depression, for example, relatively. The increase in sales of paperbound books and book club membership is substantially larger than the decrease in library circulation. The main increases in book purchasing have been in areas that suggest, in fact, that they *are* probably read. I suspect very few people buy paperbound books without at least an intention of reading them, for example, as opposed to buying reference sets for the library. All of the Gallup poll sorts of things show a very significant increase in reading over the last few years.

Certainly one's general impression in the market is that this is true. For example, there has been an enormous increase in sales of art books and elaborate picture books over the last fifteen or twenty years, which is partly related to cheaper and better techniques of producing color printing. This is probably prestige buying with very little reading, but these sales are weakening at a time when the sales of books that obviously are being bought to be read are going up very rapidly. A book like *Soul on Ice,* which we published, for example, has now sold close to a million copies. It is inconceivable a book like that would have had anything like that sort of readership ten or fifteen years ago. I am sure that almost every copy of that that is bought has been read. I would really feel fairly confident about that.

PARTICIPANT: It has been suggested that one of the main roles of a public library is to preserve literature that is not being read at the time, to make sure that copies of books are preserved, rather than just circulated, because in a few years somebody might want a book that would not be available if the public library hadn't bought it and preserved it.

PARTICIPANT: If it's any help, in our public library in Ithaca, New York, in the first five months after opening, the circulation increased 27 percent but the increase in reference use was 60 percent. To me, this indicates a greater interest and demand by our patrons for informational material, and less on popular works.

LACY: My general impression has been that increasing changes in public library concepts of their proper function have been related to the relative decline in circulation. I suppose all of us realize that any public library that chose to devote its acquisition money to buying multiple copies of current best sellers could double its circulation almost immediately, and that the decline in public library circulation represents, in part, a growing tendency that has been going on ever since the Public Library Inquiry of twenty years ago to concentrate on perhaps what one would think of as more serious social purposes, rather than the provision of light recreational reading. This has improved the quality of library use and also the reference use, but probably diminished the circulation. Most people do their detective story reading by buying paperbounds now rather than by borrowing library books. That was one of the staples of circulation.

BUNDY: I would like to respond as a former reference librarian on this business of being responsive to market. As a reference librarian, I was troubled. I didn't think the publishers were responsive to new markets, unconventional kinds of information needs. As you contemplate teaching reference, and you want to deal with groups of people that libraries haven't traditionally served, your whole paraphernalia, your tools with which you work, aren't suited to the client group that you would like to provide information to.

LACY: Well, publishing doesn't respond to needs; it responds to demands. The fact that a lot of new types of materials of this sort have been needed didn't translate itself into any multi-thousand-copy demand until very, very recently. As a matter of fact, I think the more venturesome members of the industry tended to perceive the need and to assume the demand would follow. They tended to get ahead of the demand on some of these things and had some rather unsuccessful early ventures.

BUNDY: I think we as a profession are culpable in not making that demand for client groups that didn't know how to make it. I'd like to explore the relationship of the publishing industry to the library field, because it seems to me that when you say the responsiveness to markets, you're talking about our whole paraphernalia for reviewing which has been a reinforcement of traditional ways of looking at libraries. I won't claim that the publishing industry has had control over our reviewing medium, but I think there has been a mutual reinforcement of a very restricted way of seeing needs.

LACY: That's very likely true. In the children's book field, particularly, I have sometimes had the feeling that there was a sort of sisterhood of children's book editors, children's librarians, and children's book reviewing media that had established a set of criteria of desirability that weren't necessarily very closely related to the actualities of the world. Actually, they shift back and forth in jobs. A lot of children's book editors have been children's librarians, and so on. This happens.

I think library reviewing media miss a great deal in not being much tougher on publishers. For example, for years librarians have been complaining because publishers don't use better-quality and longer lasting paper in books, and with very considerable justification. Yet very rarely does a library reviewing medium say anything about the paper in the book. If every library review medium or library journal sent out a notice to publishers and said, "No book will be reviewed in the library journal unless the review copy is accompanied by a note from the publisher on the acid content of the paper contained," and that was reported in the review, that one little thing would revolutionize publishing.

NIMER: Would it raise the prices of the books?

LACY: No. Well it might, initially. Acid-free paper isn't really any more expensive than other kinds of paper once a mill is converted to produce it. Practically all the mills that make acid-free paper now have their entire demand consumed. There would be a good deal of scramble to buy paper for a year or two until mills converted. But once a mill is converted, it just depends on what you use for filler in the papers. McGraw-Hill uses only acid-free paper in hardbound books.

BUNDY: But it's not the paper. We've been concerned with the paper too long. It's the content we should have concerned ourselves with. You say there is a time coming when publishers can produce books on demand. I think your illustration, University Microfilms, is a monopoly that's very slow in giving service and that's not the best. Are you saying publishing is going to respond to the fact that libraries indeed are producing on demand? We're not always getting copyright. Are you saying that it's out of control and therefore publishing must do something about it? Why is this the direction they are moving in?

LACY: I wasn't suggesting that publishing was necessarily going to move in that direction, that is, conventional publishing. There has grown up a whole spectrum of production enterprises. Conventional publishing probably rarely produces a book for which it can't conceive a demand of, let's say, 3,000 copies. University presses are prepared to produce materials where they can foresee a demand of maybe 1,000 copies. Over to the right of that, or left depending on your orientation, you've got Scarecrow Press, Shoe String Press, and their equivalents, perhaps prepared to produce a book for a 500-copy demand. Beyond that, the Peter Smiths and the Russells, or the Johnson Reprints, any one of the hundreds that have grown up as this technology for small editions has grown, are prepared to produce for a demand of 100 to 250 copies. Finally, there is University Microfilms and others, like Bell & Howell, who would be prepared to produce individual copies. Now, most publishers, not finding this production of individual copies a particularly rewarding and interesting thing themselves, have been perfectly willing to license somebody else to do it. Most of the industry, for example, licenses University Microfilms, though not exclusively. They will license others as well, to produce copies on a single-copy basis, on order. I think a whole range of services will rise to meet this.

BUNDY: I sound unfriendly. For the last three days, we've been skirting the question of being tied to the economic base. I guess I'm just nibbling away at the notion that the viability of publishing depends upon the profit motive.

LACY: The viability of publishing depends on the costs' being met. They don't have to be met, necessarily, from sales. They can be met from foundation grants, or from university subsidies, or whatever. There are many methods to pay the bill. They don't necessarily have to make a profit.

PARTICIPANT: A friend of mine saw your name on this list of speakers for today, so he asked me to ask you a question which is rather loaded. He's a librarian, by the way. He said that he felt that the publishing industry really didn't have the library interest at heart, because in the big picture of the publishing industry, we represent a detriment for economic growth because we take away from individual sales of publications. Do you think that he was right in that assumption?

LACY: No. He might have been thirty years ago. There was a time back in the 1920s when a major publisher introduced a motion at a meeting of the predecessor organization of the American Book Publishers' Council suggesting that the National Association of Book Publishers, as it was then called, raise a fund which would be given as a grant to the American Medical Association to sustain a program of research in the transmission of disease through the circulation of public library books, in an effort to discourage people from borrowing books and to get them to buy them. But certainly no publisher would think that way today. Library purchasing is a very substantial component of the entire market for books. If you exclude textbooks, mass-market encyclopedias, paperbounds, and book clubs, and concentrate just on the new publication of individual, nontextbook titles, I would guess half the market is the library market. Its health and well-being is indispensable to the publishing industry. It's a particularly valuable market qualitatively because it tends to even out the best seller–failure, peak-and-valley syndrome.

Let me digress for a second to say that, in general, books that are very successful in the general trade field or become extremely successful, a book that sells 100,000 copies, let's say, and is a smash best seller in its hard cover edition, will also almost certainly be a book club selection, and will also almost certainly be an extremely successful paperbound book. Most hard cover trade publishing, on the average, is carried on, at a loss before the receipt of subsidiary rights incomes. That is a typical picture for trade publishing. Publishing of new adult books, other than textbooks, would show roughly, let's say, about a 5 percent loss before the receipt of income from paperbound and book club editions. Those would transform it from a 5 percent loss to a 6, 7, or 8 percent profit.

Now, the point is that the profit from these subsidiary rights comes from a relatively few titles that are already themselves very profitable as best sellers. Probably two-thirds of all the titles published in trade publishing lose money, as a matter of fact. If you want to ask me why publishers publish them anyway, I will have to answer I don't know, but I'm glad they do. Libraries tend to balance this out. Libraries, proportionately, are an insignificant market for *Portnoy's Complaint*. They may buy 6, 7, or 8,000 copies or 10,000. Perhaps it sells 500,000 copies so it doesn't really matter. On the other hand, for a university press book, a serious nonfiction book, or an important biography, libraries may be 50, 60, or 70 percent of the demand. Without that, it just couldn't be published.

What has made the difference between 10,000 titles and 40,000 titles a year is almost entirely library demand. It has provided a sustenance for the serious specialized book in international relations, for example. We published over the last couple of years a series of twenty titles for the Council on Foreign Relations, that Atlantic China Policy Studies series. They sold anywhere from 1,200 to 7,500 copies each. I'm sure that two-thirds of those sales were to libraries, if not three-fourths. Publication of series like that is just impossible without a library market. You just couldn't do it.

Every publisher maintains a substantial library promotions department, most of them a considerable library sales effort. The publishing industry of all the rest of the world gives no library discounts or, at a maximum, only 10 percent in Great Britain. If you were a German librarian and went to a bookstore to buy books for your library, you would pay full list price. This is the only country that gives libraries substantially the same discounts bookstores get and really fusses about how hard it is to sell to them. No, God forbid, the publishing industry would collapse and die tomorrow if libraries went out.

PARTICIPANT: I have two questions. If multiple copying for fair use becomes legal, and if cause for copying becomes widespread, how will that affect the publishing industry? Number two, would you contemplate lending coming under copyright?

LACY: Let me answer the last question first because it's simpler. No, in this country, the publishing industry has always opposed the extension of copyright to loans of books. A practice exists in Sweden, for example, where libraries pay a royalty to the author in terms of the circulation of his books. You can equitably make a pretty good case for it, but practically it's just ridiculous, impossible to administer, and not worth considering. On the other question, the "if" sets up a situation that would change the answer.

The first question was: If the law should be changed so that multiple copying of books, presumably by libraries, would be legal, and if the cost of doing that were reduced to be competitive with original book publishing, would this change publishing? In the first place, I don't think there's the slightest chance the copyright law will be changed to that degree. Nobody has asked for it, not the library profession and not educators. While Congress was quite anxious, and publishers as well, to clarify "fair use" to the point that would unburden the red tape and uncertainty over many kinds of library copying, nobody wanted to use a modification of the copyright law to put libraries or anybody else in the position of publishing, of large-scale production and vending of books, without the author's permission. I don't think there's any likelihood that would happen. The situation might develop in which there was such a radical cost reduction that reprographic copying of books would become cheaper than producing the original books. This is unlikely, because no matter how efficient we get there are certain minimal costs, simply in terms of photographic paper and that sort of thing. If that happened, there probably would be a system of licensing and paying royalties to the author.

PARTICIPANT: Is there any communication between the libraries and publishing? Can the library influence the type of publishing? The concept of book selection is disappearing. We have the idea of current imprint. We buy everything that is published in the English language. How can we respond to the publishing industry?

LACY: There are a great many profession-wide levels of contact. There is an annual joint meeting of principal officers of the publishing industry and the American Library Association for discussion of general problems. Both the Adult Services Division of ALA and the children's library services associations actually have joint committees with editors in their corresponding areas of publishing to discuss kinds of books needed. I think much more effective is just what libraries are buying.

PARTICIPANT: We buy everything.

LACY: Fifty libraries buy everything. There are 100,000 more libraries in the United States. The other 99,950, believe me, are highly selective in what they buy. This is a highly determinative sort of thing. This is the reason, for example, that we used to publish 500 or 600 children's books a year, mostly fiction. We now publish about 3,500 a year, the overwhelming majority of which are not only nonfiction but highly curriculum oriented, so that, for example, a biography of de Soto fits very neatly into the unit on explorers in the social studies program in the fifth grade and is really engineered for that. That's because that's what libraries have said that they want in the most tangible way—by buying it.

Almost every major publisher has a library sales force that annoys librarians considerably by going around heckling them. One of the things they are doing is nosing around trying to find out what could possibly sell, what libraries want, and feeding a fairly steady flow of information back. We might not be very bright sometimes in responding to it, but there is a sedulous effort to find out.

NIMER: This was a partial answer to my question, which was: What kinds of mechanisms do you have for finding out what things people will buy?

LACY: Well, one of the principal ones is simply exhibiting. Every publisher exhibits at the American Library Association convention.

Most larger publishers exhibit at state and regional meetings. McGraw-Hill exhibits at something like ninety library associations a year.

NIMER: Not just in libraries.

LACY: Let me just finish the library thing—plus salesmen calling and the rest. So far as the rest of it, it is mainly a question of "Try it and see what sells and what doesn't sell."

PARTICIPANT: Let me rephrase my question a little bit. Suppose the *Physics and Chemistry Handbook* was read into the computer's memory in a university situation, or in a company situation, and suppose the university or the company department head wants that information on the console directly. Whenever workers wanted information, they would look it up on the console and get the part that they were interested in. Would you consider that an infringement of copyright?

LACY: Well, putting it on the computer in the first place without permission, yes, this is an infringement. The permission would be given readily enough for a fee. There's no resistance to doing this sort of thing. The most important proprietory body of information that my own company controls, for example, is Standard & Poor's financial data. It's a subsidiary of McGraw-Hill. That's all computer based. As a matter of fact, they give the tapes away to business schools around the country to put into computers, seeing more advantages in habituating students to using it than any loss of business in selling the returns.

The view of the registrar of copyrights, at least under the present law, which is, of course, silent about computers since they didn't exist when it was passed, does require the permission of the proprietor of a copyright to make a copy or a version of a work. The registrar has indicated that, in his view, the input of the content of a copyrighted work extending beyond the level of fair use into a computer by tape, or by punch cards, or by keyboard input would be a version that would require the permission of the proprietor. It has never been tested in the courts, but I would not really have any serious question that the courts would sustain that.

We've explored very actively what the possibilities of this are, and I guess other publishers have as well. Last year I had a bunch of fairly high-level scientists and computer experts in. All of them came to the conclusion that it really was just not a feasible thing now. It would be so much cheaper to keep a handbook on the desk of everybody who wanted to use it than to set up an expensive computer installation. It wasn't a workable alternative, even assuming free use of copyright.

BUNDY: I'm very naive about this, but if a publisher owned information vital to the public interest, it might not be in private interest to make information available. Although you said you allowed somebody to have information for marketing reasons, it would seem to me we might have to rethink this problem through. It might not be in the public interest. People who control information are monopolies. They should be subject to some . . .

LACY: Well, in the first place, you can't copyright information.

BUNDY: You seem to be saying you can do anything you want with information until you sell it.

LACY: No. No, what you sell really has very little to do with the copyright question. What the copyright law gives the proprietor the exclusive right to do is (a) make copies of his work and (b) perform it under certain circumstances, perform it publicly for profit unless it is a drama, or perform it publicly for profit or not if it is a drama, and make a version of it. There is nothing in the copyright law, except in connection with the performance of nondramatic works, where the profitability affects the copyright.

A copyright, though, is different from a patent. It doesn't apply to the knowledge or information itself, but only to the form of words that are involved. For example, if you put out a copyrighted cook book, your copyright doesn't extend to the knowledge of how to make Beef Wellington. Anybody can read the cookbook and make Beef Wellington all he pleases, and tell anybody else how to make Beef Wellington. It's different from a patent, because if you had patented a process, nobody else could use the process. In the cookbook you would have a copyright against a competitive use of the material, the particular information, the particular words. If you were making another cookbook of your own, you couldn't take the recipes from this one.

BUNDY: Couldn't I make five copies of a cookbook I paid for in my home?

PARTICIPANT: Not to sell.

BUNDY: No. He is saying selling is not the factor.

LACY: Selling is not necessarily the factor. It isn't a determining factor.

BUNDY: It's whether you catch me.

LACY: No, really it isn't that, either. Suppose, for example, I'm a composer. I've written a march, appropriate for school bands. I am offering it for sale to school bands. Now, as a matter of fact, this is one place where it's cheaper to Xerox the music, rather than to buy it, for various reasons. Suppose the school decides it doesn't want to buy 100 copies of this music for the 100 members of the chorus. It reproduces the 100 copies and gives them to the band instead of buying them. This is clearly a copyright infringement, though nobody has sold a copy of it. That is what I meant by saying selling it isn't necessarily the factor; it's exploiting the author's work without paying for doing it.

BUNDY: Maybe I'm just trying to break your system, but it seems to me we keep hearing publishers talking about authors. I've been an author. I've watched the sales and I found myself resenting it if somebody wanted me to give them a free copy. But maybe this is something that needs to go. Let's pay people for work they do and have it over and done with. Then the issue becomes what will happen to the publishing industry? But I think it's in the books we now can do it. Right now, we can make copies and you can't legislate this. You can't control it.

LACY: We may not be able realistically to control it, but it is illegal to make a copy of a work that extends beyond the rather flexible conception of "fair use." In general, what this means is to make a copy when the purpose of making it is to avoid buying the book as a realistic alternative.

BUNDY: We've been talking with some men this week who, if they had to get fifty copies of a book to some people, would think nothing of breaking all laws. I think you would be in a great deal of trouble if you went out and told some of these people in poverty areas they had to pay for the fifty copies they had made.

LACY: You might be surprised to find, however, that the publisher would say, "Sure, go ahead, if you ask my permission." The fact that one has to get copyright doesn't mean one can't do the job.

PARTICIPANT: Whenever we come across out-of-print, which is not on sale, and we need a copy in the library, we write a letter to the publisher asking for his permission to Xerox one copy for library use only. We usually get approval, but this is not always the case.

BUNDY: Now that our copy machines are outside, and we're not controlling them, we don't know what's going on. We're happy we don't.

WASSERMAN: To follow this for just a moment, there is something that's happening on a very, very wide scale. I don't know what the strategy of the publishing industry is with regard to this. I haven't been able to identify anything on the subject, but this is the reproduction of copies of materials for classroom use, particularly with the emphasis on students in formal courses. Academic subjects range over a wide variety of books and articles. The current position is to just make some copies rather than to buy the things. This, I'm sure, is a very wide-scale phenomenon in the culture now. Where do you see this leading? This is, what do you see as the implications of this? I'm sure it has an influence on the sale of the original product.

LACY: Well, I take it what you're referring to is the business of a teacher wanting to have a particular F. Scott Fitzgerald short story, let's say, which isn't conveniently available in the textbook or the anthology used by the class, so he arranges to have the library Xerox fifty copies of it.

WASSERMAN: Precisely.

LACY: I think any publisher would consider that a copyright infringement. He might, or might not, want to prosecute for it for public relations reasons. Certainly, the Authors' League would feel violently that this is a copyright infringement, much more violently than the publishers, as a matter of fact. Most publishers and a great many schools and libraries confronted with this do ask the publisher for permission to do it. Most publishers that I know grant this permission automatically for payment of a fee which usually runs a cent a page a copy, which they give to the author.

BUNDY: Wait a minute. Most don't ask! Every faculty member I know is doing it, and he's not going to the library, so the library isn't doing it.

LACY: Publishers get large numbers of requests from many librarians.

BUNDY: I would still submit that you're getting a small number of requests from a small number of very conscientious people.

LACY: This may be. There are a lot of requests that come in. Most publishers, probably a lot of publishers, just simply ignore the requests.

PARTICIPANT: Do the publishers hesitate to prosecute for fear that they will lose the case?

LACY: No.

PARTICIPANT: It is so widespread that I think if you prosecuted a university library for copying a chapter out of a book and making fifty copies, I think you'd lose the case.

LACY: No. That's an open-and-shut case. No court would consider it otherwise. I really, honestly don't think that there would be any court in the country that would hesitate to hold that as an infringement.

PARTICIPANT: Well, I'd be happy to see them follow it through, because I really feel that it is so widespread that they are afraid to tackle it.

LACY: No, I don't think that's it. There is, as a matter of fact, one quite specific case that has been decided. It was a test case and effectively argued on both sides. True, it wasn't brought by a publisher, but the situation is analogous. A man made his living primarily by selling music for school choirs and choruses which he composed himself, printed himself, and went around the country marketing. He had shown some of his material to a high school musical director in California, who found some of the material interesting and wanted to make some changes in his arrangement. He did so, and ran off 50 or 100 copies of it for his own choir, all with the best of intentions. As a matter of fact, he sent the proprietor a copy of it telling him he had done this and saying, "I hope you like the new arrangement." He was sued and it didn't go by default or anything. The school was defended by a professor of the University of California Law School who is probably the foremost academic expert on copyright in the country, and the case was lost decisively. I don't think there's any question.

PARTICIPANT: There's another human factor here. Here's an individual whose right has been infringed. It wasn't a case of a publisher. I think people take a different view against a corporation than they would a person.

LACY: The people, through the courts, recognize corporations as people when they know they represent authors. The main kind of thing that gets done this way is short stories and poems. The average poet in this country gets the overwhelming majority of his income from permission to copy his material for school use. When a school reproduces a poet's work without paying him anything, this is downright hurting. I would guess 80 percent of the income from his poetry of a poet like Robert Lowell comes not from its original publication but from its permission to anthologize. A school that, in effect, does a private anthology without payment to the poet is really taking money directly from his pocket.

BUNDY: How would you characterize, in general, the publishing industry's sense of social responsibility at this stage of the game? In specific terms, what are they doing and in what ways? Where are they mobilizing resources to put them where they're needed?

LACY: I don't think publishers are very different from people generally. Some of them are highly socially responsible. Some of them don't give a damn, and there's everything in between in the spectrum. I can give you some examples of the range. In the general race area, for example, I think most publishers today are making quite an active effort to recruit more black employees and to give them a better break in terms of promotions and so on, both individually and through the associations of publishers who have set up a special project for recruiting. Most major publishers, like the company I work for, have fairly large-scale training programs and mount a fairly strenuous effort in this area. There is a long way to go before there is anything like equity, but I think it is a fairly vigorous effort.

Most publishers now are making strenuous efforts to eliminate material from textbooks that might be considered racially derogatory or hostile. A surprising amount is sensitive. I suppose this is due much to the toughness of some school systems, like Washington or Detroit, about not buying books unless this has been done. It's due as much to that as it is to any sudden efflorescence of conscience in book publishers, just as tending to have lily-white textbooks was a simple, mindless response to demands of that time, as much as it was to any inherent racism in the publisher itself. That is, I would guess it's a fairly passive response to the market. Publishers, God knows, are beating the bushes today to publish more books dealing with race problems, even in a white radical sort of sense. Again, this is not self-sacrificial.

PARTICIPANT: No, they sell very well.

LACY: Yes, I agree. That's the main reason they're being looked for. Publishers are essentially no worse, as well as no better, than most other people of comparable levels of education or general orientation. I would expect you would find most publishers feel very much like most librarians on this sort of urban or racial issue.

BUNDY: In the industry, is there a sense of social upheaval and a need for the private sector to respond?

LACY: Yes, in some ways we were probably ahead of some others. The industry put up most of the money and supplied the initiative and ideas, for example, for the conference with the Harvard-MIT

Center for Urban Studies in 1963 on problems of the urban public library. This was almost the first conference that really dealt with the problem of library service to ghetto areas. It had similar conferences with the Office of Education in 1963 and 1964 about publishing for the marginal literate adult vocational training materials and that sort of thing.

I think in each of those cases an awareness of the emerging social need was a stimulating factor. I certainly wouldn't want to minimize the fact that publishers were seeing in this a market as well as a social need. I think the cupidity of publishers is one of the principal guarantors of its social service, and of freedom of the press in a sense. Publishers are alert to be responsible to any kind of need for which society is prepared to put up money without interjecting its own attitude.

WASSERMAN: I suppose this really is the cause for a kind of queasiness on the part of people who look at the publishing industry. It's not an industry like others, because it controls a major medium. To the extent that the medium is only sluggishly responsive to where change is and how it's inspired, I suppose those who would hope for more would expect more, and would feel more comfortable about a medium which was moving faster than the industrial construct.

From what you say, the publishing industry is moving in tandem with other elements of the corporate world, but it's different in the sense that it controls an important element of the intelligence in the culture. To the extent that it proceeds at this pace, if the culture is not being responsive, here is a utility that's not moving the culture fast enough to deal with its fundamental problems. This causes, I suppose, a kind of queasiness. Now I don't know what it does or how it does it, and what the instrumentality for this is, but I don't see publishing like I see cars or potatoes or something else. I see it as sort of central element in formulating the national intelligence.

LACY: I think it is true that publishing is tending to resemble a general corporation in its internal management corporate structure. What it stays in step with in terms of the content of what it publishes, however, is certainly not the general corporate structure. It's the educational, academic, and library community. It publishes what it can find out about, what it can discover. It publishes what that community creates, in the sense of what the writing community and the scholarly community creates, and what that community demands, in terms of what schools, libraries, and the general public buy. I guess, on the whole, publishing tends to stay abreast of the more innovative.

Let me try to say what I mean more clearly. If you took the schools in the country and arranged them in a spectrum according to what they buy, from the most conservative to the most radical, I guess that publishing would be up somewhere around the percentile that would be about 20 percent away from the most innovative and about 80 percent away from the most conservative. That is, in general, the industry in the production of educational products has tended to stay ahead of the bulk of its market and a little behind the most advanced of its market.

Publishing, to a much less degree than one would think, really controls the content of trade publishing, as distinguished from encyclopedia and textbook publishing. In that area, it remains more of a sort of recipient passer-on of what the culture can do. One final thing: publishing, even with all the great wave of mergers and consolidations, remains an exceptionally diffuse industry in relation to its total size. Only three major automobile manufacturers still remain after all the consolidations. There are hundreds and hundreds of book publishers. There are 200 or 300 really significant book publishers with a wide range of social orientation. It would be hard to point to anything that's needed that isn't published somewhere. The industry, as a whole, is able to remain quite responsive even if individual components aren't.

REID: There was an article in the *Wall Street Journal* within the last two years, which described the move of publishing houses to conglomerates. For example, Xerox bought two or three publishers; IBM picked up several.

LACY: IBM doesn't really own any general book publishers. They own Science Research Associates, which does specialized education books.

REID: Is this all?

LACY: All IBM owns. Xerox owns Ginn, Bowker, University Microfilms, and American Educational Publishing.

REID: Then some other similar organizations have picked up some publishing houses. Previous to that, some houses merged, so that a pyramiding of control is forming in the publishing industry. Some of the pyramiding comes under the control of nonpublishing previous interests. That's the first point. I don't know what the implications are. I don't know whether or not there are social implications that we can put our finger on any more. Besides that, Westinghouse now has Westinghouse Learning, and General Electric has General Learning. There is something happening in the relationship of publishing to the wider corporate world. Certainly there is a greater possibility of control of what the masses read.

LACY: Of what that publishing house publishes.

REID: Which is the same, isn't it?

LACY: No. RCA can keep Random House from publishing something, but they can't keep Viking from doing it. The same author can go to any one of a number of other publishing houses.

REID: But at least there is an additional, possible constraint. The other thing is that, by default primarily, I suspect, publishing houses have determined curriculum in the lower schools, at least. This is true, to a very great extent, mostly because teachers are passive and because the educational world has not been aggressive. Teachers haven't been writing books. They haven't been producing them fast enough. But because teachers are passive, they rely very heavily on what's between two covers. Though you may have some way of getting input from a small group of teachers about what goes into those covers in the academic world, once you get it in there, you have really done something to what happens in the classroom for a considerable period of time.

What I would like to know is, what is the process within your own selective mechanism for determining what you publish? What process recognizes this problem, if any? How do you address that?

LACY: Well, that's really a series of questions. Let me try to speak to some very briefly. One of the points was that a good many publishing houses, by consolidation and through acquisition by nonpublishing concerns, have been exposed to a situation where there may be a control over what's available to the public. This is a matter of legitimate concern, and as I said in a paper, I have worried about it a good deal myself. I haven't seen much of it happen. The only egregious case I can think of, in which the publishing of a book by a particular publisher got suppressed because of a new corporate ownership, was when Funk & Wagnalls was going to bring out a book which was a very hostile attack on American advertising, and its new owners, Readers' Digest, killed the book. I don't think they would ever do that again, because the public uproar about it did them far more harm than anything else. I didn't suppress the book, which was immediately picked up by another publisher.

In general, the ability of large corporations to prevent the publishing of a book really doesn't exist. If it gets killed by one house and it's really publishable, it's readily publishable by another. In general, the larger houses have tended to the more provocative publishing. Ralph Nader, for example, is published by Random House, which is owned by RCA. Good, solid, square McGraw-Hill publishes Julius Hobson and Eldridge Cleaver and will publish the next book by the authors of *Black Rage,* and so on. In contrast to the nonprofit publishing, the university presses and foundation presses, it has actually been the large corporate presses that have tended to publish controversial material, primarily because (a) they make money, and (b) they get into trouble by publishing this sort of book. Corporations like to make money and don't much mind getting into trouble. University presses are not interested in making money but very much worried about getting into trouble.

Now, in the textbook field, on the whole, I think the influence of publishers over curriculum content is declining, not increasing. I would guess that in the 1920s, 1930s, and 1940s, Scott, Foresman and Row-Peterson readers tended to dominate the whole pattern of reading as taught in the United States, because nobody else was thinking about teaching methods. Actually, with the important revolt in the late 1950s and 1960s against the inadequate pedagogy, both the foundations and the government are financing the new math, the newer methods of teaching biology, the new chemistry series. Further back on the horizon, the Office of Education has made grants for social studies, English, and so on. Publishers are actively competing to incorporate these new things, which have been generated this time more out of the university community.

So I would guess that the reviving strength of the educational community is tending to displace publishing as the determinative of teaching methods, rather than the reverse. The new math didn't come out of the publishing industry, whereas the "See Jane jump" did. Well, actually it also came out of Gray and the University of Chicago School of Education.

BUNDY: It was an unholy alliance with the industry.

WASSERMAN: I think this would be a good point for us to take a break.

8

THE RISE OF THE
INFORMATION UTILITY

Thursday Morning, August 14
Lecturer: David Goldberg
Panelists: Jordan Baruch

Goldberg: I don't know anything about the publishing industry, or information utilities, or anything, but I hadn't planned on talking about those anyway. They knew that when they invited me, so I feel pretty clean about it.

Nimer: You addressed the publishers.

Goldberg: I addressed the publishers, but I didn't know anything about publishing before I addressed them, or after, either. I never know what I'm going to talk about until I get there. I didn't know what I was going to talk about this morning until I had to sit through the morning session. Something like this morning makes me at first bored, and then frustrated, and then very angry, and then I blow up. I've done that in public enough times now to want to try something else. At this point, I'm not sure what else I want to try, but I guess what I have in the way of notes is to try to circle back around and try to handle the situation intellectually and keep all my hostility and anger somewhat under control.

I was on a panel at Yale a couple of months ago. I got pretty bored and frustrated. I got up and walked out and came back in again. Finally it was my turn to talk, and I asked people to stand up and kind of move around. I started talking about a micro-lab I had done there in the afternoon. I started talking about the real, suppressed hostility that I felt among the students at Yale. I had never done a micro-lab with students where there was so much physical violence right at the boiling point. As I talked about it, I started sensing how much hostility there had been in the room all night— verbal and intellectual hostility with people standing up and talking at other people in a hard-edged way.

It ended up with a student pushing the microphone in the face of the chairman of the curriculum committee, who started yelling. The students walked out, and he was saying, "What's the meaning of this? Can you explain that to me? What are you trying to accomplish?" to the students' backs. The professor never did hear what the students had to say, because the students weren't saying it the way he was used to having students talk to him. Then we spent about an hour with the students in the audience trying to tell the professor what it was all about. He never did really hear, but he knew that he had been exposed to something new, and unfortunate. Anyway, I kind of precipitated that, because I started screaming and yelling at him. I used a lot of obscenities. So I would rather not do that. I'm not sure what I am going to do.

One of the things I realized this morning is that I'm really tuned in now to the process rather than the content. I'm very responsive to what was happening here, the way it was happening, not necessarily to what was being said. I think this is increasingly important—the distinction between process and content, and the fact that we've had a content-oriented educational system and a content-oriented society. We're now equal. I think people started rebelling at the content, and then realized that the content and the process were all mixed up. Mostly young people and black people are sensitive now to the process and how it determines the content.

Anyway, I think I'll talk about the process. I'll try to do it intellectually, kind of. For me, this would be a big thing now. For the rest of you, maybe that's the bag you want to get out of. That's the bag I'd kind of like to come back to, in some way. How many have read *Understanding Media* by McLuhan?

NIMER: How many have understood *Understanding Media?*

WASSERMAN: Lacy, you published it, but did you read it?

GOLDBERG: I read it about three years ago, and I didn't understand it at the time, but I felt it was terribly important. I picked up one or two or three central ideas in it, and then kind of put it out of my mind. But over the last several years I have grown to understand it more and more and more. Finally I had to do a paper a couple of months ago on designing the living-learning unit for a new college. It just seemed to me that, of all the futuristic stuff that I've done and read about, McLuhan's book was the most significant thing around, because what he's talking about is a dramatic change in the intellectual process. What I did was look at the implications of architectural design, because when our way of thinking changes, then everything else changes too. The environment we live in has an impact on how we think. So McLuhan provided a structure for me to start viewing.

A friend of mine talks about "old culture" and "new culture." He accused me of being old culture. I think he changed his mind later. I guess this morning was a good example of old culture, old process, old ways of doing things. There are new ways of doing things that aren't nearly as well known.

I'm not sure I want to handle it this way after all.

BUNDY: You mean you feel you are not communicating?

PARTICIPANT: This is what is missing here—the intellectual presentation of the issues.

GOLDBERG: It's really very uncomfortable.

PARTICIPANT: You said you got some feeling for the process rather than content. How would you articulate what you felt to be the process? What do you think is going on and how is it going on?

GOLDBERG: The problem is that by discussing it this way, I fall back into the old culture, more or less.

PARTICIPANT: Discuss it any way you feel like it.

PARTICIPANT: Did you prepare anything before you came?

GOLDBERG: No.

PARTICIPANT: Mr. Lacy had a well-organized and a very provocative presentation. Being intellectually oriented, I appreciated this and feel that I got some new knowledge and new concepts.

BUNDY: You could have read it yourself.

PARTICIPANT: So if you didn't prepare anything before you came, well, naturally you feel . . .

PARTICIPANT: He has an opportunity to say what he feels. It is not necessary for him to prepare any speech. Whatever is on your mind, you give.

PARTICIPANT: Mr. Goldberg, you may not know too much about the publishing industry, but I'm sure with your background you're familiar with libraries. Why don't you tell us about libraries as you envision them? What do you see as their function in education?

GOLDBERG: I'm more concerned about what's going on in this room now.

PARTICIPANT: Yes, but we're all librarians.

GOLDBERG: Yes, but you're all in this room, too.

PARTICIPANT: Do you want us to go outside or something?

GOLDBERG: No, I'd be just as concerned outside.

PARTICIPANT: Would like to organize a short T-group?

GOLDBERG: No, I'd like to do something different. I know I can do those.

PARTICIPANT: May I ask you something? I think that there are many times that a person doesn't have a speech. I have been with academia for a long time, not directly, but indirectly. Why not have questions and answers? I think people are dying to ask a few things.

PARTICIPANT: Whatever you get across, I hope you get across what you are trying to do. That's my only comment.

GOLDBERG: You just never know.

PARTICIPANT: Could Mr. Baruch go first, and maybe have Mr. Goldberg respond to him?

BARUCH: It gets a little difficult being a discussant about something that hasn't been said.

PARTICIPANT: Suppose you become the discusser and . . .

BARUCH: Yes, but then we're involved in psychodrama, and that really doesn't have anything do do with this.

PARTICIPANT: Mr. Goldberg, I'm a scientist. Let's say I'm a librarian. I want to know what your new ideas on education are. How can a librarian in school progress? Or is there no chance?

GOLDBERG: You want to check my credentials? See, this is "old culture." Me, as the authority, sitting up here telling you what I think, as though I have a hell of a lot to say to you.

PARTICIPANT: Dr. Goldberg, I would like to know more about process and content. Other speakers here talked about the process, and I think you seem to know what you meant, but I'm not sure. I'm interested in knowing about process, and the difference between that and content. How would you define those two?

GOLDBERG: Let me say this first. I will fall into all the traps that I'm talking about. That's what I haven't done in a long time now. In many ways, I have so radically broken with the past, my past and the past of other people, that I missed all the traps. I wasn't guilty of the paradoxes that I'm going to be guilty of now, and I really don't want to fall back into those.

BARUCH: Maybe I can help. Can I try? As long as we've quit working.

PARTICIPANT: Do you mean you can tell us about content and show us about process?

BARUCH: This is something different. Mr. Goldberg has long been concerned with the future, according to his biography, and presumably with the prediction of the future from the situation of the present and the history of the past. I think we have heard a speech here earlier this morning of somebody addressing the world as it exists in publishing, how information gets to a marketplace from people who conceive of it, the motives and activities that go on in such a process. I think there are alternative worlds, however. Let me postulate one, and ask you to address yourself to giving the same speech that Mr. Lacy did, as a publisher in that alternate world.

What I would like to postulate is the following. There is a time in the future when thinkers are salaried, and are not paid proportionally to their output, or proportionally to the public purchase, where thinkers are salaried, and where the technology is such that the cost of rendering thought on paper is essentially negligible. In other words, where information flow takes the place in society roughly the same as water flow does at the present time, where our main concerns are control of the flow so as to be beneficial and not to drown, getting that flow where it is needed, and rendering as an economic part of society, is something that is crucial to the development of society.

I would like you to put yourself in the effective role of being in charge of the Southeast Maryland Information District, instead of the water district. What would be the concerns of a publisher in a world where the cost of transmitting information from the generator is virtually nil, and where people are paid to generate information for those who do not generate it?

LACY: In the present world, Jordan, that's essentially it. The overwhelming majority of all people who produce communication do it on a salary basis, and the cost is almost nil. The cost of the flow of print per capita in this country is a tiny fraction of the cost of the flow of water or electricity. The cost is no serious impediment to anybody's getting hold of anything he wants to read today.

PARTICIPANT: Then why do we need publishers?

LACY: For the same reason you need waterworks or an electric power company.

PARTICIPANT: I would like to respond to that model that you set up. Basically . . .

BARUCH: Don't get it as something I'm peddling, incidentally. It was to try to trigger Mr. Goldberg.

PARTICIPANT: The advantage that the publishing industry has always had in the past is that it can wrap up its particular puddle of information and distribute this throughout the United States and the world very readily. This has been the advantage of the publishing industry. Now the problem with it is that usually it has been too late, and they have segmented it so it is difficult to find the right group of puddles, if you want to stick to the water simile. Electronic means or media have the option of being able to be readily available, just like water. You can go over to your regular television set just like a faucet, turn it on, and get all this material poured out. The only problem is, if you want a particular type of information, we haven't been able to harness it.

BARUCH: The band width of the television set is just too small.

PARTICIPANT: Well, yes, right. We haven't been able to phrase the questions properly to be able to get the exact, or discrete, information we want. If we can ever reach the point where we can get selective dissemination through electronic means, this would really supplant publishing.

BARUCH: If it were cheaper. Electronic dissemination of information right now is among the most expensive ways to disseminate information. The cost of transmitting a page of printed information over a teleprinter, compared to running off an offset, letterpress, or high-speed wet press . . .

PARTICIPANT: That's true if you're thinking about using the electronic media to distribute the printed word, but certainly an audiovisual message is far better.

BARUCH: It's great for transmitting what's going on in Chicago, for example. It's great for transmitting news. It's great for transmitting entertainment. There is a wide range of information that it's not great for transmitting.

PARTICIPANT: I think that the televised aspect of what happened in Chicago in 1968 was far superior to the book. This got the message across far better than any book or magazine.

BARUCH: No question. Render unto Caesar that which is Caesar's. Let's not fall into the trap that says the proliferation of electronic technology . . .

PARTICIPANT: Let me just ask you a question. I think what we're all doing now is ignoring the dead and hoping that they will go away. The process is being ignored. What is really happening, the way I see it, is that our leader, our structure, has left us. Find something on your own. We're just falling on what you're offering as your hypothetical situation.

What I've been wanting to see for this whole week, and I think a lot of us have, what I would like to do is to go with David, go with him and just talk to him instead of just sitting around and grasping at straws and whether or not certain people feel they're relevant but others don't. This is why you get this sort of copping-out situation where people have anxiety. I don't know whether this is a communication or not.

GOLDBERG: Are you comfortable enough to talk with me even though there happen to be other people around us? Please do.

PARTICIPANT: I don't think I'm talking to you. I think I'm just talking because I would like to be heard from where I am in this particular communication setup. I think I'm not in it, because I don't think I'm related to the structure. I think that the structure is wrong, sort of. Now there is a chance for all people to communicate, without the guidance of a speech. Mr. Lacy's speech was like reading. O.K., I could have read this thing myself. I would like to react to him as a person, and this is not what's happening here.

GOLDBERG: You know, there is a rock-and-roll singer named Jimi Hendrix. I think a lot of people here know who he is. He sort of redefined what rock music is all about. He said that for ten or fifteen years rock music has done the same thing that all music did. It simply talked to people. What he wants to do with his music is that when he opens up his mouth, he wants to go inside down to what he calls the soul. I think that may be what we're talking about here this morning. All we have said so far is "la la la." We haven't got inside anything.

PARTICIPANT: There's no continuity in the group. I think change is a handy label, but we're not getting to change.

PARTICIPANT: This is an intellectual group, supposedly, of librarians. We're here to consider problems on an intellectual level. This is not a T-group session. We were not brought together for that sort of exploration, which, by the way, I agree is a very helpful way of learning. But I don't think this was the intent of this conference.

PARTICIPANT: It's good to see you frustrated.

PARTICIPANT: I'm not frustrated, except that I'm frustrated that one of our consultants comes apparently without having prepared anything.

PARTICIPANT: It's better sometimes if you don't have a paper. Maybe these people are more insecure if somebody's reading or giving a performance. They want to see you get into it, play your part . . .

PARTICIPANT: If this were a type of affective learning where we were coming together for a T-group session, then I would be all for it. It was not set up that way. It was set up with intellectual leaders from various fields.

PARTICIPANT: But we're not looking at your setup. We're interested in getting involved.

PARTICIPANT: But it was set up as a place where we were supposed to participate.

GOLDBERG: You're participants, not students.

PARTICIPANT: You asked how many of us have read Marshall McLuhan? Could I ask you a question? I have difficulty in reconciling some of the aspects of an earlier study by one of the speakers that most of our basic problems are more than 90 percent local. He said whatever project we have is local. We live on blocks, in effect. No one contested that. Marshall McLuhan talked about a global village. Could you reconcile these two contradictory facts for us and associate with that the media, or medium, if you want to make it singular? Or anything else?

BUNDY: I'm beginning to like his game.

GOLDBERG: To paraphrase the young lady, I could, but I don't feel like it.

PARTICIPANT: You sit here frustrated for three days. Obviously this was on his mind when the speaker was there. He failed to even communicate that particular fact. I think there are probably many of us who have some things that were in our minds at a particular time and still we failed to communicate it.

PARTICIPANT: You know, Mr. Goldberg, you haven't shown us that you're frustrated this morning.

GOLDBERG: You mean you haven't seen it.

PARTICIPANT: No, I see you, but I don't see you as frustrated. I see you as perhaps tired, but certainly not frustrated.

PARTICIPANT: Dr. Goldberg, let me ask you a question that Mr. Lacy raised, but said he did not have the answer to. He said that his publisher publishes two-thirds of their books at a loss, and he said he didn't know why. Do you know why they might do that? They only make a profit on about one-third of their books.

GOLDBERG: I don't know why, but I bet it is not intentional.

PARTICIPANT: I'm curious about why they would do this. They're in business, you know. How do you explain this to your stockholders?

GOLDBERG: You don't. You show them a total sheet.

PARTICIPANT: I would question whether Mr. Goldberg is frustrated. I would seem rash enough to say Mr. Goldberg is playing a little game. He is posing in this fashion to get certain reactions from the group. And he has succeeded.

GOLDBERG: Do you want to ask me?

PARTICIPANT: Not particularly. I just find it rather amusing.

GOLDBERG: I really resent this. You have said something about me obliquely. You haven't asked me directly.

PARTICIPANT: Well, are you frustrated?

GOLDBERG: I was before. I'm less frustrated now. You said something else.

PARTICIPANT: Do you generally have this low level of frustration?

PARTICIPANT: I said I think you're playing a game to elicit certain responses from the group. Are you playing a game?

GOLDBERG: I don't feel I am, no.

PARTICIPANT: Could I just say something? I'm trying to see you really. I can't say how you feel, but with all these people sitting around, I'm asking myself, "Have you ever faced a group of people?" Maybe all these people looking at you . . . This is the way I feel. Whatever you ask him is fine, but it's in such a long form it's hard for him to absorb it and come back with an answer like that. This is the way I feel.

PARTICIPANT: Ph.D.'s would hardly be upset by . . . Well, I'm sure he's appeared before groups before.

PARTICIPANT: Let me ask you that question. You brought in Marshall McLuhan. I'm very interested in it. You stated that you picked up a couple of concepts from that. Could you give us those concepts? You said you picked up those concepts from reading that book.

GOLDBERG: What is it that you want today?

PARTICIPANT: We want to hear you talk. We want to hear you get involved with us.

PARTICIPANT: We want to hear you take responsibility for your own ideas.

GOLDBERG: I have.

BARUCH: I haven't heard enough ideas.

PARTICIPANT: So why don't you say something against whoever you represent? We don't care about that part of it. We want to hear you do something.

PARTICIPANT: You're a paid consultant. We want to get our money's worth. Let's put it that way. You have a responsibility to your clientele.

PARTICIPANT: You know, we saw Ed Taylor the other night. We didn't give him an Oscar, but we're ready to give you one.

PARTICIPANT: I want to hear this gentleman talk.

GOLDBERG: You will.

PARTICIPANT: If you and I have to go to lunch together, I'm going to listen to your speech.

GOLDBERG: I get two cracks. I talk now as a discussant and this afternoon as a lecturer. You can't avoid me, hardly.

PARTICIPANT: O.K., good.

PARTICIPANT: Nobody paid you to keep quiet, did they?

PARTICIPANT: We got paid for coming here, too. I think we ought to be worrying about what we're doing with the money that we've received. Part of the point here is in terms of what the group is doing. Why pick on Goldberg right now?

PARTICIPANT: He's not answering any questions.

PARTICIPANT: O.K. So let's start answering some of the questions for ourselves. That's really what it's all about. Why throw it off on him? He was unfortunate enough to have to come today. They didn't pay him enough to come to listen to this shit.

PARTICIPANT: It has already been established that someone would throw out some suggestions or questions or whatever, and then we would start discussing. That's the format. We have accepted it. He is trying to change the format, and I like that. We need change.

BARUCH: Gentlemen, as chairman pro tem . . .

BUNDY: The chairman is about to get thrown out. Be very careful.

BARUCH: . . . I will thank Mr. Goldberg and then proceed to discuss the previous two happenings.

PARTICIPANT: How many of you want to hear him?

PARTICIPANT: If he keeps going on, someone's going to walk out of here.

BARUCH: It's really quite interesting. I'm amazed that as a group of intellectuals many of you can decide whether or not you want to hear me without having heard me. I suppose it's a sign of some sort of anger at the process that has been going on for a few days. I'm sorry I can't share it with you. I haven't been here, but I shall try to take off from where I am. It sounds very much to me as though I've been invited to discuss a publishing lecture and a nonpublishing lecture, or a publishing nonlecture, with a bunch of cop-outs.

I hear a bunch of people who really have engaged in black protest; some have engaged in white protest. I suspect there may even be some people who have engaged in other kinds of protests, but who protest against a system without being willing, as Mr. Goldberg has, to take the responsibility of trying to protest effectively. I think there is a great danger of publishers' controlling the flow of information. But from what Mr. Lacy has told us, and from what I know about the publishing field, there is very goddamn little to keep you from becoming a publisher. So if you don't like what they are doing, get off your butts, raise some capital, and do it yourself. Anybody who gets up now and says, "I want you to assume more social responsibility," in my book is naa-aah.

I'm not interested in what you want me to do. I'm interested in what you're interested in doing for yourself. Mr. Lacy said it takes a million bucks of capital investment to support a million bucks of sales. Maybe it does. What he didn't mention is how much profit comes from a million bucks of sales and whether that amount of profit will comfortably pay for a million bucks of capital. Well, from what I see on the back pages of the *Wall Street Journal,* it's eminently clear that a million bucks of sales will generate enough profits to comfortably pay for a million bucks of capital, if you print something somebody is interested in reading. Now if you say there is suppression of stuff that you think ought to get out in public, put your money where your mouth is. It's an easy matter to raise capital nowadays, despite the fact that we've got a high interest rate. Technology is driving the cost of capital investment to produce printed information or readable information down, down, down.

PARTICIPANT: Well, how come he publishes two-thirds of his books at a loss, then?

BARUCH: Because he misguesses what the public will buy. He's no smarter than you are. If you think you're smart enough to guess what the public will buy, or if you feel you've got a concentrated public or special public, go to it! The guys who publish *Biophysical Reviews* probably don't publish two-thirds of their books at a loss. McGraw-Hill publishes a hell of a lot of books. They can't be that smart all the time.

LACY: Incidentally, I probably didn't make it clear; I think I should say that I was referring to trade books. We don't publish two-thirds of the textbooks at a loss.

BARUCH: That's right. You've got a specialty market. You think you can identify with that market because you know them. You think that the color of your skin, or the fact that you've been circumcised, makes you know one particular market better than somebody else. You've got all the finesse of a horse player who thinks he knows the fillies better than somebody else does. You talk about the cost of preparation of plates in printing. No publisher that I know of runs his own printing establishment, does he?

LACY: A few, but it's rare. Doubleday does, for example.

BARUCH: By and large, you farm out the printing. O.K., there are some excellent photo offset printing houses where the cost of setup and the cost of getting material on paper is small. Now, if you think that stuff that people want is being suppressed, I invite you to use normal procedures.

If you feel that there aren't enough people who know what they want, and that the number to be served is so small that sales will be too low to support the capital cost, then I would like to offer you some alternatives. One is to carry some books that aren't aimed at this small population you're interested in, but the profit which will support these other activities. In other words, you are entitled to reinvest in your own way. The other is to set up an internal socialist system within a community.

I passed a very interesting sign in northeast Washington, a sign that says "black socialism—the right route to black capitalism." That may very well be, but here's a fine way to experiment with it, because at the guts of every one of the protest systems, including the protests we heard five minutes ago in this room, was the resentment of other people's having control of information that was pertinent to you, or to somebody whom you felt responsible for. What I would like to bring up here is the possibility that if the librarian or the teacher of library science ceases his concern with things, and becomes concerned with content, he may seek to control that content. Instead of "control," I should probably use the word "facilitate" so I don't sound like Mussolini. He may seek to facilitate the flow of that content where it's needed, or where he thinks it's needed, or more significantly, where he is willing to bet it's needed. I think if you make this role shift, you may find a discussion beginning here about Mr. Lacy's speech and about Mr. Goldberg's. He may start asking questions about where we're spending that money and how to switch affect to effect.

BUNDY: Dr. Baruch, something has happened to me.

BARUCH: You've gone to sleep.

BUNDY: Up to this point in the week I was cooperative. Now I don't want to hear you either.

BARUCH: Something's happened to me. I don't much care. I'm perfectly willing to hear the rest of you.

PARTICIPANT: Can I just ask a question? I'm wondering why you didn't say black or white, but . . .

BARUCH: Yes, I did. Several times. I said black and white.

PARTICIPANT: I'm not pushing any separate issues. I'm interested in looking at it from a two-point view. I heard you say the color of your skin and this type of thing. I'm wondering why you're looking at it in that focus.

BARUCH: Partly because I've been heavily involved with an ongoing effort to get a kind of community control for the flow of information. I happened to be focused on the black community at the time. That's my problem, not yours. I wasn't accusing you.

PARTICIPANT: If we're to have a role, it has to be beyond the matter of distributing the efforts of the establishment or further disseminating them. We have to interact here, not just give books out. We have the responsibility to link information that's available to the people in our community. This isn't anything new, but the . . .

PARTICIPANT: That's the whole point. We've said it all earlier. What are you trying to relate to now? Have the other people heard it all earlier? If this is it, we are just rehashing every single damn thing we've been talking about time and time again. It's just definitions again. It's getting very tiresome.

BARUCH: Why don't you leave?

PARTICIPANT: I think I might be able to do that.

PARTICIPANT: You said you were asking for definitions. We haven't defined a single concept up to now. I am a librarian who will go back into a library situation. I have to know what I can get out of this conference that I can implement in my particular environment. I have to understand. It's not enough to feel, because we are activists. We are operating a library, and just to be pleased or displeased is not enough.

PARTICIPANT: Did you come here to get definitions of concepts?

PARTICIPANT: No, I came to learn what I can do, how I can try to solve the problems, problems that I can't impart to you.

PARTICIPANT: Learning is a two-way thing.

PARTICIPANT: We are exposed to this thing all the time. We would like to have some kind of definition, clarification of our thoughts. Emotion is not enough. It seems to me that we are facing a major problem which is created by technology, something that is happening in the society.

BARUCH: Come on. Get off technology's back! Problems are created by people!

PARTICIPANT: I am oversimplifying, but we are living in a highly technological society. One of our problems is the difficulty to assimilate or to do something with that technology. Emotional response is not enough for the person who is going to return to his own environment and try to do something with it. That's the point that some of us are trying to express.

PARTICIPANT: I think the emotional response is much more important than anything else. The very fact that you bring the emotion of getting something from the conference, and not that of bringing something to the conference, I think is a very important emotion. It is going to lead to your frustration.

I listened on the first day to what people said they wanted and expected from this conference. Nobody really said what they expected to contribute. Everybody said, "Well, I'm here to find out, or to solve a problem." Or "I have this hanging over my head, and I want somebody to tell me how I'm going to solve it." This is not what you need. Nobody can tell you how to solve your particular problems. What you need is the attitude of seeing what you can get out of it, tackling one thing at a time, failing many times, failing perhaps two-thirds of the time, and learning from those failures.

PARTICIPANT: I really agree with you there, because I think if I go back to my library with just one new feeling, I think I will have accomplished something. All this intellectualizing is just verbiage.

BUNDY: That's not what she said. You took it all wrong. She didn't say to go back with a new feeling, she said to come with one.

REID: If you drive into a garage with brakes that are slipping, so that you're afraid to get out on the highway, and you find that the engineers are talking about concepts, relationships, extrapolations, what do you do? You say, "Look, come and look at my brakes. Damn it, I want to get this fixed. This is what I want to do. This is my problem."

PARTICIPANT: Maybe you should get out of the car and get a bicycle.

REID: You might not have to do that. You might have to say, "It's my understanding you're working for me if I pay you, so look at my problem."

PARTICIPANT: It's unfair partly because we are supposed to be doing something. We are supposed to be the people who repair those brakes and we are refusing to. We must do something to fix them.

REID: It's the same thing. You've got a problem and you don't know what to do, right?

PARTICIPANT: Yes, but I can't take my library problem to the garage and ask the serviceman to fix it for me. I have to fix it myself.

PARTICIPANT: That's not true.

REID: Not knowing what to do is your problem. What do you want to do?

PARTICIPANT: There's a difference. The man in the car has a goal. He knows where he's going. He is a man who has direction.

PARTICIPANT: We may be in a car, but we don't have a map in our minds. And what people are really coming here for is to find out where they should go.

BARUCH: I've gotten something out of this conference. This is the first inkling I've ever had that librarians had feelings.

PARTICIPANT: It's so easy to do things when you know you want to do something. It's like a computer. Something burns out somewhere. The repairmen spend hours trying to find out where the damned thing is burned out. When they do find out, it's easy to fix. Most things are that way. If you know what you want to do, this man can tell you how to do it. He's damn smart. He knows all kinds of technical things, but we're supposed to be talking about change and all these things. Let us hear what the hell you want to do.

I'm not really sure I know that I want to do, but I know that every time I go to these funny things, like the Congress for Change, this kind of thing, or ALA, and I get drunk enough, about 1:00 in the morning I start talking to somebody, or making love, or something; somehow I get a little bit more of a feeling of what the hell is it all about.

We're worried about circulation going down. Maybe circulation ought to go down. I don't go to public libraries because they charge me an overdue fine. On a paperback, I end up paying $1.00. That's why your circulation goes down. I mean, if you ask a question that simplistically you can get an answer. There are questions that are not that way, and I don't know that anybody really is . . .

PARTICIPANT: How can you communicate what you want to change unless you start talking?

PARTICIPANT: I didn't say I wanted to change something. I said I wanted to know what the hell it is that as librarians we are thinking of doing. Maybe we ought to do exactly what we are doing. Libraries are limited vehicles. With a bicycle, you can't go eighty miles an hour.

BARUCH: May I make a suggestion? The way things are changing I don't think it is realistic to assume that the librarian is tied to the library. I don't think it's essential that the librarian be tied to the library. The thing I was trying to say before was that the librarian has alternatives facing him. The only thing, I think, that any of us who . . .

PARTICIPANT: Excuse me. You didn't leave! You are sitting there because you don't really want to be left out of what *may* happen.

BARUCH: I suspect this is remarkably analogous to your professional activities, too. Let this be the intelligence agency, and you people can be the counter-intelligence agency.

PARTICIPANT: What is that supposed to mean?

BARUCH: Nothing! it is just supposed to be a nasty comment. I was mad. I'm trying to give in to my anger. This is really what you were doing too, so don't be too hard on me. It's the only thing some of us can do who talk here. We can't talk about changing the library because we are not familiar enough with libraries.

What we can do is bring to people's attention the existence of some alternatives. Whether you see your life in a way that wants to make use of these alternatives is entirely up to you. Whether these alternatives are relevant to your problems depends on how well we guess. I hope I can guess as well as Lacy does, and only two-thirds of the alternatives that I bring forth are irrelevant. I think the idea of becoming a publisher is a relevant alternative. It is certainly a relevant alternative to libraries that have Xerox machines.

PARTICIPANT: I don't think you ought to feel attacked by people trying to do something else. Maybe this other thing doesn't belong here, but it's going on. I didn't like your speech, Mr. Lacy, but you were beautiful when you responded to people's questions. I didn't like your speech because I don't like statistics about publishing.

LACY: I don't either, to tell you the truth.

PARTICIPANT: It seems that some people start to think that because there's something going on here, it must be against the thing they do, and it's not. There are two kinds of things here. People are thinking, "Let's hear a state-of-the-art talk about telecommunications." There are other people here who are not expecting that, who are not wanting it, or who are thinking about something else. I hung around because they were going to talk about that sort of thing.

BARUCH: I'm being perfectly honest. I'm doing this for a completely selfish reason. This afternoon I've got to give a speech about something, the evolving system or something. I'm very much like Goldberg. I haven't written it yet either, but on the other hand, I don't eat lunch. What I'm trying to find out from the group here is what the hell they want me to talk about this afternoon. I can use my time as discussant in the morning to do that. It makes me look good in the afternoon. It's perfectly clear that they don't know. I'm not going to talk about their feelings. If people don't give me some clues . . .

PARTICIPANT: Who are "they"? Is it we? What is setting up this communication barrier? Who are we? We you? They us? Or we they within the faction here? I mean they we. I would rather break that down.

PARTICIPANT: I think we are now discussing the very essence of the thing that has bothered us for the whole time. I agree with you that neither statistics nor this very theoretical discussion is the thing that we want. But I think what we do want is to communicate among ourselves. Some people respond emotionally to certain emotional situations, but not all of us have this talent. We would like to know what the whole thing is about. You need to define some way of communication. There has to be a small vocabulary of words that all of us could agree on.

REID: There is a small vocabulary of words. They are words that you use the minute you walk out that door. Why don't you use them now?

PARTICIPANT: Like what?

REID: Shit!

PARTICIPANT: That's the word that I don't understand.

REID: You don't understand that word?

PARTICIPANT: No, I don't. To me, personally, that word has an implication that has nothing to do with my profession, but I sense that it says something to you. I'm trying to find out what that meaning is. That's my difficulty from the very beginning. There we are. Back to definitions.

REID: I know what I want to do. Can I tell you what I want to do? I would like, somehow, to do something in the black community that would enable black people to know the things they really need to know to have more power. That's what I want to do. Now that isn't as specific as I want to get, but at least I know the general department store that has the maps. I think it has something to do with what you all do during the day, because I think you do something with information. That's what I want to do!

PARTICIPANT: That statement is intelligent to me. I understand what you say.

REID: Now what do you want to do?

PARTICIPANT: I'm listening.

REID: You don't have a damn thing in mind you want to do. Right?

PARTICIPANT: What do you mean, I don't have a damn thing in mind?

REID: You don't have anything in mind you want to do.

PARTICIPANT: Why this question?

REID: Because I told you what I want to do. We're communicating now. Now, what do you want? . . . He's refusing to talk to me.

PARTICIPANT: No. Are you asking me why I came here?

REID: No. I said, what do you want to do?

PARTICIPANT: I need more than two minutes to answer your question.

REID: Take it!

PARTICIPANT: I don't think I'm tuned up to the mood of the group to present, to discuss . . .

REID: Don't cop out! You said he copped out. Don't blame non-communication on anybody else.

PARTICIPANT: I'm not blaming anybody. I'm just trying to establish the communication.

PARTICIPANT: You're in the group to convey your ideas and to express why you're here to the group.

REID: So far he has conveyed something. I don't know what it is.

PARTICIPANT: You've got something, and you don't feel it's right to say it or something?

PARTICIPANT: No.

PARTICIPANT: Say it!

PARTICIPANT: No.

PARTICIPANT: Say it!

PARTICIPANT: Wait a minute! He's said what he had to say.

PARTICIPANT: What do you want me to say? Do you think that the problem of change is something that I can answer in one sentence? Do you think I can solve the problems that we are facing as librarians in fifteen minutes without preparing something so it is intelligible to you? We can keep talking. That's probably one way. That's probably in the sense that you mean. We create an atmosphere in which we keep talking, talking, and talking, and something will come out.

REID: That won't do it! Nothing will come out because an atmosphere is created. Something comes out if there ever is anything inside. You can't get all of those things in, this week. Only if something was inside wanting to come out, can you provide some handles that are ever going to be used.

BARUCH: Young lady, are you insisting that people need to know what they want to do in order to be effective?

REID: I merely think that somewhere along the line you've got to make a commitment and say, "This is what I want to do." If you try to do it and can't, you figure out, "O.K., maybe that isn't what I wanted to do" or "I screwed it up. I don't know how to do it!" But you know! Yes, commit yourself!

PARTICIPANT: A lot of times you don't know what you want to do until you hear what somebody else wants to do, or what they don't want to do, or that they don't know what they want to do. I don't think you have to know what you want to do. Not knowing what you want to do is just as valid, too.

PARTICIPANT: It's funny; people become doctors because they want to make people well. People become librarians and don't know why the hell they became librarians. At least doctors know what they're going to say they want to do.

PARTICIPANT: Fervor is a little bit foreign to the intellectual task of the librarian. I don't see why I have to have some evangelical commitment. I want to run a good university library which will take cognizance of the needs of the undergraduate, the graduate, and the faculty.

BARUCH: Can we take that very statement for a moment, because that one happens to be very close to my heart? You want to run a university library (I think I'm using your words) that will take cognizance of the needs of the students, the faculty, and somebody else, researchers. Yet what I'm afraid frequently happens is that we run a university library that takes cognizance of the administration's view of the needs of the students.

PARTICIPANT: No. I'm here to find out how I can more aptly discern the needs of the students. That's why I'm here.

BARUCH: Let me ask you a different question. I think one of the things we have to face is, if you did discern that, how would you then deal with the administration? How would you get them to allow you to run a university library that dealt with the perceived needs of the students, despite their variance with the administration's perception of the needs of the students?

PARTICIPANT: I'm not sure they would vary.

BARUCH: I'm not sure they would either. I'm giving you a question.

PARTICIPANT: I would persuasively try to present these student points of view to the administration, saying, "We're not meeting the need to this extent." It seemed to me that we could have learned some of those things this week in the intellectual context, but I must say we haven't learned them.

BARUCH: I was at Brandeis one day when a group of students came in and expressed some dissatisfaction with the library. They did it by dumping the books on the floor. That's not a very constructive way of expressing the change that they would like to see, but I think it is a constructive way of expressing a need for a change that is probably severe enough to be listened for and examined further.

PARTICIPANT: I don't think that would have been necessary if someone had been listening or if those students had tried to talk to the librarian. Did they?

BARUCH: It's like the story of the donkey and the two-by-four. Sometimes you've just got to get his attention. Frequently people don't listen. It's even been happening here this morning. Occasionally we've had people not listening.

PARTICIPANT: Well, I'm not sure that administrations of any sort, of any level, are as unresponsive as some people like to picture them.

That's what I'm saying. I'm saying that some people have as their aim just to disrupt. They don't give a damn about improving the situation. I think this is so.

BARUCH: I think that's a comfortable hypothesis.

PARTICIPANT: I think it has been going on for some time. In my situation, some of those who yelled the loudest for wanting the library to stay open until 1:00 A.M. before exams, when we held it open, didn't appear. Now, I tested their hypothesis. They said we want longer hours . . .

BARUCH: You found one hypothesis, one claim, that wasn't substantiated. Lacy runs the whole business batting only 33 percent.

PARTICIPANT: I mean these kids who yelled the loudest over longer library hours did not come in to use the library when we had longer hours. I know them personally. They're friends of mine.

It was worthwhile. It was a valid point. We will continue to hold the library open, but I repeat that those who yelled the loudest didn't have red eyes from studying until 1:00 in the morning.

BARUCH: But is it possible they were yelling about something else? Is it possible what they were really saying to you was, "Look, the library is something very close to our educational experience. We would like some student control over what it does. We'll tackle first something we know even you dense librarians and presidents can understand. We'll tackle leaving the library open late before exams. This will give us an element of control." There is a need on the campuses now for students to feel a self-expression, a control of the environment. Many administrators know this, and I'm sure lots of librarians do.

PARTICIPANT: I agree with you. I think that library administrators and other administrators are trying to respond to this as they get the cues from the students. Now in this Congress for Change I thought we were going to learn how to discern those cues obliquely, or directly, or any other way. Maybe they are saying one thing and meaning something else. Maybe we can learn to interpret this foreign language.

PARTICIPANT: This is not the Congress for Change.

PARTICIPANT: We keep talking about responding to student demands and this kind of thing. One thing that has always bugged me is why libraries don't have salesmen. We ought to figure out what our product is. We ought to go sell it to people. When I used to work at a library reference desk, I used to try to put things up that would bring people in. I used to run out and take a book and show it to somebody.

I said, "Hey, this came in. Did you see it?" I used to bug people. At first, they weren't used to it because librarians didn't do this kind of thing. I used to work in a bookstore. In bookstores, it's O.K. to do this kind of thing because they sell books that way. I always figured librarians should sell them that way, too. Why the hell do students ask you to stay open late? I would like to see libraries open a whole lot later. If they don't come in, show them movies, do something that's going to bring them in. But bring them in!

BARUCH: Where do you work?

PARTICIPANT: I work for the Library of Congress.

BARUCH: What do you do there?

PARTICIPANT: I argue with my boss all day.

BARUCH: O.K. But what do you do there?

PARTICIPANT: Sometimes I write programs. Sometimes I do systems work.

BARUCH: Why did you go to the Library of Congress?

PARTICIPANT: For a very poor reason. We constantly hear about the word commitment. Sometimes I get the feeling that there is only one kind of commitment that is acceptable. All other commitments are rejected. Let's talk about the commitment. You mentioned that the library should be open more and more hours. Our library is open twenty-four hours. We are trying to understand what our commitment is, and we are doing it. We are doing a lot of things. What is better, to stay outside of the library institution and be committed to some kind of feeling for something, doing nothing and just discussing it, or going back to the library and having it open twenty-four hours? Some of us came here with that experience. We are trying hard to respond to new commitments, but we cannot respond completely until we understand each other. That's, in essence, why I'm asking about definitions. I'm not asking about what is obvious. I'm trying desperately to understand what you mean.

PARTICIPANT: I think that's the way a lot of us feel; I don't know how many, but I know that I would agree with this gentleman. It isn't that we're here trying to fight students. We're here trying to understand how we can not only respond, but maybe anticipate their needs. But then we get this big bag about commitment and change. What in the hell do you want us to be committed to? What do you want us to change?

PARTICIPANT: I'm still interested in seeing the curriculum changed.

PARTICIPANT: A lot of difficulties that we are facing have arisen because we come from different environments. We come with different things happening in our communities. Sometimes I raise a question, and then I am corrected, because what I think is right is only right in my own particular institution. It's not right in the environment of many of you.

There is such a diversity of backgrounds, there is such a diversity of interests, that the communication is almost impossible. That's what I'm asking for. This morning I asked about the process of book selection. I made an error. In our university situation, the book selection concept is disappearing. I was completely unaware that this was happening only in 500 libraries. There are a number of things that I am presupposing by not being aware of the situation in other libraries.

By the same token, you are assuming that what is happening in librarianship is only that which happens in your own library. When I look at the library at the University of Maryland and learn that there are 120 people in technical processing and I reflect that I am doing the same kind of processing with thirty people, then I start understanding why you are objecting.

BARUCH: You missed a splendid opportunity before. When somebody asks you why you are with the Library of Congress, you should say, "Because I can't stand acquisition programs."

PARTICIPANT: That's got nothing to do with why I went to the Library of Congress. We do have acquisition programs there. People are just as ugly and dumb as the people in other libraries with acquisition programs. It seems to be the nature of my experience with acquisitions. That's why I don't like statistics.

PARTICIPANT: Why don't you become an acquisition librarian?

PARTICIPANT: Because I'm not sure that's the answer. That's like saying, "Why don't you become an accountant and make accountancy as exciting as hell?"

PARTICIPANT: I'm not an accountant, but I am a librarian. There are some things I am professional in, and I hope to change them some.

PARTICIPANT: Here's the point. I haven't thought a whole lot about acquisition librarians as people you have to have around. The fact that they're ugly doesn't necessarily impede their functions—not the fact that they may annoy other librarians. They don't bother students, which is a grace.

This guy asked a valid question: "Why am I at the Library of Congress?" I really don't know. Dr. Bundy talks about library education. That's not wholly irrelevant, because to educate a librarian you've got to know what a librarian is. I didn't really learn it at Columbia. I learned a hell of a lot, but I really didn't learn that. I guess that's what some people are kind of talking around.

Miss Bundy's paper, this ethics thing, raises a whole lot of points that are not ethics. There are procedural points, too. At Teachers' College, when a student asked me a question, I would find him an answer. I used to get reprimanded for it all the time. I was told it was the wrong way to do things. You don't find answers for students. Students should be taught to find the answers themselves. But the guy had to have it quick. It's this kind of thing, it seems to me, that people can get so hung up in.

PARTICIPANT: We are trying to present a view which is not the view of those few who are very strongly dedicated to one commitment. They didn't want to listen. They left. Now, how can we communicate?

PARTICIPANT: Some of them said they'd be back.

PARTICIPANT: Yes, but how can we communicate? There is an assumption that if I don't agree with you, I must be your enemy. That's not true. You don't want to listen to us.

PARTICIPANT: But we are sitting here listening to you.

PARTICIPANT: I'm not saying anything personal. I'm not referring to myself. I have the feeling that there is a commitment which is very strong, and I don't understand it.

PARTICIPANT: Some people believe there is some magic in consensus and having everybody agreeing with you. There's no magic in it.

PARTICIPANT: No, but the first thing is to understand before you agree. All I am striving for is to try to understand.

PARTICIPANT: There should be some value in our society in discussion. One group simply says, "We refuse to discuss," and walks out. Then communication has ended.

PARTICIPANT: What's the sense in saying they are refusing to discuss? They are discussing. They've gone off to discuss something perhaps quite different from what's being said here.

PARTICIPANT: Maybe they want confirmation in their own views. They don't want different views.

BARUCH: As a matter of fact, it looks like you're on your way out the door.

PARTICIPANT: I'm hungry.

BARUCH: I just want to take a very brief minute to pick on this young lady who wants to set up a way for the black community to get its information. I happen to feel that that is a very important goal. It goes along with a kind of responsibility to get the tools to do it rather than just claiming you want to do it. I think some of the shit you've got to shovel is the kind of stuff that Dan Lacy has to go through. You've got to goddamn well know how much it costs to print something before you commit yourself to print it. You've got to goddamn well know whether anybody reads it before you accept it.

I think what is necessary in this, as in most vocational schools, is to learn the kinds of tools well enough so that you can use them for your ends. There is nothing inherent in the problems because of technology. Technology is a bunch of tools. They're dangerous tools because they've got big, sharp edges, and they cut a big swath. But you can't just scream about technology coming; you've got to learn to handle it. I think you missed a superb lecture this morning about how to get into the publishing business, because somehow it turned you off. If you had viewed yourselves as potential publishers . . . I think some of Lacy's competitors might well have given an arm and a leg for some of the information that came out, or could have come out in a discussion period. So I'm a little teed off at people who have commitments and no guts.

REID: I learned two useful things that have impressed me. They relate to this thing I'm interested in. I don't know what to do with them, yet, but now I see, at least, we don't have to go to McGraw-Hill. We can do an offset job. We can do better than that. If we have something that makes money, we can get McGraw-Hill to work for us because they're for sale. Maybe smaller people are for sale. All right, there's a gal who has little kids write books for nonreaders, because nonreaders read what children write. Teachers haven't discovered this, but she has. She's building up her library this way. I'm pleased to find out it's not like "Way down here, what are you doing way up there?" There are some in-betweens, little steps that can be taken locally. I'm a little encouraged.

There's another thing that I learned today: that is the contrast between the corporation and the university. In spite of the fact that they're similar, their risk-taking is different. I grew up during the 1930s and 1940s. My knowledge about this is no longer applicable. Where people are for sale, you can use them.

PARTICIPANT: Can I say something, please? because I'm hurt. You talk about a white community, a black community. Where is the foreign community? Why don't you incorporate that, too? There are a damn lot of foreigners around here. I happen to be on the other coast.

PARTICIPANT: I don't feel like an outsider.

PARTICIPANT: I do. And I always will.

REID: Maybe this is your problem.

PARTICIPANT: I think there is a foreign literature. There is a foreign literature in law, but nobody ever talks about it.

BARUCH: Sure, we talk about it.

REID: You talk about it.

BARUCH: If you all talk about your needs in this area or what you think are your needs in this area, a whole bunch of us will be happy to talk about it with you. We don't talk about it, because we're not that perceptive.

PARTICIPANT: Perhaps. I'm not as eloquent as you. I cannot discuss this as well as you, but I think there is something in what the young lady was trying to say. That's all.

BARUCH: Keep discussing! I'm going to adjourn.

9

INFORMATION TRANSFER, DISSEMINATION, AND THE EVOLVING STRUCTURE

THURSDAY AFTERNOON, AUGUST 14
LECTURER: JORDAN BARUCH
PANELISTS: MARY LEE BUNDY
                JOSEPH C. DONOHUE
                PAUL WASSERMAN

BARUCH: I was asked to talk today about the technology and the developing system for using it. The kind of information I gained this morning, though, says that there are real problems and that you feel them acutely. I say "you," because I don't share them with you. I'm not a librarian. What I will try to do is tell you about some projects that are going on without any intent to convince or to convey any more than information about possibilities, in the hope that some of them may provide you with tools for solving your problems. I would like to offer these to you just as a view of what is going on. Those of you who are not interested in this kind of tool for problem solving, please feel free to walk out.

We talked this morning a little bit about the possibility of going into the publishing business. We talked a little bit about the fact that things were changing. Let me step off into the world of computers for a moment. Even though I talked this morning about how expensive computers are for the storage and regurgitation of information, there are some things computers do very well. One of the things that computers do very well, and quite economically, is to look things up

327

in large files. Most of you are familiar with selective dissemination systems, selective retrieval systems, retrieval systems in general. There are a group of us in the universities who have started to look at what we call a personal information management system. It's a form of reaction to something we perceive as information pollution today. There is a great deal of information around today that I'm not interested in, that I don't want to read, that I don't want to be distracted by, where the probability of payoff for me is small enough that I choose to avoid the risk. I would like a technique to express these prejudices, to help me select what I want to read.

Has anyone here tried to take a drink from a garden hose during the summertime? It's a good way to drown. The best way to take a drink is to sort of pinch off the hose, so that it's only coming out in the size trickle you can handle. The same thing is true with information. There is much being presented. We were told this morning that the publishing industry in this country publishes approximately 800 new titles a week. I read fast, but not that fast. Of those 800 new titles a week, there is probably one that is of great interest to me, or maybe only one title in every ten weeks. If I have to spend a great deal of my time filtering that which is presented, I'm snowed. As a matter of fact, if an abstract of each of those 800 books was presented to me every week, I couldn't read all the abstracts in order to select which book I want to read. So I need some other tool.

One of the tools one can use is a small slave. You can tell him, "Here is a black crayon. Here is a certain set of descriptions that I'm interested in. Cross out all those abstracts that don't fit those descriptions. Then I'll go ahead and read the rest of the abstracts. From those I'll cull the one or two books that I want to read." A couple of things are wrong with that. Slaves are hard to come by nowadays. Machines are not. They are getting very, very much less expensive. Machines are also easy to instruct to do this kind of a boring job continuously week by week.

The problem is that most of the machine systems are relatively unmodifiable. It becomes very expensive to change my mind about what I'm interested in. So machines can foster a kind of stasis in one's interests. A group of us have been wondering if there is a way of taking very small machines that will be economical, at least for reasonable-sized groups, putting file manipulation programs on them, and making it possible for an individual to modify his interest profile.

These programs will let the individual freely express what he is interested in. The machine will then take that expression, search the files, and make it very inexpensive for the individual to change what he is interested in, to modify it. Can we adapt such a machine, or give it the ability to call up large central stores of information and update its own files?

I would like you to visualize this as a hierarchy. Some day an outfit like McGraw-Hill, instead of running a bunch of printing presses, as you were told this morning, will have stored information of one kind or another, some of it—much of it in fact—being references to books, meaning things that are printed, or at least visually observable. This publishing house will have a large store of such information, and the University of Maryland, at several spots throughout its campus, will have some small machines where an individual can go and say, "I'm interested in a new method of smelting of metals." His machine will call the McGraw-Hill machine, which will look up that information and relay it to the smaller one, which will add it to the individual's personal files.

Now, not everybody can get very excited about methods of smelting, but people can get pretty excited when they want to look up information in a file relating to political movements, or relating to what's going on in other communities, or relating to what's going on in other social systems. Eventually we will find that information can be marketed over this kind of a network from a central source to small machines. The individual sits with his small machine and does the kind of searching and screening that makes it possible for him to select some meaningful information that he wants to pay a lot of attention to, like reading or something like that.

That's a brief remark about some computer activities. Unfortunately, or fortunately, it's really all I want to say about computers. There are many, many esoteric uses of computers that really don't have much bearing here. There are lots of experiments, of which you are all aware, on information storage and retrieval in computers. They are, economically, so far away from use by the individual that I don't even consider them a tool structure yet. They may be the raw material out of which tools will some day be wrought to work on your problems, but they don't exist yet, for all intents and purposes.

A couple of other activities do exist that I think are useful. One of them is a form of micro-publishing which I do want to mention.

I am sure you are all familiar with microfilms and micro-images. You've had them coming out of your ears, because people keep telling you how they ought to be used more in libraries. Yet nobody really wants to use them in libraries. Well, there is a group that is concerned with trying to tailor micro-published information to the individual user so that it is as comfortable and as sensual an experience to use as a book is, to make it as convenient as a book, but for a different reason.

There are many of us who believe that libraries, as such, have their historical roots in the fact that books are expensive. The library started because it was not really possible to own all the books you wanted as an individual; therefore you joined with others in a communal ownership system. The micro-publishing field has gotten to the state where the technology makes it possible to duplicate things on a level where some of that background is up for challenge. It may, in fact, be possible for an individual to own all the books he wants. If that be true, then the nature of a library may change. In other words, if the cause for the institution is modified, it is likely that the institution will modify also.

What I believe will happen is the following. I believe that publishers will keep on publishing books. They have a value. I believe that many of those books will also appear in a microform. The microform I am particularly talking about is a four-by-six piece of film with 500 pages or so on it. I think that people will read these, using portable hand-held readers that represent an individual investment of $50 or $100, something in that range. But the point is, you won't read microforms by sitting in front of your desk and getting a crick in your neck. You will read them in the john or the bathtub, or in bed, the way you read books. Hopefully, they will be free enough from vibration so that you can read them on the BMT subway.

It is my hope that we will have, in the next four or five years, centers that have little master microfiche, many, many thousands of them, such that when a student comes in and says, "I want books x, y, and z" the attendant (and I won't call the attendant the librarian now because I visualize a different role for the librarian) will take out one of these masters and plop it in a slot in a reproducing machine. It will reproduce itself as another microfiche, which the attendant will hand to the student. The student will take it away. He will own it. Depending on the social structure in which this is going on, the student may pay for it or the center may absorb the cost if it is a part of the school and a part of the student's tuition.

A group from the universities in EDUCOM have been talking to the publishers about not doing this behind the publishers' back or stealing anything but, quite the contrary, as a possible new alternative in the publishing field. Publishers are not wed to printing presses. What we would like to do is make it possible to focus this kind of activity so that when a student gets a microfiche copy the publisher's cash register rings. The publisher gets a royalty. In fact, our whole goal is to let that royalty be set by the publishers in an open market. Some publisher will say, "This book is worth a 75¢ royalty every time it is reproduced." Since there are several hundred publishers, however, another publisher with a book on the same subject that isn't selling quite as well will say, "I will put mine on the market for a 35¢ royalty and sell twice as many." And he may, or he may sell a great deal more than twice as many.

We are looking at an experiment. Rather than a library as a circulation device, we are looking at centers that are local manufacturing plants. If such centers come into existence, if the centers themselves are very cheap, if the central activity that puts the centers together also puts out catalogs of the books, and if we make it easy for the users of the centers to say, "Hey, why the hell isn't this book included?" and set up a process whereby that book does get rapidly included, then I would like to ask, what is the role of the librarian in a milieu like that? Certainly not acquisitions! Certainly not cataloging! Certainly not running a circulation desk!

Many of these centers would start in school environments, formalized education environments. Some of the young librarians we have talked to visualize themselves as resource consultants for the rest of the academic group, for the teaching staff, and so on. Some of the even younger librarians see themselves as resource consultants for the students. Some of the very young librarians view themselves as resource consultants for the community in which the school is embedded and feel that the school now has a chance of becoming an information center for the community. Mr. Lacy said, this morning, "There is really no economic reason for not owning any book you want, or at least for not being able to get your hands on what you want to read."

There are awfully big economic reasons for not being able to get as many books within my arm's length as I want to have within my arm's length. Partly because I am fairly lazy, as I suspect some of you others are, my knowledge envelope that surrounds me is not very large. I can lay my hands on things. I keep a messed-up desk where I know where everything is. I have file cabinets close at hand which are practically empty, except for used bottles. But this envelope is small. I need that envelope to be small and dense. Books like this are very dense. These micro-books enable you to have a great many books. If, in fact, we can get micro-books to sell for less than a half a buck apiece, then the student who now spends $100 on 10 books may find himself spending $100 on 200 books which he retains. So I offer you this kind of activity. Depending on your personal views, you may accept it as a tool, or as a thread, or as an inconsequential piece of information.

One third piece of activity I think you might be aware of is a thing we would like to call interactive television. This activity is going on under the sponsorship of the Corporation for Public Broadcasting. One of the tough things about television is that it is a one-way communication tool. Somebody pours stuff into a network, or a station, and it comes out this twenty-one-inch stovepipe into your living room. The only interactions you have with it are the seven positions of the switch and an off switch, so you have a choice among eight things. With the advent of cable television, the crack I made about it this morning just isn't true any more, if one says that not all the stuff that comes out of the television set has to be lots of motion, jazz, and spoken words, but can be a little more sedentary. Many of you are familiar, I think, with things like slide shows where you have an audio-tape and a set of slides that flash on a screen. They are very effective teaching tools.

On a single television channel you can present 100 slide shows. Many of the modern cable television sets are now up to twenty channels. Many of them will have 96 channels by the end of 1970.

We, in the educational establishment, have asked that the Federal Communications Commission require cable TV owners to reserve 20 percent of their capacity for educational use. We really don't know what the hell we would do with it if they gave it to us. Since they don't know what they're going to do with the other 80 percent, they are perfectly willing to give it to us. And that's what has happened. They are going to make 20 percent of the cable TV capacity in this country available for educational use.

There are designs for receivers with a few buttons on them where a person can sit and, by pushing several buttons, can communicate his response back to a computer which is tied to the television station. He can modify what he sees, change channels. Did any of you go to Expo and see the Czechoslovakian movie? Here is a movie taking an action. Here is one of the things you can't do with television as it now stands.

One of the things we feel is tremendously important to teach, particularly in the community, is that an individual—and I'll go one step further: not an individual, but I, me, my ego—is an effective change agent; I can do things and the world changes when I do them. It is not really a great big thing to turn off the television set, although you might get some help out of that. What we are trying to teach is that I can experiment in a nonhostile environment with living with my own decisions.

Let me give you an example. You are all familiar with the case method of teaching business courses. We have a group preparing the business course for an interactive television presentation. It goes like this. The business starts with four partners. They begin to fight. At the end of ten minutes of presentation, a decision has to be made. There is a very limited menu of decisions. You can increase production; you can decrease production; you can increase sales effort; you can go out and borrow money; or you can get new equity capital. There are a limited number of things you can choose. The program will be designed so that at this point these alternatives flash on the screen. The student will be asked to pick one. He will do this by pushing a button, much like programmed instruction. For x minutes he will live with a pictorialization of what happened as a result of his choice, and he will come to another branch point. Many students will live through the failure of their businesses. We don't have a lot of the intervening scenes, but some of the last scenes have the sheriff locking the door.

The point is, one will be able to experience a business failure without being a business failure and without suffering some of the irreversible things that happen. One will also be able to experience business successes. Several things are important if this kind of technology is going to come to pass, and librarians, who will some day develop into the social scientists of the information field, are going to have to ensure that some of the things that are needed in such an environment happen. For example, it will be improper if the only presentations to a community are those made by the Harvard Business School or some other group. It is imperative that the social structures that deal with technologies also deal with the members of the community, who must be allowed to express their perception of an activity. The community must be able to experiment with it. We feel that by educating community people in what's going on at a very early stage in the technological development, they will be able to take advantage of it when it becomes a reality.

The same thing is true with the micro-book activity that I described earlier. It's imperative, obviously, if you're going to turn out a lot of new titles each month, that the community that is being served has a way of expressing its preferences as to what gets turned out. The same thing is true of the personal information management system, although that's a lot less clear. People will start to share their commonly owned files. We will see a kind of communication taking place that hasn't existed up to now.

I wanted to explore very briefly with you three developmental activities that are going on. I don't know enough about your problems to tell you a great deal about the applicability, although I will be happy to respond to effective or affective questions. I will also be happy to talk about other things that you may know are going on in technology that it hasn't occurred to me to tie to the library world.

PARTICIPANT: The Public Broadcasting Act of 1967 allocates at the present time about $7,000 or $8,000 toward local community radio stations and/or television stations. Is there any possibility that this may be greatly extended? As far as public libraries are concerned, this is one way in which a public library could have resources to make it possible to route information to a community.

BARUCH: You're asking the $64 million question! To predict what this administration is going to do with education is a rather hazardous occupation.

PARTICIPANT: I might mention, for those of you who aren't aware of it, that this particular act would cover 75 percent of the expense of establishing a community radio station or community television station, so that if you wanted to start an FM station in your community, it would cost $20,000.

BARUCH: That's interesting. One of the reasons we're interested in cable TV is because we can knock the cost down a hell of a lot further than that. We're interesting in piggybacking on commercially used facilities. There is a lot of capital investment that has to be put in place anyhow. Although you learn in industry not to do incremental costing, this is just the way many of us live. We will try to make diligent use of equipment that's there anyhow. It becomes rather economical.

PARTICIPANT: I see challenges that come out of your statement that affect us as practicing professionals. Your statement also has implications for education. This is the whole concept of who delivers, who is involved in the delivery of information. You included, as does Mary Lee Bundy, the interpreter role, the analytical function, as being part of the delivery of information. Many of us are not prepared either to do this or to supervise a complex which will include this. We don't have to be able to be interpreters, but we must be able to recognize a good interpreter.

Does this group have some suggestions or comments to make along these lines? Inevitably, it seems to me, next year or ten years from now technology is going to make it possible for an entirely different kind of impact on what is delivered physically. Is our profession going to be in on the interpretations? I don't know whether or not, for example, in academia, professors are prepared to see interpretation coming out of libraries and information centers. They might want to preserve that function for themselves.

BARUCH: I don't know if librarians have to go the interpretation or translation route. Information, by itself, is becoming a focal commodity in the lives of the students and in the lives of the people in the community. We need a set of professionals who have in their grasp a great deal of information about information. I don't mean information scientists, because that's a different world, but we need people who are information specialists, if you like. I think that is a role for librarians. When I say a resource consultant, I don't mean somebody who either gives answers or teaches you how to get the answers, but acquaints you with the alternatives that exist in this pipeline of information.

BUNDY: We've been using "interpreter," though, to mean a double role. The interpreter has an information community whose needs are interpreted to the information system.

BARUCH: I would like very much to shorten up the line. That still implies an intercessionist to me, and I'm scared of priests or any other kind of intercessionist. I would like to shorten that up and make it possible for the individual to tell the information system what he wants and let the information specialist, the librarian, take on the role of educating him in how to do that.

BUNDY: This may be a phase, but right now we don't even have information systems that reach some people. We need these systems.

BARUCH: Sure, but I was talking about goals. A goal that I'm talking about is to get the individual coupled to the information system as closely as possible, with the librarian serving to teach him how to communicate with the system, rather than interposing himself between the individual and the system. An analogy to this is the programmer. I don't know if any of you have had anything to do with computers via programmers. Programmers sit between me and this great powerful computer, and I'm not going to be happy until I can talk to the computer directly. What I would like the programmer to do is to move over and teach me how to communicate with the computer, rather than interposing himself between me and the computer.

BUNDY: There is a fallacy there, however, because the individual doesn't have that kind of power, nor does he know the engineering of the system well enough to say that it could be doing more for him. The interpreter, if he is at all professional, will continue to serve in the role. You would see librarians as servants of the system, primarily. I'm just defending the interpreter.

PARTICIPANT: Let me start from a more basic point. According to my understanding, if we look at incremental systems, the material that is processed is very deep and needs different handling techniques. Report literature needs different processing techniques. We do not process it as we process books. All these data are changing the nature and function of librarians. Computers and other hardware are not just tools. The quantitative change has been so great that it has brought in a qualitative change. Unless we become aware of this fact, we will very soon be sidetracked by other people who will be handling this information problem more efficiently, as it should be handled.

I was really hoping that in your talk about computers you would bring in the other side from a different perspective and provide us with a proper role. The computer is not just like the electric typewriter. We should consider this equipment not as just another machine, but in proper perspective, so that we can bring in the necessary change to the nature of libraries.

BARUCH: There is a difference in kind, instead of a difference in degree, when one introduces certain kinds of tools. The steam engine was another tool; so was nuclear energy. They have caused a major rethinking of some of our social structures and some of our social activities. Modern information technology promises to come into being in the not-too-distant future. It does not exist today, despite the fact that you and I may have easy access to consoles. The technology that promises to come into existence will have a far more earth-shaking effect than anything we have discussed, such as nuclear energy, steam engines, or even new experimental social structures.

Perhaps I can best give you the flavor of some of this by talking about quantities, times, things that we're familiar with, but please, one of the big dangers in my field, the computer field, is an enormous urge to oversell what we're doing. It's a disease. We suffer from what I can best call the tense problem. We frequently use the present tense verb when we mean the future, past tense when we mean the present. There is more optimism per square foot in this field than in almost any other.

So with that preamble, let me remind you again that the kind of information science and technology we're talking about is coming. It is not here! I can only say it's coming, probably. The computers we do have make it possible for an individual to search through files at the rate of several hundred thousand entries per second. For example, I have a computer terminal. I used to have one at home. It gives me access to files in the order of 100 million characters. Now, when one can do this, it is a very significant difference from going through the card catalog. It's a tool that generates a difference in kind. The guy who has that terminal has a clout of power that the guy without a terminal doesn't have. And the guy who has the terminal with a key that lets him write on those files in addition to reading them has even more clout than the guy who can only read them. So when we say there is a difference in kind, there is indeed.

This brings up the concept of a two-way library. There is an association of special librarians, a set of libraries, special libraries, technical libraries, where the intersection of the set of users who are library readers and the set of users who are authors is very high. Many of the readers are authors; many of the authors are readers. In a library where the number of combined author–readers is high, wouldn't it be nice if we let these authors-cum-readers make notes in the margins of the book as they read and have their marginalia become part of the retrievable library? That is very, very possible using electronic means.

One of the experiments we have tried is the following. We set up a file, put abstracts in it, and got a bunch of sophisticated users, and gave them the right to annotate those files as well as to read them, with one proviso. Whoever writes anything must sign it. As a matter of fact, we go a little bit further than that: he has to sign to get on the machine, and the machine signs what he writes, so he can't cheat. This has proven a most interesting experience. As a matter of fact, we set up a computer for a totally different use—computation in medicine. This was just a little activity going on in the corner. The computer is now devoted to this entirely and nobody gives a damn about computation in medicine.

PARTICIPANT: Why do you have them sign their names?

BARUCH: Well, because it's important for me to be able to see who said something so that I can look for other things that he may have said about other similar materials. This becomes a linkage, a significant piece of information. It is not a punitive measure. If you like, let him sign it numerically with no code to tell who he is as an individual. What I'm interested in is a linkage among entries to show that a set of entries came from a common perceptive viewpoint.

It is a set of linkages, a trail. This kind of two-way library, I think, will become a wave of the future in the special library. Now, how about the libraries where we do not customarily have a large intersection between users and readers? If it were very cheap to make it possible for the reader to annotate the files, would he? I think this is one of the experiments we will find in the nonspecial library coming up.

In the electronic libraries, we will find abstract materials, linkages, review articles where all individual users of the library can annotate them, and where I, as a user, can use a filter to avoid being inundated by all of this information. I, as a user, can use a screen made up of users' names, writers' names, or writers' numbers so that I only read that which I am interested in or which contributes to my biases or something in which I have some experience. This kind of use of a library is different in kind. This concept of a library entity is different in kind.

There are a couple of things to say about this library I've been describing. You could say it is really only a bibliographic file, that users are not really making marginal notes in the books, but rather are writing on the library cards. That could be. The difference comes once you have played with the file. You can now say, "Gee, this body of information interests me. Send me all those things on microforms, and I'll pay for them." You get a very interesting concept of the library, one that is quite different.

It requires a different set of views of the professional and a very different set of views of time and space, because the physical location of such a library is completely unimportant. Those of you who viewed the mode access computation know that, unless you have to pay the phone bill, where the computer is is just not very important.

PARTICIPANT: At this point, let me give an example of a system. We have copied the NASA transfer system on our tape. We have microfiche copies of the documents. We have interest profiles of the users. We run specific searches. This is a library, according to my understanding of a library, and it could be any other library, even a children's library. The cost of fourteen cents per search is minimal and there is no librarian required for that work.

BARUCH: That doesn't necessarily make you very popular here. Keep talking.

PARTICIPANT: That's right. This is why I believe that unless we change the nature and status of a librarian, unless we change the knowledge parameters of librarians, unless we change our interests and our professional responsibilities, we will betray the library students who are unsuspectingly coming into the library schools hoping that some day they will be information handlers. They will be people who will be handling information transfers.

DONOHUE: I would like to respond. You raised an issue that Mr. Baruch alluded to: namely, the role of the librarian in face of this technology that's now available. I'm grateful for the kind of presentation he made of what technology is available and some of its possibilities. I don't think it takes anything away from this kind of thinking to point to the fact that you are now beginning to talk about implementing some of the things that Vannevar Bush envisioned in the 1940s, such as service to the individual by creating a memory trail of the individual's own thinking and reading. In the intervening twenty years we have gone ape over the big system, the bibliographic control over a million documents. The poor guys getting the printout now have a million documents to deal with. You are coming to the point now where you are *really* talking about what Dr. Bush was envisioning twenty years ago and which nobody has yet provided.

BARUCH: Let me interrupt and go one step further. Part of the reason I talk like this is because I spent the last nine years dealing with very large computer systems in medicine. They were central, time-shared, all the right buzz words. Only one thing wrong with them. Nobody wanted to use them. There was this great solution. We just never really found a problem for them. So after a while, you know, you get hit on the head often enough, you back off, and say, "Why doesn't anybody want to use it?" Some of the reasons came out.

One of the reasons is, of course, there is a tremendous loss of autonomy in using such a system. It's large. It's elsewhere. It's others'. It has things in it I don't use. It doesn't have all the things in it I want because to put those in would be expensive for other people. The result was one of the questions that got raised: "Would it be better to get small systems that were less powerful that people used, than large systems that were more powerful that people didn't use?"

We've gotten interested in Van Bush's concept, which went from him to this student. His student was my thesis adviser, so it's not too surprising I sound a little bit like him.

DONOHUE: Who is that?

BARUCH: Gordon Brown. I mention this because some of this is a sad experience. One of the reasons I hesitate to oversell some of the large systems is because they can so easily get oversold.

DONOHUE: I would like to submit that I think that possibly the reason it went wrong was that there was no set of information managers, if you will, who really had an expertise. I'm not selling short the library profession's background of knowledge about knowledge. I happen to think it's the most relevant body of knowledge that exists, primitive as it is, but we were not able to exercise the role with enough competence in something that is now coming to be known as information science.

Frankly, I'm a bit disturbed to hear you imply something that I hear from a lot of librarians, and that is there are information scientists and there are librarians. If the librarian is not in some sense a participant in the creation of an information science, he is going to become to the computer technologist the same kind of slave he has been to the book publishing industry all these years. He is going to be a passive recipient of a bunch of stuff, and it's going to be his job to pass on, as best he can, elements from this to the users.

There are three elements that are essential to being a librarian. He's concerned with the nature of the human record. (It happens to be a concern with a particular kind, print and near-print. But that's trivial.) He is concerned about the user of the record and about the user's need, and he is also concerned about the process by which the user gets the information. We are in danger now of overlooking some of these elements.

REID: Joesph, can I ask something, or at least stretch one of your roles? I might say to the group that I don't mind pressing my own interests. We found that the simplest medium that was supposed to help the fellow take the learning process appeared where youngsters were already a growing concern in terms of money, but didn't appear where they were not in that posture, where youngsters were having all kinds of trouble already. Libraries have more hardware and little typewriters than cities have.

DONOHUE: You're saying that the cities needed them more?

REID: Yes. I'm saying there is a differential here. Let's come out of the city–suburb contrast. Let's just get into the little college–big university thing, where you know you are going to reflect the same thing and perpetuate the same thing.

BARUCH: Now you're in my area. Those are my customers.

REID: This differential in access to information and the increased participation of the individual in the process of screening out the pollution, which you talk about, so he can get to what he wants to use, is going to increase the differential.

BARUCH: O.K., in other words, the rich get more. The Department of Defense, NASA, and the universities, where they already have sophisticated librarians working for them, are going to get more, and more, and more. No! Wrong!

REID: Wait! It will, unless . . .

BARUCH: Unless you take an active role.

REID: There is a social role as well as a personal thing.

BARUCH: You sit on your butts, MIT is going to get more money and the little college down the street just isn't. The community college is going to get still less.

There is one interesting thing, though. I run a consortium, if you can call being president of the consortium running it. I'm the nearest one to being run by the consortium, I guess, is a better way of saying it. It has about a hundred universities and colleges in it. They recognize that this disequilibrium is a danger. They are committed to the concept that education needs spreading, so the three projects I described just now arose. If you examine them, they do the large schools the least good.

They are projects that arose out of necessity, we felt, to meet the needs of the smaller school and educational entities that don't yet exist, things we call community learning centers, that don't exist at the moment. Each of these projects is aimed at that kind of a target. For example, Harvard College library really couldn't care less about another 100,000 volumes on microfiche, but Roxbury Community College sure as hell does. A school that has three IBM model 360s is not particularly concerned about a fairly sophisticated file managing system that you can get your hands on for $40,000, but a small school is, particularly if it allows it to do significant things in adapting it. Interactive television is a way of getting responsive education out into the community, outside the school environments altogether.

PARTICIPANT: Allen Kent and a whole group of people are selectively tackling the problems of the organization of information, but not the problem of matching information to people.

DONOHUE: I think we have to realize that information scientists may be people who have never heard of the term "information science." The linguist who is concerned with patterns of children's learning in relation to their possession of certain kinds of books is an information scientist.

PARTICIPANT: The one who worries about relating those findings to staffing the library in an inner city environment is an information social scientist.

DONOHUE: Librarians have tended to think of themselves as a different breed. They believe they have no relation to information scientists. We have tended to make this hard-and-fast distinction and to act as though librarians had nothing to offer the scientific process.

BARUCH: That is no more true than it would be right to assume the social scientist has nothing to offer the physical sciences, or that the social sciences can ignore the impact of the physical sciences on social structure. Right now, to my mind, the kind of social scientist I'm talking about is a step above information scientists in that he must be concerned about the substance of information science and he must be concerned about the substance of what goes on among people and about matching the two together. He cannot ignore one half or the other. Any librarian who says, "What's important to me is getting things to people" without worrying about how these things come into existence, is a half-assed librarian. You can't stay that way.

DONOHUE: You have to draw some lines. You have to say, "This is my job. There are other things that are not my job." I don't think book publishing is the librarian's job. I think we have a lot to offer by way of valuable information as to what books ought to be published. We will be entering a new aspect of information science in doing it. There is nobody in the world with a wider range of data, but the librarians have not, by and large, done anything with the data.

BARUCH: I think you and I see a clear role for librarians.

DONOHUE: I'm responding to the notion of a complete separation, because . . .

BARUCH: I'm not objecting to the concept of a speculation. I think it is less useful to use the same title for two activities which are not truly one-to-one. I would like to make up a high-status title for librarians that is also reasonably descriptive of what the hell they've got to do in the coming years.

PARTICIPANT: Do you think the word "librarian," then, is not a high-status word?

BARUCH: What do you think?

PARTICIPANT: I'm asking you, because you're making a distinction between . . .

BARUCH: By and large, I think a librarian is a low-status word in our society. I have some nice sociological studies to show you if you would like proof of that. There is a psychological test called the dab test. Have yourself a ball some day. Don't tell people what you do for a living, and ask them to draw a librarian.

PARTICIPANT: A word isn't going to change the status of a librarian.

BARUCH: No, but changing the word may make clear that the librarian has a new and real role in a developing field. If the librarian identifies himself with that new role, there will be no hurdle to get over.

I don't want to argue the sociology of various names.

PARTICIPANT: People tend to have constraints about their views of what is possible and what kinds of contribution they can make.

BARUCH: In the community of people with whom I deal, "college president" has gotten to be a very low-status title.

PARTICIPANT: Perhaps "plumber" has more status than "college professor" or "president."

BARUCH: Not more status, more income!

PARTICIPANT: Perhaps; it depends. I think librarians, as a rule, don't think very highly of themselves. This is number one. Number two, a year ago in *Library Journal* there was a discussion about salaries, and the result was, "We don't need more money because we don't deserve it."

PARTICIPANT: In special libraries, the librarian is a very important tool. The users know the information is there, but they don't have enough time to go and dig it up.

DONOHUE: It's a high-priced errand boy you're talking about.

PARTICIPANT: You can call it whatever you want, but you can't live without it.

DONOHUE: I'm suggesting that there is another role for the librarian.

BARUCH: It's interesting the word that she used. She said, "a tool."

DONOHUE: I was going to react to that, but I thought you were speaking of the library.

BARUCH: No, the librarian.

PARTICIPANT: Joe, administrators are service agents.

PARTICIPANT: Some administrators think of people as tools no matter what they do.

PARTICIPANT: I'm talking about the role. "Administration" is a high-status word in our field, but administration is a supportive role.

PARTICIPANT: In too many cases, it's a manipulative role.

PARTICIPANT: If you are creative, you are no longer a tool.

DONOHUE: I want librarians to have clout. They've got to have the competence and the knowledge to say, "I have scientific evidence to show. . . ." They should stop gassing about status and titles. Who gives a damn about the title? If you're doing the job, you'll be respected. I don't care if they call me a plumber, or whatever. If you go in with the clout that comes from having the same kind of knowledge that gives an engineer, a physicist, or a statistician his clout, he is not giving you a collection of opinions of other physicists. He is giving you something that can be duplicated by other people. This is what I want of librarians. I want them to be participants in an information science. They've got a wealth of data. They've got more damn data than anybody else has in the world about the processes of information.

PARTICIPANT: I don't know anyone who has a greater wealth of data about algebra I than an algebra I teacher, but they have difficulties getting it across. The Coleman report indicated that the apparatus in the school is relatively insignificant in the students' achievements.

DONOHUE: I'm not familiar with the Coleman report. Do you mean it doesn't matter what kind of apparatus the library has?

PARTICIPANT: You don't have to continue to operate the way libraries always have. Conceivably, you can use these materials so it makes a difference.

PARTICIPANT: Education has been evolving. The nature of information has changed, the way of handling it has changed, but we haven't changed. We are letting other people take over our profession. We are professional people, not glorified secretaries, but we do not act up to our place. The courses that are offered in most of the library schools are so watered down that they are just glossing over most of the contents. The instructor keeps telling his students that they can't get down to the nitty gritty because of the low level of the class. Students from the mathematics school are coming all the time to be information scientists, but the courses are watered down because of the existence of other library school students who can't cope with the mathematics.

PARTICIPANT: Do you know what the answer to that is? One cause has been created by people who say, "In order to achieve any status as an information handler for physicists, you've got to be a physicist," so they throw out the librarians and bring in the physicists. In another six months the physicists are bored. There is another reason. In this field, we hold in such contempt our own bag of tricks that we have said there is no place for undergraduate preparation in this field.

BARUCH: We talk about information science and librarians as information scientists. I don't think there is an identifiable, codified, basic, underlying discipline to the library vocation.

DONOHUE: Neither is there to medicine.

BARUCH: I don't want to argue about that, either. I will challenge whether we are not in some sense being deluded when we talk about ourselves as information scientists, the same as those who are actively engaged in the effort to find such a discipline. I believe a really solid course of some fundamental study into what the Greeks used to call the roots and growth of knowledge should be required before you can start any talk about being library scientists without being accused of exaggeration. Before we get too hung up on how we become information scientists, I would like to scrap the thought of an information science existing. It doesn't.

I happen to be a specialist in file structure. One of the reasons I am a specialist is that I can make up file structures faster than most other people can. I do not have an underlying fundamental discipline that tells me how to match a file structure to a need. It's a case of continual invention. My cohorts in the field are no better than I am. Having scrapped the concept of information sciences for the moment, can we now discuss the existing information technology— the hardwares and the softwares?

In the concept of information technology, what the hell does a librarian do? When I used to go to a library, there were three activities I went through. First was the activity of discovery. I had to find out that something existed. Second was the activity of acquisition. I had to get my hands on it. And third was the activity of assimilation. Once I got my hands on it, I had to read it and understand it.

There are lots of people concerned with the application of technology to discovery. There are far fewer concerned with the application of technology to acquisition. There are even fewer concerned with the application of technology to assimilation. There are barely any concerned with the application of all of this to relevance in a social study.

In this milieu, isn't there some role for librarians that is absolutely fundamental for the continued existence of society, given an information technology?

DONOHUE: I can't add much to that. What you're talking about is information science, even if you don't want to use that term.

PARTICIPANT: Then we're fooling ourselves by setting up doctoral programs for information science and librarians.

BARUCH: Right!

PARTICIPANT: If there is no such discipline, we're fooling ourselves to try to prepare for it.

BARUCH: I'll tell you a secret. A doctoral program doesn't prepare people for anything. Doctoral programs are sources of slave labor for uncovering a science. One doesn't start a doctoral program because there is a well-founded science. A doctoral student is supposed to be at a stage of maturity where he can afford to live with doubts and uncertainties. So now he too can join the search for information science. I didn't say to give up that search.

For a long time, we designed filters for radios and television without ever having a theory of filter design. Eventually a few people came along with a theory of filter design and taught us how to optimize it. It never changed the filters very much. I think we are in the same state with information science. We know an awful lot about what's going on, but we do not have a codification, a formalism, and a discipline yet. We need a doctoral program to fool around with that, whether you want to set it up as part of a library program or not. I would set it up in a library program. It's a good place to put students who can't relate to people.

PARTICIPANT: I can think of legitimate problems that can be handled by a doctoral program. Without delineating an example, I would say that a doctoral program should prepare the student to be able to handle a problem. That surely is in the library science.

BARUCH: It's truly not a scientific activity.

PARTICIPANT: Not specifically.

BARUCH: There is no formalism. There is no way of demonstrating the completeness of any file protection scheme you come up with as a solution. Lacking that, you don't have a science.

Somebody recognized that if people are going to have large files, there is a social need for the protecting and insuring the integrity of those files. I would like to see librarians identify themselves as the people who uncover these problems, even if they can't solve them.

PARTICIPANT: You want librarians to tell you why the doctor doesn't like the big scheme, why he would rather have a small one?

PARTICIPANT: Here we go asking the questions again that we were discussing before.

PARTICIPANT: There are lots of reasons for that.

PARTICIPANT: He is asking us to identify the fact that the doctor doesn't work well with the machine. Throw that problem back to the engineer!

BARUCH: I see some technology coming along. Like they used to say in the old burlesque act, "Either it's going to get into the act, or it's not." If it doesn't, we don't have to pay any attention to it. If it does, we've got two possibilities. It's going to be good for the user, or it's not.

There has to be an agent someplace, the librarian or somebody in his stead, who is concerned with the best matching of knowledge technology with people and people's needs. Let me point out that if the librarians don't assume this task, it will still get done. People like Dan Lacy will do it. Maybe he'll name it marketing, in his view of the information world. He may not have quite the same motives. He may not have quite the same understanding of the social structure. He may not have the same responsibility toward the social structure the librarian does. I would prefer to see it happen in this kind of an academic context rather than the commercial or governmental one. So I offer you a possible role, but I don't offer it as a solution or a salvation.

WASSERMAN: For the rest of the session this afternoon, I thought it might be interesting for the group if we shift. We'll begin the last half of the afternoon with Jordan Baruch being the responder. I've asked Joe if he would tell us about his project in Baltimore in enough detail so that the group has a sense of what he's up to. Then we will ask Jordan to comment or react to the technological implications of it. So, Joe, would you tell us about your project?
DONOHUE: The Public Information Center Project is funded by the State of Maryland Department of Education, Library Extension Division. It is being developed by the School of Library and Information Services in cooperation with the Enoch Pratt Library in Baltimore. The notion behind it is one that Dr. Wasserman has been advocating for a long time, that of extending the information resources of the public library system far beyond the traditional constraints, even considering the special things that public libraries do now.

There are two major kinds of constraints for public libraries. One is that their activities have been conducted, for the most part, within their own walls. The other is that they have generally been tied to what we consider traditional media. There are some exceptions to these constraints—children's stories in the oral tradition, bookmobiles as an exception to operating within your own walls, things like film programs and rental of films. But these are still tied to providing the information that happens to be in the public library's own holdings.

The Public Information Center Project is an attempt to break out of both of these constraints, with an accent on information. Enoch Pratt and the Maryland library school are setting up a Public Information Center. We are going to operate in two phases. First, we will investigate the community needs and the community resources with regard to information. Second, a demonstration project will be set up to extend the scope of the information services of the library. The assumptions behind this are that in the city, the metropolitan setting, conditions are changing rapidly and creating all kinds of social stresses which increase the society's need for disseminating information to all citizens, not just to the technical community and the school community. The citizen as citizen, and not as student, official, or professional or other occupational role, needs urgently many kinds of information that is not in books. It's not in the vertical file of libraries. Librarians have recognized this for a long time. They keep three-by-five card files of resource people, information frequently asked for, and so on. We believe it is appropriate and desirable to provide a formal mechanism by which this kind of information can be identified, captured, put into a memory with ready accessibility.

What we are going to do is go out to a community, particularly to the social agencies. Since we can't do all things in a year's demonstration project, we have decided arbitrarily to hone in on the health and welfare type of information. This is still cutting quite a broad path. With the cooperation of the Health and Welfare Council, and other councils which coordinate the activities of community agencies, and through direct contact with the agencies themselves, we're going to create an inventory of information resources.

We're going to create a file. This file will probably be at two levels. We'll have what you might call the ready reference file. It will provide the kind of organizational data on the agencies that can provide specific services in health and welfare areas. We'll have a backup file in greater depth on each of these agencies and collateral material so that when you need the kind of information you can't provide with the directory approach, the kind that require greater research and in-depth study, we'll have this available, too.

Part of the problem is to define our proper role. Particularly in the health and welfare area, it is necessary to decide what we should and shouldn't do, where to draw the line between being an information man and being a case worker. I'm not temperamentally a case worker, and I am certainly not competent to do case work. Furthermore, in discussion with social workers and other people who do provide substantive services to people, I have found that they reach a certain point where they can't handle the information problem to their own satisfaction. They are trying to be both social workers and information managers, and they can't do both adequately, so they too are beginning to see a division of labor as desirable.

We are now in the process of working out a definition of roles between ourselves and organizations such as the Health and Welfare Council. They already operate a referral service which puts the individual in touch with the agency that can help him. They follow it up to make sure their referral doesn't become the run-around. On the other hand, we plan to concentrate on the information aspects.

We think that this will provide stimulation to the library's own personnel to zero in on certain social problems and to bring to bear on these problems the fantastic resources that a large public library system has, both in terms of the materials and in terms of the information capabilities of the personnel. We have some ideas that the branch libraries may want to work on. And the departments in the central library will be a principal resource for information in building our file. We will be building this data base, however, not simply as an adjunct to the agencies with which we work. We will use whatever they give us plus what we can dig up for ourselves. We will create a data base which will be available to the public on an individual basis, to the agency, to the council, and to the press or other media.

This is an undertaking of large scope. The aim is to turn over the keys to the library by the middle of next year. Once it becomes an operating function of the Enoch Pratt Library, they may want to structure it somewhat differently. That's O.K. We're just building a model. We're going to turn over the working model to them before the end of the contract year. Already there is some interaction with our teaching program. I am half-time on this project and half-time teaching in the school. We started out quite independently in another effort, which we call black recruitment. Because of some interest in that, I found myself on the committee. Jim Welbourne recruited a young man who is in the data processing business. He is a systems design man, a very sophisticated guy. He happens to work for an organization that has a lot of capability in on-line data acquisition and dissemination. I discussed the public information center with him along the line of "What can we do together?" As we're calling the shots on this, in a sense, it was "What can we do for you?" However, before that guy finished talking with me, the roles were reversed, because he had some impressive ideas about using his knowledge and his company's capabilities. Hopefully, they will go along with this. He will continue his association with his company and work on a developmental program to provide a model for public information center activity, similar to what the government agencies are developing for the scientists who want to sit in Dallas and query the MIT library files.

Using the network that is already established in the Maryland system, perhaps we will be able to provide some remote access to information. For example, suppose there is a case worker in Washington County or on the Eastern Shore who needs certain information. He can, through his public library, query our center, which will rapidly return to him either the name of the person or the organization that can do something for him, or the research materials he needs. You can use your imaginations to see how far this can go.

I'm not dismissing the bibliographic mode as unimportant, but there are many more resources. Agencies in government, like the State Department, the Agricultural Department, the CIA, and the DIA, are interested in and have developed some on-line systems. One of the reasons for this is that they have a fantastically large data corpus which is not in book or report form. It doesn't have a good, clean bibliographic name and address. It seems to me that as librarians we've got to concern ourselves more with this kind of data, which is so urgently important.

Perhaps I'm biased, but it's highly important to me that the guy who has a pressing social need in the middle of Baltimore have at his disposal tools and techniques that are now available only to the defense industry and to the scientists and engineers. I would like to get some responses from our guest because he knows ways of doing the kind of thing that I'm interested in doing, and to hear from you participants because I feel this is our responsibility, as librarians.

BARUCH: This is a great introduction to a much more general problem that faces you as librarians. By and large, as librarians you deal with local user groups, and I don't necessarily mean geographically local, and highly distributed sources. Publishers exist all over the place. Your information flows from many places. Communications people are starting to set up one–many and many–one communication systems. For example, a system such as Mr. Donohue has described clearly should be able to take advantage of the many, many data bases that exist around the United States. The librarian at Enoch Pratt will have to become someone who is cognizant of the structure, the source, and the intent of many of these data bases. For example, Project Talent has a suburban data base that the Maryland schoolteachers ought to be able to use. There are things called poison information centers where immediacy of response is often a matter of life and death. There are many machine-stored files.

It would be nice if the concept of a referral center, which is really the nub of what you are talking about, evolved to the concept of a switching center where the user need not know the existence, location, or form of a piece of information. He needs only to come and express his problem; then this switching center can connect him with something or someone where he can deal on a one-to-one relationship. This growth of a switching center will probably be one of the next stages in this project. There are going to be several of these. Then there is going to grow the next stage system which asks, "How do these interconnect over a common network?" Because what we are going to find is that those people in chemistry keep classifying things for chemists, and the people in biology keep classifying things for biologists. How does somebody who is interested in psychopharmacology make use of both what the chemists and what the biologists have classified, not to mention the psychologists and the doctors? This kind of switching will be the next stage of development.

WASSERMAN: You are talking about two different things, essentially. When you talk about chemistry, you are talking about a reasonably circumscribed discipline. You're talking about an information communication system of knowers who are knowledgeable in a highly technical sphere and who have common interests that can be sorted out by discipline. There we have, I think, a different basis for a national system. There is an organization of people with a common technical concern with the field.

What we are driving at here is a different kind of instrument, one which is concerned with intelligence that is discipline-free. Information that people require for their technical performance is being packaged and structured effectively and efficiently already by the societies, by the indexing services, by the bibliographic forms, procedures, and technologies which are funded and resourced to death. That's where all the dollars go.

Nobody is worried about the culture. You've got an instrumentality; you've got an institution. It's a public library. There it sits in the city. It controls artifacts in every sphere, primarily books and other forms like books because they're comfortable and convenient and because people know how to deal with them. But the need in that culture has shifted. Where the book was once the artifact that contained intelligence, it's no longer where it's at. It's no longer where the intelligence resides.

Considering these facts, who plays the role of being the intermediary for the other requirements in our changing culture? That's what this is all about. It's not for science, not for the disciplines that are nurturing their own requirements, but for people who need to know about all of the complicated things that happen in contemporary life that a city has answers to if somebody sorts them out. Here we are playing this role.

BARUCH: Please don't oversell what science has done to its fund of information, Paul. There is a great deal going on in the sciences—abstracting services, codification services, et cetera—and it's a major fiasco. The reason it is a major fiasco is because of the problems of getting information outside of one's specialty. For example, the man in the city who happens to be an accountant has a pretty good feel for what's going on in accounting in the city, but he needs to know about the fire department and he doesn't know where to go or who to ask. He doesn't know how to find out about getting a tax abatement or what to do about rat control or mosquito control in his community. The rat control information is put into the system by people who know rat control. They codify the system for other rat controllers. The people who put in the stuff about mosquito control do the same thing. They are entomologists, because you have to pass a test as an entomologist before you can become a mosquito control man.

You need somebody who can look at the entomologists' file from the point of view of a householder. That's exactly the same thing that is required in physics and chemistry. I need somebody who can look at a chemical file from the point of view of a biologist. The idea that he knows any more about the chemical file structure than the householder knows about environmental control is just wrong.

One of the reasons we are having severe trauma in the scientific information area is because we have been spending enormous amounts of money on something like *Chemical Abstracts*. We've got chemical abstracts coming out all the time. They are all abstracted, codified, and keyed on the basis of the Geneva classification system of organic chemical molecules. Petroleum engineers who have to use *Chemical Abstracts* are interested in petroleum and coordinate compounds. They don't have the foggiest idea of how the thing is organized and couldn't learn if you tried to teach them. They need an interpreter as badly as this man you are talking about. I'm suggesting that there may be sources of funding for the kind of thing you're looking at that are broader than the sources of funding for the State of Maryland. You're looking at a problem that has functional analogues in areas that have some money.

PARTICIPANT: As Mr. Donohue said, though, it is not the citizen as scientist, or the citizen as student, or the citizen as anything else, but it is the citizen in the city with common problems because he lives in that environment.

BARUCH: I would prefer to use the term "a person in the community of people." This holds for citizens; it holds for disciplinarians in a community of disciplines; it holds for states in a community of states. What I'm excited about is that here is somebody who is starting a functional referral service dealing with information rather than with artifacts. This is a significant step.

DONOHUE: I'm excited by the possibilities for us professionally of what you're saying. You are saying we need somebody to interpret chemical literature for the biologist in the biologist's terms. I think what we need is something a little bit different from that, enormously different really—someone who looks at knowledge on a motor level. He need not be, in fact he must not be, somebody who takes the chemical literature and interprets it as a biologist, but rather somebody who interprets it in a general enough sense to "mark and park" it so that both groups can deal with it. This is not just something we do by the seat of our pants. It is something that requires study in epistemology, logic, mathematics, and who knows what else.

BARUCH: You are talking about a true classificationist. We've got to raise them. We've got to breed them.

DONOHUE: This thing disturbs me. I keep referring to the data base, the knowledge that librarians have and other people as well—the press for example. People who have been information professionals have done much of it purely pragmatically. But isn't information something that can lend itself to an objective, disciplined approach? We have data, but we must mine it for principles of operation which can be validated and which will form the basis of an information science discipline, which we can apply then with some confidence.

WASSERMAN: The discourse is shifting levels of abstraction, I think, to the point where it is getting pretty garbled. Let me try to get hold of a couple of points. One, you make an interesting point when you talk about the need for an intermediary to act for someone from one discipline who needs information from another discipline. That's where librarians have performed best, because they have known a little about a lot of things. When someone was out of his field the little that librarians have known has made them reliable intermediaries. If a witch doctor needed information about chemistry, generally the librarian knew more about chemistry than he did, so the librarian could play an intermediary role there. In witch doctory, you know, they know their own stuff and they don't need a librarian.

BARUCH: I've got to interrupt you. I'm not looking for an intermediary. That is just what I'm not looking for. I'm looking for somebody who will teach the chemist what the logic of organization is concerning the biological files—how to get his hands on the sources, how to discover what the connections are between the sources and the files. I do not want him to be a half-baked chemist who can talk to a biologist.

PARTICIPANT: But then he must know the convention used for each one of the files.

BARUCH: He must have enough of the disciplines so he can absorb those conventions as they come, so that he can become a force in shaping those conventions, so that he can become a consultant to people who are building new conventions, so that he is, in fact, one who deals with the structure and roots of the knowledge.

PARTICIPANT: It seems to me to be an impossible task.

BARUCH. Not at all.

PARTICIPANT: You're asking him to be familiar enough with each discipline to know how it is organized and to know the utility of its files. The librarian must span the whole spectrum of subject areas in order to do this, a whole spectrum of differently organized . . .

BARUCH: Isaac Newton defined gravity. He did not have to understand apples and hairs and gun shells and rockets and a whole bunch of other things. He was after root structures. This is what I am saying the librarian now has to do in the form of the organization of knowledge: seek out the root structures. He does not have to be an almost-specialized chemist or an almost-specialized biologist. He must be somebody who can talk with the chemist in terms of the organizational philosophy of the chemical literature as an implement.

PARTICIPANT: Let me suggest a different kind of formula and see what you think of this. A group of specialist librarians join forces. One whose specialty is the organization of chemical literature works on a day-to-day basis with practicing chemists. Another specialist librarian does the same thing for physiologists. All the librarians are connected together by their common interest in ways of handling and organizing knowledge.

BARUCH: What will be the language in which they communicate with each other? It will be the language of the structure of the knowledge with which they deal. Therefore, each of those librarians must be able to deal with that. The fact that some of them will also become medical specialists and biological specialists, I consider incidental. The thing we're missing in this pseudoscience that we have to have is this fundamental knowledge of description language.

One of the things we tackled as a task was how to convert the tapes of *Chemical Abstracts* to MARC [machine readable cataloging] tapes. This is a perfectly simple kind of problem, except that we're missing the language. We can do it for a special case. No problem! Now, we would like to generalize that solution. How can we instruct the machine to convert any form of tape to a MARC tape, leaving voids where there are informational voids? Ergo, what one needs is a procedural language to describe to a machine what is a field, what is the structure of the field, what are characters, what are elements, and so on. We don't have such a language yet. There is one currently being developed. That language will form a good first step for the librarian in dealing with this big problem.

If such a language did exist tomorrow, how many library schools would incorporate it as part of the curriculum? I think that is a valid question.

WASSERMAN: You have put the problem into a different context. I don't think that's the basic problem. You've leaped ahead, it seems to me. Joe Donohue says there is a far more difficult problem of politics and economics and human persuasion . . .

BARUCH: Absolutely!

WASSERMAN: Don't blink it away and say absolutely! The problem **really is to fig**ure out the mechanism for getting the intelligence to the point where you can sort it out evenly and to get human beings to agree that the responsibility resides here.

BARUCH: I am not blinking it away, Paul. I recognize it. This is the hard part of life, however. You and he and I have the other task of training the people who are going to work in the area. Right now, we ain't doing it!

WASSERMAN: We're trying. We have some things we're doing here with knowledge that is very embryonic, I'll concede. We do have some things going here like this.

PARTICIPANT: Where are these things being taught, Mr. Baruch, this sort of basic course?

BARUCH: Are many of you familiar with multidimensional taxonomic classification? We've talked about search schemes, selective dissemination schemes where a man gets a card and checks off things he's interested in. One of the things you'll learn very quickly if you try to run an SDI [selective dissemination of information] system is that people don't know what they're interested in. You would like to keep track of what they throw away in case there is a great deal of this. You've got the whole problem of modification.

Here is another game you can play, other than giving somebody a check list of things that he's interested in. You can do the following. You can prescribe a set of 2,000 books and describe them on anchored scales with different dimensions. This one deals with science; this one deals with race relations. You can have a bunch of dimensions. Now you can play the following game. Give these to a person in pairs and say, "Which of these two are you interested in?" This is a forced-choice test. You can take a thousand such forced choices and draw a locus of interest in a multidimensional space. Now here is a book and you say, "Who wants it?" Well, suppose you're at x distance in this multidimensional space, x feet. Anybody whose interest clump lies within five feet of this book ought to find out about it.

This is quite a different kind of SDI system. It can't be done with a punched-card computer. It can be done with one that is essentially on-line fact or analysis. A very complex kind of work. It's exactly the same kind of technique, however, that was used in clumping students in Project Talent. Those same skills are used in clumping books in a multidimensional space of books. It would be great if schools of library science were concerning themselves now with the technology and the possible usefulness of some of the multidimensional sorting techniques. Clumping has been around for a long time. Factor analysis has been around so long it has gone into disrepute in some areas.

I would be very excited if we could get library schools to adopt this. A few medical schools, for whom it's almost a matter of life and death to adopt this, have recognized that diseases aren't entities, but they are expressions of distance from a clump of symptoms that we normally recognize with a label.

These things are happening. They're happening outside the substantive world. They're happening in the world of information science. I would like library scientists to be so up on what's going on that the transition from that to running a library, or to running a special library, or to running an information center, is almost a matter of course.

PARTICIPANT: Mr. Donohue, are you familiar with the San Francisco general programming of information? They took a car into the ghetto area on a three-times-a-week basis, stopping any place where somebody flagged the car down and answering reference questions.

DONOHUE: No, I'm not. Is this for reference questions or referral?

PARTICIPANT: Referral.

DONOHUE: I would be very upset if they gave the guy a bibliographic citation.

PARTICIPANT: It's a referral situation. In other words, they ask the question on a Monday. They come back with the answer on Wednesday. I can't elucidate too greatly on it because I read only one article in the *Wilson Library Bulletin* some months ago about it.

DONOHUE: Is this run by a library?

PARTICIPANT: Yes, it's run by the San Francisco Public Library.

DONOHUE: Quite frankly, I'm a conservative about libraries. I feel that we've got to do what we can do best. I have some reservations about how much we ought to go out looking for problems.

PARTICIPANT: I think you misunderstand. The city gives the public library a car three times a week. If I'm driving down the street and some eight-year-old boy comes up to me and says, "Who won the World Series in baseball in 1955?" I would have his answer for him the next time I drove through there.

DONOHUE: I wish you had chosen something that it would not be so easy to demolish. The kinds of things we ought to be turning our attention to are matters of dire need first.

PARTICIPANT: For all I know, they might be doing that.

DONOHUE: They might. I don't want to demolish this thing, because I do appreciate the idea behind it, if applied to important problems.
PARTICIPANT: I'll see if I can find the article and bring it to you personally.
DONOHUE: It does point up this problem that I'm working with now. We've got to find objective ways, as well as ad hoc responses, to define what our job is, and what its limitations are.

This has implications for our training of library school students. Do we train them to be social workers? Do we train them to be computer programmers, or politicians, or financial experts, or whatever? People used to say that to be a good librarian, you must be a whole list of things. Well, I say, "Nonsense!" We don't have to do that. We're sunk if we all try to be all of that or even some of it. But we do have to learn something about how to deal with the knowledge in those fields that is particularly relevant to us in our operations, as well as to the information we're trying to transfer.

If you drive that car down the street in San Francisco, in certain districts you will get questions that are genuine reference questions. If you drive it down other streets, you're going to get guys coming up to you and grabbing you by the lapels and saying, "I need help, or I'll kill myself. Do something!" At that point, all the books you have are likely to be irrelevant. You've got a human being with a human problem and you may say, "Nuts to the books; I'll go and try to help him."

But this is what worries me—when we go into the domain of the social worker, or try to be the teacher, or the pastor, carrying books. We've got to realize our limitations. Quite frankly, I have had very serious misgivings about our own High John project. I've voiced them. The people who have developed High John under sometimes scathing criticism are not blind to these issues. They say, "Yes, that really is a problem, and we're trying to define it." That, I think, is a better response than saying, "That's a problem, so let's not go into it."
PARTICIPANT: Haven't you imposed any limitations on this resource file that you've got?
DONOHUE: I said we would start with health and welfare.
PARTICIPANT: With that, suicide is a health problem, in a way.
DONOHUE: Yes, it is a health problem—in terminal cases a serious one. But I'm trying to proceed on the notion that if something is being done well already, we won't try to do it. I think the pie is

awfully big. There is plenty for everybody. And I want what we do to relate as closely as possible to my vision of the librarian's role.

To me, a librarian is essentially the records manager. Don't take offense. When he departs from that, he loses scope and focus. Records management is a very limited notion to some people, but not in the library sense. It implies a deep understanding of the nature of the record, of the user's need for the record, and of the process by which the user makes real contact with the record. It includes identifying, collecting, and organizing the record, and operating systems that make the record useful. I would further restrict that and exclude some records. Historically, librarians have dealt with records of written and oral language, and think that's a plenty big area. The painting, the sculpture—these are artifacts that have similar but different problems, and I'm content to leave them to museum curators, who are also records managers.

PARTICIPANT: You have used the words "records and management." Why couldn't you say information handling?

DONOHUE: Because I'm not an information handler. I'm a communicator. In my professional role as librarian, I am concerned with communication, but specifically as it uses some kind of records. I believe that the essential problem of the librarian is effective communication through records—not of information per se, but information which is related to and contained in records.

This distinguishes me, very conveniently from my point of view, from the man who is a dancer or a commentator, or from you and me in face-to-face communication. For example, here is Elizabeth Schwartzkopf in the boondocks this week singing. She uses all manner of records, music scores, books, all that sort of thing, but when she's on that stage her act of communication has nothing to do with records any more. It's immediate. *Our* act of communication, on the other hand, is one that is inevitably and essentially tied to the records.

BARUCH: May I help a little bit? You're talking about information handling, and Donohue is getting a little negative about it because it implies custodianship of the content of that information. He views himself as a specialist in the structure of information rather than its contents.

DONOHUE: That's true; I'm more interested in how it's hung together than in what it says. But the distinction I'm making here is a different one.

PARTICIPANT: What is the difference between a blind Venetian and a venetian blind? You have to be that much aware of the topic, at least.

BARUCH: Nobody is arguing about ignorance of topics. We're just not that smart, yet. One can be concerned about the difference between venetian blinds and blind Venetians without expressing a commitment to medicine or interior decorating. He can be concerned with it, because he is concerned with the structure. That I think, is a perfect role for a librarian.

DONOHUE: He said I'm responding negatively. I hope it doesn't come over to you that way. But I am negative to a false distinction, which has been made and promulgated in the information retrieval field until I'm sick to the teeth of it. That is, "Oh, the library is concerned with records. Information retrieval is concerned with information." But this is nonsense. All communication involves some medium, or record, or both. I haven't found the man yet who retrieves information without some artifact, whether it is in the form of extracts or bits or . . .

BARUCH: In fact, they are manipulating records rather than information. I think this is almost a good stopping place. May I end by telling a story?

We've used the term "methods" several times. You as librarians know a substantive definition of method. We moved to a new house fairly recently, and I had the problem of throwing away an old trash can. I don't know if anybody has ever tried this. It's very difficult. You can't put it out for the trash collector. He just leaves it there. What we finally did was to put a sign on it. It said, "Please take!" He took the sign. My daughter's remark was, "Dad, what you need is a disposable trash can." She is absolutely right. We are looking here for a meta–information science, the technique of dealing with the information fields rather than with the fields themselves.

10

THE LIBRARY PROFESSION: POLITICS, POWER, AND COLLECTIVE BARGAINING

FRIDAY MORNING, AUGUST 15
CHAIRMAN: MARY LEE BUNDY
PANELISTS: ELDRED SMITH
RALPH BLASINGAME, JR.

PARTICIPANT: I would like you to think about the implications of what we've been hearing for practice. In twenty-five words or less, what is the greatest implication for practice?

BUNDY: I don't think it has to be specific. Sometimes specificity lends clarity to generalizations, but it is the other way around, too. This morning we have a session which I had planned to introduce and give a shape to. I think now I'm going to back off from this, probably because I'm not sure whether my participants would follow the shape I gave it. I would, however, propose, if it's agreeable with you, that in the question period we might try to focus on why we asked these gentlemen to come.

We have looked at the culture. We have looked at society and its needs. We have looked at some of our tools—information transfer and the publishing industry. We also need to look at our professional tools for a change. Over and over again I hear librarians saying, "What can I, as an individual, do?" So much so that it is very alarming to me the number of librarians I meet who are indeed planning to get out of the library field because they have been unable to find a way to be effective in their bureaucracy. So this morning we have

362

invited these gentlemen to come and talk about our tools, specifically
library unions and our professional association, to learn how they can
be useful for us in trying to effect change in our local organizations.
SMITH: I'm going to assume at the beginning that we recognize a
need for change in library practice and that we also recognize the
shortcomings of the library bureaucracies in achieving change. I want
to suggest some vehicles by which nonadministrative librarians, people
who are not in control of bureaucracies, may (1) develop needed
change programs outside the restrictions of the normal bureaucratic
channels, (2) press for needed change programs within their libraries,
and (3) modify the organizational patterns for their libraries to provide
for current service needs.

Basically, there are two types of such vehicles that are now functioning. One is the librarians' union; the other is the librarians' associations,
as differentiated from library associations. I want to compare these
in terms of their relative viability in developing and implementing
programs, and in terms of their various strengths and weaknesses.
Library unions are certainly growing at the present time. There are
two that are particularly active: the American Federation of Teachers
and Academic Librarians and the American Federation of State, County,
and Municipal Employees in Public Libraries. The latter seems, to
me anyway, to have the greater impetus at the moment.

The strengths of the union are several. They provide a vehicle for
librarians to get together and plan programs as peers outside the normal
library bureaucratic channels. This depends, of course, on the democracy
of the local itself. But within a local, it's fairly easy to ensure democratic functioning. This may become a problem within the union
bureaucracy itself as you get beyond the local; but within the local,
if the members are serious about using it as a viable vehicle for change,
you can make sure that it functions in that way. Second, the union
may be the only way to deal with rigid and change-resistant administrators, particularly in terms of implementation. This is because the union
is supported by the power, legal knowledge, and so forth of organized
labor. Finally, unions can provide support for library programs within
a community. They can provide an added dimension of community
library action.

Unions, however, have a number of weaknesses. I think it's important to examine these if we're trying to evaluate whether this is the
proper vehicle to use. One is simply the continuing reluctance of many

librarians to join them. This is lessening, but it's doing so gradually. Until it lessens perceptibly, the unions are not going to have the kind of impact that wholesale change requires. There are a number of minor difficulties about unions, such as dues structure and so forth, but these don't really seem to me to be problems once the viability of the unions is accepted. The third problem, and this is probably the major one with unions, is the commitment involved in the relation of a union to the whole body of organized labor. Organized labor represents, really, another bureaucracy, so it means that, in effect, you are moving into another bureaucratic organization in order to cope with your own. As I said, you can make sure, if you're serious about the union, that it functions well at home, but when you begin to depend upon the power of organized labor, you begin to have commitments to it, and these can conflict.

The obvious conflict, which is frequently raised, is the strike versus the librarian's service commitment. This isn't a simple matter. In other words, a strike can be a viable mechanism for improving service on a long-range basis if it leads to a significant change in the system, in its goals, but it can be an immediate conflict. It doesn't necessarily have this kind of long-range effect either. It depends on what it is being used for. In particular, within organized labor there may be strike commitments for goals and problems that do not seem particularly pertinent to the librarian, such as supporting other elements of labor, and so forth. On the other hand, it has to be kept in mind that this is the basic strength of the union. The willingness to support other areas of organized labor itself.

Librarians' associations are basically quite different from the union. Their strengths tend to be rather opposite to those of the union, as do . . .

BUNDY: Forgive me for interrupting, but I don't know of many librarians' associations.

SMITH: Right. I'm not referring to library associations. What I'm speaking of are associations such as the Association of Librarians at the City University of New York, the Librarians' Association at the University of California, the librarians' associations that are developing in Canada and elsewhere, frequently (at least this is the phenomenon in Canada) in direct opposition or direct competition with the library associations. In other places, they were developing to solve specific local problems within a local system.

Like the union, the librarians' association within a specific library can provide a forum to discuss and plan outside the normal library channels. It may work better with a cooperative administrator. The question might be raised, "If one has a cooperative administrator or administration which is itself committed to change, what's the point of having an organization outside of the bureaucracy that's also committed to change?" I think it provides an added dimension, a vehicle for librarians to develop programs that are not strictly in keeping with the overall library plan, a different perspective, a means for librarians to get together outside of their normal work relations and discuss common problems.

Another strength of the librarians' organization is its lack of ties with organizations outside the library field, and in many cases outside a specific library. This gives it much more independence, of course. On the other hand, this is the basis of its fundamental weakness. It lacks any outside leverage to exert against the library administration if change is being resisted. There is a great danger within a librarians' association of cooptation, the formation of a company union with an administration that may seemingly be cooperative but basically is not so.

The most significant comparison between these two organizations, it seems to me, however, is not those that I have discussed but really what the likelihood of their impact on the total library organization is. Can they modify that organization to make it more viable for professionalization and for the kinds of significant professional service that we have been discussing here? I think that it's becoming very clear that there is a basic conflict between the bureaucratic organization of libraries and the abilities of the individual librarian within his organization to function as a creative professional person. If this is true, then the bureaucratic structure of libraries itself has to be changed, specifically in such areas as decision making—who makes what decisions, who has what latitude in decision making, judgments on service, judgments on personnel, how the librarians are appraised, on what basis, and so forth.

Associations can develop a professional pattern within a library and press for the incorporation of this pattern into the library structure itself. At the University of California, where I am, this is currently being attempted by the librarians. We have formed an association on the nine campuses of the University. It is based on the structure of the academic center, which functions for the faculty in this respect.

Its purpose is to set standards for collection development, for information service, for bibliographical control, for peer review of appointments and promotions, for peer review of grievances; and to accomplish this through peer meetings of all of the librarians and through committees selected by the librarians.

A union has real problems in attempting to achieve this kind of alteration in the library structure. In the first place, it has to give up its outside commitment if it's going to attempt to create an organization that can be incorporated into a library. In effect, this means giving up its basic source of strength and ceasing to be a union. The basic approach to unions, which is one of bargaining, tends to reinforce employer–employee relationships. I'm not saying that it can't achieve substantial professional improvements, but it can't have a real impact on improving library policies and practices. Basically, the relationships remain the same within the library and really tend to harden. It can support bureaucratic rigidity through various commitments of its own, such as commitment to seniority, for example.

These are all problems that are being faced by professional unions in general, unions of engineers, scientists, and so forth, as well as of librarians. It is a problem that professional unions are aware of, and are attempting in some respects to cope with, but it's a difficult problem. A long-range viability of the union as an agent of change in the profession is very much involved with the ability of the unions to work out this problem.

Finally, I would like to look at these two kinds of organizations as vehicles for change within the profession generally, on a national level. A national librarians' union which would involve not simply much more organization, but some kind of joining between the two unions that are now operating in the field, would have the same strengths as the local unions do, only more so. It would have greater power. It would have access to greater, more expensive legal assistance. But it would have the same problems also, with the exception that a national union could possibly have more impact on the labor bureaucracy, could possibly work for substantial changes in labor's attitude to professional unions, providing that it was able to control its own bureaucracy as it developed. Perhaps it could gain sufficient independence to solve the problems of a professional union, if it was once again able to focus on this. A national librarians' association could possibly solve the problem of the needed muscle to support the goals of local associations. Perhaps, like the AAUP, it could support the integrity and standards of the profession and its individual members on a nationwide basis.

The situation at the present time is a very fluid one. Either the association or the union may be a very viable mechanism to help with immediate problems in a given library. Both are certainly growing at the present time. We have to keep a long-range view of change in the profession in mind, in evaluating either one of these organizations. Above all, this kind of change requires a commitment from the librarians, from ourselves, to work hard for the changes that we want, in an organized way, to develop viable goals and work for them, to develop programs, and to take risks. Ultimately, if we're going to have change, we've got to be willing to move into the change arena ourselves to work with some kind of group that is committed to this kind of process.

PARTICIPANT: I notice you are a member of both kinds of organizations. You are a member of the state librarians' association, which is noncommunity, and you are a member of the local on the Berkeley campus. Now which of these do you think is going to emerge as the one that will be most acceptable, to bring about needed change in the profession?

SMITH: Acceptable to whom?

PARTICIPANT: I mean which do you think will get the job done that you want done?

SMITH: That's just the question. I think that within the university right now the impetus lies with the association. If the association is able to accomplish the kind of goals that it has set for itself, which include really modifying the library structure and developing a vehicle for a more professional situation, it obviously is going to win out, but there are serious questions about how long it will be able to keep going in this direction.

BUNDY: What are the vehicles? How do you accomplish ends against resistant administrations? Are there alternatives to the strike? Or would you actually employ the strike in librarians' associations?

SMITH: In a librarians' association, no. The association has not considered using the strike. One of the things that has happened at the University of California has also happened at the City University of New York. There has been a kind of peculiar relationship between the union and the association. The union moved in initially, followed by an association. The union, in many ways, has softened up the situation, has provided a threat to the bureaucracy which the association is able to capitalize on.

This didn't happen as part of some major plan. It has created a lot of antagonistic feelings. Highly committed unionists are rather unhappy about seeing their organization used as muscle for the association. The university is fearful of some enormous plot whereby the union is really manipulating the association in an attempt to work its way in. But I think what has basically happened is that these two organizations have tended to support each other, at least in the initial stages.

PARTICIPANT: Would you envision that the union might just fade away, if change comes about through this other, more moderate approach?

SMITH: It's going to be a long time before the union withers away there. One of the reasons for that is that there will be a lot for the union to do even if the association is successful in its initial stages. There are a lot of areas the union can work in, and is working in.

BUNDY: Could there be a division, such that the union is concerned with working conditions and librarians' associations are concerned with professional service?

SMITH: Yes, except both of the organizations have come to realize that the two cannot be that easily separated. But the kind of action that comes easiest to the union is to develop a salary proposal, or something similar.

PARTICIPANT: I know the academic status question in California has been resolved. Did the California Library Association, or the ALA, assist in this in any way?

SMITH: The California Library Association is supporting the academic status of the state college librarians. They have agreed to levy sanctions, although it is very unclear as to what these sanctions will be, against the state colleges, if the state colleges do not grant academic status.

PARTICIPANT: They do have academic status. Isn't it a matter of faculty status?

SMITH: The state college librarians have academic status of a kind. The program that they have is for various kinds of implementation of the status. What they are asking for are implementations that are very close to the kinds of rights and privileges that faculty have. They have kept away from asking for faculty ranks and titles.

The salary proposal is somewhat different. This is the problem of academic status. You can have academic status as a name, which lots of libraries apparently do, or you can have it implemented in terms of what it means substantially to the elite of the academic community, the faculty. Or you can have it implemented in terms of what it should mean to the librarian. These are three different models.

What we've got now in most libraries is a kind of an academic status in terms of name. The universities say, "All right, you've got academic status. You're part of the academic community." And maybe you have the right to use the faculty club, et cetera, but in terms of salaries, in terms of a role in decision making, in terms of sabbaticals, in terms of the work year, in terms of tenure or security of employment of any substantial kind, there is really very little of that in most of these libraries.

These are the goals that the California Library Association has approached. These are really the goals of the Librarians' Association. The university is working for it, too, although we've taken a somewhat different tack because conditions are different. We've approached it essentially through the organization of the university and are trying to get a role in decision making first, and then develop from this the academic role of the librarian.

BUNDY: Now when you say "role in decision making," do you mean within the library or within the university?

SMITH: Both.

BUNDY: When you go to the faculty center coming from the professional library school, you're not going as a member. You're going to represent your interests.

SMITH: Right. It would be a librarian's senate, which would sit on the various campuses with the faculty setup and probably joint committees of various kinds. One of the things that we're very interested in, for example, is library representation on the committee dealing with courses and curriculum. This is a very sore point with the faculty.

BUNDY: Can you interest the faculty enough to even engage in joint committees on an equal basis?

SMITH: That's right.

PARTICIPANT: I don't understand why you want to separate the librarians' decision-making bodies from the academic center. In Albany, the university librarians have attained full rank and title. The university library has been made into a school, so it has the rights of representa-

tion that a school would have within the university, like the School
of Social Welfare, or the School of Library Science.

BUNDY: But in point of fact, it does not.

PARTICIPANT: How do you hope to influence decisions by a parallel
organization? Don't you want to get right in there where the action
is? Why do you want to be separate but equal?

SMITH: It depends on the decisions you want to influence. Most
of the decisions that we're currently interested in are the decisions
that focus within the library.

PARTICIPANT: I think there is another distinction in a major university
like Berkeley. The basic degree that is accepted for promotion to assistant professor at Berkeley is a Ph.D. I don't think the librarians
want to face up to the responsibilities of getting Ph.D.'s in order
to be a member of the academic center.

PARTICIPANT: We worked on that at Albany, too. We found that
there are certain departments in the university that do not require
Ph.D.'s for high rank, such as music and physical education.

PARTICIPANT: Albany is not Berkeley.

PARTICIPANT: This could probably be worked out.

SMITH: There's a problem at Berkeley, and at the University of California in general. You've got a large and varied academic community.
It's not just the faculty and the librarians, but a sizable contingent
of researchers, professional research extension specialists, and so forth.
All these people are academic personnel. Together the nonfaculty
academics are as large, if not larger, in number as the faculty. The
faculty are very jealous about their specific role within the senate, particularly in terms of courses and curriculum. It is their senate, and
they have resisted the other groups' moving in.

   This is one problem. We could confront this by insisting on belong-
ing and trying to fight on that issue, but connected with this is another
problem. What is the role of the academic librarian? Is it a role
as a quasi-faculty member? Is it a different role within the academic
community? This is really a basic idea behind our drive for a librarian
senate. The role of the librarian, although basically academic and certainly connected with teaching and research, is different from that
of the faculty. Different questions deserve attention from the librarians
themselves. An example of such a question would be library service
as opposed to instructional policy or collection development. These
are essentially library problems, bibliographical control.

What's the best vehicle for dealing with these? Can we deal with them through the library bureaucracy? Our conclusion has been that we can't, not fully, not effectively, not in an academic way. The effort here is to create a vehicle that will enable us to do this. We have also proposed joint committees with the faculty to deal with matters where we are mutually involved.

WASSERMAN: I see a number of problems in what you're saying to us. If I understand it correctly, you are talking about a model that is sort of an inside structure in relation to objectives. Could one differentiate the relative functional utility of an outside force in one kind of setting against an internal force in a different kind of setting? Perhaps a public library, collective bargaining, with all its trappings, might be the most expeditious mechanism, by virtue of its being that kind of an institution with a certain kind of culture and orientation, while in an academic situation the union may have distasteful connotations.

I wonder about the local situation as a factor in this. That is, that the association seems to be a less belligerent body in the sense of not being identified with collective bargaining in a tough sense. It seems to provide more of a workable arrangement, a relationship between professionals within the organization, as differentiated from the kind of hard stance which is reflected by collective bargaining traditionally.

I wonder about the problem of multiplicity. I guess I worry about that as a factor. You've described two organizations in one setting. And we haven't even said anything about what Ralph Blasingame is going to talk about, and that is another organization in which we are either involved or alienated. Here we have three structures, with no leadership that I can identify for any of them. Where the hell is it going to come from? Who is going to be with the association and the unions, and the national association, if there is such a thing? We're so bankrupt in leadership anyway. We're talking about many, many organizations. All of them seem to be cutting at a different piece of the problem, and I guess I find this troublesome.

SMITH: Leadership is a tremendous problem, I'll agree with you. I think it's not correct to characterize the local situation in California as bereft of leadership. As a matter of fact, one of the encouraging things about it is that it has produced some leaders.

BUNDY: There's a good point right there. Multiplicity of organizations is productive of leaders. We haven't had our training grounds for leaders.

SMITH: Right. The leaders who tend to go up through ALA have the same problem in leadership that there is in the large library system. In order to make it you have to come to terms with the establishment, play the establishment game. In many ways, this is antithetical to a lot of problems in professionalizing. The leadership problem is a complex one. As Mary Lee has said, right now these kinds of associations may prove to be productive of leaders rather than the opposite.

WASSERMAN: You made the point about taking the long-range view. I wonder if this field can afford such a position. That is, in the long run we'll all be dead. In a field which has such a deep-seated malaise, can we afford to watch this happen, and watch that happen, and not be concerned with the immediacy of the issues, and the strategy for more effective modification and adaptation and variation? I have some question about this.

SMITH: I don't mean to restrict one's attack to immediate problems, but to develop a long-range view of the direction that we want librarianship to move in and to cope with these problems in those terms. I don't mean a fixed one, necessarily. I would hope that we can approach this in a flexible way so that as we cope with immediate problems, they will make an impact on us and we can adjust our long-range view. One of the difficulties I've seen is a tendency to deal gropingly with what is immediately there, without putting it into any kind of perspective. I don't mean a fifty-year plan, but maybe a five-year plan.

PARTICIPANT: I'm confused about something that you brought out. At the ALA, it was eminently clear to those of us who attended meetings on faculty status for academic librarians that the mood of the country was in that direction, full faculty status. The ALA, as I recall, passed a very definite resolution calling for full faculty status for all academic librarians in all academic situations.

BUNDY: I hate to be cynical, but what did that cost them?

PARTICIPANT: But now he is softening it, and he says, "No, the California college librarians are not going for full faculty status. They're going for this intermediate stage."

SMITH: It's not intermediate, not unless you see it as some kind of hierarchy.

PARTICIPANT: But you are suggesting we are going to get this solidified organization, rather than have our own center, and maybe we'll get that. I'm not for that at all. I feel that we ought to go all the way for faculty status at this time. At my institution, we are members of the senate and we have sabbaticals. We have leaves of absence, and so forth. I don't believe in stopping. If the University of California, because of its peculiar structure, wants to do that, O.K., but for other colleges and universities, I think we have to go the way of Albany.

PARTICIPANT: I don't know if Wisconsin is a progressive state or not, but we do have full academic rank in our university. Right now there is a trend developing outside of the library to separate the teaching faculty from the nonteaching faculty. This goes all the way into the whole restructuring of the system. If that happened we would maybe have the rank, but we would be ranked as nonteaching faculty. We would be deprived of a number of things that we already have.

SMITH: You have what the teaching faculty has?

PARTICIPANT: We have two kinds—an academic rank and something special in academic stages. We are qualified for the full rank but we have full rank from instructor.

SMITH: What does your status give you other than rank? For example, do you have the same kind of leave programs?

PARTICIPANT: At this point, we do.

SMITH: Do librarians get leaves?

PARTICIPANT: Not so far, but we can petition.

SMITH: You can petition, but do you ever get them?

PARTICIPANT: We're working on it. In Madison there is another thing. There are two major universities—one young, the other older. We have the same rights, but the use of the rights is somewhat different. We are more liberal in giving grants. That reflects policy probably.

BUNDY: Speaking as a faculty member, I'll tell you why I really don't approve of librarians' being members of a faculty. Basically, I think librarians are anti-intellectual. I'm putting this harshly, but they really don't understand academic freedom. If you let the librarians in and give them full voting rights, you've given the administration 200 votes. I think he's describing for us a way to grow up. Let us enter on a different basis than going in as poor relations. You may effect some working condition improvements, but you're poor relations in the faculty senate. In many subtle ways they are telling you this. How many librarians have headed an important academic committee? You're playing a service role. He's saying you would play it better if you enter as a partner. I've always been for academic status, but I'm toying with this idea.

PARTICIPANT: One of the arguments that is being made comes from students. They want to separate the teaching faculty from the nonteaching faculty. They don't want the nonteaching faculty to interfere with the teaching process of the university.

BUNDY: We have an interesting parallel with our students now. We have an ad hoc committee where the students are considering participation on the faculty committees and in the general faculty. If they become active participants, do we really have a faculty meeting any more? That's one of the choices, and it's the one they've selected. I'm not sure they wouldn't be better advised to do sort of a parallel to this, which is develop a strong student government, and enter into joint committee relationships. The dangers of cooptation are so many if they come in, no matter how much they demand student rights. I'm not convinced they wouldn't better achieve goals by a parallel organization, interacting on a different basis.

PARTICIPANT: I don't agree with that at all, because I've seen it work at Albany. All of these fears I've heard from other people. Now the very same people that I remember as thinking in one way have changed completely in their feelings and opinions.

BUNDY: You're not talking about the students, because your students are coopted on your committees, according to your faculty.

PARTICIPANT: That's true for the school committees, but I'm talking about the university faculty committees. I've sat on some where there were students, and it really makes a tremendous difference. They add a certain dimension of experience that changes the faculty attitude toward the decisions they have to make. They are coparticipators. They bring their own experience to it. They do not in any way turn into Uncle Toms at the last minute. They give their own point of view and it's different.

BUNDY: All right, but let me give you the difference and let's see. The physics department of Maryland has a group of students who have chosen the other route. When they have an issue they wish to discuss with the faculty, they send representation from their government to that faculty committee. It makes a difference, because they send people who are committed to it, willing to put time on it. They make sure that the student sent as a representative is not a student of the professor who is the chairman of the committee. After all, let us face the realities of life. This student also has to get through school. They are protecting their own weakness in a sense. They're saying,

"O.K., let's be sure it doesn't happen. You, you, and you are going to this one." They avoid all the work of the academic committee. They don't want to sit there and go through all the bread-and-butter things that have to go on in a committee. They select the issue, the time, the place, and the people they'll send. I'm just proposing it as an alternate model, trying it out.

SMITH: I would like to come back to several things. First of all, I think that this business of nonteaching faculty is a contradiction in terms. If you're faculty, you're faculty, and that means teaching, it seems to me. You've got a group that calls itself nonteaching faculty. Isn't it much healthier for the group, in terms of developing its own program, its own role, to call itself what it is? This is one of the basic arguments for librarians to push for librarian status as academic personnel rather than faculty members.

About this business of what went on at ALA: I was very much involved in this. The decision to push for faculty status was developed on the floor and was a kind of compromise. It was something that I personally went along with, because I didn't want to see what we were accomplishing, small though it was, torn to pieces over that kind of debate at that time.

PARTICIPANT: Mr. Galloway seemed to make very much of the word "faculty." He was representing the state college librarians.

SMITH: Dean Galloway is highly committed to faculty status.

PARTICIPANT: The trend is that way. For instance, there is a new man at the University of Kansas, Dave Heron, who seems to be committed to faculty status. His librarians do not have it, and he is exploring ways to get this started. There are other major centers in the United States that are moving in this way. I would hate to see it torpedoed by this.

SMITH: You're not torpedoing anything. I talked to Dean Galloway about this. In the attempt of the state college librarians to achieve this, he did a study of various institutions that supposedly had faculty status. He couldn't find a one, a single institution, outside of the junior colleges, where the status of the librarians was really fully faculty status.

PARTICIPANT: Then he didn't inquire at Wichita State. I'm there and I inherited a very fine situation.

SMITH: You have the academic year for your librarians?

PARTICIPANT: No, we are paid on a twelve-month year.

SMITH: Do you get a salary comparable to the twelve-month faculty status?

PARTICIPANT: Now, yes. Not for those who have been there for some time, because we just became a state institution. But we are now on the salary scale. If anyone is promoted to assistant professor in our library, they must come up with the assistant professor's salary for a twelve-month person. We get study leaves.

SMITH: How many assistant professors do you have?

PARTICIPANT: I think there are about nine assistant professors, various associate professors, two professors, and the rest are instructors.

SMITH: And the professors are administrators?

PARTICIPANT: One is. I am.

BUNDY: In academia we have a tradition that you have your professorship and your tenure through it, not in your position as head librarian and not in your position as a dean or a department head. Your job for life is guaranteed by your academic status. I would just like to throw out the thought that we might improve library situations in the college world by introducing this notion. This has nothing to do with you. No one is automatically the head of any library for his career time.

PARTICIPANT: Our tenure is not dependent upon anything except the fact that we've achieved tenure in the library.

BUNDY: So you're not guaranteed a job for life.

PARTICIPANT: Yes, I am.

BUNDY: As head librarian?

PARTICIPANT: I don't know as head librarian.

BUNDY: O.K., that's the point I'm trying to make.

PARTICIPANT: I have tenure. Many of my people who have been there for some time have tenure. It comes about through the same tenure committee that considers tenure for faculty members.

PARTICIPANT: Mary Lee, do you know of any department head who is not a professor?

BUNDY: My point is, they can be replaced. We replace deans and department heads every day of the week. But we don't replace head librarians. They think they have a job as head librarian for their career time.

PARTICIPANT: I don't think this is the point, Mary Lee. There are places where tenure and these things do come to the faculty, and sabbatical leaves to the librarians as members of the faculty.

SMITH: I would like to get this back from the business of purely status problems.

PARTICIPANT: It isn't purely status.

SMITH: That's what we've gotten onto. Let us shift to the question that the whole conference is about—change. If you want to have substantial changes in library operation and service, if you want to develop a more creative service program, what is the best vehicle for doing this? Do you do it as a part of the faculty senate? Or is it better to have this kind of governing body maybe in addition to participation in the faculty setting within the library?

PARTICIPANT: It seems to be better. I have two librarians on the senate who were elected to the senate. One of the librarians has been the president of the AAUP. There is no distinction in our university between a librarian and a physics professor.

SMITH: Let me give you an example of what I mean. For several years now, some of the librarians at my university at Berkeley have been concerned about the lack of ability to use the library that graduating students and graduate students at the university have. We wanted the library to develop a formal program for instructing students in how to conduct library research. We proposed this to the library administration, were resisted, and were turned down for a period of a couple of years. Finally, as a result of many of the things that happened locally there, there was developed an experimental program within the university, an experimental college, whereby new courses could be generated by the students and others. This was accepted as a part of that program, once again in opposition to the library administration, who felt it was taking the librarians away from the sorely needed day-to-day tasks that they were performing in the library. He was supported, I might add, by both the union and the librarians' association

It has now been in operation for the past year. From almost all the feedback from the students, and from faculty members whose students have been involved in it, it has been a very productive program. Some of the departments, particularly the English department and the history department where undergraduate library research is a significant part of their program, are very pleased with it. This is the kind of service innovation that I'm talking about, the kind of innovation that was impossible with the old library structure, which tended to focus its attention on the traditional bureaucratic goals, setting the traditional service limits, utilizing its personnel in the traditional way.

PARTICIPANT: They did the same thing at Berkeley. You are talking about an administration that was just not responsive.

SMITH: That's right.

PARTICIPANT: With the new administration or in another library that has a different administration, you don't have those obstacles.

SMITH: I doubt very much if this type of program would have been developed by the old administration that is now supporting it. I'm not saying this critically. Well, I *am* saying it critically. I think that this is the whole point, really. The librarians need some kind of vehicle that is willing to give serious consideration to innovation.

PARTICIPANT: The faculty may feel this more.

SMITH: The faculty is very pleased with it now, but the faculty senate as a whole would not have been a good vehicle for developing this. They would have seen it as competition with them.

BUNDY: Of course, in a way you aren't saying anything different. A school can develop mechanisms for decision making within it and still be a participant in the university faculty structure.

SMITH: That's right. In terms of making change within the institution of the library, there has to be a different kind of organization in the library. It can be a modification of the kind of organization that exists. You can build into the bureaucracy a kind of professional organization. This is the sort of thing that industry is trying to do, where they employ a high percentage of professional personnel in research and development, and they are accomplishing it. This is one way. This can conceivably be done by an imaginative administrator, but I just don't see much of it going on. Another way is for the librarians themselves to work to achieve this by developing their own model which can deal with specific programs, such as this program for the experimental course, and at the same time can press for alternate change of the bureaucracy itself.

BUNDY: You're putting it in service terms, which are our goals, but you really are talking also about a transfer of power from the administration into the hands of professionals, including the thing I resist the most, the need to participate in promotions, salary increases, hiring, and firing. Is that your most resistant sector? It seems to me they would let you play with reference if you wanted to, but try to take away the right to give the salary increase, or censor one of your own group instead of them.

SMITH: It depends on who the "they" is. If you've got a very rigid and bureaucratic head of reference, he's not going to let you play with reference. But it's true that the peer review appointments and promotions are a tough hurdle also.

PARTICIPANT: In your concept of the library union, do you include administrators or do you exclude them altogether?

SMITH: In this system the professional administrators would be involved, but they would be involved as professionals, not as administrators.

PARTICIPANT: Take the medium-sized university library. Practically every librarian is an administrator, a decision-making person. How do you make this clear?

SMITH: Well, if you've got every librarian as a substantial decision-making person, you are having an impact on the organization. That seems to me to be quite viable in itself, if it's working.

PARTICIPANT: One of your librarians at Berkeley told me that he was very active in unions, but that now he has been made head of the undergraduate library, he is withdrawing from the union, because he now considers himself administration. He doesn't feel that he should belong to the union. This may just be a personal decision.

BUNDY: I'd like to disagree with Eldred Smith. Once you cross a certain line, and you have responsibility for other people and keeping a shop open, you need the checks and balances of the reference librarian who isn't committed to those aims, who's committed to a client aim. The checks and balances don't automatically occur because the head of reference may spend an hour a day at the reference desk. He's just taken on a different set of commitments. He still needs, I would argue, the checks and balances of the professionals.

SMITH: He needs to be in it.

BUNDY: Not on top of it.

SMITH: No, right, but involved in it.

BUNDY: Well, we have this problem with Paul Wasserman. The dean of the library school is also a faculty member. We have faculty committees of which he officially is an ad hoc member without vote.

WASSERMAN: Why do you denigrate the capacity of the person who plays the administrative role?

BUNDY: I'm going to finish if you'll let me. One of our problems is that we have just so much talent. Among them is Wasserman. If we kick him out because he is an administrator, we've lost an important resource. Our problem is we can't deal with him on equal terms. He's better able to do it than we are. We can't forget he's the guy who decides our raises, so we fail to get the benefit of him as a faculty member.

WASSERMAN: That's your hangup, not mine.

SMITH: We had a long debate about this when we worked on the structure of this organization. Should we or should we not allow administrators to be involved? At what level should we cut it off? Our decision was we should not allow administrators to be involved, but encourage them; that this would provide a different environment, that the administrative rigidity was reinforced by the bureaucratic organization. To get them into this new organization would be to change the environment and would help us cope with our hangup in terms of our particular attitude toward them.

BUNDY: All right, Eldred, that's exactly it. What you're saying could be Uncle Tomism, or it could be what you want it to be, dependent on the professionals and their ability to deal with this and throw out status.

SMITH: The basic problem is to create a vehicle where the professional can function as a professional. If he needs a vehicle to protect him from himself as a professional, then he just can't cut it.

BUNDY: Maybe he needs it for a while. Maybe he needs to develop, as the students seem to need a vehicle to develop, enough confidence to enter into a relationship where they're not constantly having status rule the game.

PARTICIPANT: As a public librarian, I've got a problem in regard to unions. It is somewhat related to what Dr. Wasserman was talking about earlier—leadership. I don't know the situation on the West Coast as I do the East Coast, so that's what I'll talk about. Much of the leadership on the East Coast comes from the administration. To form a union from the underlings seems almost ludicrous at this point because so many of them don't particularly care about changing what exists. The agents for change, more often than not, are in the administrative capacity. How do we reconcile ourselves at this junction?

WASSERMAN: I think you can differentiate out perhaps the situation in the small setting, where what you're characterizing may be more true than in the bigger bureaucracies, where, by virtue of their complexity in scale and size, the administration in the process of being coopted into the establishment, maybe, commits the administrator to a different set of values and priorities and needs than presumably those who play professional roles. You have the capacity to function more in a so-called professional role in a small situation as administrator, than when you are in a large structure and you are more administrator than you are professional. You are coopted by that establishment to reflect its goals and values unless you have very, very deep-seated commitment to something called professionalism. Our tragedy in librarianship is that we've not identified the professional basis and the professional core. Administration has been our professional contribution where there has been such. Therefore, the administrator sees that as what he has to contribute organizationally, and not as a librarian. I think the two can be differentiated.

PARTICIPANT: Well, I'll put my question in simple terms so you can answer me in more simple terms. I have a small staff. I have only seven people. They don't belong to a union. As an administrator I should not want them to go on strike, but in actuality I think it would be the greatest thing that could happen to me if they went on strike; yet I shouldn't be thinking like that as an administrator. How do I reconcile myself as a leader, as an administrator to the union? What do I do?

WASSERMAN: That's a complicated problem. The problem that we have with librarianship is that we don't have any kind of an incentive structure in librarianship that recognizes anything except administrative performance. Just like other fields, people sort of gravitate upwards.

Those people who could be making a very important contribution, particularly in their professional roles, don't have identified for them by the field or by anybody else the importance of staying with that technical professional role. The consequence of that is that very, very good people get out of what they're doing and go into administration. Sometimes they are very adept in the administrative role. Sometimes they're inept in the administrative role. They would have been better encouraged to stay in a technical role, but the tragedy of a culture that rewards administrative contribution and denigrates technical professional contribution relative to administrative contribution is that this is the way things are. Now in librarianship, it seems to me, enlightened administration has the responsibility for trying to change that.

Maybe I'm not answering your question, but something is still on my mind from the previous discussion. To the extent that the administrator recognizes this problem, he works to improve the capacity of the organization to provide status and incentives and whatever other perquisites he can for the professionals and keeps them out of administration unless they are of the temperament and of the stuff of which administrators are made, which are not necessarily the same as those of which effective professional contributions are made.

In response to your situation, where you find your relationships is a matter of professional conscience, I suppose. One has to make a choice. Either the values of your professional contribution are important or your servant relationship to the power structure is important. This is really the dilemma of the administrator in a public setting He is responsible to a public body, and he is, in effect, their servant. I guess that's why he can't be a member of the union, because presumably he works for somebody else whose interests are not the same.

I suppose in a small situation, ultimately, it's to the benefit of the organization and its goals to encourage unionization in order to make change, because that's in the interest of the culture too. To the extent that the administrator is a servant of the culture rather than his professional goals, he is doing a disservice to the capacity of that organization to perform what it's supposed to perform. So I would say encourage the union.

SMITH: I mentioned the problem of the professional union. I think you've also got the problem of the professional administrator. It's no less a serious problem that the professional administrator has to find means for making administration a professional vehicle. If administration keeps him from functioning professionally, keeps him from developing the professional role of his organization and professional staff, then it is no less inimical to librarianship than a union is, when it tends to winnow down the professional commitment because of a possible commitment to the union bureaucracy.

BUNDY: Birenbaum gave us a role as the professional administrator with clear goals in mind, willing to role-play, so that he might unconsciously say to the administration, "I really want to strike." Without those clear goals and without a certain kind of personality, I think it's right.

PARTICIPANT: In a conflict situation like this, wouldn't you think it best if this young man could get into a much larger organization where he isn't the administrator? Then he could form the union and be the union leader.

BUNDY: You're right! If he's just plain uncomfortable with the role, he should get out.

PARTICIPANT: I'm playing off my professionalism. I take a certain amount of pride in an ability to administer. I'm selling out to the union in a number of ways.

PARTICIPANT: Unfortunately, that's where the salaries are, too. We are rewarded monetarily for being administrators, whereas we're not for being bibliographers.

BUNDY: I guess I agree with him. There's no way to win. For instance, Father Baroni is sometimes referred to as the archbishop's pet radical. This isn't what we saw. You can't win either way.

SMITH: You should keep in mind that this is a challenge in itself. You must not focus on the fact that there is a sellout. You must try to fuse the two and make administration a professional vehicle. That's the big challenge.

BUNDY: Maybe Ralph Blasingame will have some help for us.

BLASINGAME: The topic listed on the program is everything and nothing—power. You can spend all day talking about power and not learn anything. You can say, "Power is the name of the game," and say everything generally and nothing specifically. Let me try to make some general observations, suggest an analytical model, and then see what you have to say. Some things that would be well to bear in mind, I think, are these. First, we have the leadership that we want. Do we object to it? Not really. We have put up with it for so long that we have to come to the conclusion that the profession of librarian-ship—excuse me, the occupation of librarianship—has selected its leaders consciously, because it has done it for such a long period of time.

A student of mine last year in a seminar did a paper on the back-grounds of chief librarians in the twenty-six largest cities in the United States. She didn't send out questionnaires, but worked with what data she could get. Every since 1930, which was the base date for her study, with two exceptions, the heads of all of these libraries have come either through a series of administrative positions within those libraries or, more commonly, through a series of headships of larger and larger libraries. This is such a firm pattern that you must look at it and say, "That's the way we want it to be!"

A long time ago Mary Parker Follett wrote an essay on constructive conflict. This is item number two in my general list, in which she said we solve conflicts in three basic ways. We solve them through domination. A prominent person or group makes the problem go away, at least for the time being, by refusing to consider it. Second, more commonly, we cooperate. Each group involved in the controversy gives up something. Everybody comes out with something to work with, some means of getting on with the business at hand, but it isn't really satisfactory to anyone. She proposes a mode of conflict solution which she refers to as integration—not talking, of course, about integration of the races. Her suggestion is that conflict situations contain within themselves solutions which are satisfactory to everyone, which promote everyone's interests.

Of the three methods, because of the relative strength of interest groups, cooperation becomes necessary and is by far the most common method. But domination is what we really like. Within the normal bureaucratic structure, an individual who manages to dominate a problem by making it go away receives a certain amount of self-satisfaction out of this. For that reason it is the most popular and the best-liked method of problem solution. Integration, she suggests, is a method of problem solution in which we haven't any practice. There's no one around to tell us how to do it because no one has paid much attention to it.

Now, to go on a little bit, within the profession of librarianship we all look too much the same. Most of us come out of English literature or American history, I would guess. We come up through fairly good high schools; we go to second-rate colleges for the most part. We take subjects that do not require that we analyze anything very carefully. So, as a group, the members of this occupation do not have analytical modes of thought. We dissent fairly often. We argue. We get emotional, but we don't know how to analyze. In this sense, then, we are nonintellectuals and, in many cases, anti-intellectuals. That is to say, if you define an intellectual approach to problem solving as an analytical approach, then we are anti-intellectual. As a consequence, too, we find it very difficult to identify issues and to trace the issues through and to observe what happens over some extended period of time with respect to the various issues. We react, very commonly, in a visceral fashion.

Now I have put on the board one suggestion as to how you can analyze organizations. The block in the center represents the organization, any organization. You can call this a special library. You can call it the American Library Association. You can call it the town council, anything you want to. It is an attempt to abstract the context within which organizations work and to examine a little bit about what happens within them.

Within the organization, you have at least two broad groups of people who exercise influence, or at least would like to exercise influence. The gatekeepers really do exercise influence. These are the people who, in one way or another, determine what the demands and supports are. They determine which of those inputs will be translated into real decisions and which will be translated into symbolic decisions, or gestures. Each organization also contains what one might call "within-puts," that is, persons operating within the organization, not necessarily in a formal gatekeeper position, who look out to the environment and say, "What really would make us relate to the environment?" They come back within the organization and say, "How would we alter this organization to respond to those things?" Basically, each of you must have claimed to yourself in registering for this seminar that you are a "within-put" in these terms. I'd raise a serious question as to whether you really are, but at least you must have visualized yourselves as "within-puts."

Now any organization operates within an environment—an immediate environment, and a next environment, and so forth. We operate within innumerable environments. The town public library operates in its community. It operates in its county. It operates in its political structure. It operates in its region, state, nation, et cetera. Very often we think these environments are discrete. When you want to know how to run your public library, you make a community study. And what is that? That's a study of the town, isn't it? Everybody knows that! Of course all these other environments impinge on that town.

Incidentally, let me mention a book called *The Conduct of Inquiry,* by Abraham Kaplan. Mr. Kaplan attempts to spell out a general approach to research in the field of behavioral sciences. It's a difficult, at times a turgid, book, but I think a very important one. If you want to understand the interrelation of environments and the various factors within environments, you really should read Kaplan or something like that.

It is out of the environments that we get inputs—demands and supports, broadly speaking. You can interpret these in any way you want to. We talk about needs, for example. I'm not sure that that is a demand. A need is something that the people within the organizaton very often ascribe to the people in the environment, whether they express it or not, and even whether it is real or not. So we very often get things that we think are demands, which are not really demands at all. But we do get actual expressed wants. Let's distinguish between needs and wants, just for the moment, and say that needs are those things which we would ascribe to people—need for information, for example. Wants are those things which they translate into an allocation of their resource—their money, their time, what have you. Supports, of course, we think of as being largely financial, but we have many different aspects—psychological supports, emotional supports, and actual allocation or resources.

I present this to you as one of many potential models that you might keep in mind to try to find out what really happens in organizations, and why they exist, and why they do what they do. I have tried to say that some of these demands and/or supports are fed more or less directly through organizations and come out as more or less unmodified decisions. A town sets up a library and people expect it to circulate books, and so it does circulate books. It modifies the decision somewhat, perhaps, and imposes what may be moral, or immoral, restraints on what books it's going to have. It won't have all the books. It won't make them all available. So the decision doesn't pass exactly straight through, but it comes through pretty nearly in pure form. At the other extreme, we would have decisions that come through as entirely symbolic.

At this point, I would suggest to you that services to disadvantaged persons through public libraries are, for the most part, symbolic. The symbolism is not necessarily unimportant. In fact, we pay much too little attention to what we do as symbol and what we do as reality. We ought to be able to separate them and understand that we do create symbols at times and that there is great value in that in some instances. In the particular case I mentioned here, one could use symbolic as a pejorative term.

With this in mind, let me suggest that it is very popular these days to analyze organizations in black box terms. You look *just* at the inputs and *just* at the outputs and make a judgment about the institution's organization on the basis of what you see. The feeling is that, as soon as you get in with the organization and begin to listen to the rationale, begin to listen to all the voices that you hear explaining why they do this and why they don't do that and how this is done and what all the restraints are, you really become confused. You become coopted in the real sense. If you listen to all this, you can't any longer really understand what has happened. Back off! Forget the internal operation. We're going to look at just what goes in or what comes out.

Looking at the library field, we have what I would call a prototype institution. Its origin pretty clearly was in the great cities, a few of the great cities, let's say. The city was the first consequence of the long-term process of urbanization. It drew people out of the countryside and had to accommodate them with a means of production. The city developed an economy, which demanded innovation, demanded skill development, demanded a certain amount of information. Within the city, we have seen the development of a great many institutions—the museum, the library, the zoological garden, the zoo, what have you, which are all voluntary, but they are, nonetheless, contributory to the economy of the city. That structure firmed up awfully early. It jelled very fast, partly as a result of the lack of administrative theory at the time, but partly also because of this desire on the part of individuals to achieve dominant position, and partly as a result of stress on economy of operation.

We find the library in a city developing first as a bureaucracy. There's nothing wrong with a bureaucracy. That's just one way to run things. We use the term in a derogatory fashion today, and very often individual bureaucracies should be derogated. But nonetheless, it is merely a statement about how an organization operates. That is to say, it operates on the basis of division of function; it is organized around the various skills that persons may develop in order to achieve an end. So we find the typical library having functional departments—catalog departments, acquisition departments, reference departments, circulation departments, and so forth. We find that these are organized generally in pyramidal form. In other words, there is one guy at the top within each department.

By its very nature, the bureaucratic form of organization places great stress on administration per se. This is perhaps the root of our problem. We have taken people who are essentially ignorant of administration and put them in the positions of great importance. They have, in many cases, I think we have to say out of self-protection, elevated themselves because they didn't know what else to do. This style of organization also tends to generate techniques. We know how to buy books. We know how to catalog books. We know how to circulate books. We don't know much about information, really, but we know a lot about materials, so a lot of material concepts tend to dominate our service policy.

Incidentally, it won't be until we get away from that whole hangup that we will really have a library service policy that can work towards certain objectives, the grand designs that are for the benefit of mankind generally. This organization has traditionally been supported by a single city. It has existed by sufferance and that's all. The states have said, "You may have a library," and that's it. The federal government until very recently didn't say any more than that, if that. It had no reason to say anything. Only very recently have we gotten away from the idea that a library serves a geographic area, usually a very limited area, strictly limited because that's where its money comes from, with a few exceptions.

In the late nineteenth and early twentieth century, when we began to evangelize the library, the only model we had was the big-city library. So, ignoring the fact that the smaller town and/or county didn't have the economy that demanded the information, didn't have the skill development, didn't have the leadership, we went out and duplicated this institution thousands and thousands and thousands of times. We kid ourselves about how many libraries there are. There are an awful lot of libraries that we ignore. Any library with less than a thousand-dollar book budget doesn't appear in the American Library Directory, and yet there may be far more of those than there are of libraries with over a thousand-dollar budget.

This prototype library also has had a great effect on the academic library. Most university libraries are very much like the public libraries, not in detail, but in structure. They are bureaucracies. They are divided by function. They are supported by a single institution. It is really only because of this similarity of most libraries organically that we have been able to think of a library profession and of training for librarianship. What we really do is train people for this style of organizational management.

Incidentally, as long as we have that style we don't have to be specialists. All we have to specialize in is reference, whatever that is, or cataloging, or acquisition. We don't have to know anything about the important matters that are before the nation and the world today, in terms of scientific development, technological development, degradation of the atmosphere. We can ignore all this. We are the last Renaissance men. We say that all the time because it makes us feel good.

When you look at the professional associations, what you've got, of course, is a repetition of the basic organizational model. You have a group that consists of bureaucrats, who learned long ago that inasmuch as they didn't have any specialty, they couldn't have any policies. So we don't have any policies in the American Library Association that mean anything. Why not? Because that's the easiest way to administer if you really don't know how.

Let me give you a few examples of what I have in mind. As a professional association we have no legislative power. We get involved in legislation all the time. We have no power. In the reorganization of ALA, responsibility for legislation in local, state, and federal bodies was assigned to a unit within the library administration division. On the personal plea of Emerson Greenaway and Roger McDonough, this responsibility was reassigned to an ALA committee. It's a very important designation—ALA committee. You're not responsible to anybody if you're an ALA committee. The whole (that is, local, state and federal legislation) responsibility was assigned. I was on the board of LAD [Library Administration Division] at the time, and Mr. Greenaway told me, "We're not going to carry the local and state responsibility."

Of course, he carried out this intention. He never did administer that responsibility. All he was ever concerned about was federal legislation, and not even a policy there. You can tell that if you look carefully at what happened within the American Library Association. Absolutely no question about it! We have no policy, and so we are open to invasion by individuals who do have policy. The most important group, of course, is the publishers.

Not long ago the American Library Association and a lot of other groups managed to get Congress to restore some monies back to LSCA [Library Services Construction Act] and some other programs. We offended a committee chairman very badly in that concept, and he said so. We have never paid any attention to that. It has never been reported in the *ALA Washington Newsletter,* for example. Why did we offend him? Because we reversed his committee's position, in his view, without adequate justification. I would agree with him.

There was another little hint that you should have picked up. There was a move to assign these sums of money to the Secretary of Health, Education, and Welfare, ultimately to the Office of Education. We opposed that. We said that it would be very bad because it would give the Secretary of Health, Education, and Welfare too much power. We said that in the *ALA Washington Newsletter*. Can you imagine how the Secretary of Health, Education, and Welfare will feel when he reads it? Someone will read it. He won't, but someone will, and will be offended for him. *Publishers' Weekly,* commenting on the same situation, said that giving this money to the Secretary of Health, Education, and Welfare would be bad for publishers. That's the significant remark.

In other words, our failure of policy development here has turned us over to the publishers and made us in every real sense their handmaiden. I could point to some other instances. Last year when the American Library Association was terribly short of money, the pressure was taken off after the conference by a grant of $175,000 to ALA by the H. W. Wilson Company. This was theoretically to operate certain manpower programs, but what it did really was to take the pressure off.

We don't have a policy with respect to intellectual freedom. It is easier not to have a policy with respect to issues such as this. Administrators don't like intellectual freedom. They really have to belong, or think they have to belong, to some other establishment, some higher establishment, something out in one of the other environments. They don't really have to if they want to do a good job, but mostly they want to keep their job, so they think they have to. Consequently, they really express disdain for the whole concept of intellectual freedom. During the five years that I sat on the executive board, for example, the matter of setting up a division and then setting aside a sum of money for defense of individual librarians trapped in censorship issues came up time after time after time. For three years we had a position that wasn't filled.

Why does this happen? The amounts of money were constantly taken up. We would budget the position. We set up $5,000 which is nothing. Then we'd say, "You see? That's our symbol. That's our symbolic decision." Then we would take it all away. We wouldn't fill the position. We would take the money out and put it in something else.

In my view, the questions that should have been raised at Atlantic City [at the ALA meeting] are these: Why don't we have power? Why don't we do things? Why are the decisions with respect to the great issues of mankind always symbolic? Why are the decisions with respect to cataloging codes always real? The question basically should never have been, How much money does ALA need? The question should have been, What does it do with its money?

The young activists will have to take their share of the blame here. We allowed ourselves to get involved in the rationale within the organization. We failed to step back and say, "Wait a minute! What are the environments within which the organization operates? What are the inputs? What are the outputs? Which are real and which symbolic? And why are they so?" I would like to suggest to you that nobody is going to get to these issues. It's too difficult. We don't know how. We don't have analytical methods. We tend to discard all of this abstraction as somehow unreal. It seems to me we cannot be real in our judgment of what institutions do unless we can abstract ourselves from the details.

NIMER: In the very beginning you said that we have the leadership we deserve and that we want, because we've had it for such a long time and, therefore, it is conscious. It seems to me that because we've had it a long time it is not conscious. It is only when you make a direct action that it is conscious.

BLASINGAME: How do you think these people got there?

NIMER: Well, maybe the consciousness was there twenty-five or thirty years ago, but we've had a vacuum ever since.

BLASINGAME: It still is. Let me answer this way. If you and I were thrown into a personal association, and if I dominated you every day for a month and you didn't do anything about it, then I would have to say that's what you want. Up to the point where you quit and walked out or else beat me in the head, you would be accepting that situation.

NIMER: Suppose you were dominating me for a month and that maybe *was* what I wanted. Then three people walked into the situation and then more and more people came in. It takes somebody with fresh vision to see this is not what should be.

BLASINGAME: You're suggesting there are people coming in with fresh vision, presumably, but if they still allow me to dominate, then that's what they want.

NIMER: They're new and untried.

BLASINGAME: Not forever.

NIMER: They are judging the situation. They say, "He's been there a long time. He has dominated and she is being dominated."

BUNDY: It depends on where they come from. If they came from a lifetime of being dominated and they went to that situation, they would probably accept it also. You're saying that they have no perception of any other world, and therefore, it wasn't a conscious choice.

NIMER: But they come from education, don't they?

BLASINGAME: This is a world in which the individual is terribly dominated, but he participates in this great institution which keeps on its shelves all the thoughts of mankind, certainly not all of which suggest that man ought to be dominated by someone else. Librarians never read the books, or at least they never put what they see into practice. That's my point. As long as you don't do that, as long as the institutions continue to survive, then I have to assert that the individuals within the institutions are accepting this kind of leadership. They've found what they want.

BUNDY: I once questioned a library school class about their opinions of the people who run ALA. They said, "Well, they are our leaders. That's why they run it."

WASSERMAN: Just as you need informed intelligence to calculate alternative strategies within the structure of library bureaucracies, you need intelligence to focus upon the tragedy of the library bureaucracy which is ALA. I think our problem is that we don't have that kind of intelligence in any kind of leadership. I see rhetoric. That's what social responsibility is until it's translated into pragmatic action, either within the framework that you have described nationally or within the several bureaucracies.

BLASINGAME: Let me give you a couple of things that have come to my attention. A young man came to Rutgers to organize a chapter of the Social Responsibility Roundtable. The only exhibit he had in his hand was a newsletter put out by the New York chapter, in which that chapter absolutely uncritically opposed the proposed budget cuts in the three New York systems. Well, hell, here's the group that he's talking about being socially not responsible and he is ready to go out and uncritically support them. His next point was that had there been a chapter like this in Newark when the Newark public library was threatened with being closed, they could have done the same thing.

There isn't any less socially responsible organization within my knowledge than a public library. Why would they want to do that? I'll tell you another instance. Somebody in Pittsburgh put out a petition. They wanted local librarians to put it out on their desks and get patrons to sign it. It was in support of the appropriation for the Library Services and Construction Act. The wording was so wild that it was really unbelievable. If they didn't get $47.5 million, it was going to destroy the American public library. A great deal of that money has been very badly used. We never look at how it has been used. Furthermore, it is an absolute figure which in the face of inflation has been declining in value ever since it was first appropriated. They wanted to ask some patrons to say that if Congress doesn't appropriate that very small amount of money (when you get down to per capita funds, it is very small), it's going to wipe out the American public libraries. That act was, in my opinion, irresponsible.

PARTICIPANT: To me, this document that has been circulating around the table today is a case in point. I signed my name because I wanted information. I'm basically in sympathy with the things that it says, but I feel that it should have been much more carefully formulated.

BLASINGAME: Then you shouldn't have signed it.

BUNDY: I didn't sign it.

PARTICIPANT: It was circulated because we can sit, and we can talk, and we can rationalize, and yet nothing occurs. I think the Social Responsibility Roundtable is an excellent example of social irresponsibility in some fragments of their activities. But overall, no! I rationalize it strategy-wise. At some point there comes a time when you have to say, "Well, it has its laws, but we have to do something."

BLASINGAME: But you see, you're taking an either/or situation. I'm trying to say that as long as you do that, you're going to fall in behind the people who are leading the profession now, because they put it to you that way every time. What Paul Wasserman has said to you is that what you have to do is figure out *all* of the options. You're not doing that. Nobody is doing that.

PARTICIPANT: But don't you fall into the intellectual trap? When you think of all the options, you begin to think of all the alternatives to the options.

WASSERMAN: Don't throw out any analysis until you have sorted it out. That's dangerous.

BLASINGAME: It's never even gotten started. Time after time after time I've insisted that matters go into the minutes of the executive board. When I joined that august body it was a private club. I suspect it is again. It was common for the old people in the profession to use the executive board to vent their spleen on various individuals. They would say, "I want this off the record." Then they would say really terrible things about other people who weren't there to defend themselves, or whose friends weren't there. It was the practice not to record any dissent within the executive board, unless someone insisted that it be recorded. If I voted "no" on an issue and everyone else voted "yes," the group turned on me and tried to get me to change my vote so they wouldn't ever have to put any dissenting voice in the minutes. So I regard as one of my damn few accomplishments on the executive board the fact that a lot of dissent got into the minutes. But nobody ever read them.

BUNDY: They seem to be circulating a lot more things to us nowadays.

BLASINGAME: They circulate a lot of things, and nobody reads them, for the most part. Council members, for example, typically do not read the material that is sent to them well in advance of the meeting. You go into a council meeting and nobody knows what the hell is in the minutes.

PARTICIPANT: As long as the library profession is made up of the type of people that it is, there is no organization that can be founded, no way of restructuring the ALA, that will actually serve the best interests of the profession or of the clientele of the group.

BLASINGAME: I wouldn't agree with that at this stage. As for myself, I don't have any further desire to try to change the American Library Association through direct personal action. I've been here longer than I'm going to get to stay, and I'm just not going to spend the rest of my time at that sort of thing. However, if you, as young people, want to change the American Library Association, I think you can do it, but you can't do it unless you become students of the situation, unless you do the dirty, grubby work of finding out what really happens, finding out who really is appointed to this committee and that.

PARTICIPANT: Tell us how to get inside.

BLASINGAME: You have to read the minutes of both the council and the executive board, to begin with. A long time ago, six or seven years ago, the International Relations Committee was rapidly running out of money. They were, at the time, the only committee that had its expenses paid to meetings other than meetings held at the summer conference. They just happened to meet at a time when the executive board was meeting, and they just happened to meet in the same place. They had this wonderful scheme. They had a big Rockefeller grant, which was running out. They were going to hold back the overhead charges on all future contracts to support the international relations program. Think now of a group that hadn't been successful in getting any contracts finding this wonderful means of supporting itself through overhead charges, which were running between 2 percent and 4 percent. Totally inadequate! They were going to use that money, which they didn't have, to support their own activities.

They got this decision through the executive board over my wild protest. I had been put in the position where I felt they weren't going to survive, and that this was going to be turned back to me because I had opposed this stupid allocation of no funds. So I suggested that the American Library Association should write into its operating budget enough money to support a minimal office for the International Relations Committee, consisting of a director and one clerical assistant, with the clear understanding that they would have to bring to the board as the first order of business a statement of what the association ought to be doing in the international relations field with its own money.

We gave them $40,000. You know what they did first? They rushed right out and signed a contract with AID to send people traveling around the world at a time when the newspapers, the scholarly journals, everybody was writing about the problems of this type of contract. This followed the upheaval over the Defense Department sociological studies in South America. It followed Michigan State's upheaval. Michigan had gotten heavily involved in a CIA project, and some of the people there didn't know it. The atmosphere within which such a contract should have been signed, could have been signed, just wasn't there, but that was their first order of business. We never got a statement of policy as to what we should do in this field.

PARTICIPANT: Are you suggesting that we could do best by staying within ALA and trying to revise it?

BLASINGAME: I'm very dubious about whether this institution is subject to change, partly because it is so thoroughly dominated by a very small group of people. More recently I've been discouraged by observing the attacks on the association, which are in every real sense visceral and not analytical. You'll never change it on an emotional basis. Never. If we don't see something more than these emotional attacks, I think you ought to abandon the American Library Association.

BUNDY: What if we see an exchange of power? Keep the same structure, perpetuate it, but see an exchange of hands?

BLASINGAME: I would see happening within the association very much what has happened within the large public libraries, probably in the universities too, which is that people move up and are gradually socialized until when they get to the top they all have the same attitudes. They are thoroughly homogenized. You're not going to get any change. You may get a change of faces, although that is happening very slowly.

PARTICIPANT: Then the problem is not in the bureaucracy per se, but in the people who are at different levels in the bureaucracy.

BLASINGAME: Including those at the bottom, yes.

PARTICIPANT: So if you can change the people in the bureaucracy, you could use the bureaucracy to facilitate change. That would be an exchange of power.

BLASINGAME: Let me come back and say there is nothing wrong with bureaucracy per se. This is just a way of operating. You can make any way of operating work to the ends that the people within the organization strongly feel it should, providing that they have the organizational know-how to make it work that way so the bureaucracy per se is not an impediment.

BUNDY: As a library educator, what do you think of the notion that we are all things to all people? As library educators, we now begin to wish to formulate policy. Our issue was that we wanted to give preference to fellowships for students over institutes. We were told we might upset the ALA applecart; we might hurt the possibility of getting funds. We were chided for even suggesting that there might be a policy coming out of the educational group, and it was suggested that this was disloyalty to the overall group.

BLASINGAME: Typical tactic.

NIMER: You painted a very dismal picture of ALA, and some reasons why it was so in terms of the kind of people who work in it. Are there professional organizations that are a prototype of the kind you would like? I don't think there are. Isn't the AAUP, or any one of the other professional organizations, very similar to the ALA?

BLASINGAME: From what I know of the AAUP, the answer is, no, it is not. Maybe it's just that I don't know it very well.

WASSERMAN: Here is the frustration of this culture. We have people who genuinely want to change. They find what you have described, that what's wrong with this culture is personified in the people who lack the skill and the capacity to be otherwise. Their frustration is frustration in the face of the identification of evil and the impossibility of making it otherwise. I agree with you completely. We are limited by our capacity. We must not deal with it viscerally but deal with it intellectually. Librarianship is more poverty striken than most businesses because it doesn't attract many people into the field who have this capacity to begin with. It certainly doesn't do anything very substantial to increase that capacity in the course of educational acculturation.

BLASINGAME: It works exactly the opposite, I would say.

PARTICIPANT: I didn't really understand his statement about the lack of analytical capability.

BUNDY: We're the old culture, the radicals of the 1930s.

BLASINGAME: I teach a course. "Teach a course"—that's kind of an extreme statement; I sit there while the students, at least a few of them, try to learn something. I use this model as a beginning point and try to talk about urbanization and what's happening and what is likely to happen in the future. It's my experience that when the students get through with this course, that's that. A few of them are excited about it. A few of them, I hope, may continue this analysis, but most of them come to the school with the frame of mind that this is one more hurdle they've got to jump over. They're going to jump over. They're going to jump over it and, when it's finished, that's that.

BUNDY: The other response that Paul and I get in administration is, "You're being critical, therefore you don't like the public library." Would you say to the engineer who told you the left wing of your Boeing 707 was about to go, "You don't like Boeing airplanes, or you wouldn't be critical of them"?

PARTICIPANT: That's exactly what happens today in organizations, isn't it? The person who offers suggestions for changes is the person who is criticized.

BLASINGAME: I haven't been invited to serve on any ALA committees. I wouldn't accept the invitation were it given because I have other

things to do with my time, but, yes, one is very quickly frozen out.
I don't regret it, as for myself, but I regret it as a mode of behavior
for the organization. I think it is self-destructive, essentially.

BUNDY: When I did the article on who runs the ALA, a political
scientist, Robert Presthus, said, "Well, they've got only so many choices.
They can attack. This they will never do. It brings an issue out in
the open that they don't want brought out in the open. They can
put you on the nominating committee and coopt you. Or they can
ignore you." They ignored me. There has never been any kind of
response from ALA.

BLASINGAME: Let me give you another illustration. The statement
is made that a few people control the association. David Clift [ALA
Executive Director] says, in apparent response, that one person out
of seven serves on a committee in the American Library Association.
Absolutely irrelevant, but people accept it as reasonable.

PARTICIPANT: Why is it irrelevant?

BLASINGAME: The control of the association and service on committees are not related.

PARTICIPANT: I didn't conceive it as that way. I thought if you were
on committees you did have something to say.

BUNDY: Look how those committees are budgeted.

PARTICIPANT: I'm not on a committee, but I assumed that when
I got on one, I would have something to say.

BLASINGAME: You would have something to say about that committee.

PARTICIPANT: They would put you on a committee, but without responsibility, sort of like the model cities.

BUNDY: The executive secretary of the large national organization
and all bureaucracies is a very powerful position. One reason is just
because he stays around. The president of the ALA comes in and
comes out. What can he do in one year? In the history of ALA,
the executive secretary was only once run out.

BLASINGAME: In 1947 or 1948, the executive secretary, Milan, had
retired. He was run for the presidency and Skip Graham was nominated
from the floor. Skip was elected. I think we are building up to one
of two things: erosion of the American Library Association, which
frankly I would welcome because it is the only way you can tell the
people that you don't like what they're doing, or some kind of revolution which might take the form of some new organization.

PARTICIPANT: Couldn't there be a nomination from the floor at this point?

BLASINGAME: You've missed the point. The president of the American Library Association is enormously powerless.

PARTICIPANT: As a profession, we get hung up on the American Library Association. It's an easy bugaboo. Yet there's a much deeper problem, and you've implied that. Frankly, I'm again going to ask you, where do we take the implications that you've given us this morning? Where do we take them? Do we take them to the admissions office of the library science schools?

BLASINGAME: Perhaps I should have started off by saying that any time one deals with people, one deals with the most marvelously complex situation imaginable. Indeed, it is beyond imagination. Even for a person skilled at looking at behavioral patterns, all the different things that people can do and think and the reactions they can have are beyond imagination. So, what do we do? First, please don't try to restrict it to some simplistic approach, as you were earlier. You must stop that. That's the first thing to do.

PARTICIPANT: It's not easy to do.

BLASINGAME: That's right, especially because you are encouraged to think in these either/or terms, through your whole sixteen or seventeen years of education. It's either good or it's bad. You've got to quit that. That's very hard to do.

PARTICIPANT: By the same token, with all due respect, you are implying we have to come out of the black box.

BLASINGAME: You have to step back away from the situation, treat it as a black box, and stop getting involved in the argument.

PARTICIPANT: It's that borderline. When do you enter the black box?

BLASINGAME: You can get in in any number of ways. The easiest way to affect the American Library Association today would be to refuse to pay your dues. You want to organize something? Organize a dues strike! They'll wake up in one hell of a hurry, because money is what counts.

BUNDY: They only survive from your membership. If you can pull that away from them, and if students will start walking out of classes . . .

PARTICIPANT: I think it is going to happen, even if it isn't organized.

BLASINGAME: You have to have something along with this. You can't just have a dues strike and then no policy that you want to have implemented.

SMITH: I would disagree with that. If they suffer financially enough, then within the black box they'll begin to worry, and say, "How are we going to get in contact with that environment again?"

BUNDY: There ought to be a force working on a policy, while another force is . . .

SMITH: Isn't the problem that the environment itself isn't really sure what it wants out of ALA? This, going back to what you were talking about before, is really at the heart of the trouble of the Social Responsibilities group. They are very unhappy, but this unhappiness is not being channeled into a constructive program.

BUNDY: You are both saying the same thing. He is saying they're neither politically effective, nor are they policy makers.

WASSERMAN: On the other hand, I would not ally myself with you, Ralph, on the notion that the better alternative is to destroy this organization.

BLASINGAME: I don't think you can destroy it, Paul.

WASSERMAN: You destroy it by withdrawing its capacity to perform. Then perhaps another organization is given rise to, with all of the problems and dangers inherent in the one that we've already got.

BUNDY: They will start to listen. The one thing they must have is those memberships, because they can't function without them.

BLASINGAME: That is an assumption.

WASSERMAN: No, no! They will understand that the people don't want to pay the dues. They won't understand the implications of the act.

BUNDY: Then they should go out, Paul.

WASSERMAN: I want to save the society and its institutions, and I don't want to do it by tearing them down.

BUNDY: We're not destroying them; they are destroying themselves.

PARTICIPANT: This could be interpreted in two ways. If I don't pay my dues it may be that they will say, "Gee, the dues are too high." They might not get the message at all.

PARTICIPANT: On the first page of the *ALA Bulletin,* you read about how terrible library salaries are. On the last page of the *Bulletin,* you read that they are going to raise our dues to $25. In between, you find no justification for one or the other.

BUNDY: When that association takes a stand on salaries, it's something a professional would belong to for that reason.

WASSERMAN: It's not an association, it's *us!* *We* have the power for it to be otherwise, if we would understand . . .

BUNDY: If we will exercise it.

WASSERMAN: Yes, precisely!

BLASINGAME: If young people really want to operate in a different association, they can. I'm specifically opting out, except conceivably as an adviser, because I don't have that time left any more. The techniques are fairly simple. One of the techniques would be to discover what the real decisions have been. People can give you some guidance in this. My associate and I spent a great deal of time getting beaten around the head and shoulders, but we found out an awful lot about what really happens inside and what the decisions have been. There will be some others, not very many.

The next move would be to look at the details. Read carefully what comes across your desk and question every last word of it. Why do they take this action? Why do they say this? Most of the claims, for example, for ALA's success in Congress are phony. They jump on somebody's bandwagon, and then they came back to you and say, "Look what great people we are." So you have to question everything you see.

Second, you will have opportunities at various conferences to insist that certain new items of business arise. If you get upset about the lack of policy with respect to international relations, by God, put it on the agenda. Make them discuss it and say, "Why haven't we got a policy?" Have a vote and say, "Let's have a policy by next year, or we'll ask for your resignation." You can do it. You can get at it through council if you will elect enough council members. That's a very difficult procedure, but it's still profitable. Now if you elect them, then they're going to pour a lot of time into it. They're going to have to caucus. They're going to have to decide for themselves what the issues are. They are going to have to stand on their own two feet in the council meetings and raise hell. That can all be done.

WASSERMAN: Implied in this is the recognition that representation is a representative process, and before people are selected for it, as they are now, on the basis of names which are totally irrelevant to their performance in this role, they should say something about what it is they have to say for you, and through the organization, for you. Now it is a sort of popularity contest in which people are chosen for I don't know what reasons, but it is a magical, mystical process.

Maybe they base it on the part of the world or country in which they live, or whether they are male or female, or how big a library they administer. All these reasons have no relevance whatsoever to the way in which they control the activity of this organization.

People can demand a point of view. Why shall I vote for you? What do you mean to me? In the process of being elected the present way, the people nominated recognize that they mean nothing to anybody. They are just puppets; they're just people who perform irrelevant roles.

PARTICIPANT: Someone made a suggestion that each person who ran for council should put down a statement, instead of just a biography. This I believe. I always look to see which library school they came from.

BUNDY: But that's the problem now between the ones in power and ones out of power. If I ran for something, what would be my issues? I would have to do all this work, as he says. Get access to people inside, before I could clarify the issue. The people in power know the issues. They are avoiding most of them, but if they had to do it, they could do it better than I could, because I'm on the outside.

WASSERMAN: But if you don't do that, you don't deserve to represent anybody.

BUNDY: There is another reason why these men are heads of organizations. They have the time. They are in jobs where they can take the time. They can travel on company money. Many librarians who might usefully serve don't have this kind of money or resources.

WASSERMAN: Once again we come back to how much time we want to spend and how much we want to work and how much we are willing to spend of ourselves in these processes. To the extent that these people have the time to do whatever they're doing with social responsibility, which is very interesting and very important, that time can be spent in intelligent activity that is purposeful and not rhetoric.

BLASINGAME: That's true.

BUNDY: SDS is way ahead of them. They're really moving.

SMITH: There were some plans made on a very informal basis at Kansas City, which got sort of plowed under, to develop a nonestablishment slate in ALA which would have two purposes: (1) it would run on a program, and the program would be those very things that we want ALA to do; and (2) it would be put on the ballot by petition, which is possible. It seems to me if you want to hit ALA in the most dramatic and probably the most effective way, this is the way to do it, not by going through the establishment machinery. Strike at this business of its lack of goals and purpose.

BUNDY: They're running the same slate. John Forsman is going to be on both. What does that tell you?

SMITH: That's where social responsibility has its place, then.

BUNDY: Yes, but the official group is going to run John Forsman too. Now, where are we?

PARTICIPANT: It is unfair that one additional factor is the librarians themselves. My own experience is that the people who are most resistant to change in our institutions are the librarians. What percent of the time do we look at ourselves and not think about how important we are or how big a group we are? How many of the incoming librarians, the old librarians, how many of them really care? They want to put in their eight hours of whatever they have and forget about it.

BUNDY: You notice he's not telling us to go to the rank-and-file librarianship. He is telling us to engage in a power struggle with a relatively few people, on the part of a relatively small number of people.

PARTICIPANT: How about sending a message to the library school in regard to selection of future candidates?

BLASINGAME: I don't take Gallup polls, but as a result of traveling around, I get in touch with a lot of people. It is my view that there is a general unhappiness with the current situation. There is no leadership to focus the unhappiness. We have a relatively large group of people who would follow common sense at this point. They will not follow empty rhetoric.

I would also like to suggest one other thing. We have treated this, the size of the challenge, in a kind of pessimistic way, but there are some optimistic characteristics about it too. One is the challenge itself. We are in a position right now, in the profession, where we can respond to the challenge. We can develop programs that have some chance of success. This can be a tremendously rewarding thing. The opportunity lies before us. I would hate to see us simply be overwhelmed by the challenge.

SMITH: I will add a couple of comments to that. Ultimately, any change starts with the individual. To you who wish to have some influence on the future, you might start reading the books that you take care of. You'd better read Kaplan; you'd better read Simon, you'd better read a lot of people that in all likelihood you have never been forced to read. We are going to make different choices. It seems that people at Maryland are under constant pressure to be in the national milieu. We might make a choice to create a milieu here for something we think is very important, which is the entry route for our profession, but we're torn. We see so many needs.

BLASINGAME: There is still the time between dinner and bedtime, which we, for the most part, squander.

BUNDY: For instance, an individual choice for me might be to get off most of the establishment committees I'm on, and try to do more with the unofficial committees, which are making the changes. I'm not saying I will, but I'm saying these are choices we face to get that hour between dinner and bedtime. Some of us at Maryland haven't had that.

PARTICIPANT: What was the name of that author you suggested?

BLASINGAME: Read in the areas of public administration, political science, the newer sociology.

WELBOURNE: Because of what we have in this profession, because the movement, the change, is so scattered and so unknown to itself, it is not enough to come up with an enlightened point of view and present it to the membership as it exists today and expect it to be implemented. You have to organize first around those things that people will accent. It may not be the kind of very pointed, directed, enlightened sort of thing that we envision . . .

BUNDY: Jim, I disagree with you. The changes he told us today have not been made. They really have not. The changes in library education are just beginning to be made.

WELBOURNE: A group can be dominated. Look at those members who remain silent. They give force to that domination themselves. You sit here, Mary Lee Bundy sits there, Paul Wasserman and others in the field do also. Where can we go? Yet you cop out and say you think it's up to young people. They will re-create the field. By that very process, the conservative outlook wins out. By the time the young people re-create the field and take the enlightened pose, they will have already been coopted by the establishment. Organize around whatever you have to get people organized! Mobilize the change element! Bring together your sophistication in the field and that group and work together; then all right, that's free.

BLASINGAME: That's a very good point. Let me say some things out of my experience what may be of some value. You live in a political world. All human interactions are, in one way or another, political. We live this way. This is the way we get along. We govern ourselves. You can't do anything in this environment without understanding the issues and then organizing. You're exactly right.

As to which issues will catch attention, I've become, out of experience, quite flexible. There are an awful lot of issues that would catch attention. In the long term, I think people respond better to a reasoned approach to policy questions than they do to emotional approaches, however strongly they may feel at the moment. You say I've opted out. To a considerable degree that's true. I said to myself at one time, "You're not really getting anywhere." I have spent a long time at this. Let me just go on and tell you the specifics. We got the Library Code, the first library code ever to pass any state legislature, which had all sorts of goodies in it for libraries, through the legislature. The Pennsylvania Library Association never found out what was going on, but we got it through the legislature because at least they stayed quiet. The first thing that happened was that the whole thing was torn apart by a few individuals. They just couldn't stand to divide the power that they had already gathered, you see, no matter what the benefit. The benefits were tremendous, but they couldn't stand to divide it. I looked at that and I said, "Don't spend your life with this." This is a very tough business. I was neglecting my family very seriously at a very critical time and I said, "The hell with it! I will try something else. I will try the academic approach, which had always interested me anyway."

So I very consciously shifted roles. Now if you want me as an adviser, if you want me to tell you what my experiences are and to suggest things that you wish to do, I am right with you. But I really made a permanent change in my life style. I'm not about to go back. I again would repeat, you get to the point where you realize suddenly that you're over the hump, you know. You've had more time than you've got left. You have to say, "What are you going to do now?" That becomes increasingly valuable time. You don't have to worry about that yet.

WELBOURNE: People don't want advice. They want power. Part of your knowledge is very valuable, as is your commitment and your interest in the field. To say, "All right, I'll order a better world for you people by advising you" is nonsense. We're going to do something. We understand we have problems, but we're committed to doing something. What tools, what strengths do you have to recognize and point out weaknesses? Your role is either to lead or to advise others what to do.

BLASINGAME: I don't think you understand what I intend, but go ahead.

WASSERMAN: One cannot be everything simultaneously. One cannot use human personal resources in a multiplicity of ways and be effective. If someone like Ralph puts his energy and his commitment into the role he plays, that is as powerful a contribution as putting it into the politically active arena that you're talking about. One man can't be twelve men. One man dedicates energies for one kind of star and follows it, not twenty stars dissipating energies in every direction. Don't degrade his role. That's a powerful role, an influential role.

WELBOURNE: I question the magnitude of the stars you're talking about, not necessarily the numbers. You can sit here and look at all your resources. You can place them on a priority scale. You can list the legal points that can move this profession. I asked you to measure up to where your action role is.

WASSERMAN: Jim, you're making a judgment that working in the political arena is a more valuable solution to the problem than influencing minds that are coming along in numbers. That's a contribution, too.

BLASINGAME: I can only say that as a result of my personal experience, I've decided that it is not more important to work in the political arena. Maybe what I'm working at is not going to turn out to be any more important, but I have to find that out for myself. I can't switch back. What I am trying to do is take a longer-range type of action by working with students who can act on broader fronts than I can working alone.

WELBOURNE: I can't understand it.

BUNDY: Jim, maybe you're not saying the right words, or maybe it is hopeless.

SMITH: If this is the only problem we've got, we're in great shape. There are some people who want to theorize and others who want to act, but the problem we have is not with these groups. It's with that enormous group that doesn't want to do a damn thing and that isn't doing anything. That's the group we should focus our attention on. Let's all kind of work together on that.

PARTICIPANT: One method of changing an organization might be to parallel it with a purposeful study, make policies, and work toward changes in the original organization itself. I'm thinking in particular of something that occurred within the Democratic party. The ADS set a parallel to it as a means of effecting change. Would this be applicable to the ALA?

BLASINGAME: Probably it would. A considerable degree of self-discipline would be required on the part of persons involved. Perhaps anything that results in meaningful activity takes that. One of the problems that I would suggest to you, however, is that you may have aspirations for the American Library Association which are quite unrealistic. You may think of it as representing the profession, whereas, if you read the constitution or the charter of ALA, you will find that its purpose is to represent the interests of libraries. There is an institutional orientation contained in those words which is going to be hard to beat. It is quite possible that after some attempts in this direction you might well say, "What we need is a new organization." I'm not suggesting you shouldn't try it, but I wouldn't spend the rest of my life on it.

BUNDY: There are other organizations. There is the ASIS, which is considering a possible merger with SLA, the Special Libraries Association. These organizations have importance. They have ideas. They have people who can contribute. They hold what could well be the information profession. So when we talk of ALA, we're still talking only to ourselves; we're talking about traditional librarianship. You have to put these other groups into the equation. It would seem to me it would be very unwise at this stage of the game to form any association that didn't take into consideration the information technology from the very beginning, not try to bring them in later. They have tools, talents, money, and more prestige and respect in their short lifetime than we seem to have been able to muster in our long lifetime. There is a possibility of a marriage here, an alliance between interests. You can't leave that out of the equation, because then you've left librarianship to taking care of books.

BLASINGAME: It might also be reasonable to think of an organization which would represent librarians and which could find it possible to restrict its interests. One of the problems with the American Library Association, and I see something of this in many other associations made up essentially of humanists, is that they all get to be a mile wide and a mile thick. They want to cover everything and they don't do anything very well. It may be best to think of an organization of professional persons, if that's the way that you want to put it, who have social concern, and cut out everything else.

PARTICIPANT: There would have to be some base requirements for membership, such as being a librarian. The trouble with ALA is that it includes anybody who has even a mild interest in libraries.

BLASINGAME: One of the basic problems with the American Library Association is that it tries to include too many environments. We have the governors of libraries and the administrators of libraries and the service personnel of libraries all in the same organization. Essentially these are different environments.

WASSERMAN: It may be that there would be some utility in looking at the developments in librarianship as stages in a cycle of evolution in which, during its earlier phases, it needed the kind of support and underpinning that came only out of the solidity of the institutional form, because those who functioned in it were irrelevant and limited functionaries anyway, and the only people who really spoke or could speak with any authority were those who had control of that institution. It may be that we have come in our evolution to the point where we now are ready to assume a more mature and responsible role as human beings interested in the institution, rather than vice versa.

PARTICIPANT: How can we get this feeling within the organization if we're still going to include nonprofessionals, trustees, all these people who have supported libraries?

BLASINGAME: You're suggesting, aren't you, Paul, that we might take a step beyond that and start a really different chain of thought through associations?

BUNDY: One thing I might bring up right now is the question of a national librarians' association. I'm not yet sure everyone here would accept the distinction or the need for it. Assuming that you did, let's talk for a minute about ways and means. There was some notion that it could happen rapidly. Others felt that it takes a lot of careful thought and planning.

BLASINGAME: My feeling right now is it might be best to lay a concerted assault on the American Library Association. We have kicked around the problem quite a bit. I see it as twofold. One is the goals and two is the organization to reach the goals. Despite the fact that there is a lot of discontent, we haven't really established goals very clearly. We've got a certain amount of organization, but it's not organization really to reach any specific goals. Within the limits of ALA at the moment, it might be easier to attempt a concerted asault on the organization, perhaps around the issue of getting members into the council or around some other significant issue which would help to develop the program, on the one hand, and to develop the organization nucleus necessary to push that program through, on the other hand.

In other words, we need a committee of concern that's fairly sizable and spread out across the country. If that fails, and right now my feeling is it's more likely to fail than not, you have achieved a basis for an organization by this means. You've also got a program that has been tested against ALA. It will also clarify the issue for a lot of librarians who are not sure now whether ALA is the proper means. They will not be sure until they see that ALA will not respond to issues when those issues are clearly brought before it. At that point we could seriously plan a librarians' association. If we do it now, we will wind up spreading our resources too thin. A lot of people just don't want to quit ALA. Other people are already going off on a number of different tangents.

BUNDY: We found at Maryland that people who will bear a new venture, like a new school, are not the same kind who come along later when it's established, when it has its accreditation. There is nothing wrong with the second kind of people. Some people are just better for the first and some the second. So you begin to get an organization that isn't anything.

BLASINGAME: One wouldn't necessarily lead to the other.

PARTICIPANT: Didn't we talk about this the other day? Saul Alinsky had the notion that any organization should die within three to five years, after it's done what it was supposed to do.

BUNDY: I would be perfectly happy with that. We could form a nice parallel institution to force change with one objective being you don't want this kind of organization to grow. It would get us out of some of the dangers of perpetuation.

PARTICIPANT: The difference between that and social change within ALA is that a separate organization could force the issue more readily.

BUNDY: I have discovered something in talking with people on accreditation committees who are not librarians. The only organization they have ever heard of is the ALA, so they take their accreditation standards. They accept the code of ethics. They take the ALA legislative platform. They haven't really thought about it. I say to them, "Look, there are other associations now in the arena. This organization may not speak for the members." I'm beginning to think that's the next direction. In accreditation circles I have found a great deal of openness to the idea that ALA should not be the sole accreditation agency. It may be our mother and father, but it's not somebody else's.

PARTICIPANT: It's probably presumptuous of me to speak about the ALA, since I've only been a member about three years, but someone asked this morning how to get in in order to work from within. In my limited experience, one of the big problems is that the whole profession is so apathetic. People really don't want to work. This isn't particularly true of a certain group.

For example, in the Committee for the Disadvantaged that I'm on, there were three people who were asked to be members of this committee. We wrote to them right after ALA, two black and one white. They were picked not on that basis, but they were all actively working. Two of them were really quite young in the profession. We haven't even had the courtesy of a reply from these people expressing interest in serving on the committee.

Last year I worked on a subcommittee. The main reason I am now chairman of the committee, I think, is that nobody else would meet any deadlines, nobody would really work. This is one of the reasons you get the same people in positions of leadership. My big problem has been deciding what to agree to work on, because the same people do get asked all the time. There is a reason for it.

BUNDY: Unfortunately, I agree with you. I've heard this for many years in the profession. The in-group says they have to stay in because no one else will join them.

PARTICIPANT: We picked people from all parts of the country. They were young. We thought they would have a great deal to contribute. Why don't they even answer the letter?

BUNDY: Did it ever occur to you it might be the very act of picking? We all pick each other.

PARTICIPANT: Somebody has to decide. I suggested one of the people because I knew she was young and I knew she was doing a great job in Florida working with the blacks. I thought she would be good on the committee.

BUNDY: Some universities have invited students to participate on committees where the administration picked the students. They found the same indifference about coming to meetings and working, et cetera. We are hopeful that if the students themselves elect the people they want to come, we'll get a different response.

PARTICIPANT: How do I do that? How do you go about doing that? How do you know except by the work they are doing what their interests might be?

BUNDY: That is what bothers me. There are 30,000 members of ALA. I refuse to believe you couldn't find three people out of them. Even in the disadvantaged movement, there must be 200.

PARTICIPANT: These three people were picked on the basis of the work that they're doing. Do you think people should write in and say, "I would like to be on a committee"? They won't do that.

PARTICIPANT: There are other ways of doing it. In the state association in Maryland, I asked the JMRT [Junior Members Round Table] group in our association to tell me who they wanted on the state committees. This works very well. They all respond. They are all active. Maybe that's the way to do it.

PARTICIPANT: There was a bulletin about a year ago from the executive secretary or somebody, saying, "If you are interested in working on any committee, please send us your name."

BUNDY: Let me tell you a story about that. There was an administrative assistant to the president of ALA, not the current president. The man was head of a very large metropolitan public library. He began the business of advertising in ALA, "Write, if you would like to be on a committee." My friend, the administrative assistant who no longer is, told me that people wrote in. Hundreds of them wrote in. They all wanted to be on international relations, et cetera. There was a tremendous response. He was starting to open the letters and sort them out, when the president of the American Library Association said, "What are you doing? Here is the list of committee members." This is a pretty callous use of power.

PARTICIPANT: I didn't know the results of it. I only know what I read in the bulletin. I was a little reluctant. I wanted to write in but I thought, "Who am I to say, 'Please put me on a committee'?" So I didn't write.

PARTICIPANT: I'm trying to put myself in that situation. If I were asked to join one of those committees, I would have several objectives. First of all, I'm not sure what the committees intend to do. The goals of the committees are not clear enough to attract my interest.

Then the work spent on the committees takes me away from what I am doing right now.

BUNDY: He's right. Since they have no purpose, this is a status thing. Since they have no money, they may be geographically located so they can't even get to meetings.

PARTICIPANT: Still, you would probably have the courtesy at least to write and say, "You don't have definite goals, so I'm not interested." Nobody said to me, "Now we have to be careful who we get on these committees."

BUNDY: You know who are good people to have on committees. They don't have to make it explicit.

PARTICIPANT: By implication you are saying, "I'll pick people who go along with the establishment."

BUNDY: That isn't an evil thing. That's like saying I might prefer to relate to Ralph or Eldred rather than a twenty-one-year-old here. We think alike. We've come through similar experiences. We share points of view. That's not really an evil thing, until it becomes dysfunctional for this profession.

PARTICIPANT: I would personally prefer that we add the letter "s" to our society and make it American Libraries Association, a coordinating body of different groups and activities which merge naturally. Let's respond to the need as a transitional group that tries to do something with it, has a coordinating pattern to facilitate activities, and get units in contact with each other. Do this, instead of building a tremendous national association which is so detached from our original problems that it's useless.

BUNDY: The ALA has never, in spite of persistent efforts, let the association become regional so that people could get together and form alliances and friendships on a basis where they might take action.

PARTICIPANT: As far as library schools are concerned, it seems as though anything east of Kent State is one region and anything west of Kent State is another region, and that the twain will never meet.

BUNDY: If the association and its members couldn't decide to move their headquarters from Chicago, Illinois, to one of two metropolitan centers, Washington or New York, how do you expect great change from them?

PARTICIPANT: The membership did decide.

BUNDY: They decided to stay in Chicago. If they can't make a decision to shift their base to where the action is . . .

PARTICIPANT: This is a different kind of decision.

BUNDY: That's what I'm saying.

PARTICIPANT: The executive board wanted to move but the membership said no. It seems to me the membership was responsive. Didn't they take a vote?

BUNDY: That's what I'm saying. If the rank-and-file membership in the association can't make that change, I wonder what other changes they're going to be capable of, if any.

PARTICIPANT: You're just saying you don't agree with their decision, but they did decide. I didn't agree with it either, but they voted.

PARTICIPANT: What Mary Lee Bundy is saying is perhaps it shouldn't have been a democratic thing at all.

BUNDY: You're saying this is a debatable issue. Maybe it is. To me, it was a symbolic issue. The centers and the headquarters for money in this profession for information development are in Washington and New York. The ALA preferred to stay in Chicago. There is no great information center in Chicago.

PARTICIPANT: Even though the bureaucracy said, "We're moving to Washington," the people rose up in revolt and said, "No!"

WASSERMAN: A lot of this is extraneous discussion. I would like to come back to something that Ralph suggested as one of the problems. It is the multiplicity and the range of activity that is conducted in library settings. Perhaps one problem is the sorting out of functions and responsibilities that now exist, which are technical purposes with organizational implications and which are purposes, strivings, and needs of a professional class of people who have common concerns, interests, and issues within its framework. The question is whether hospitality can be provided within the framework of the same organization to the aspirations of the individual qua professional, and the aspirations of the institution as an institution. This is the question posed by your suggestion to try to change ALA this way and see if it will work. What you're asking is if it can work.

BLASINGAME: It seems to me we really need an issue that confronts this question directly. We need some kind of proposal that can be brought to ALA as an initiative measure that would strike right at the heart of the problem. See what ALA is able to do with it. If they can't handle it, then indicate that they can't and why they can't and why we need to go outside ALA.

PARTICIPANT: I think we've gone past that point.

BLASINGAME: I don't see that. In what respect?

PARTICIPANT: Year after year we say to the ALA, "You're unresponsive to us in all respects." And they say, "Oh no, we're not. We do whatever you want." Now, and at least as far as I can read, I've never seen them once respond the right way.

BLASINGAME: But the problem is, how many people feel this way? I'm pretty well convinced also that ALA is not viable. The real problem is getting enough librarians into another organization. This happened once when the Special Libraries' Association was formed. If we could really take a look at that and see what was involved there, we could perhaps use it as a model for what we want to do now. What do we do? Do we issue a call for a librarians' association? I could see doing that to raise the question, but to say, "Let's form it," I don't think you're going to get anybody to support that.

PARTICIPANT: Look at it another way. A lot of new ALA members said, "We never get to say anything," so ALA formed a junior members' association.

BUNDY: But look at what Junior Roundtables was. Delayed adolescence! You shouldn't have asked for Junior Roundtables, you should have asked for the council.

PARTICIPANT: We knew we couldn't get the council, so . . .

BUNDY: One of the tragedies of this profession is that we have a Social Responsibilities Roundtable. If we had a Social Action Roundtable, it might be different. But when our goals have become a roundtable, that's a tragedy.

PARTICIPANT: Of course, it's rhetoric once again.

BUNDY: It should be at the top of the organization. We have a social responsibility. We are a profession. We legitimatized it and then put it down to the status of a roundtable.

PARTICIPANT: Maybe you can take advantage of the increasing memberships next year. Maybe you can provide for it in some kind of a temporary organization where the membership is deposited until certain things are changed.

PARTICIPANT: Give them membership at wholesale. That will be a good point.

BLASINGAME: What kind of membership? Who are you going to comply with?

PARTICIPANT: Say, "You can join us for x number of dollars."

PARTICIPANT: There will be a number of people here who tend to be extremely dissatisfied, yet they don't want to disassociate themselves from ALA. They don't want to feel that they quit over a question of money. Maybe we should deposit that money in some temporary transitional organization which would start representing our views at the same time.

PARTICIPANT: How much should they deposit?

PARTICIPANT: Whatever they paid up to now, which is quite low.

BUNDY: Let me just wonder along. You are immediately going to be involved in the idea of organizational problems. How much money you need to survive. How much the executive secretary costs. Again I guess I'll come back with Ralph and say, "Until you get a goal and a purpose, you're just organizers."

PARTICIPANT: I certainly think it is correct to question how the money is being spent, but I also think most people are questioning it. We're calling ourselves a professional organization. My husband, who is a lawyer, spends more on his state bar fees than any of us are asked to pay for our national organization, and then the American Bar Association is something else.

BUNDY: I think some of the issues are economic, but they are not a case of dues. Let us form a national librarians' association and we'll take a position on salaries. The beginning salary in this field could become $10,000. Take a position. Tell members, "Don't go to insitutions that don't give $10,000, regardless of . . ."

PARTICIPANT: I wrote Paul Wasserman a letter about my salary because I couldn't find out anything from ALA.

BUNDY: That's one issue. Another issue is job placement, so that innovative people can get matched up with innovative organizations. This is not the failure of an administrators' association, because it is not to their advantage to do this. They're the guys who hire us at the lousy salaries. They're the people who would rather we stayed than not. Those are professional issues. You start with economic issues.

SMITH: My experience has been in California, where we've got an organization of approximately 600 librarians from the university rolling. In order to do that, it took a tremendous commitment from about a half dozen people. They just worked like the devil. We had a lot of things going for us. We had a particular climate where the librarians were incensed. We had certain commitments from the administration of the university to change. We got over 150 librarians together initially at ALA to support this, but it would be extremely difficult to do this on a national level. We are all members of the same family, so to speak. We are all University of California librarians. We have a telephone tieline we can use to call on. Communication is easy.

Try to do this on a national level. At this time, it looks hopeless to me. It just looks hopeless. In the first place, you've got to get a core of highly committed, highly able people who are going to be willing to devote the tremendous amount of time required. You've got to get the money to support them in their activities. You've got to develop a real communications network around the country. You've got to develop a viable program. You've got to be able to support a national meeting.

BUNDY: About this business of passing a petition around, signing your name to something like that is an act of cowardice these days. You're afraid not to, but it hasn't committed you to anything. You've got to get people one by one. It takes hours.

WASSERMAN: I don't like the economic issue for a number of reasons. For one thing, it is a spurious issue. It's like status. We can't legislate salaries. The consequence of that would be the replacement of the irrelevance that we've performed with people who have less certification for it but who will do the same thing. Unless we deliver in the market-place a service that has an economic value, we can't enforce . . .

BUNDY: Then you would just close this profession down because we cannot recruit the people that this profession needs at these salaries. You've got to think of the people coming along. To say we're not worth it is to say . . .

PARTICIPANT: Are you talking about changing our image?

WASSERMAN: I'm talking about the fact that we can't enforce a national minimum salary and say that "unless someone gets this, he won't do anything." Because that would mean there wouldn't be people doing these things. People can be hired to do most of the things that are being done in libraries right now for half of that.

In the special library field or the technical library field, they're not hung up on master's performance. They don't know, frequently, that you need a master's degree to be identified as a librarian. People are hired for the contribution they make in the organization. If we were to legislate a salary saying, "No special librarian can be hired for less than $10,000," or whatever the figure would be, they would hire anybody who said he was this, particularly the lower-level functionaries who have carried out these roles.

In effect, what I'm saying is that you reach the level of economic value on the basis of the contribution you make. How do you do this? How do you get people to perform at that level? You do it by changing what people do. You do it by professionalizing the functions. You do it by appealing to people about the need to make contributions in work settings by doing things that are not now the going thing.

BUNDY: Let me be cynical. People only begin to respect what they've paid for. Every time you push for your salary, you push for the guy next to you, and the guy coming up after. Every time I push for my salary, I am pushing for better faculty at Maryland.

PARTICIPANT: But Dr. Bundy, they always apply for the openings. The openings set up the seller. How can you divide . . .

BUNDY: This is not true any longer. It is our market. I can have four jobs tomorrow. You can have a dozen. That's our market now, and we are very slow to realize it. When people just begin to want you, the first thing you do is test it out. Say, "O.K., give me money." It's a growing, aspiring profession. It's a natural thing to do.

PARTICIPANT: You don't have a minimum wage for doctors or lawyers. They're paid because they're worth it.

BUNDY: It's our market. The people who want more money are the people who have creative energy. When your most creative people want more money, give them more money. Don't say, "Ninety-nine of those librarians are no good, so I won't pay you."

PARTICIPANT: The only way you could do it is for librarians to voluntarily become unemployed.

BUNDY: They would have to be prepared.

PARTICIPANT: May I say something? I don't know if you're aware of this or not. In California we all got a 5 percent or 6 percent raise. The librarians won. The people who have only one year's experience didn't get it. In order to accomplish something, five of us are going to leave. If five people can leave, I suppose some other people can leave. They ought to have a little bit of money to live on. I agree with Dean Wasserman that we can't put a $10,000 on a national basis, but you can ask for more money. I am very naive about this and I am terribly young and I don't know enough. But this is what's happening.

PARTICIPANT: If ALA did supply a good placement service to manage the records, you would find out where the good salaries were, and you could leave the positions that had the poor salaries.

PARTICIPANT: In our situation, we take a person and within a year we expect that person to show his potential. If the person turns out to be good, we give him quite a large increase in salary because we recognize value and we want to keep him in the library. So the starting salary is really a question of competition with other libraries just to get somebody for a trial period. The money is not the problem. Once we find out that a person is worth keeping on a job, we're willing to pay for it.

BLASINGAME: I would like to suggest a different core issue than salaries. It seems to me to be an extremely important one. This is reorganizing the libraries, reorganizing the use of librarians, and reorganizing such things as the decision-making function in libraries. This has to be tied to service, the kinds of service that are provided and the kinds of service that people need. A program such as this could be taken to ALA on the basis that as our primary institution it's their responsibility to do everything that they can to push for specific kinds of reorganization. These should be proposed in the program and related to specific kinds of service. Then give ALA a year to do it. Don't give them an ultimatum, but present this program supported by a petition. If it isn't done, then make this the issue of another association.

BUNDY: We are on politically as well as morally better grounds if we take the service issue. On the other hand, I'm not sure I'd even take the service issue. I'd take the client.

11

CHANGE RESPONSES FROM LIBRARIANSHIP: EDUCATION, RESEARCH, AND PRACTICE

FRIDAY AFTERNOON, AUGUST 15
PANELISTS: MARY LEE BUNDY
             PAUL WASSERMAN
             BROOKE SHELDON

BUNDY: Our format is education, research, practice. What are the implications of what we've heard this week? Because most of you are in practice I think we want to spend most of the time on that, so I'm going to say quickly a few things about library education. Paul will talk on library research, and then we'll ask you to begin talking about practice.

Fortunately for all of you, maybe, I lost my speech. I have been thinking through what I have learned this week. It might be important for us to think for a minute of how we extract from an experience like this concepts to take back. Some of the people who came here this week related to us as human beings. I saw no direct relevance to my job at all. That doesn't mean they may not have the biggest impact on me; I just can't say immediately what it is. Then the people I related to most personally and professionally are probably Freedman, who talked about professional education, and Birenbaum. I'll discuss what I feel were the implications of what they had to say to library education.

In these meetings we really reinforce our prejudices rather than change basic attitudes, so I probably have only reinforced the attitudes

I had already. I hope I deepened my understanding of some things. I think I found four or five practical things to do immediately. I kept saying, "Mr. Birenbaum, you've cheered me up." And he said, "I tell you the institutions are crashing. The society is in upheaval. And I have cheered you up?" "Well," I said, "you told me what I thought." I've been going around talking to people and telling them that this is an urgent situation and I was somehow wrong. This isn't an urgent situation. Things are going on much as they have before. What's a riot here or there? After all, we had union riots back in the 1930s.

WASSERMAN: Indeed, the rationale for continuing in your role as Chicken Little is that the sky *is* falling.

BUNDY: The second reason Dr. Birenbaum cheered me up, I guess, is that I felt I, that is the profession, wasn't in a boat alone. When there are creative men like him heading our academic institutions, then I think we will work together toward something. We have this terrible "down under" feeling in the profession. What can the library do in the total environment? It isn't being responsive. I mean, you almost have no choice or chance. You are in a suicide mission really, almost literally, so I guess I reinforced the need for change.

One thing keeps going through my mind. Ruth said it. She prefers to think of this society in a developmental sense. She does not want to believe that this is the age of discontinuity. She wants to see it as a growing up. Maybe that's a more positive way of looking at it, than in Chicken Little's land. In the long run, it doesn't matter which way you look at it; I have the feeling the outcomes might be the same. Someone like me who is restless, dissatisfied, has high levels of aspiration, probably isn't needed most of the time. At the time when change is needed, you may need this type of person. It is no credit to the person. He must be this. He is this.

What I'm leading up to is, do we want to revamp traditional library school curriculum, which is one way to force change, or do we want to develop some totally new program? I've been involved in a committee this year just for thinking purposes, so we wouldn't get all tied up in the question of whether we should keep "History of the Book" as a course or not. We put our curriculum away and we went at it another way. If we come back to our curriculum and deal with it, I think we will deal with it as a political expedient. If it is politically expedient to tie what we're trying to sell to that curriculum, we will.

You know what really goes on in curriculum studies in library schools or any other schools. Everybody is protecting his domain and the new elements are trying to get in. They're trying to get control of the required courses. It looks very intellectual because we are academics and we intellectualize. We have long conversations on the influence of the information sciences. In the meantime, we're all protecting our territory. We may really come up with something a little different, but it's the same people teaching. Even though we have said we wish to shift reference entirely, the same guy is teaching reference who has taught it for twenty years. You can't impose new concepts on him. So having spent one year in tremendous activity, reorienting the curriculum, typically we all go back and do what we did before. Those of you who have been through library school are the results of this process.

Perhaps we should not be fighting inch by inch to get rid of "History of the Book" and replace it with "Libraries and Social Change" as an alternative. Let's think of new ways of curriculum development. Since we've already been working on this, I just fed into this institute some things I wanted to be sure got into the curriculum. For instance, we were exposed this week to men with a very sophisticated understanding of politics. Later, as we talked, we discovered we didn't even understand the inside of our own association that well. At Maryland, we do have a course on the public library in the political process. What do students need to know to go out and change this profession? One thing they must have is a level of political sophistication that we have not given them in the past, so that's an ingredient. Ralph proposes analytical tools. At Maryland, we have sought to give students analytical tools, at least in the behavioral area. We are probably weakest in the analytical tools in our own professional area—cataloging and reference.

We are toying with the notion of private practitioner. Freedman said that they are not going to prepare people solely to work in social work agencies. Some social workers are going to be prepared to work outside the agency. A librarian might work out of a community center in a variety of settings. He would be closer to the client group. He would go back into resource centers for materials occasionally but he would be unhanded from the commitments of libraries. This doesn't mean that library education doesn't still need to educate the people who stay inside the resource center, but it does mean this might be a whole new avenue, so that we don't fall into plugging another reference librarian in behind another reference desk.

We have been studying this approach in our ad hoc committee. We said, "Let us invent the work roles of the future." We said that ten years from now we don't want librarians to be doing what they are doing now. We agreed not to fight over whether it is information specialist or reference librarian or what. We put some words on it and I hope the words won't throw you off. We developed three broad work roles—the information interpreter, the information processer, and the information manager. There are a whole variety of subroles within these broad categories. I won't go into detail, but our point was that if we can define what it is we want professionals to be doing, then we will be ready to work with our curriculum more knowledgeably. We will say, "What do you need to know to perform these work roles?" It has been a very exciting experience. We have invented all kinds of work roles—undergraduate information specialists, et cetera. Later when we sell it, we may say this is really the expanded role of the reference librarian.

Last night, a group of us met to talk about the ethics statement. We had a good suggestion from Eldred Smith to include examples because it seems so bland at first reading, and people aren't going to see the implications immediately. I think it is a dangerous instrument. Over and over and over again, we hear that the problems of our time are moral and ethical. Well, in library education we must consider those moral, ethical problems. We middle-class people must not regard them as something we don't talk about, something not nice to talk about, which we almost literally do. We must bring these in.

Ultimately, assurance is competency. This is why I'm interested in students' having clients in library school. When students register in library school the first day, each student should be given a client or told to go among the 30,000 students at the University of Maryland and find a client. This client would be his for the semester to give library service. You could say he doesn't know enough to give library service. That's true. What would he begin to do? In every class he went to in library school, he would be sitting there thinking about his client. He would begin to ask a different set of questions. He would come in with questions and inquiries. He would know whether those reference tools are relevant. This is what he doesn't know now. Now he senses he doesn't want to learn those books, but he doesn't have a substitution. Once people leave practice, they find it becomes vague; they can't ask the right questions. I think it would be a dynamic force in our professional courses if we had students who had to go meet their clients in an hour. Does anybody want to respond to this?

PARTICIPANT: It would give him the client mind-set which is so basic to our code of ethics. If the student thought of the library school in terms of clients, then you couldn't eradicate that from his mind in the bureaucracy. I think that's the important thing.

BUNDY: I do too, and I think that's what we should support from now on. We might get into bureaucratic problems if we still gave grades. Probably few students would do it if we didn't give them three credits. We would have to solve these problems. Then we might want to see an outcome. One possible outcome would be to talk to the client at the end of the semester and see what he thinks. Maybe we'll also do that. We'll recruit people into librarianship.

PARTICIPANT: Is there any point in the client's being a disadvantaged person in certain instances? Or is that a separate issue?

BUNDY: To be honest, I would say an undergraduate is disadvantaged at the library. And that's 30,000 at the University of Maryland.

WASSERMAN: Asking the client to review performance, however, is not really a fair gauge where he has no capacity or taste for it. Let me give you an illustration. When I was at Cornell, they had a magnificent school of hotel administration. I was one of the contributors to the grade for the student in Smorgasbord 105, so I wandered through the line. There was a boy with his white cap on, grinning at me hopefully. He gave me whatever it was he had been responsible for concocting. My palate wasn't discrminating enough, I don't think, to be a responsible agent for assigning a value to it. So I think you need different measures.

BUNDY: We've got some measures. At the end of the semester the student should be able to turn in an interest profile on his client to show that he got to know him well enough to find out his interests and what he needs to know.

PARTICIPANT: The client could at least say, "He helped me" or "He didn't help me."

WASSERMAN: Our level of expectation from librarianship is so minimal that the very process of being interested enough to pursue someone is a positive fact. That's not a fair discrimination, you see. It's better than anything anybody ever heard of who had anything to do with a library. That's better than nothing. So I'm not arguing with the notion; I'm just arguing with one little technical point.

BUNDY: In education they are doing this now more and more. They are beginning to have the students tell something about the course. They don't have to say whether the teacher's level of scholarship was that good, but they can tell something about his delivery. They're a factor in the situation. Say there were 100 students involved. Even if you didn't give them an organization, they might begin to see that they were all answering the same questions. They might create a bureaucracy. They might subdivide and allow one student to take all the questions on African studies. Interesting things could happen. One might develop a bibliographic expertise.

I already can see what's wrong with the whole thing. Only two credits for this! This is the story in library education. You bring in a novel idea, and you only get three credits for it. This happened in our High John project. Those students gave their lives, their free time, everything else for three credits. It was not easy to go back to the conventional classes, to take it down and give it back. You really had to care to take the High John course. I guess that's the price you pay for every pioneering effort.

PARTICIPANT: Dr. Bundy, what worries me about this approach to education, and it worried me when I listened to Dr. Birenbaum too, is it sounds to me that we are putting the emphasis on skills and on practices, rather than the philosophy behind it.

BUNDY: Then I guess I'm not explaining myself well. Skills are everything man knows. Dr. Birenbaum was saying the students are sitting in on philosophy classes. In other words, in order to approach that client you might have to go back and learn something about psychology or the student culture. Instead of sitting there and learning philosophy, library administration, and organization of knowledge, you would focus around the need to answer today's questions.

PARTICIPANT: Some students accept part-time jobs in libraries in order to have experience, on-the-job training.

BUNDY: Yes, but it should not be technical. I hope it would be professional, but not technical.

PARTICIPANT: I did something like this when I was in library school. I took a job in a public library system while I was still in library school. It gave me a sense of reality. I would sit in class all day long and hear philosophic gook about what it meant to be a librarian.

Then I had to go to work and I realized that 60 to 75 percent of what I learned in class was totally irrelevant to what I was doing on the job. Maybe, if nothing else, it would show the library school a proper direction in education.

PARTICIPANT: But there are so many directions in libraries. I worked, for example, as an assistant in an art library. I thought I would become an art librarian. I took a lot of art courses. I never had a chance to find a job as an art librarian. I wasted lots of credits.

BUNDY: I guess I'm not expressing well what the students would be doing and how we would use that concept. You see, I have always resisted this notion of practice. In the first place, this idea gets us out of the bureaucracy. It identifies us with the client. It gives us a purpose for learning. It doesn't say we don't learn philosophy, that we don't learn reference, but it gives us a reason for learning. It doesn't say I will no longer listen to any lecture that doesn't directly relate to my client. It just says there is more possibility that an instructor will get to me.

WASSERMAN: But the agenda, the need, is set by the limits of one individual, if this is what you are talking about. What Dr. Bundy is saying, in effect, is if I follow a music major around, I am then conditioned to go and study a lot of things related to that individual's need. But an informed intelligence may better prescribe for me what I must know generally to function in my professional role.

BUNDY: There are several things to what you've said. However, we must eventually practice somewhere, with somebody, at some time.

PARTICIPANT: But I think that if I had some very general basis to build upon, it would be easier to change than if I had one practical experience and then had to change to another practical experience.

WASSERMAN: I don't think anybody is quarreling with the concept in the abstract. I think there are always going to be differences in degree and in resolution, in pragmatic terms. My sense of it is that it is an interesting idea and would be worth some experimentation. That's not the same as saying, "It's a perfect idea! Great! That's our answer!" It's no better answer than a lot of other potential answers. It's an interesting idea and it has some potential payoff, I suspect.

BUNDY: All right. That leads me to what will be my last thought for all this. I think we can relate to each other here although I am in education and you're in practice. Maybe High John is an example. Should you start to do things with too little planning, too little experience, or should you wait until you have fully developed programs and plans and experience? If you happen to be in a school or a library that is going to do something for the first time, you must be willing to leave the boundaries. You are now a risk taker. You no longer have any proof that it will work, because it's never been done. You might look for models in other fields. I do this. I see another field doing it, and I say, "Well, good! Let's try it in librarianship." If it does nothing else, it will upset librarianship a little. It may not be a perfect fit, yet maybe for me the ethical question is, "Should we start or should we wait until we feel fully prepared to start?"

WASSERMAN: I think the risk in our field is the not taking of risk. That is, I think that in a field like librarianship, in a culture like the American culture now, the greater risk may be found in not chancing some alternatives. To the extent that one has the imagination to seize on options that have not been fully perpetrated, one is playing the riskier role technically and professionally. I think that not risking failure is more chancy and more risky for any profession in this time.

PARTICIPANT: All experiments must not succeed. I mean, the very fact that it is an experiment means we are risking that it may fail.

BUNDY: But then there is the consideration of the fact that it is other human beings we may be risking and not just ourselves. Paul and I were once told that it wasn't just our risk and our jobs, it was people in the community and kids that won't have a library if we fail. It came up again when we started recruiting black librarians. This time I was so bruised by High John I said, "No, I will not take a risk again with another human being." But someone pointed out that in the normal competitive struggle in academia, if the curriculum is never changed, all the damage is undoubtedly being done and people are already getting hurt anyway. So we must do something.

WASSERMAN: The culture of librarianship and the culture of library education are cultures where chance-taking proclivities are very, very limited. We not only shrink from risk taking, we take a kind of malicious and fiendish delight in the demolition of those who take some chances, because their failure gives us the rationalization for our passivity and inaction. I think that's a tragedy in any business or profession.

BUNDY: For example, there are very creative people who are attacked constantly but never on the basis of what they are creative about—only as individuals. Other people don't like their attitude; they may not like the creative person's loud mouth; they don't like other things. Well, when a profession treats its innovators like that, what hope is there? You have to understand the psychology of the innovator. The innovator doesn't seem to give a damn, but he does. This is what he's trying to tell you. It can hurt.

Why don't we do things? Why don't we join the next movement coming along? It may just be the next movement coming along, and this is the answer. For me, right now, in this profession, I want payoff. I'm not going to wait a long time, though, until I see a sure thing. I'm still willing to bet, and I think I might be getting better intuitively at betting. I think this ethics thing is a good bet, but it's still a bet. I took three weeks and two people's time, off and on. If it fails, we've lost three weeks of time. This is not the same as the three years of energy that went into High John, so I'm taking smaller bets, and I hope placing them better. For me, this is the answer at the moment. I change from day to day.

WASSERMAN: Shall we shift to research? I don't want to say very much about research. I don't think of this group as especially interested in research as much as it is in education, but I think the implications of this week have something to say to us with regard to our research. The sterility of the things we study and worry about and experiment upon in librarianship was clearly and starkly put into perspective for us by many of the ideas that were generated by the people who talked with us this week. I think our traditional research in librarianship has been addressed, in the main, to irrelevant issues rather than to those which are exceedingly relevant. From irrelevant research on questions that in no conceivable stretch of the imagination could bear upon our range of alternatives and the way in which we evolve as a discipline and as a practice, we must shift toward an end that perhaps may in some ways not only be conceived of as research, but more as action and more as developmental and more as experimental combinations of learning and trying and doing.

Some of what we've said this week has really reinforced my belief that some of the things that we have been trying are important. We must try to shift some of our perspective toward trying and doing developmental kinds of things, not the traditional kinds of research, but rather attempts to chance alternatives. I think there is a room in librarianship for experimentation and development. To name one

illustration, there is the question of product development. If you look
at publishing, you can see in it the capacity for us to experiment
with ways and means that we have the intelligence to exploit for
our own purposes and for our own ends, which has not often been
recognized or realized.

Our speaker yesterday, Jordan Baruch, discussed a social science
of librarianship. These have been the questions that have been engaging
us this morning. These are the kinds of issues about which we know
so very, very little in librarianship. We have no perceptions of these
facts and factors that Ralph Blasingame identified, as a consequence
of the research we do in librarianship. I feel better about our concern
in the doctoral program, which we are trying to put into being, because
it is a commitment to at least one important portion of these issues.
In the social, political, organizational, ecological, sociological concerns
of libraries, library organizations, librarians as professional practitioners—in all of these areas we have no basis for action, for performance, other than intuitive. Our research has not addressed itself to
these concerns. It has addressed itself to historical issues and bibliographic issues. These other issues are extraordinarily important, it seems
to me—all the more important as a consequence of what we've heard
the people all week telling us about. They are telling us to be tied
to the needs of this discipline and to the needs of the institutions
with which we're concerned.

BUNDY: Another tie-up with research that isn't research, as we used
to think about it, came out of this morning. I invented it at lunch.
I don't know enough to invent it, but I know ways now of simulating
situations. I thought to myself, "Wouldn't it be fun to get a library
school to simulate being the American Library Association with a responsibility for national library affairs?" Make one group the dissident
group, young radicals. We could then act out action programs in our
model ALA after we figure out where the strategic areas are. We
could see what a group of people in this situation could do.

I heard of a similar class at Cornell six months ago, maybe a year
ago, where they were simulating business, industry, and the black community. My brother visited the class, and at the time he visited it,
they could each play any role they wanted. The blacks chose to play
the black community. Some were industry; some were government.
Well, the point of the game was to pass something along and see
the effect on the economic sector, then to see the effect on the black

community. At the point at which my brother visited the class, they had drawn a curtain. The blacks were sitting on one side; government, industry, and the church were sitting on the other. The blacks were saying, "We don't care what you're doing for us. We don't want it."

I mentioned that it was at Cornell, so this could be a dangerous game to play, but nevertheless, I would like to throw it out. We now say that in library education the whole world is really ours. Let's throw out any traditional thing that should be in a curriculum.

WASSERMAN: I think another lesson of this week for me has nothing to do with research, but it has much to do with education and practice. That is the need for link-up and involvement between what we are doing in the university and what is being done in the institution we are concerned with, or the practice we are concerned with. In some ways our aloofness, one from the other, is breaking down, but I think I have had reinforced for me the idea that we must ponder very, very clearly and directly the implications of all of what we do, think, propose, and philosophize about in the academy, and that all that we do must be tied very, very clearly to practice and the consequences of it. I would hope also that the other side (if it is another side; those in practice show that it is simply another reach into the same thing) would appreciate the potential contribution from scholarship to its ends, and that's not always the case. I think our needs are so inextricably interwoven that we need closer ties and closer groups than we have yet achieved at the university. This is something that I think is vitally important to us.

PARTICIPANT: I thought I would go away from here this week saying I would never hire a Maryland graduate. If we don't try to get inside the other's feelings and see what each is trying to do, it could be very bad for both sides, both extensions. I don't think it will continue. I'm looking forward to some exciting doctoral dissertations coming out of this group, and I'm looking forward to meeting some exciting librarians coming out of this group. But an administrator could be scared.

BUNDY: Of course, what we have done was to bring you from practice into our one-upmanship game in which we sort of held control. That is, we made you play the game the academic way. You had to sit down and talk about it. I think you expressed this feeling to me. When you come out of practice you're not used to sitting five hours a day theorizing, so we put you at a disadvantage. Our intention was good.

PARTICIPANT: Paul, let me contradict you to some extent about what has been said before this week. For instance, Dr. Birenbaum was talking about learning by doing and the patient relationship and so forth, and Mary Lee said then we couldn't do that, that there is no such thing as a prototype library.

BUNDY: I wiggled my way out later. It took a while. Then Ed Taylor gave it to me.

PARTICIPANT: You mean the one-client relationship center. Why is that better?

BUNDY: It grew out of that ethics statement. We were searching to build the key professional relationship with the client, not with the bureaucracy. We might have hesitancy about going into a conventional bureaucracy. We were using the model that Freedman used, in which some people are prepared for agency work and social work, but a certain number of people now coming out of schools of social work are being prepared to function outside the agency but still inside the profession.

PARTICIPANT: Is all this going to establish a bridge between the library school and the faculty?

BUNDY: When this ad hoc committee on the curriculum began working, we began to evolve information work roles. Then we said that they can't be practiced in libraries. I don't think so. I think they will demand starting salaries of $15,000. They'll have to. I think there is going to be acceptance. I think people will be grabbing for them. Administrators have been hard pressed by client groups that haven't been getting service. Well, I could still be on the staff and work in the union. I couldn't work for the dean of students because he is obsolete, according to Birenbaum. I could still function in the university, and still be a librarian in every sense I know, without working in a library. I think the head deans and administrators will want these floating librarians very much. What do you think?

PARTICIPANT: Yes, I think so; and I think also if library school graduates are going to join the bureaucracy, it's better to send them ready to approach it critically, rather than to send someone who feels that that's just the way librarianship is. The bureaucracy itself can be changed. That's something that is not always easy to realize, but it is really true.

BUNDY: When I worked in libraries, I was constantly getting confused. Was my job to keep the reference books in order on the shelves,
or to help some guy and tear the reference books down? I told myself,
"No, I really can't help this guy now, because it will put something
in disorder for the next guy." It was always the next guy, so I never
did really demolish anything to help anyone. Then I realized I was
caught in the trap. I had to keep everything in order for the next
guy and he never was going to be there. Well, it's possible to get
out of some of those conflicts. Now, you could follow your client
anyway. You could manage to work within the system. I'm just suggesting another environment. The departmental librarian at the university
may still have more of a collection than my floating librarian would
have, but the danger might lie in beginning a book collection. It
would be to your advantage not to have books for your client. A
collection would involve you in organizational problems, and you might
become a bureaucracy in a small way.

SHELDON: Ralph Blasingame described the librarian this morning
as anti-intellectual, an idiot liberal arts major and nonanalytical person,
so in that sense I guess I could represent the practicing public librarian.
We had a great deal of discussion about why we came and we had
trouble in agreeing on this, but I think that at the very beginning
after the first couple of days many people said there was a sense
of dissatisfaction. There was some agreement then. If we came with
any idea of getting answers, we realized we might as well forget
it, because there are no answers.

However, I do think many of the speakers gave us ideas that we
can take back and perhaps implement, relating them to our own community. Your idea about the client is a good idea. The idea of knowing
the community was our way in 1954, when I was in library school.
We did a community survey. That's much better than doing a thesis.
You really had to get out into a given community and learn all these
things. This week I began to think, "Well, really there aren't any
new ideas," and I found this all through the week. We had some
very innovative people working in community groups and so on, but
not anything really terribly original. Now this isn't true in the educational level in your areas. I got a lot of new ideas, which I didn't
get from the community end. Perhaps some of your public librarians
would argue with me about that. Did anybody really get a new idea
about reaching any segment of the community that we haven't reached?

BUNDY: If you're in a public library, did you have a feeling that you would go back and look at your collections with a different perspective?

PARTICIPANT: Absolutely! The whole picture, not just the collection! You can't just put your finger on a single point and say, "This is what I've learned, and when I go back I'll say this is what I've learned." I think I've learned how to operate a little bit better within the power structure that I'm in conflict with all the time. I have a little better understanding of what it is and how to operate within it and maybe even how to be a little more effective within that power structure than I am right now. I think I've learned a little bit. Just how I'm going to use it, I couldn't tell you right now.

BUNDY: After I listened to Father Baroni I felt better about some of the things I haven't felt right about at High John. I created this new goal. I don't feel right giving people books when they don't have milk. When I was a teacher they told me to teach them to read; never mind if they're hungry. I think that Father Baroni's message was if they're hungry, they eat first, and then they worry about reading.

SHELDON: He had another important message too, which I think is applicable. He said it doesn't matter about the second-hand underwear and so on, but the only thing that is really going to do any good is changing the attitude of the middle class. He even gave some concrete suggestions for doing it. He said, "Change their attitudes! Have them elect someone who will go in and change the system." He suggested one method which I really think is applicable to libraries: the television program. He was suggesting it can be done in homes. You have a program and then you have a group. I think the libraries could do the same kind of thing, when we get this interactive television that is supposed to be coming along. We could view the program, the social issue, have the group discuss it, and then have immediate feedback back and forth. I don't know why this isn't applicable to libraries.

PARTICIPANT: Some of us already do things like that.

SHELDON: Preston Wilcox gave us three suggestions. He said, "Get books that relate to the people in the community." He said, "Get into the community." These are both things that we are doing. He said, "Librarians should listen." We weren't even following at that point, because we all started saying, "These are things that we do," but the point is we are not doing them, or people like Edward Taylor and Preston Wilcox would not come here and say this is what libraries should be doing. If we were doing these things, these people would know it. If we're doing them, we're doing them only in very isolated cases. I don't know what we can do about this, but I think we have to face the fact that they're not new ideas, but we haven't really put them into effect.

PARTICIPANT: Maybe we can appreciate this, but there are many of our staffs who do not. If each staff member became involved in one organization with social relevance for the community, we could inspire them to come out for participation in further attempts.

BUNDY: What about Dr. Galler's notion of the adaptive organization? Have you got an organization where the first order of business is to get itself in a position to make change?

PARTICIPANT: I think most of us are there in one form or another no matter what organization we work in.

BUNDY: You've got a staff who resist this. Are they resisting social responsibility or are they resisting almost anything?

PARTICIPANT: I think some of them are too much the retired librarian type, but others will really respond if the opportunity is made available to them.

PARTICIPANT: Is it easier to affect your staff by doing something yourself while in a position of leadership and then asking the staff person to assume this responsibility? This would be an indication that you wouldn't have asked this person to do this thing if you didn't have a high regard for his intelligence, ability, and flexibility. I think one thing that happens sometimes is that one person who is responsible has some ideas and the staff people don't get the ideas. They are told they ought to be doing something. Maybe they don't respond, or the person who is responsible feels this is germane to their activity but not germane to the top, which, of course, organizationally is true, except sometimes in order to get staff involved one has to do it. For example, a librarian of a fairly large branch was the first person in the library to be involved with the community at the project commitment. I don't know how effective that commitment is there, but that's neither here nor there. The point is that the first person at that particular branch who went to the organization meeting and who took an assignment on a subcommittee was the librarian, the chief of staff and operations. The next time he went to a meeting he took a staff person along. I'm sure that he had made up his mind that what he would do would be to spin off his responsibility, but you have to have a responsibility to spin off. You may have to create it. He created it by being involved. By being involved he gave it status, respectability. There was no question that you would get your brownie points by doing what the guy himself thinks is important. This is one way to get the staff involved.

SHELDON: As Spencer Shaw says in talking about dealing with exceptional children, you cannot expect every librarian to work with exceptional children. The administrator has the duty of getting persons or a person on his staff who will do this. He has the obligation to get the money and to back the program. I see this as the administrator's role. Then with his backing, staff resistance is overcome.

BUNDY: What both of you have said is realistic. But I'm not just sure in the long run that it's going to be the same thing as what Eldred Smith has been talking about, which is a shift into the decision making in order to get innovation and to be receptive to the ideas coming up. Perhaps that is the supreme task of the administrator.

PARTICIPANT: The administrator should create a milieu in which fresh ideas are accepted and rewarded. By example, the administrator created a situation where the librarian said, "Well, I can be safe in joining."

PARTICIPANT: Let me say something about this because I was one who got involved in project commitment. It wasn't the director of the library.

PARTICIPANT: What's very interesting, though, is that the director of the library thought you did a great thing.

PARTICIPANT: He did, yes, but there are people who were waiting around hoping that the thing wouldn't work. It's fine to have directors supporting initiative, but you still have the problem of other people sitting around and hoping that the damn thing won't work.

BUNDY: It forces you into the terrible business of wanting many people there on a particular night to prove something that maybe wasn't the point at all.

PARTICIPANT: So the only choice is to look for new librarians and have a program of new librarians coming into the field.

BUNDY: Yes, but you are saying this has got to go on for a few more years until these mythical people come. You've still got to go on.

PARTICIPANT: How much support do you have to have?

PARTICIPANT: You just have to have a tough mule hide about these things and go ahead.

SHELDON: The new librarians are not really mythical. When Virginia Kerr was promoted to branch librarian, she was asked to go to a certain area. Several other branch librarians said, "You poor thing. If you're lucky maybe you'll be transferred out of there soon." She said, "I asked to go to this branch because this is the kind of thing I want to do." I don't think we're totally devoid of people who want to do this kind of work. Why not hire them?

PARTICIPANT: Maybe we don't have enough.

SHELDON: You're right. Several people said that technology is only a tool and that libraries must take a position on the issues. We have missed the boat there. One thing that was reassuring about Dr. Galler was that he made us realize that museums are experimenting a little bit by presenting all parts of a problem, and so on.

BUNDY: I was cheered up by that fact.

SHELDON: Yes, I felt a lot better. Relatively speaking, I think we've gone a lot further in our role towards reaching out. Dr. Galler called libraries and museums crypto-universities. I felt that was probably a good term.

BUNDY: He kept saying a museum was a kind of library except for knowledge generation. I couldn't quite see us as knowledge generators, but I think our classificationists could. They say, "We'll put it together differently, which will help people learn."

WASSERMAN: I would say that we can be knowledge generators if we conceive of that as our role and function. That's what I meant a little while ago when I was talking very cryptically about publishing as a phenomenon. One consequence of our expertise can be the generation of products and services which are shared widely.

BUNDY: He means reference tools.

SHELDON: I felt that this had interesting implications in the kind of people we may get from the library schools. Someone else said the B average criterion for getting into library schools shows only that a person has the ability to jump through certain hoops. I have long felt that we need to reach some of these people who are more people related at the sophomore level, so that they can pick up a language or so. We are losing a great bet here. I go and talk to an education class at a college in New Mexico every year, and every year I get about eight people who express interest in librarianship. They want to be school librarians. These kids are very outgoing and I think reasonably bright, but they don't have the language requirement.

If we could have reached them at the freshman level we could easily have talked them into taking Spanish or another language to meet that requirement.

WASSERMAN: Perhaps there is a more fundamental question. Is the language requirement a carryover from a time when it had some utility? I think that is one of the open questions we face in library education. It may be that much of the time spent working in a language is time misspent. This is a problem for the schools to address themselves to.

PARTICIPANT: But until you change that, we have to advise people to take a language.

PARTICIPANT: Dr. Wasserman, is the graduate school here at the University of Maryland autonomous?

WASSERMAN: In some ways. In terms of language, yes. We could decide we don't want people to have a language.

BUNDY: But that's not the alternative. The fact is that we don't want people without languages.

WASSERMAN: We could decide it's not a master's requirement and the graduate school would support us. This is *our* problem. You're taking our problem on by default because we're not thinking through our problems.

PARTICIPANT: Until you change your requirements according to the catalog, we would have to say we want you to go to Maryland but you must have a language.

WASSERMAN: One of the things I meant by building a bridge between practice and the university is that you have a voice in this decision. If what you need in practice is not language but something else, you can tell us and we will listen to you. In our superior and infinite wisdom we have no business making judgments out of context with reality. If the reality is that a language is no longer relevant, well, let's throw it out.

BUNDY: I could report that we are in the process of eliminating the languages. The way we do it is by beginning to make exceptions. As we pile up the number of exceptions, the next stage will be a review of the policy. We just aren't there yet.

WASSERMAN: You see, one of our problems is the infinite variety of libraries for which people are being prepared. Some libraries need foreign language capacity.

SHELDON: I'm not even suggesting that the standards be lowered. On Monday I thought I heard you say, "We really can't help the kind of people we're getting." This is where I violently disagree. I think the schools can help it. I'm very much a conservative. I don't suggest lowering the standards, particularly, but instead, reaching kids while they're freshmen if a language is important.

BUNDY: I like the other thing a little bit better. If they are going to coordinate as outgoing people, let's have a new standard. Instead of having a language, let outgoingness be a criterion, or have other alternate possibilities.

PARTICIPANT: I liked what you said the other night about languages. Here we are learning French and German when we can't even speak the language of the ghetto.

PARTICIPANT: One of.the problems is that there is not enough variety in treatment and in production in the library schools. The market needs a great variety of librarians. It's going to need more and more librarians. For some, language will be very important. For others, other skills will be important. Instead of just giving up the language requirement, perhaps we need to do away with language except where it's needed and try to substitute other capabilities in other areas.

PARTICIPANT: There may be a parallel to training the librarian in a client relationship who must then struggle with bureaucracy in order to fulfill that client relationship. We need to train librarians to the optimum and then send them out with a mission to overhaul the field.

SHELDON: Father Baroni's point was let us give the professional what he needs to enable him to perform, including campaigning for the minimum wage. I believe the consensus was to give all points of an issue but to become politically involved also, if necessary.

PARTICIPANT: Where do we draw the line?

SHELDON: What field is not ours?

PARTICIPANT: We have to limit ourselves to providing information. I don't think I would go into the business of teaching.

BUNDY: It would reduce the hangup of not reading.

SHELDON: If there isn't anyone else teaching reading in the community, then the library ought to do it. Let me give you an example. In Santa Fe, in the schools, there is only one program for a student who dropped out of school. He could go back and take shop. In 1964, the library started reading courses. We advised this. This year six hundred people are enrolled in additional education in the schools. Somebody had to get it started.

PARTICIPANT: That's not the function of the library.

PARTICIPANT: The public library was once known as "the poor man's library."

SHELDON: We advertised, "Come and learn reading and receive a diploma." The whole lower floor of the library was packed. Why shouldn't this be a legitimate function?

PARTICIPANT: Aren't you saying that the library should provide the resources, at least—that it should begin the job?

SHELDON: We didn't intend to take over the function of the schools. I went around and knocked` on people's doors. They didn't think the schools could afford them. I don't think they will ever go back to the level where there won't be some kind of additional education program in the Santa Fe schools. Our role is over now.

PARTICIPANT: Do we have to fill all social needs?

BUNDY: Until you are willing to line up some needs, we are almost forced to look at a range of needs.

REID: Some services are more socially acceptable than others. I received an unsolicited notice in the mail that there would be a series of lectures in the library not far from where I live. I don't see the difference between sending out notices and going and talking to people saying that there would be a series of reading classes at the library. The library reached me.

PARTICIPANT: That is not the function of the library.

REID: They thought I would be interested in something that they were doing. What could be more promotional than teaching people to read?

PARTICIPANT: Why should I teach children to read? I think I should try to improve the school system.

SHELDON: When we started at Santa Fe, it had the highest illiteracy rating in the country. We did not really know that the Title II or Title III would come along. This is so basic that it is the function of the library.

PARTICIPANT: We support community programs but we don't dance.

REID: It seems to me from your discussion that you have other clients with needs that you satisfy. You have access problems of a different type here. I'm talking about specific needs. This is access at a different point.

PARTICIPANT: I live very near Carnegie Hall. Wonderful programs! I take my family. This activity is not the primary function of the library.

WASSERMAN: I think your approach to need is directed to process. It might be directed to other things, human requirements.

PARTICIPANT: I see my function as a librarian to provide support for various programs, not to try to perform their activities.

SHELDON: There is another point to this. We have to get the money. Somebody said the city council does not think of us as one of the major forces of the community. This kind of a program really reflects the community need. This is the kind of program that might bring the library into focus.

PARTICIPANT: You are putting on some window dressing so that you can get some money.

WASSERMAN: That's not the state of the world. If I function in a library where someone can't use what I have because of lack of certain skills, I am concerned with the educational process as a human being. You're concerned with the technical process.

PARTICIPANT: I'm a librarian.

REID: If you were in a university library serving the School of Medicine and you were provided a console for access, and if a clientele didn't relate to that console, wouldn't you feel a responsibility to help them to relate?

PARTICIPANT: Systems are too large for the individual position. Before designing the system, you should go through a systems analysis. I have a feeling that you are trying to usurp other people's professions and responsibilities and you are thereby neglecting your own profession. We should understand our own profession better.

SHELDON: Do you think that boys should come in and watch a film in a library?

PARTICIPANT: Use all the hardware that you can! That is one of the programs that we can provide to the community to support the community program. Here we have stretched our responsibility so far. We do this for promotional services.

PARTICIPANT: I respond to the same problem. Isn't this the time to think of some other specialization, a program to introduce commitment?

SHELDON: Going back to the discussion this morning, every man has to choose his role. He can't be a hundred people at once. We have to keep up, but we also have to concern ourselves with a certain aspect of our profession. If people like you can get this information to us quickly, that is great, but we should be more socially committed.

PARTICIPANT: The librarian should be trained to do his job.

WASSERMAN: We have been hoping that we could work something out in the area of expertise.

SHELDON: We have always had teachers in library schools who taught library skills, but they haven't actually given us a sense of commitment.

PARTICIPANT: Training is important. You learn about cataloging but not about the psychological aspects of it. We are asking for a librarian who is strong in sociology.

BUNDY: Some people have been turned off completely for ten or fifteen years. For me, it was all too vague.

PARTICIPANT: I would like to start doing something today.

WASSERMAN: I would like to take this opportunity to thank you for staying until the bitter end. We might be accused of manipulating you, but we hope that in the process of being manipulated you have learned. Thank you very much.